Hybridity and its Discontents

'Hybridity' started life as a biological term, used to describe the outcome of a crossing of two plants or species. It is now a term for a wide range of social and cultural phenomena involving 'mixing', and has become a key concept within cultural criticism and post-colonial theory.

Hybridity and its Discontents challenges many of the established ideas about hybridity. Through careful examination of a number of manifestations of hybridity – in cross-cultural encounters, sexual relationships between differently racialised social groups, borrowings and exchanges in art and music, and the emergence of new subjects and identities as a result of global shifts of cultures, capital and commodities – the contributors trace the intricate process of hybridization itself, drawing out the multiple uses and meanings of the term in its social and historical contexts.

Avtar Brah is Director of Social Studies in the Faculty of Continuing Education, Birkbeck College, University of London.

Annie E. Coombes is Director of Graduate Studies in the School of History of Art, Film and Visual Media at Birkbeck College, University of London.

Hybridity and its Discontents

Politics, science, culture

Edited by Avtar Brah
and Annie E. Coombes

London and New York

First published 2000
by Routledge
11 New Fetter Lane, London EC4P 4EE

Simultaneously published in the USA and Canada
by Routledge
29 West 35th Street, New York, NY 10001

Routledge is an imprint of the Taylor & Francis Group

Typeset in Galliard by RefineCatch Limited, Bungay, Suffolk
Printed and bound in Great Britain by
Biddles Ltd, Guildford and King's Lynn

British Library Cataloguing in Publication Data
A catalogue record for this book is available from the British Library

Library of Congress Cataloging in Publication Data
Hybridity and its discontents: politics, science, culture / edited by
Avtar Brah and Annie E. Coombes.
        p.   cm.
    Includes bibliographical references and index.
    1. Hybridity (Social sciences)   2. Multiculturalism.
    3. Miscegenation.   4. Assimilation.   (Sociology)   I. Brah, A.
II. Coombes, Annie E.
    HM1272.H92   2000
    306—dc21   00–020158

ISBN 0–415–19402–4 Hbk
ISBN 0–415–19403–2 Pbk

Contents

Illustrations

Notes on contributors

Avtar Brah is Director of Social Studies in the Faculty of Continuing Education at Birkbeck College, University of London. She is the author of *Cartographies of Diaspora, Contesting Identities* (1996), and co-editor (with Mary J. Hickman and Máirtín Mac an Ghail) of *Global Futures: Migration, Environment and Globalisation* (1999); and *Thinking Identities: Ethnicity, Racism, and Culture* (1999). She is also on the Editorial Collective of *Feminist Review* and the Editorial Board of *Ethnic and Racial Studies*.

Annie E. Coombes teaches art history and cultural studies at Birkbeck College, University of London, where she is Director of Gradute Studies in the School of History of Art, Film and Visual Media. She is the author of *Reinventing Africa: Museums, Material Culture and Popular Imagination* (1994), and her book *Histories in Transition: Visual Culture and Public Memory in Contemporary South Africa* is forthcoming with Duke University Press. She is also on the editorial collectives of the *Oxford Art Journal* and *Feminist Review*.

Donna Haraway is Professor in the History of Consciousness Program at University of California at Santa Cruz. Her publications include *Primate Visions: Gender, Race, and Nature in the World of Modern Science* (1989) and *Simians, Cyborgs and Women: The Reinvention of Nature* (1991).

Sandra Klopper lectures in the Historical Studies Department at the University of Cape Town. Her research interests include the so-called traditional arts of several southern African communities and various contemporary forms of popular culture. She recently mounted an exhibition of hiphop spraycan art at the South African Museum in Cape Town, and has just completed a manuscript based on Peter Magubane's photographs of rural South African traditionalists.

John Kraniauskas teaches Latin American literary and cultural studies at Birkbeck College, University of London. He is co-editor of the *Journal of Latin American Cultural Studies* and on the editorial collective of *Traces*. He is currently completing a book on the transnationalisation of cultural studies.

Jo Labanyi is Director of the Institute of Romance Studies (School of Advanced Study, University of London) and Professor of Modern Spanish Literature and Cultural Studies, Birkbeck College, University of London. Her publications include *Spanish Cultural Studies: An Introduction* (co-edited with Helen Graham, 1995); *Gender and Modernisation in the Spanish Realist Novel* (2000), and the chapter on Spain in *Heroines without Heroes: Reconstructing Female and National Identities in European Cinema, 1945–1951* (ed. Ulrike Sieglohr, 2000).

Charlie Owen is a Senior Research Officer at the Thomas Coram Research Unit of the Institute of Education, University of London. His main research interest is the secondary analysis of official statistics. He also researches preschool daycare services, including isssues of gender. He is co-author of *Men in the Nursery* (Claire Cameron, Peter Moss and Charlie Owen), published in 1999. He also teaches research methods and data analysis, both quantitative and qualitative.

Ann Phoenix is a Senior Lecturer in Psychology at the Open University. In 1997/98 she was a visiting professor at the University for Humanist Studies in Utrecht. She has published widely on issues of gender, 'race', ethnicity and class. Her books include *Young Mothers?*, *Motherhood* (Ann Phoenix, Anne Woollett and Eva Lloyd), *Black, White or Mixed Race?* (Barbara Tizard and Ann Phoenix), *Shifting Identities, Shifting Racisms* (Kum-Kum Bhavnani and Ann Phoenix) and *Standpoints and Differences* (Karen Henwood, Chris Griffin and Ann Phoenix).

S. Sayyid is Lecturer in School of English, Sociology, Politics and Contemporary History in the University of Salford. He is the author of *A Fundamental Fear: Eurocentrism and the Emergence of Islamism* (1997).

Deborah Lynn Steinberg is a Senior Lecturer in the Department of Sociology, University of Warwick. She has written extensively on scientific and popular cultures of the gene, eugenics, sexuality and the body, and (with Debbie Epstein) on televisual cultures and the talk-show genre. Publications include: *Bodies in Glass: Genetics, Eugenics, Embryo Ethics* (1997); *Border Patrols: Policing the Boundaries of Heterosexuality* (1997), co-edited with Debbie Epstein and Richard Johnson); and *Mourning Diana: Nation, Culture and the Performance of Grief* (1999, co-edited with Adrian Kear).

Ann Laura Stoler is Professor of Anthropology, History, and Women's Studies at the University of Michigan, Ann Arbor. She is the author of *Race and the Education of Desire: Foucault's History of Sexuality and the Colonial Order of Things* (1995), and co-editor (with Frederick Cooper) of *Tensions of Empire: Colonial Cultures in a Bourgeois World* (1997). She serves on the editorial boards of *Comparative Studies in Society and History, The Journal of the History of Sexuality, Historical Sociology*, and *Critical Anthropology*.

Her book *Carnal Knowledge and Imperial Power: Race and the Intimate in Colonial Rule* is forthcoming with University of California Press.

Nicholas Thomas has written widely on history, anthropology and art in the Pacific. His recent publications include *Possessions: Indigenous Art/Colonial Culture* (1999) and, with Mark Adams, *Cook's Sites: Revisiting History* (1999). He is Professor of Anthropology at Goldsmiths College, University of London.

Amal Treacher is a Senior Lecturer in Psychosocial Studies at the University of East London and is on the Editorial Collective of *Feminist Review*. She is currently documenting and theorising children's autobiographies and is the editor of *The Dynamics of Adoption*.

Lola Young is Professor of Cultural Studies at Middlesex University. Her publications include *Fear of the Dark: 'Race', Gender and Sexuality in the Cinema* (1995).

Introduction: the conundrum of 'mixing'

Annie E. Coombes and Avtar Brah

The idea for this collection came out of a series of interdisciplinary seminars held at Birkbeck College, University of London, entitled 'From miscegenation to hybridity?'. The seminar generated heated debate and drew discussion from a wide spectrum of academics, students and professionals. Their enthusiastic response to what was evidently a controversial topic suggested a need for a more considered analysis of this term and one which located it within specific historical and geographical contexts.

This project has a certain urgency since the concept of 'hybridity' has now acquired the status of a common-sense term, not only in academia but also in the culture more generally. It has become a key concept in cultural criticism, in post-colonial studies, in debates about cultural contestation and appropriation and in relation to the concept of the border and the ideal of the cosmopolitan. The phenomonon that the term 'hybridity' seeks to address produces varied responses. At times it has resulted in an uncritical celebration of the traces of cultural syncretism which assumes a symbiotic relationship without paying adequate attention to economic, political and social inequalities. On the other hand recent work on the music industry, for example, argues that music is one of the more productive sites for hybrid interactions which could be described as both cultural exchange *and* commodification without being reduced to either one or the other (Gilroy 1993; Sharma and Sharma 1997; Hebdige 1987; Jeater 1992; Lazarus 1999). Obviously at another level, 'hybridity' signals the threat of 'contamination' to those who espouse an essentialist notion of pure and authentic origins. This lends the term a potentially transgressive power which might seem to endorse the celebration of its traces as transgressive *per se*. The chapters in this volume complicate such readings by subjecting the process of hybridization itself to critical scrutiny and encouraging the reader to take account of the multiple uses and meanings of the term depending upon the configuration of social, cultural and political practices within which it is embedded at any given time.

Of course the hybridity debate, and its inextricable historical association with sexuality and fertility through the discourses and legislation of assimilation and segregation, shares certain features with the current debates on multiculturalism. (See Bennett 1998 for an exemplary collection of essays and introduction to the debates). In particular it shares the problems of the kinds of tokenism which aestheticizes politics by providing endlessly differentiated cultural experiences on an expanding menu of delectation while the subjects of this feast continue to experience the kind of discrimination which makes their own material existence at best precarious and at worst intolerable. On the other hand this recognition of 'cultural diversity' has paradoxically provided a platform for claiming political rights by enabling some constituencies to mobilize around an ethnic particularity in what other commentators have described as 'strategic essentialism' (Spivak 1993; Hall 1990; Parry 1994; Lazarus 1994). The pitfalls and contradictions of such strategies are graphically illustrated in the South African context following apartheid, where the legislative support for the recognition of ethnic particularities (be they San, Griqua or Zulu) may come dangerously close to reproducing the ideology of 'separate development', which policies laid the foundation of the apartheid state (Mathieson and Atwell 1998). This example provides one of the clearest confirmations of the project of this book which is the necessity of historicizing the concept of hybridity and of acknowledging the geopolitical contexts in which the terms of the debate circulate.

One of the differences between the ways hybridity and multiculturalism are addressed is that multiculturalism always contains a policy dimension missing in the hybridity debates, where the term masquerades as a solely cultural descriptor, and where, crucially, culture is often represented as autonomous from any political or social determinations. Indeed one of the difficulties of the ways in which hybridity has been mobilized in the cultural sphere is precisely that the institutional frameworks through which it circulates are insufficiently theorized (García Canclini 1990; Coombes 1992). The chapters in this volume are particularly attentive to this dimension of the debate.

Most importantly, in this volume we felt that it was essential to foreground the ways in which hybridity is constituted and contested through complex hierarchies of power, particularly when used as a term which invokes the mixing of peoples and cultures (Brah 1992). Importantly, it is only through recognizing the ways in which these terms have been given different and often conflicting meanings at specific historical moments that we can understand the stakes in the present debates on hybridity versus essentialism.

Because these debates impinge on so many areas of social and cultural practice, this collection draws on the expertise of scholars in a number of different disciplines and professions. We viewed an interdisciplinary approach as a structural necessity rather than a gratuitous eclecticism because the terms of the debate are, by definition, centrally concerned with questions of 'race', ethnicity, gender, sexuality and class. We both felt strongly that these social and psychic categories are not analysable through the confines of discrete disciplines. To this end the book foregrounds the intersection of discourses and practices mobilizing hybridity across the social, biological and medical sciences as well as the humanities.

Miscegenation and racial purity

Because of its current popularization through cultural criticism, 'hybridity' is often misunderstood as a purely contemporary concern. The genealogy of the term is, of course, more accurately associated with the development of the natural sciences and in particular botany and zoology, where it referred to the outcome of a cross between two separate species of plant or animal. In the eighteenth century, when classification of the natural world and its material products became a veritable obsession, the concept of the hybrid was expanded to incorporate humans. Even before Social Darwinism had permeated nineteenth-century society the categorization of different human populations into taxonomies of 'race' was already a central theme within Europe through the work of individuals such as J. F. Blumenbach, J. A. Compte de Gobineau, Georges Cuvier, Charles White and Robert Knox (M. Banton 1987). One of the structural features of the ensuing debate was a concern with the point of origin of the species which played itself out as the infamous war between the polygenesists and the monogenesists. As Robert Young summarizes:

> It was the increasing vigour with which the racial doctrine of polygenesis was asserted that led to the preoccupation with hybridity in the mid-nineteenth century. This was because the claim that humans were one or several species (and thus equal or unequal, same or different) stood or fell over the question of hybridity, that is, intra-racial fertility.
>
> (Young 1995: 9)

The debate concerning the effects of interracial union was of course fuelled by the progress of western colonialism and imperialism and the priorities of 'managing' the colonized subject for the purposes of providing cheap and effective labour or to minimize the disruption to the chosen model of indirect or direct rule (Yuval-Davis and Anthias 1989). As a result, one of the features of colonial contact, particularly in the nineteenth century, was the emergence of a set of administrative directives and strategies designed either to promote assimilation with the colonized or to ensure that a stricter code of segregation was observed. The outcome of such strategies was not always self-evident. Benedict Anderson, for example, cites the case of Pedro Fermin de Vargas, whom he describes as 'an early nineteenth century [Colombian] liberal' and who advocated interracial breeding between whites and Indians as a means of 'hispanicizing' the population and eliminating those characteristics which apparently marked the Indians as 'a degenerate race' (Anderson 1983: 21). And such thinking cannot be easily consigned to the past. Up until the 1960s a similar goal was intended in Australia, through the assimilation project where aboriginal children up to the age of four were forcibly taken from their mothers and placed in adoptive white families. Such initiatives, however, have never been without some unforeseen consequences which did not always favour the progenitor. From the point of view of the colonizer, the danger with any programme of assimilation which ultimately might result in sexual unions amongst peoples from different cultural and social backgrounds was that the resulting offspring of any such union might eventually outnumber the colonizers and subsequently 'contaminate' not only their cultural legacy but the genetic stock itself. In his *History of Jamaica* Edward Long exemplifies this concern and its interdependence with anxieties about how inter-racial union in the imperial centre might disrupt other hierarchical social structures such as class, seen as essential corollaries to effective colonial rule. He writes in 1774:

> The lower class of women in England are remarkably fond of the blacks, for reasons too brutal to mention; they would connect themselves with horses and asses if the laws permitted them. By these ladies they generally have numerous brood. Thus, in the course of a few generations more, the English blood will become so contaminated with this mixture . . . as even to reach the middle, and then the higher orders of people.
>
> (Loomba 1998: 159)

Ann Stoler in her chapter on the politics of exclusion in colonial Southeast Asia draws attention to the 1930s French colonial policy of encouraging young women of mixed Southeast Asian and European parentage to marry Frenchmen and follow them into the bush, 'where young women from the metropole would be hesitant to follow their husbands . . . [and would form] the foundation of a bourgeoisie, attached at one and the same time to their native land and to the France of Europe'. As she points out, however, there was always the residual fear: 'What could be done with this mixed population, whose ambiguous positioning and identifications could make them either dangerous adversaries or effective partisans of the colonial state?'

Enoch Powell's infamous 'rivers of blood' speech and Margaret Thatcher's 'swamping' speech are testimony enough to the longevity of such anxieties as they resurfaced in the more recent past in relation to the possible effects of immigration on 'British' culture, assumed here to be homogeneous, white Anglo-Saxon. And of course such volatile rhetoric has historically always been a feature of the racist campaigns of the far right. It is also important to remember however, that the introduction of debates on the virtues and dangers of assimilation were not always the prerogative of the colonizer. From an early date the discourse of cultural assimilation has also been appropriated by the colonized subject and wielded to considerable effect as a weapon in the armoury of anti-imperialist intellectuals and educated elites (Coombes 1994: chapter 2; Gilroy: 1993).

One of the objectives of this book is to demonstrate that the historical and contemporary neuroses about intercultural union, which circulate especially (though not exclusively) where the peoples involved display visible signs of difference such as skin colour, are inevitably grounded in the impossible assumption of originary unity and racial purity.

The chapters in Part I all focus on instances where sexual relationships between racialized groups are a central issue. The chapters confirm how anxieties about miscegenation and the preservation of racial purity have often underpinned discussions about cultural and social intermixing. We have deliberately selected contributions which straddle both the historical and contemporary in order to foreground a number of questions about the relationship between the historical legacy and the contemporary experience of living in a metropolitan context with long-established multiethnic communities. For example, why are some sexual liaisons only ever discussed in terms of the ways they confirm or transgress the fictional myths of racial purity? Why is it that sexual relations between certain communities, and not others, have historically provoked extreme anxiety and why do such relations continue to exert such panic? How does this panic still gain ground despite the liberal-humanist rhetoric of 'tolerance' and despite the fact that *cultural* diversity has become one of the major icons of the global market?

Part I includes contributions on how discourses of racial purity and assimilation were implicated in the emergence of new forms of symbolic cultural and political practices in colonial settings, for example in Indonesia and for the nationalist project of Franco's Spain. Ann Stoler analyses how 'métissage' was legally handled, culturally inscribed and politically treated in the contrasting colonial cultures of French Indochina and The Netherlands Indies in the 1890s. Her account highlights the contradictions it presented and the ways in which it disrupted the distinctions of difference which sought to maintain the neat boundaries of colonial rule. She proposes that in linking domestic arrangements to public order, family to state, sex to subversion and psychological essence to racial type, métissage might be read as a metonym for the biopolitics of the empire at large. Jo Labanyi concentrates on an example of cultural production from Spain in the 1930s and 1940s in the form of the folkloric musical. She argues that hybridity, in this context, through the promotion of identifications with culturally mixed heroes and heroines, should be understood as an attempt by the Franco regime to procure consensus for its totalitarian model of nationalism through the assimilation of subaltern cultural forms. Crucially, it was an attempt which, she believes, failed to recuperate these cultural expressions. Ann Phoenix and Charlie Owen unpack the complex contradictions presented by the lived experience of 'mixed parentage', through a study of social identities of young men and women living in London in the 1980s. Their demographic analysis demonstrates that people of 'mixed parentage' constitute a small but increasing percentage of the total British population. It also shows that this grouping within minority ethnic populations is proportionately larger. Phoenix and Owen found that the young people in their survey were categorized on the one hand as if they were simply 'black' and on the other hand as if they were neither 'black nor white'. However, it is clear from their research that the young people themselves had a more sophisticated understanding of such labelling and used the terms of colour flexibly as their identifications shifted over time and from context to context. Amal Treacher provides an autobiographical account of negotiating identities when the pressures of mixed parenting lead to separation and displacement both physical and psychic. Making use of Julia Kristeva's argument that as a consequence of the 'intractability of the unconscious' we could all be said to be both strangers to ourselves and continually confronted with the strangeness of the Other, Treacher analyses her own experience of this 'strangeness' by exploring the effects of the rupture of leaving her 'home' in Cairo for another. In particular her concern is to analyse the effects of the 'dynamics of skin colour on the formation of identity' for a child of mixed heritage and the complex fantasies of identification which take place in this context. Most importantly, both Treacher's and Phoenix and Owen's chapters are inevitably also an exploration of the way that 'lived experience' can prove transformative rather than simply constraining.

Consequently, Part I highlights some of the difficulties of living with the negative associations which are the historical legacy of 'miscegenation'. But it also challenges these derogatory legacies by providing research which testifies to the possibilities of a lived experience which goes beyond the limitations of a subjectivity forged only in relation to one or other side of some binary divide.

Engineering the future: genetic cartographies and the discourse of science

It has long been argued that a belief in the pre-eminence of science, technology and medical innovation envisioned as the motor force of social progress has been central to the development of 'modernity'. Over the centuries a great deal of emphasis came to be placed upon the need to understand, and thereby engineer and control, 'nature' through the application of science. In other words, nature was disembedded and assumed identity within certain influential discourses as something that was separate and distinctive from culture. The nature/culture dichotomy that followed this fissure persists to this day, despite its various deconstructions, as does the corresponding iconic significance attached to scientific rationality and a view of science as a guarantor of 'objective truths'. Indeed, there are those who regard science almost as a secular 'God' of modernity. This representation has not been without some pretty dire consequences for humanity and the environment. One such example is the scientific taxonomies through which human variation has been constructed in essentialist terms of 'race' or 'sex' so that these categories become a signifier of inherent and immutable 'difference'. In these cases, science can become an alibi for legitimizing processes of inferiorization, exclusion, subordination and inequality; arbitrary relationships can be made to seem preordained, natural, always already given; and observation or statistical correlation may be confused or conflated with causation and explanation.

However, the notion of science as some kind of 'transcendental signifier' has more recently been seriously contested by those who wish to understand science as a cultural discourse. Here, scientific discourse, like any other discourse, is seen as having its own regulative mechanisms, its own specific procedures and its own methods for judging claims that it professes. Far from being prophesies of absolute certitude, scientific claims are regarded as invariably contingent, provisional, open to corroboration or refutation, with the possibility of being superseded (Harding 1990; Rose, Kamin and Lewontin 1984; Hall 1992; Haraway 1989).

As a cultural discourse, science is far short of being 'neutral', and is deeply marked by power relations. The chapters in Part II all demonstrate this point.

Donna Haraway's chapter is a trenchant, ironic, and even playful critique of the narratives, epistemologies and technologies embedded within the practices of leading-edge techno-science at the end of the second Christian millennium. Just as a Judeo-Christian point of view was central to 'perspectivism' which under-pinned early modern and Renaissance art and map-making, it is similarly at the heart of the supposedly secular interpretations of the computer game SimLife and other similar simulation games. Haraway analyses current discourses of gene mapping where 'life' – materialized as information and signified by the gene – can admit no metaphors or tropes. The gene leapfrogs its role as an interacting part of an incredibly complex process to become an 'auto-telic and self-referential thing-in-itself'. Haraway critiques what she sees as 'fetishism of the map', because fetishism is about mistakes or denials where a fixed thing stands in for processes of change, contingency or reiteration associated with actions and relations of power-differentiated beings. Fetishes obscure or literalize the non-literal and symbolic nature of themselves and of all representation. Hence, gene-maps, according to Haraway, are liable to become fetishes when they are made subject to a specific kind of reading: one which facilitates a mistake or a denial so that, instead of being understood as a trope, the gene is reified as 'process' and is turned into 'thing'.

Drawing upon the collective strengths of Marx, Freud and Whitehead, Haraway teases out the economic, psychoanalytic and philosophical strands with-in gene fetishism. Her essay demonstrates how contra-narratives to gene fetishism can help develop a critical relationship to the production of techno-scientific epistemologies without either constructing them as a veritable enemy or celebrating them as the key which will invariably unlock all the mysteries of the universe.

To walk this tightrope is not easy. In particular, the current penchant for popu-larizing scientific discourses poses certain dilemmas. It brings to light the difficul-ties of translating scientific tropes through the language of popular culture. The entry of terms such as the 'language of genes' into popular discourse and imagin-ation foreground questions of intertextuality and discursive articulation. What, for example, are the effects of popularization of particular scientific enterprises? What kind of vocabulary is utilized, and what kind of shared cultural codes are invoked to make the esoteric in science accessible to the public? Which publics are targeted in particular projects? What is the relationship between social relations and conceptual trajectories of scientific cultures and broader popular discourse? What hegemonic power relations are produced and mobilized through specific popularization strategies?

Deborah Steinberg's chapter is informed by such questions. She examines the nexus between professional and popular sensibilities surrounding the science of genetics through a textual analysis of the 1991 Reith Lectures entitled *The Language of the Genes* and delivered by Steve Jones. She analyses the narrative and metaphoric conventions deployed by Jones in order to translate genetics for the popular, albeit elite audience of the British Broadcasting Corporation's Radio

Four. She explores the significance of the Reith Lectures in British culture, followed by a semiotic analysis of the 1991 series of Reith. Steinberg argues that the use of the metaphor of 'language' and 'literacy' serves to convert a fairly formal event into a seemingly familiar and intimate communicative relationship between Jones and his audience. The chapter unravels the contradictions involved when, on the one hand, genes are conceptualized as reproductive bodies and, in this sense, construed as key constituents of 'race' and nation, and, on the other hand, are disclaimed for racism and nationalism. She suggests how it would be possible to understand the processes of disavowal operating here in terms of the 'fetishism of the gene' of which Haraway speaks.

This is not to say that Steve Jones is engaged in some game of duplicity. Far from it. Rather, it is a point about the workings of the cultural subconscious without which conscious agency cannot function other than largely in a voluntaristic fashion. It is also about the way in which the biological discourse of 'race' and 'nation' is treated as unproblematic, as if 'scientific racism' is all in the past and its discredited history is widely available to the general public and fully accepted, when neither is the case.

The chapter raises some difficult questions about authorial intentionality, for one would not doubt the sincerity with which Jones aims to undermine racism. It foregrounds the fact that what matters most is not so much the intention of the speaker but the nature of the discourse produced via the articulation of meanings constituted and disseminated through cultural, economic and political institutions and practices.

A focus on discourse rather than intention is important for another reason. Once a discourse is reiterated and popularized within a cultural formation so that it becomes sedimented in the form of Gramscian 'common sense', it is then available as subject position even to those who are constructed within it as 'Others'; that is, the discourse could, potentially, be appropriated also by these 'Others'. What the outcomes of such appropriations might be would, as we have already noted, depend upon the context. A case in point here is the 1960s appropriation of the term 'black' by African-Americans. In this political space, 'black' came to be invested with positive connotations which posed a major challenge to previous negative meanings associated with it in racialized discourses. A key aim of this political movement was to engender pride in being black. But being black, in our view, is not the same as being a member of a 'black race', the latter construction having been part of the hierarchical racial taxonomies that crystallized in the West during the sixteenth and seventeenth centuries. The idea of a biological race has long been discredited but, as we have already noted, its usage has far from disappeared.

Lola Young's chapter maps out the dilemmas involved when the discourse of 'race' is utilized by black scientists in order to argue the supremacy of the 'black race'. Young analyses two well-known texts within this canon, *The Isis Papers: The Chemical Key to the Colours* by Frances Cress Welsing and Carol Barnes' *The Key to Black Greatness*. Young argues that, although such a body of work as the above might be intended as a counter-discourse to scientific racism, the methodologies used bear remarkable similarities to textual strategies of racialized scientific inquiry. Cress Welsing and Barnes do critically address gene theory but the locus of their concern lies in melanin, the substance which gives rise to skin colouring. Whiteness is seen as a lack of sufficient melanin and is associated here with negative attributes. As against polyvocality and heterogeneity, the texts consequently invoke a view of 'authentic' black cultural practices and an essential black subject. Given the range of skin colouring, linguistic and cultural diversity among African peoples in Africa as well as in the African Diaspora, being black, Young contends, cannot ever be solely about the measurable amount of a particular chemical in the body. 'Black may be thought of as always already "hybrid" and any attempt to use it as a homogeneous, self-contained category is contingent on a political interpretation not a biological one.' She points to the well-established history of the idea of 'race' and 'hybrid', where metaphor and analogy have played a major part in making inappropriate comparisons between incommensurate categories and subjects, as when there was a slippage from the use of the term 'animal husbandry' to intergroup sexual activity. Identifying a similar elision within the contemporary trend of applying the concept of 'hybridity' to human cultural and artistic endeavour, Young cautions against its careless use.

Cultural translation

Much contemporary criticism has focused on hybridity as the sign of the productive emergence of new cultural forms which have derived from apparently mutual 'borrowings', exchanges and intersections across ethnic boundaries. Indeed the contemporary art market thrives on the commodification of the results of these supposedly cross-cultural and interethnic exchanges. Most of the centres of contemporary art in western Europe, North America, Canada and Australia have hosted large exhibitions foregrounding such cultural products, and many smaller organizations have been launched on the basis of such an enterprise. Commentators have variously lambasted such attempts as the bare-faced appropriation of entrepreneurial capitalists or as the dawning of a new era of mutual respect which moves the old liberal rhetoric of cultural relativism onto a more concrete and material footing. Other research has sought to analyse the more contradictory and complex trade-offs and negotiations that may take place in such instances. The controversial production and marketing of Australian aboriginal art is a case in point, where the creation of a thriving market for acrylic painting and prints has been both criticized as a profitable ploy highly controlled and directed by those who manage the production and sale of the work but where it is also acknowledged that the funds from the work have facilitated different kinds of projects which have been highly beneficial for the communities involved (Willis and Fry 1988–9; Benjamin 1996; Myers 1991). The use of aboriginal work as an international icon of Australianness remains painfully incommensurate with the abysmal state of aboriginal civil rights eroded through a long history of persecution. Nevertheless such liberal pluralist strategies have had evidently progressive repurcussions by providing ballast to support aboriginal claims in terms of both land rights and political enfranchisement more generally.

Our contention in this book is that the earliest history of travel, exploration and colonialism has always entailed various kinds of serendipitous, mutual, strategic and subversive cross-cultural borrowings and more transgressive masquerades. Such exchanges or inversions should not be seen as a solely contemporary phenomenon. Recently Paul Gilroy's *Black Atlantic* explored the ways in which different versions of European and North American culture, philosophy and political analysis both informed and have been informed by the work of intellectuals and professionals who made up the African and Caribbean diaspora and of the transformative effect of their work on the metropolitan centres that became their home. (Gilroy 1993; see also Brah 1996 for a discussion of the complexities of diaspora and the nature of lived intersubjectivities in Britain). Earlier research was concerned to demonstrate the ways in which the colonized subject often knowingly exploited a presentation of self which reappropriated and transformed given colonial identifications and mobilized them for their own ends (De Moraes Farias and Barber 1990; Hobsbawm and Ranger 1983; Hall 1992).

Discussion about the possibilities and impossibilities of reappropriating colonial forms has often been framed around the question of language in relation to literatures. To what extent it is possible to claim an effective anti-colonial critique while writing in the language of the oppressor was a question posed in relation to the writing of Aimé Césaire and the négritude movement in France in the 1950s (Césaire 1950). More recently the debates have resurfaced in the arguments for and against the use of English between the Nigerian novelist Chinua Achebe, who has argued for the creative hybridization and reappropriation of the English language in many African states and the pragmatic need to use a language common to many African nations, and the Kenyan author Ngugi wa Thiong'o who has vociferously argued the case for writing in Gikuyu because of the irretrievable colonial violence propounded through the imposition of English (Loomba 1998; Achebe 1975; Ngugi 1986). For some time now a debate has been raging in Britain concerning what constitutes 'English' literature on the school curriculum. Some protagonists are arguing for the need to acknowledge the legitimacy of forms of English often referred to as patois, pidgin or creole and to understand these as the creative response to cultural contact and exchange between Britain and the cultures of the Caribbean for example and consequently an important contribution to new literary forms capable of enriching the 'English' language and reflecting the dynamic constantly changing nature of living language. Such positions pose a number of serious challenges to a constituency devoted to sustaining a notion of Englishness which is exclusively white and Anglo-Saxon. Any fixed notion of an academic canon, of course, and the question of a universal aesthetic are also called into question by such moves to reinvent 'Englishness' in the image of the highly heterogeneous and diverse communities which actually make up the nation.

In post-colonial theory certain aspects of appropriation of the language and culture of the colonizer have been discussed in terms of 'mimicry'. Homi Bhabha in a series of influential articles has argued that this should not be mistaken as simply wholesale capitulation to the colonial imperative but should be seen rather as a means of evading colonial control (Bhabha 1994 and 1998). Bhabha's argument turns on the idea that because colonial culture can never faithfully reproduce itself in its own image, each replication (act of mimesis) necessarily involves a slippage or gap wherein the colonial subject inevitably produces a hybridized version of the 'original'. In other words, hybridity is intrinsic to colonial discourse itself, and consequently colonial discourse potentially undoes itself. The importance of the question of agency here is crucial. While recognizing that psychoanalysis has proved fundamental for the theorization of subjectivity, desire and identity, a number of commentators have foregrounded the dangers presented by the exclusive use of a linguistic and psychoanalytic model for analysing the workings of colonialism. They insist on the need also to recognize agency as a conscious choice and as a means of rescuing the colonial subject from perpetual victimhood by acknowledging their ability to act as progenitors of resistance against the violence of colonialism in different ways (Parry 1994; Spivak 1993; Chakrabarty 1992). In feminist theory the related though not identical concept of 'masquerade' has, to the contrary, always contained a strong sense of agency unlike its formulation as 'mimicry' in post-colonial theory (Rivière 1929; Irigaray 1985a and b). Many of the chapters in this volume engage with both the psychic and the material dimensions of this problem.

The chapters in Part III engage with different aspects of these debates and in particular they address the complex issue of how to theorize the question of agency and understand the relationship between the concepts of appropriation and invention as they occur in instances of cross-cultural exchange. Annie E. Coombes's chapter explores the issue of agency by focusing on the possibilities for reclaiming a monument made impossible in the context of post-apartheid South Africa because of its association with the foundations of the apartheid state. Mobilizing the concept of 'translation', she asks how far it is possible to disinvest such a monument of its Afrikaner nationalist associations and reinscribe it with a new set of resonances which effectively produce it as a monument to the ingenuity of the black majority in South Africa and conversely as a staging post for the invention of a new Afrikaner identity by a constituency which self-consciously wishes to disassociate itself from the old regime. Nicholas Thomas's chapter emphasizes the importance of acknowledging the conscious workings of agency in relation to adapted forms of traditional bark clothing and other textiles emerging out of the impact of missionary contact in the Pacific. He argues against understanding the resultant hybrid textiles as objects which embody exchange or transformation as the inevitable result of contact with another culture but rather as objects which made possible new forms of embodiment and collectivity. 'Material arrays of hybrid forms, in other words, can be seen not as indices of mixed identities but as technologies that enable people to act in novel ways, and have novel relations imposed upon them.'

One of the other features of much of the research analysing instances of hybridization is that it focuses on examples where hybridity is seen solely as a condition of relations between the colonized or diasporic communities and aspects of western culture or the culture of the colonizer. Few case studies explore the internal dynamics of hybridity constituted across and within social, political and cultural entities and not exclusively in relation to the West (Brah 1996; Canclini 1990; Coombes 1992). Consequently it becomes a condition which serves to reinforce the notion of a static and unequal set of power relations where one (marginalized) group reacts to the culture of another group in political dominance. Many of the chapters in Part III seek to dispel this distortion.

Sandra Klopper explores the 'Africanization' of the fashion industry in South Africa partly as a response to Thabo Mbeki's call for an 'African Renaissance' and partly as a complex re-evaluation of the past and of South Africa's changing relationship to the rest of the African continent. In tandem with Coombes and Brah, she analyses hybridity as an internal condition and looks at the ways in which the contradictory signs of hybridity in the emerging fashion industry are the result of a concern with South Africa's future role in and relationship to other African countries rather than a concern with how it might be viewed by the West.

Reconfiguring nation, community and belonging

In an increasingly globalized world, the term 'hybridity' has become the means for reflecting upon the relationship between 'the local' and 'the global' and the multiple ways in which globality, region and locality feature in economic, political, and cultural forms and practices. The concept of 'hybridity' as it informs the analysis of the links between the local and the global operates polysemantically, bringing together disparate themes ranging from imperialism to subject formation, and different theoretical traditions covering a variety of disciplines including psychoanalysis, literary criticism, philosophy, sociology, anthropology and history. Thus, the idea of 'hybridity' as John Kraniauskas suggests, 'is also the site of a politics of theory in which alternative uses of the term – and alternatives to the term – fight it out, are articulated and unravelled'. In his chapter, Kraniauskas stages a productive conversation between 'post-colonial' and 'Latin-Americanist' perspectives on cultural studies through a focus on the work of two theorists, Homi Bhabha and Néstor García Canclini, whose work he sees as exemplars of these two schools of thought. These critics are also identified as representing two distinctive theoretical strands: psychoanalytic and literary (Bhabha) and, anthropological and sociological (García Canclini). Kraniauskas foregrounds Dipesh Chakrabarty's image of a 'border-land of temporality' as especially apposite to understanding the work of Bhabha and García Canclini because both 'not only visit borders in their texts . . . but develop 'border epistemologies' too', and both feature disjunctive 'post-colonial' time and space as the constitutive inside of contemporary geopolitics.

As regards Bhabha's work, Kraniauskas highlights its intimate connection with psychoanalysis, arguing that 'postcoloniality here actually works like the Freudian unconscious'. He points to Bhabha's imaginative deployment of the concepts of 'disjuncture' and 'disavowal' which together yield his notion of 'third space'.

However, Kraniauskas takes issue with Bhabha's analysis of agency, finding his conceptualization of agency 'asocial, in other words, an unmediated force operating totally unconsciously'. Hence, he addresses García Canclini's work as a counterpoint to Bhabha's psychoanalytic reading.

From the point of view of a discussion of 'hybridity', García Canclini's work is seen as offering an alternative conceptual repertoire; one that could open a field of operation 'beyond psychoanalysis and deconstruction'. This work, according to Kraniauskas, provides a 'transdisciplinary gaze' (socio-anthropological) on 'transculturated worlds', fostering ways of thinking about Latin American modernization not as an alien and dominant force that works through the substitution of tradition but rather as a project of multi-directional renovation from inside. García Canclini's interdisciplinary 'hybridity' does not simply mean the borrowing of terms from different disciplines. On the contrary, it encompasses their mutual transformation, as when he confronts, and thereby transforms, Gramsci's political concept of 'hegemony' with Bourdieu's sociological concept of 'reproduction'. He locates Latin American modernism at the intersection of 'heterogeneous temporalities', involving processes of 'intercultural hybridization' and 'hybrid sociability'. One cannot just enter and leave modernity since it is a condition that has marked us all globally. The most one can hope for, García Canclini argues, is to 'radicalise the project of modernity'. A significant limitation of both Bhabha and García Canclini, according to Kraniauskas, is that their cultural concerns 'obliterate political economy'.

In S. Sayyid's chapter the work of Al-Azmeh on Islamicism becomes the focus of an argument against the tendency to conflate a rejection of essentialism with a critique of universalism. Anti-essentialism without a critique of universalism, argues Sayyid, could simply serve as another means of endorsing western hegemony. Al-Azmeh's anti-essentialist position – that there is no transhistorical Islamic essence – is shown to be shot through with essentialist tendencies of its own. Moreover, despite its avowed anti-essentialism, the Al-Azmeh discourse constructs the West as embodying 'universal values' whilst Islamicist practices are reduced to being instances of 'particularity'. Sayyid points to global asymmetrical power relations which underline such myths and describes the strategies as examples of 'western supremacist discourses'. He also draws attention to the problematic use by Al-Azmeh of terms such as 'racism in reverse' or 'reverse orientalism' when describing the rejection of liberal metropolitan discourse by South Asian settlers in Britain.

A non-essentialist position consistent with itself would provide a different story. As Sayyid argues, the contest between Islamicists and their opponents is not simply a conflict between 'fundamentalists' and 'liberals' but rather a contestation between 'western asala' and that of 'Muslim asala'. Both are discursive constructions and are part of attempts to remake the world in their own image, albeit in the context of unequal power relations.

Avtar Brah's chapter expands on this discussion by mapping, through a complex and sensitive meditation on identity, how we experience each other and ourselves through the psychic, social and political structures of racialization, gender and class. In her chapter the concept of Britishness/Englishness is inter-rogated. In particular her concern is the analysis of how such concepts are being reconfigured and reconstituted at the end of the millennium. In part, this is also, of course, an exploration and a critique of stories of 'origin'. Brah analyses the processes which underpin this reconfiguration and argues that, even in instances where such processes of change are disavowed by those directly implicated, the impact of such changes are often internalized unconsciously as modalities of sub-jectivity. As a means of unravelling the complicated subject positions which are involved in encounters between racialized subjects, Brah analyses the circum-stances that produce an unanticipated connectedness to a working-class white woman in Southall. In this way Brah's essay brings us back to two of the central themes of this collection, the unexpected and contingent results of lived experi-ence and the fact that we are not inevitably contained by that which seeks to produce us as bounded subjects.

Bibliography

Achebe, Chinua (1975) *Morning yet on Creation Day*, New York: Anchor Press/ Doubleday.

Anderson, Benedict (1983) *Imagined Communities: Reflections on the Origin and Spread of Nationalism*, London: Verso.

Banton, Michael (1987) *Racial Theories*, Cambridge: Cambridge University Press.

Benjamin, Roger (1996) 'Aboriginal Art: Exploitation or Empowerment?', in Rex Butler (ed.), *What is Appropriation? An Anthology of Critical Writings on Austral-ian Art in the '80s and '90s*, Sydney: Institute of Modern Art and the Power Publications.

Bennett, David, ed. (1998) *Multicultural States: Rethinking Difference and Identity*, London and New York: Routledge.

Bhabha, Homi K. (1988) 'Culture's In Between', in David Bennett (ed.), *Multicultu-ral States: Rethinking Difference and Identity*, London and New York: Routledge.

—— (1994) *The Location of Culture*, London and New York: Routledge.

Brah, Avtar (1992) 'Difference, Diversity and Differentiation', in James Donald and Ali Rattansi (eds), *'Race', Culture and Difference*, London: Sage Publications.

—— (1996) *Cartographies of Diaspora: Contesting Identities*, London and New York: Routledge.

Césaire, Aimé (1950) *Discourse on Colonialism*, New York and London: Monthly Review Press, 1972.

Chakrabarty, Dipesh (1992) 'Postcoloniality and the Artifice of History: Who Speaks for "Indian" Pasts?', *Representations*, 37, pp. 1–24.

Coombes, Annie E. (1992) 'Inventing the "Postcolonial": Hybridity and Constitu-ency in Contemporary Curating', *New Formations*, 18, Winter, pp. 39–53.

—— (1994) *Reinventing Africa: Museums, Material Culture and Popular Imagin-ation in Late Victorian and Edwardian England*, New Haven and London: Yale University Press.

De Moraes Farias, P. F. and Karin Barber (eds) (1990) *Self-assertion and Brokerage: Early Cultural Nationalism in West Africa*, Birmingham: Centre for West African Studies.

García Canclini, N. (1989) *Culturas híbridas: estrategias para entrar y salir de la modernidad*, Mexico City: Grijalbo.

Gilroy, Paul (1993a) *Small Acts: Thoughts on the Politics of Black Cultures*, London and New York: Serpent's Tail.

—— (1993b) *The Black Atlantic: Modernity and Double Consciousness*, London: Verso.

Hall, Stuart (1990) 'Cultural Identity and Diaspora', in Jonathan Rutherford (ed.), *Identity, Community, Culture, Difference*, London: Lawrence and Wishart.

—— (1992) 'New Ethnicities', in James Donald and Ali Rattansi (eds), *'Race', Culture and Difference*, London: Sage Publications.

Haraway, Donna J. (1989) *Primate Visions: Gender, Race and Nature in the World of Modern Science*, London and New York: Routledge.

Harding, S. (1990) 'If I should die before I wake up: Jerry Falwell's Pro-Life Gospel', in F. Ginsburg and Lowenhaupt Tsing (eds), *Uncertain Terms*, Boston: Beacon Press.

Hebdige, Dick (1987) *Cut 'n' Mix: Culture, Identity and Caribbean Music*, London: Methuen.

Hobsbawm, Eric and Terence Ranger, eds (1983) *The Invention of Tradition*, Cambridge: Cambridge University Press.

Irigaray, Luce (1985a) *Speculum of the Other Woman*, Ithaca: Cornell University Press.

—— (1985b) *This Sex Which is Not One*, Ithaca: Cornell University Press.

James, Deborah (1990) 'Musical Form and Social history: Research Perspectives on Black South African Music', *Radical History Review*, 46, 7.

Jeater, Diane (1992) 'Roast Beef and Reggae Music, the Passing of Whiteness', *New Formations*, 18, Winter, pp. 107–22.

Lawrence, Errol (1982) 'Just Plain Common Sense: The "Roots" of Racism' in The Centre for Contemporary Cultural Studies (eds), *The Empire Strikes Back: Race and Racism in Seventies Britain*, London: Hutchinson.

Lazarus, Neil (1994) 'National Consciousness and the Specificity of (Post)colonial Intellectualism', in Francis Barker, Peter Hulme and Margaret Iversen (eds), *Colonial Discourse/Postcolonial Theory*, Manchester and New York: Manchester University Press.

—— (1999) *Nationalism and Cultural Practice in the Post-colonial World*, Cambridge: Cambridge University Press.

Long, Edward (1774) *The History of Jamaica, or, General Survey of the Ancient and Modern State of That Island with Reflections on its Situation, Settlements, Inhabitants, Climate, Products, Commerce, Laws and Government*, London: Lowndes.

Loomba, Ania (1998) *Colonialism/Postcolonialism*, London and New York: Routledge.

Mathieson, Susan and David Atwell (1998) 'Between Ethnicity and Nationhood: Shaka Day and the Struggle over Zuluness in Post-Apartheid South Africa', in David Bennett (ed.), *Multicultural States: Rethinking Difference and Identity*, London and New York: Routledge.

Myers, Fred (1991) 'Representing Culture: The Production of Discourse(s) for Aboriginal Acrylic Paintings', *Cultural Anthropology*, 6, 3.

Ngugi wa Thiong'o (1986) *Decolonising the Mind: The Politics of Language in African Literature*, London: James Currey.

Parry, Benita (1994) 'Resistance Theory/Theorising Resistance or Two Cheers for Nativism', in Francis Barker, Peter Hulme and Margaret Iverson (eds), *Colonial*

Discourse/Postcolonial Theory, Manchester and New York: Manchester University Press.

Rivière, Joan (1929) 'Womanliness as Masquerade', *International Journal of Psychoanalysis*, 10, pp. 303–13.

Rose, S., J. Kamin and R. C. Lewontin (1984) *Not in Our Genes*, Harmondsworth: Pelican.

Sharma, S. and J. Sharma (1997) *Disorientating Rhythms*, London: Zed.

Spivak, Gayatri Chakravorty (1993) *Outside in the Teaching Machine*, London and New York: Routledge.

Willis, AnneMarie and Tony Fry (1988–9) 'Art as Ethnocide: The Case of Australia', *Third Text*, 5.

Young, Robert J. C. (1995) *Colonial Desire: Hybridity in Theory, Culture and Race*, London and New York: Routledge.

Yuval-Davis, Nira and Floya Anthias (1989) *Women-Nation-State*, Basingstoke: Macmillan.

Part I
Miscegenation and racial purity

1 Sexual affronts and racial frontiers: European identities and the cultural politics of exclusion in colonial Southeast Asia

Ann Laura Stoler

This chapter is concerned with the construction of colonial categories and national identities and with those people who ambiguously straddled, crossed, and threatened these imperial divides.[1] It begins with a story about *métissage* (interracial unions) and the sorts of progeny to which it gave rise (referred to as *métis*, mixed bloods) in French Indochina at the turn of the twentieth century. It is a story with multiple versions about people whose cultural sensibilities, physical being and political sentiments called into question the distinctions of difference which maintained the neat boundaries of colonial rule. Its plot and resolution defy the treatment of European nationalist impulses and colonial racist policies as discrete projects, since here it was in the conflation of racial category, sexual morality, cultural competence and national identity that the case was contested and politically charged. In a broader sense, it allows me to address one of the tensions of empire which this chapter only begins to sketch: the relationship between the discourses of inclusion, humanitarianism and equality which informed liberal policy at the turn of the century in colonial Southeast Asia and the exclusionary, discriminatory practices which were reactive to, coexistent with and perhaps inherent in liberalism itself.[2]

Nowhere is this relationship between inclusionary impulses and exclusionary practices more evident than in how métissage was legally handled, culturally inscribed, and politically treated in the contrasting colonial cultures of French Indochina and The Netherlands Indies. French Indochina was a colony of commerce occupied by the military in the 1860s and settled by *colons* in the 1870s with a métis population which numbered no more than several hundred by the turn of the century.[3] The Netherlands Indies by contrast, had been settled since the early 1600s, with those of mixed descent or born in the Indies numbering in the tens of thousands in 1900. They made up nearly three-quarters of those legally designated as European. Their *Indische* mestizo culture shaped the contours of colonial society for its first two hundred years.[4] Although conventional

---

From *Comparative Studies in Society and History*, 34, 3 (1992), pp. 514–51.

historiography defines sharp contrasts between French, British and Dutch colonial racial policy and the particular national metropolitan agendas from which they derived, what is more striking is that similar discourses were mapped onto such vastly different social and political landscapes.[5]

In both the Indies and Indochina, with their distinct demographics and internal rhythms, métissage was a focal point of political, legal and social debate. Conceived as a dangerous source of subversion, it was seen as a threat to white prestige, an embodiment of European degeneration and moral decay.[6] This is not to suggest that the so-called mixed-blood problem was of the same intensity in both places nor resolved in precisely the same ways. However, the issues which resonated in these different colonies reveal a patterned set of transgressions that have not been sufficiently explored. I would suggest that both situations were so charged, in part because such mixing called into question the very criteria by which Europeanness could be identified, citizenship should be accorded and nationality assigned. Métissage represented not the dangers of foreign enemies at national borders, but the more pressing affront for European nation-states, what the German philosopher Fichte so aptly defined as the essence of the nation, its 'interior frontiers'.[7]

The concept of an interior frontier is compelling precisely because of its contradictory connotations. As Etienne Balibar has noted, a frontier locates both a site of enclosure and contact, of observed passage and exchange. When coupled with the word interior, frontier carries the sense of internal distinctions within a territory (or empire); at the level of the individual, frontier marks the moral predicates by which a subject retains his or her national identity despite location outside the national frontier and despite heterogeneity within the nation-state. As Fichte deployed it, an interior frontier entails two dilemmas: the purity of the community is prone to penetration on its interior and exterior borders, and the essence of the community is an intangible 'moral attitude', 'a multiplicity of invisible ties'.[8]

Viewing late nineteenth-century representations of a national essence in these terms, we can trace how métissage emerges as a powerful trope for internal contamination and challenge conceived morally, politically and sexually.[9] The changing density and intensity of métissage's discursive field outlines the fault lines of colonial authority: in linking domestic arrangements to the public order, family to the state, sex to subversion, and psychological essence to racial type, métissage might be read as a metonym for the biopolitics of the empire at large.

In both Indochina and The Netherlands Indies, the rejection of métis as a distinct legal category only intensified how the politics of cultural difference were played out in other domains.[10] In both colonies, the *métis-indo* problem produced a discourse in which facile theories of racial hierarchy were rejected, while confirming the practical predicates of European superiority at the same time. The early Vietnamese and Indonesian nationalist movements created new sources of colonial vulnerability, and some of the debates over the nature and definition of Dutch and French national identity must be seen in that light. The resurgence of European nationalist rhetoric may partly have been a response to nationalist resistance in the colonies, but it cannot be accounted for in these terms alone.[11] For French Indochina, discourses about the dangers of métissage were sustained in periods of quiescence and cannot be viewed as rhetorics of reaction *tout court*. This is not to suggest that there was no correspondence between them.[12] But anti-colonial challenges in Indochina, contrary to the discourse which characterized the métis as a potential subversive vanguard, were never predominantly led nor peopled by them. And in the Indies, where persons of mixed descent made up a potentially powerful constituency, the bids they made for economic, social and political reform were more often made in contradistinction to the demands of the native population, not in alliance with them.

Although the content of the métis problem was partially in response to popular threats to colonial rule, the particular form that the securing of European privilege took was not shaped in the colonies alone. The focus on moral unity, cultural genealogy, and language joined the imagining of European colonial communities and metropolitan national entities in fundamental ways. Both visions embraced a moral rearmament, centring on the domestic domain and the family as sites in which state authority could be secured or irreparably undermined.[13]

At the turn of the twentieth century, in both metropole and colony, the liberal impulse for social welfare, representation and protective legislation focused enormous energy on the preparatory environment for civic responsibility: on domestic arrangements, sexual morality, parenting and more specifically on the moral milieu of home and school in which children lived.[14] Both education and upbringing emerged as national projects, but not as we might expect, with a firm sense of national identity imported to the periphery from the metropolitan core. As Eugene Weber has argued for late nineteenth-century France, 'patriotic feelings on the national level, far from instinctive, had to be learned'.[15] As late as 1901, six out of every ten French army recruits had not heard of the Franco-Prussian war.[16] Thus the Gallicization of France and its colonies through compulsory education, moral instruction and language was not a one-way process with a consensual template for that identity forged in the metropole and later transported by new metropolitan recruits to colonial citizens. Between 1871 and 1914, French authorities were preoccupied with the threat of national diminishment and decline, with the study of national character a 'veritable industry in France'.[17]

French anxieties over national identity are commonly attributed to the loss of Alsace-Lorraine in 1870, but of perhaps equal import was the collective assimilation of over 100,000 Algerian Jews under the Crémieux Decree of the same year.[18] Debates over who was really French and who was not intensified over the next twenty years as increasing numbers of working-class Italians, Spanish and Maltese in Algeria were accorded French citizenship. A declining birth rate (accelerating in the 1880s) placed a premium on expanded membership in the French national community but prompted a fear of internal aliens and pseudo-compatriots at the same time.[19] The Dreyfus affair coupled with concerns over the suspect loyalties of the new French of Algeria gave particular urgency to debates about the cultural contours of what it meant to be French.[20]

Heightened debates over the mixed-blood question in the Dutch context converged with domestic and colonial social reform, crystallizing in a civilizing offensive of a somewhat different order. It targeted the 'dangerous classes' in both locales – Holland's paupered residuum (as distinguished from its respectable working class) and the Indies' growing population of impoverished (Indo) Europeans, the majority of whom were of mixed descent but legally classified as European. The domestic project joined liberals and conservatives, Protestants and Catholics in a shared mission, with middle-class energies concentrated around the 'uplifting' of the working-class family and its moral reform. This 'civilizing offensive' focused in large part on child welfare and particularly on those 'neglected' and 'delinquent' children whose 'upbringing' ill-prepared them for 'their future place in the social system' and thus marked them as a danger to the state.[21]

Although national anxieties were not at the same pitch as in France, there is evidence that, at the turn of the century, Dutch national feeling – what Maarten Kuitenbrouwer has called an 'extreme nationalism' – underwent something of a revival', then later subsided again.[22] In tandem with the domestic offensive was also an imperial one that spanned concerns about Dutch paupers in the Indies and 'vagabond Hollanders' in South Africa both. Efforts to counter 'the perils of educational failure' and the increased mixing, marrying and interaction of poor whites with colonized populations in the two locales gave rise to increased investments in the education of poor white children and assaults on the parenting styles those children were subject to at home.[23] The securing of Dutch influence in South Africa on the eve of the Boer War centred on strategies to instil a cultural belonging that was to mark the new boundaries of a 'Greater Netherlands' embracing Flanders, South Africa and the Indies.[24] In both metropolitan class and imperial projects, questions of national identity, childrearing and education were on the public agenda and intimately tied.

Thus, the question of who might be considered truly French or Dutch resonated from core to colony and from colony to core.[25] In the Indies and Indochina, cultural milieu, represented by both upbringing and education, was seen to demarcate which métis children would turn into revolutionaries, patricides, loyal subjects or full-fledged citizens of the nation-state. As T. H. Marshall has argued, 'when the State guarantees that all children shall be educated, it has the requirements and the nature of citizenship definitely in mind'.[26] Métis education raised issues about retaining colonial boundaries and regenerating the nation. At issue were the means by which European *beschaving* (civilization or culture) would be disseminated without undercutting the criteria by which European claims to privilege were made.

As such, the discourses about métissage expressed more pervasive, if inchoate, dilemmas of colonial rule and a fundamental contradiction of imperial domination: the tension between a form of domination simultaneously predicated on both incorporation and distancing.[27] This tension expressed itself in the so-called métis problem in quintessential form. Some métis were candidates for incorporation, but others were categorically denied. In either case, the decision to grant citizenship or subject status to a métis could not be made on the basis of race alone, because all métis shared some degree of European descent by definition. How then could the state mark some candidates so they would be excluded from the national community while retaining the possibility that other individuals would be granted the rights of inclusion because French and Dutch 'blood prevailed in their veins'? I explore that question here by working off of a seemingly disparate set of texts and contexts: a criminal court proceeding in Haiphong in 1898; the Hanoi campaign against child abandonment in the early 1900s; the protracted debate on mixed marriage legislation in the Indies between 1887 and 1898; and finally, the confused and failed efforts of the Indo-European movement itself in the Indies to articulate its opposition to 'pure-blood' Dutch by calling upon race, place and cultural genealogy to make its demands.

In each of these texts, class, gender and cultural markers deny and designate exclusionary practices at the same time. We cannot determine which of these categories is privileged at any given moment by sorting out the fixed primacy of race over gender or gender over class. On the contrary, I trace an unstable and uneven set of discourses in which different institutional authorities claimed primacy for one over another in relationship to how other authorities attempted to designate how political boundaries were to be protected and assigned. For mid-Victorian England, Mary Poovey argues that discourses about gender identity were gradually displaced in the 1850s by the issue of national identity.[28] However, the contestations over métissage suggest nothing linear about these developments. Rather, class distinctions, gender prescriptions, cultural knowledge and racial membership were simultaneously invoked and strategically filled with different meanings for varied projects.

Patriarchal principles were not always applied to shore up government priorities. Colonial authorities with competing agendas agreed on two premises: Children had to be taught both their place and race, and the family was the crucial site in which future subjects and loyal citizens were to be made. These concerns framed the fact that the domestic life of individuals was increasingly subject to public scrutiny by a wide range of private and government organizations that charged themselves with the task of policing the moral borderlands of the European community and the psychological sensibilities of its marginal, as well as supposedly full-fledged, members.

At the heart of this tension between inclusionary rhetorics and exclusionary practices was a search for essences that joined formulations of national and racial identity – what Benedict Anderson has contrasted as the contrary dreams of 'historical destinies' and 'eternal contaminations'.[29] Racism is commonly understood as a visual ideology in which somatic features are thought to provide the crucial criteria of membership. But racism is not really a visual ideology at all; physiological attributes only signal the non-visual and more salient distinctions of exclusion on which racism rests. Racism is not to biology as nationalism is to culture. Cultural attributions in both provide the observable conduits, the indices of psychological propensities and moral susceptibilities seen to shape which individuals are suitable for inclusion in the national community and whether those of ambiguous racial membership are to be classified as subjects or citizens within it.

If we are to trace the epidemiologies of racist and nationalist thinking, then it is the cultural logics that underwrite the relationship between fixed, visual representations and invisible protean essences to which we must attend. This convergence between national and racial thinking achieves particular clarity when we turn to the legal and social debates in the colonies that linked observable cultural styles of parenting and domestic arrangement to the hidden psychological requirements for access to French and Dutch citizenship in this period.

Cultural competence, national identity and métissage

In 1898 in the French Indochinese city of Haiphong, the nineteen-year-old son of a French minor naval employee, Sieur Icard, was charged with assaulting without provocation a German naval mechanic, striking his temple with a whip, and attempting to crush his eye. The boy was sentenced by the tribunal court to six months in prison.[30] Spurred by the father's efforts to make an appeal for an attenuated prison term, some higher officials subsequently questioned whether the penalty was unduly severe. Clemency was not accorded by the Governor-General, and the boy, referred to by the court as 'Nguyen van Thinh *dit* Lucien' (called Lucien) was sentenced to bear out his full term. The case might have been less easily dismissed if it were not for the fact that the son was métis, the child of a man who was a French citizen and a woman who was a colonial subject, his concubine and Vietnamese.

The granting of a pardon rested on two assessments: whether the boy's cultural identity and his display of French cultural competence supported his claim to French citizenship rights. Because the Governor-General's letters listed the boy as Nguyen van Thinh dit Lucien, they thereby invoked not only the double naming of the son, privileging first Nguyen van Thinh over Lucien, but suggested the dubious nature of his cultural affinities, giving the impression that his real name was Nguyen van Thinh, although he answered to the name Lucien. The father, Sieur Icard, attempted to affirm the Frenchness of his son by referring to him as Lucien and eliminated reference to Nguyen. But the angry president of Haiphong's tribunal court used only the boy's Vietnamese name, dropping Lucien altogether and put the very kinship between the father and son in question by naming Icard as the 'alleged' father.

Icard's plea for pardon, which invoked his own patriotic sentiments as well as those of his son, was carefully conceived. Icard protested that the court had wrongly treated the boy as a '*vulgaire annamite*' (a common Annamite) and not as the legally recognized son of a French citizen. Icard held that his son had been provoked and only then struck the German in retaliation. But more important, Lucien had been raised in a French patriotic milieu, in a household in which Germans were held in 'contempt and disdain'. He pointed out that their home was full of drawings of the 1870 (Franco-Prussian) War and that like any impressionable (French) boy of his age, Lucien and his imagination were excited by these images.

The tribunal's refusal to accept the appeal confronted and countered Icard's

claims. At issue was whether Nguyen van Thinh dit Lucien could really be considered culturally and politically French and whether he was inculcated with the
patriotic feelings and nationalist sentiments which might have prompted such a
loyal response. The tribunal argued that Icard was away sailing too much of the
time to impart such a love of *patrie* to his son and that Icard's 'hate of Germans
must have been of very recent origin since he had spent so much time sailing with
foreigners'.[31] The non-French inclinations of the boy were firmly established with
the court's observation that Lucien was illiterate and knew but a few French
words. Icard's argument was thus further undermined since Icard himself 'spoke
no annamite' and therefore shared no common language with his offspring.

Although these counter-arguments may have been sufficient to convince the
Governor-General not to grant leniency, another unclarified but damning reason
was invoked to deny the son's case and the father's appeal: namely, the 'immoral
relations which could have existed between the detainee and the one who
declared himself his father'.[32] Or as put by Villeminot, the city attorney in
Haiphong charged with further investigating Icard's appeal, the boy deserved no
leniency because 'his morality was always detestable' and the police reports per-
mitted one 'to entertain the most serious suspicions concerning the nature of the
relations which Nguyen van Thinh maintained with his alleged father'.[33]

Whether these were coded allegations of homosexuality or referred to a possibly illegal recognition of the boy by Icard (pretending to be his father) is
unclear. Icard's case came up at a time when acts of 'Fraudulent recognition' of
native children were said to be swelling the French citizenry with a bastard population of native poor.[34] Perversion and immorality and patriotism and nationalist
sentiments were clearly considered mutually exclusive categories. As in
nineteenth-century Germany, adherence to middle-class European sexual
morality was one implicit requisite for full-fledged citizenship in the European
nation-state.[35]

But with all these allusions to suspect and duplicitous behaviour perhaps what
was more unsettling in this case was another unspeakable element in this story:
namely, that Icard felt such a powerful sentiment between himself and his son and
that he not only recognized his Eurasian son but went so far as to plead the case of
a boy who had virtually none of the exterior qualities (skin tone, language or
cultural literacy), and therefore could have none of the interior attributes of being
French at all. What the court seemed to have condemned was a relationship in
which Icard could have shown such dedication and love for a child who was
illiterate, ignorant of the French language and who spent most of his time in a
cultural milieu that was much less French than Vietnamese. Under such circumstances, Icard's concern for Lucien was inappropriate and improper; his fatherly
efforts to excuse his son's misdeeds were lauded neither by the lower courts nor
by the Governor-General. On the contrary, paternal love and responsibility were
not to be disseminated arbitrarily as Icard had obviously done by recognizing his
progeny but allowing him to grow up Indochinese. In denying the father's plea,
the court passed sentence both on Icard and his son: both were guilty of
transgressing the boundaries of race, culture, sex and *patrie*. If Icard (whose

misspellings and profession belied his lower-class origins) was not able to bring his son up in a proper French milieu, then he should have abandoned him all together.

What was perhaps most duplicitous in the relationship was that the boy could both be Nguyen van Thinh in cultural sensibilities and Lucien to his father, or, from a slightly different perspective, that Lucien's physical and cultural non-French affinities did not stand in the way of the father's love. Like the relationship with the boy's mother, which was easily attributed to carnal lust, Icard's choice to stand up for his son was reduced to a motive of base desires, sexual or otherwise. Neither father nor son had demonstrated a proper commitment to and identification with those invisible moral bonds by which racist pedigrees and colonial divides were marked and maintained.

Cultural neglect, native mothers and the racial politics of abandonment

The story invokes the multiple tensions of colonial cultures in Southeast Asia and would be of interest for that alone. But it is all the more startling because it so boldly contradicts the dominant formulation of the 'métis question' at the turn of the twentieth century as a problem of 'abandonment', of children culturally on the loose, sexually abused, economically impoverished, morally neglected and politically dangerous. European feminists took up the protection of abandoned mixed-blood children as their cause, condemning the irresponsibility and double standards of European men, but so too did colonial officials who argued that these concubinary relations were producing a new underclass of European pau-pers, of rootless children who could not be counted among the proper European citizenry, whose sartorial trappings merely masked their cultural incompetence, who did not know what it meant to be Dutch or French. The consequences of mixed unions were thus collapsed into a singular moral trajectory, which, without state intervention, would lead to a future generation of Eurasian paupers and prostitutes, an affront to European prestige and a contribution to national decay.

If we look more closely at what was identified as abandonment, the cultural and historical peculiarities of this definition become more apparent. In his com-prehensive history of child abandonment in western Europe, John Boswell commonly uses 'abandonment' to refer to 'the *voluntary* relinquishing of control over children by their natal parents or guardians' and to children who were exposed at the doors of churches or in other public spaces and less frequently for those intentionally exposed to death.[36] Boswell argues that ancient and con-temporary commentators have conflated abandonment with infanticide far more than the evidence suggests. Nevertheless, perceptions and policies on abandon-ment were integrally tied to issues of child mortality. Jacques Donzelot argues that in nineteenth-century France abandonment, often led to high rates of child mortality and that the intensified policing of families was morally justified for those reasons among others.[37] This does not suggest that abandonment always led to death nor that this was always its intent. The point is that in the colonial context, in contrast, discussions of abandonment rarely raise a similar concern for infanticide or even obliquely address this eventuality.

The abandonment of métis children invoked, in the colonial context, not a biological but a social death – a severing from European society, a banishment of 'innocents' from the European cultural milieu in which they could potentially thrive and where some reformers contended they rightfully belonged.[38] Those officials who wrote about métis children argued that exposure in the colonial context was to the native milieu, not the natural elements, and to the immoral influence of native women whose debased characters inclined them to succumb to such illicit unions in the first place. Moreover, abandonment, as we shall see, was not necessarily voluntary, nor did both parents, despite the implication in Boswell's definition, participate in it. The statutes of the Society for the Protection and Education of Young French Métis of Cochinchine and Cambodia defined the issue of abandonment in the following way:

> Left to themselves, having no other guide than their instincts and their passions, these unfortunates will always give free rein to their bad inclinations; the boys will increase the ranks of vagabonds, the girls those of prostitution.
>
> Left to their mothers and lost in the milieu of Annamites, they will not become less depraved. It must not be forgotten that in most cases, the indigenous woman who consents to live with a European is a veritable prostitute and that she will never reform. When, after several years of free union with Frenchmen, the latter disappear or abandon her, she fatally returns to the vice from which she came and she nearly always sets an example of debauchery, sloth, and immorality for her children. She takes care of them with the sole purpose of later profiting from their labor and especially from their vices.
>
> For her métis son, she seeks out a scholarship in a school with the certainty that when her child obtains a minor administrative post, she will profit from it. But, in many cases, the child, ill-advised and ill-directed, does not work and when he leaves school, abandons himself to idleness and then to vagabondage; he procures his means of existence by extortion and theft.
>
> Abandoned métisse girls are no better off; from the cradle, their mothers adorn them with bracelets and necklaces and maintain in them a love of luxury innate in the Annamites. Arriving at the age of puberty, deprived of any skills which would help them survive, and pushed into a life by their mothers that they have a natural tendency to imitate, they will take to prostitution in its diverse forms to procure the means necessary to keep themselves in luxury.[39]

Here, abandonment has specific race, cultural and gender co-ordinates. Most frequently, it referred to the abandonment of métis children by European fathers and their abandonment of the children's native mothers with whom these men lived outside of marriage. The gaze of the colonial state was not directed at children abandoned by native men but only at the progeny of mixed unions. Most significantly, the child, considered abandoned whether he or she remained in the care of the mother, was most frequently classified that way precisely because the child was left to a native mother and to the cultural surroundings in which she lived. But the term abandonment was also used freely in another context to condemn those socially *déclassé* European men who chose to reside with their mixed-blood children in the supposedly immoral and degraded native milieu. In designating cultural rather than physical neglect, abandonment connoted at least two things: that a proper French father would never allow his offspring prolonged contact nor identification with such a milieu and that the native mother of lower class origins would only choose to keep her own children for mercenary purposes.

If abandonment of métis offspring by European men was considered morally reprehensible, the depraved motives of colonized women who refused to give up their children to the superior environment of state institutions were considered worse. Thus the president of The Hanoi Society for the Protection of Métis Youths in 1904 noted that 'numerous mothers refuse to confer their children to us . . . under the *pretext* of not wanting to be apart from them, despite the fact that they may periodically visit them at school'.[40] But if maternal love obscured more mercenary quests to exploit their young for profits and pleasure, as was often claimed, why did so many women not only refuse to hand over their children but reject any form of financial assistance for them? Cases of such refusal were not uncommon. In 1903 the Haiphong court admonished a métisse mother who was herself 'raised with all the exterior signs of a European education' for withdrawing her daughter from a government school 'for motives which could not be but base given the mother's character'.[41] Resistance also came from the children themselves: In 1904, the seventeen-year-old métisse daughter of an Annamite woman cohabited with the French employer of her mother's Annamite lover, declaring that she *volontairement* accepted and preferred her own situation over what the Society for the Protection of Métis Youths could offer.[42] Numerous reports are cited of métisse girls forced into prostitution by *concubine*, that is, by native men who were the subsequent lovers of the girls' native mothers. These cases expressed another sexual and cultural transgression that metropolitan social reformers and colonial authorities both feared: namely, a 'traffic in *filles françaises*' for the Chinese and Annamite market, not for Europeans.[43]

The portrait of abandonment and charitable rescue is seriously flawed, for it misses the fact that the channelling of abandoned métis children into special state institutions was part of a larger (but failed) imperial vision. These children were to be moulded into very special colonial citizens; in one scenario, they were to be the bulwark of a future white settler population, acclimatized to the tropics but loyal to the state.[44] As proposed by the French Feminist caucus at the National Colonial Exposition of 1931, métisse young women could

> marry with Frenchmen, would accept living in the bush where young women from the metropole would be hesitant to follow their husbands, . . . [and would form] the foundation of a bourgeoisie, attached at one and the same time to their native land and to the France of Europe.[45]

This perspective on mixed marriages was more optimistic than some, but echoes the commonly held view that if métisse girls were rescued in time, they could be effectively educated to become *bonnes ménagères* (good housekeepers) of a settled Indochina, wives or domestics in the service of France. Similar proposals, as we shall see, were entertained in the Indies in the same period and there too met with little success. However, in both contexts, the vision of fortifying the colonial project with a mixed-blood yeomanry was informed by a fundamental concern: what could be done with this mixed population, whose ambiguous positioning and identifications could make them either dangerous adversaries or effective partisans of the colonial state?

Fraudulent recognitions and other dangers of métissage

The question of what to do with the métis population prompted a number of different responses, but each hinged on whether métis should be classified as a distinct legal category subject to special education or so thoroughly assimilated into French culture that they would pose no threat. In French Indochina, the model treatment of métis in The Netherlands Indies was invoked at every turn. In 1901, Joseph Chailley-Bert, director of the Union Colonial Française, was sent on a government mission to Java to report on the status of métis in the Indies and on the efficacy of Dutch policy towards them. Chailley-Bert came away from Batavia immensely impressed and convinced that segregation was not the answer. He was overwhelmed by the sheer numbers of persons of mixed descent who occupied high station in the Indies, with wealth and cultivation rivalling those of many 'full-blooded' Europeans. He argued that the Dutch policy not to segregate those of mixed descent nor distinguish between illegitimate and legitimate children was the only humane and politically safe course to pursue. He urged the government to adopt several Dutch practices: that abandoned métis youth be assigned European status until proof of filiation was made, that private organizations in each legal grouping (i.e., European and native) be charged with poor relief rather than the government; and that European standing not be confined to those with the proper 'dosage of blood' alone. In the Indies he noted that such a ruling would be impossible because the entire society was in large part métis and such a distinction 'would allow a distance between the aryan without mix and the asiatic hybrids'.[46]

Monsieur A. July, writing from Hanoi in 1905, similarly applauded 'the remarkably successful results' of the Indies government policy rejecting the legal designation of métis as a caste apart. He argued that France's abolition of slavery and call for universal suffrage had made a tablua rasa of racial prejudice; however, he was less sanguine that France's political system could permit a similar scale of naturalization as that practised by the Dutch, since not all young métis could be recognized as *citoyen français* for reasons he thought better not to discuss. Firmin Jacques Montagne, a head conductor in the Department of Roads and Bridges also urged that French Indochina follow the Indies path, where the Dutch had not only 'safeguarded their prestige, but also profited from a force that if badly directed, could turn against Dutch domination'.[47] Based on the account of a friend who administered a plantation on Java, he urged that métis boys in Indochina, as in the Indies, should be educated in special institutions to prepare them to be soldiers and later for modest employment in commerce or on the estates.

These appeals to Dutch wisdom are so curious because they reflected neither the treatment of the poor Indo-European population in the Indies, nor what administrative quandaries were actually facing Dutch officials there. In the very year of Chailley-Bert's visit to Batavia, the Indies government began a massive investigation of the recent proliferation of European pauperism and its causes. Between 1901 and 1903 several thousands of pages of government reports outlined the precarious economic conditions and political dangers of a population legally classified as European but riddled with impoverished widows, beggars, vagrants and abandoned children who were mostly Indo-Europeans.[48] The pauperism commission identified an 'alarming increase' of poor Europeans born in the Indies or of mixed parentage, who could compete for civil service positions neither with the influx of 'full-blooded' Dutch educated in Europe nor with the growing number of better-educated Indonesians now qualified for the same jobs.[49]

The Dutch did investigate Indo-European adult life and labour, but the focus of the commissions' concern was on children and their upbringing in the parental home (*opvoeding in de ouderlijkewoning*).[50] Among the more than 70,000 legally classified Europeans in the Indies in 1900, nearly seventy per cent knew little Dutch or none at all. Perhaps the more disturbing finding was that many of them were living on the borderlands of respectable bourgeois European society in styles that indicated not a failed version of European culture but an outright rejection of it.[51]

The causes of the situation were found in the continued prevalence of concubinage, not only among subaltern European military barred from legal marriage but also among civil servants and European estate supervisors for whom marriage to European women was either formally prohibited or made an economically untenable option. Although government and private company policies significantly relaxed the restrictions imposed on the entry of women from Europe after the turn of the century, non-conjugal mixed unions, along with the gendered and racist assumptions on which they were based, were not about to disappear by government fiat. In Indochina, French officials had to issue repeated warnings against concubinage from 1893 to 1911 (just when the societies for protection of métis youth were most active), suggesting the formation of another generation that threatened not to know where they belonged.[52] The pauperism commission condemned the general moral environment of the Indies, targeting concubinage as the source of a transient 'rough and dangerous pauper element' that lived off the native population when they could, disgracing European prestige and creating a financial burden for the state.[53]

But Indo-European pauperism in the Indies could not be accounted for by concubinage alone. The pauperism commission's enquiry revealed a highly stratified educational system in which European youths educated in the Indies were categorically barred from high-level administrative posts and in which middling Indo-Europeans were offered only a rudimentary training in Dutch, a basic requisite for any white collar job.[54] European public (free) schools in the Indies, like those in Indochina, were largely schools for the poor (*armenscholen*) attended by and really only designed for a lower-class of indigent and mixed-blood Europeans.[55]

A concrete set of reforms did form a response, to some extent, to concubinage and educational inequities, but European pauperism was located in a more unsettling problem: It was seen to have deeper and more tenacious roots in the surreptitious penetration of inlanders into the legal category of European.[56] Because the European legal standing exempted men both from labour service and from the harsher penal code applied to those of native status, officials argued that an underclass of European soldiers and civilians was allegedly engaged in a profitable racket of falsely recognizing native children who were not their own for an attractive fee. Thus, the state commission argued, European impoverishment was far more limited than the statistics indicated: the European civil registers were inflated by lowlife mercenaries and, as in Indochina, by *des sans-travail* (the unemployed), who might register as many as thirty to forty children who did not have proper rights to Dutch or French citizenship at all.[57]

The issue of fraudulent recognition, like concubinage, hinged on the fear that children were being raised in cultural fashions that blurred the distinctions between ruler and ruled and on the fear that uneducated native young men were acquiring access to Dutch and French nationality by channels, such as false filiation, that circumvented state control. Such practices were allegedly contingent on a nefarious class of European men who were willing to facilitate the efforts of native mothers who sought such arrangements. Whether there were as many fraudulent recognitions of métis children in Indochina, or *kunstmatig gefabriceerde Europeanen* (artificially fabricated Europeans) in the Indies as authorities claimed is really not the point. The repeated reference to fictitious, fraudulent and fabricated Europeans expressed an underlying preoccupation of colonial authorities, shared by many in the European community at large, that illicit incursions into the Dutch and French citizenry extended beyond those cases labelled fraudulent recognition by name. We should remember that Nguyen van Thinh dit Lucien's condemnation was never explicitly argued on the basis of his suspect parentage, but on the more general contention that his behaviour had to be understood as that of an *indigène* in disguise, not as a citizen of France. Annamite women who had lived in concubinage were accused of clothing their métisse daughters in European attire, while ensuring them that their souls and sentiments remained deeply native.[58]

Colonial officials wrestled with the belief that the Europeanness of métis children could never be assured, despite a rhetoric affirming that education and upbringing were transformative processes. Authorities spoke of abandoned métisse daughters as *les filles françaises* when arguing for their redemption, but, when supporting segregated education, these same authorities recast these youths as physically marked and morally marred with 'the faults and mediocre qualities of their [native] mothers' as 'the fruits of a regrettable weakness'.[59] Thus, abandoned métis children represented not only the sexual excesses and indiscretions of European men but the dangers of a subaltern class, degenerate (*verwilderen*) and lacking paternal discipline (*gemis aan vaderlijke tucht*), a world in which mothers took charge.[60] To what extent the concern over neglected métis children was not only about the negative influence of the native milieu but about the threat of single-mother families as in Europe and America in the same period is difficult to discern.[61] The absence of patriarchal authority in households of widows and native women who had exited from concubinary domestic arrangements was clearly seen as a threat to the proper moral upbringing of children and sanctioned the intervention of the state. Métis children undermined the inherent principles upon which national identity thrived – those *liens invisibles* (invisible bonds) that all men shared and that so clearly and comfortably marked off *pur-sang* (pure blood) French and Dutch from those of the generic colonized.

The option of making métis a legal category was actively debated in international colonial fora through the 1930s but was rejected on explicitly political grounds. French jurists persuasively argued that such a legal segregation would infest the colonies with a destructive virus, with a 'class of *déraciné*, déclassé', 'our most dangerous enemies', 'insurgents, irreconcilable enemies of our domination'.[62] The legal rejection of difference in no way diminished the concern about them. On the contrary, it produced an intensified discourse in which racial thinking remained the bedrock on which cultural markers of difference were honed and more carefully defined.

This was nowhere clearer than in the legal discussion about whether and by what criteria children of unknown parents should be assigned French or native nationality.[63] Under a 1928 *décret*, all persons born in Indochina (that is, on French soil) of unknown parents of which one was presumed to be French could obtain recognition of '*la qualité de français*'.[64] Presumed Frenchness rested on two sorts of certainty: the evaluation of the child's 'physical features or race' by a 'medico-legal expert' and a 'moral certainty' derived from the fact that the child 'has a French name, lived in a European milieu and was considered by all as being of French descent'.[65] Thus, French citizenship was not open to all métis but restricted by a 'scientific' and moral judgment that the child was decidedly non-indigene.[66] As we have seen in the case of Nguyen van Thinh dit Lucien, however, the name Lucien, the acknowledged paternity by Icard and the patriotic ambiance of the household were sufficient only for the child to be legally classified as French, not for him to be treated as French by a court of law. Inclusionary laws left ample room for an implementation based on exclusionary principles and practices.

The moral outrage and crusade against abandonment attended to another underlying dilemma for those who ruled. Métis youth not only had to be protected from the 'demoralisation of the special milieu' in which they were raised but, as important, educated in a way that would not produce unreasonable expectations nor encourage them to harbour desires for privilege above their station simply because French or Dutch blood flowed in their veins. The aim of the Hanoi Society for the Protection of Métis Youth was 'to inculcate them with our sense of honor and integrity, while only suggesting to them modest tastes and humble aspirations'.[67] Similarly, in the Indies, Indo-European pauperism was commonly attributed to the 'false sense of pride' of Indos who refused to do manual labour or take on menial jobs, who did not know that 'real Dutchmen' in The Netherlands worked with their hands. The assault was double-edged. It blamed those impoverished for their condition but also suggested more subtly that, if they were really Dutch in spirit and drive, such problems of pauperism would not have arisen.

The cultural frontiers of the national community

Fears of white impoverishment in the colonies were held by many different constituencies: by social reformers concerned with child welfare, by European feminists opposed to the double standard of European men, and by colonial officials who fiercely debated whether increased education would diffuse the discontents of the European poor or, as with the peasants of France, turn them into empowered enemies of the state.[68] However, none of these fears was very far removed from the more general concern that European men living with native women would themselves lose their Dutch or French identity and would become degenerate and *décivilisé*. Internal to this logic was a notion of cultural, physical and moral contamination, the fear that those Europeans who did not subscribe to Dutch middle-class conventions of respectability would not only compromise the cultural distinctions of empire, but waver in their allegiances to metropolitan rule.

Such fears were centred on mixed bloods but not on them alone. In the Indies, at the height of the liberal Ethical Policy, a prominent doctor warned that those Europeans born and bred in the colonies, the *blijvers* (those who remained), lived in surroundings that stripped them of their *zuivere* (pure) European sensibilities, which 'could easily lead them to metamorphize into Javanese'.[69] A discourse on degeneracy with respect to the creole Dutch was not new in the Indies but in this moment of liberal reform took on a new force with specific moral co-ordinates. This discourse was directed at poor whites living on the cultural borderlands of the *echte* (true) European community, at some European men who married native women, at all European women who chose to marry native men, and at both European and Indo-European women who cohabited with, but chose not to marry, men of other nationalities.

These specific fears may have been intensified by the surge of political activity at the turn of the century, coalescing around an Indisch population of 'mixed-blood' and 'pure-blood' Dutch of Indies origin. Their distinct economic interests, cultural style and legal positioning produced equivocal loyalties to the colonial state. The Indische voice, evident in a range of new publications and associations, identified itself in two ways: by its cultural rooting in the Indies rather than The Netherlands and by an ambiguous appeal to the notion of race. At a time when the native nationalist project was not yet underway, this Indische press articulated a new notion of a fatherland loyal to, but distinct from, the

Dutch fatherland and firmly opposed to the Dutch-born elite who managed the state. Between 1898 and 1903 various Indisch groups rose, fell, and reassembled as they each sought viable programmes to promote the 'uplifting' of the Indo-European poor without linking their own fate to them. To do so, they resorted to principles of racial hierarchy that accorded those of a certain upbringing, sexual morality and cultural sensibility a right to privilege and to rule.[70]

What underwrites this common discourse is a new collusion between race and culture: as race dropped out of certain legal discriminations, it reemerged, marked out by specific cultural criteria in other domains. The contemporary discourse on the new racism in Europe situates 'cultural racism' as a relatively recent and nuanced phenomenon, replacing the physiological distinctions on which earlier racisms had so strongly relied.[71] The 'novelty' of the new racism is often located in its strong cultural inflection, embedded in wider structures of domination, based in the family, and tied to nationalist sentiments in ways that make it more relevant to a wider constituency and therefore more pervasive and insidious to weed out.[72] But are these features of the 'new racism' really new at all? I would argue, on the contrary, that they are firmly rooted in a much earlier discourse that linked race, culture and national identity, a discourse elaborated at the turn of the twentieth century in Europe's 'laboratories of modernity' – the colonies – not at home.[73]

It is striking how critical the concept of cultural surroundings (*milieu* in French, *omgeving* in Dutch) in this period was to the new legal stipulations on which racial distinctions and national identity were derived. Paul Rabinow makes a strong case that the concern about milieu permeating French colonial thinking on education, health, labour and sex in the late nineteenth century can be understood only in terms of the scientific *episteme* on which it relied.[74] Medical guides to the acclimatization of Europeans in tropical regions frequently warned that Europeans would lose their physical health and cultural bearings if they stayed in the tropics too long. Debates over whether European children should be schooled in France or The Netherlands were prompted by efforts to create the social habitus in which sentiments and sensibilities would be shaped.[75] These debates drew not so much on Darwin as on a popular neo-Lamarckian understanding of environment in which racial and national essences could be secured or altered by the physical, psychological, climatic and moral surroundings in which one lived. The issue of *omgeving* and the linkages between national, racial and cultural identity were, however, most thoroughly thought out in the colonial legal discourse on the criteria for European status and inscribed, not in the laws themselves, which self-consciously disclaimed racial difference, but in the cultural logic and racist assumptions underpinning the legal arguments. What is apparent in these documents is a tension between a belief in the immutability and fixity of racial essence and a discomforting awareness that these racial categories are porous and protean at the same time. More unsettling still was the cultural perception that the essences embodied by the colonized and colonizer were asymmetric. Thus Javanese or Vietnamese might at any moment revert to their natural indigenous affiliations, while a Dutch essence was so fragile that it could unwittingly transform into something Javanese.

Jus sol, jus sanguinis and nationality

'In the civilized world, no one may be without a relationship to the state.'[76] J. A. Nederburgh, one of the principal architects of Indies colonial law in 1898, engaged the question of national identity and membership more directly than many of his contemporaries. He argued that in destroying racial purity, colonialism had made obsolete the criteria of *jus soli* (place of birth) and *jus sanguinis* (blood descent) for determining nationality. Colonial *vermenging* (mixing or blending), he contended, had produced a new category of 'wavering classes', large groups of people whose place of birth and mixed genealogies called into question the earlier criteria by which rights to metropolitan citizenship and designations of colonial subject had once been assigned. Taking the nation to be those who shared 'morals, culture, and perceptions, feelings that unite us without one being able to say what they are', Nederburgh concluded that one could not differentiate who had these sensibilities by knowing birthplace and kinship alone. He pointed to those of 'pure European blood' who

> for years remained almost entirely in native surroundings [*omgeving*] and became so entirely nativized [*verinlandschen*] that they no longer felt at ease among their own kind [*rasgenooten*] and found it difficult to defend themselves against *Indische* morals and points of view.[77]

He concluded that surroundings had an 'overwhelming influence', with 'the power to almost entirely neutralise the effects of descent and blood'.[78] Although Nederburgh's claim may seem to suggest a firm dismissal of racial supremacy, we should note that he was among the most staunchly conservative legalists of his time, a firm defender of the superiority of western logic and law.[79] By Nederburgh's cultural account, Europeans, especially children 'who because of their age are most susceptible and often the most exposed' to native influence in school and native servants at home, who remained too long in the Indies 'could only remain *echte-Europeesch* (truly European) in thought and deed with much exertion'.[80] While Nederburgh insisted that he was not 'against *Indische* influence *per se*', he recommended that the state allocate funds to bring up European children in Holland.[81] Some eight years later, at the height of the Ethical Policy, another prominent member of the colonial elite made a similar but more radical recommendation to close all schools of higher education in Batavia and to replace them with state-subsidized education in Holland to improve the quality of the coloured (*kleuringen*) in the civil servant ranks.[82] Both proposals derived from the same assumption: that it was 'impossible for persons raised and educated in the Indies to be bearers [*dragers*] of Western culture and civilization'.[83]

Attention to upbringing, surroundings and milieu did not disengage personal potential from the physiological fixities of race. Distinctions made on the basis of *opvoeding* (upbringing) merely recoded race in the quotidian circumstances that enabled acquisition of certain cultural competencies and not others. The focus on milieu naturalized cultural difference, sexual essence and moral fibre of

Europeanness in new kinds of ways. I have discussed elsewhere how the shift in the colonies to white endogamy and away from concubinage at the turn of the twentieth century, an intensified surveillance of native servants and a sharper delineation of the social space in which European children could be brought up and where and with whom they might play not only marked out the cultural borders of the European community but indicated how much political security was seen to reside in the choices of residence, language and cultural style that individuals made. Personal prescriptions for inclusion as citizens of the Dutch state were as stringent and intimate as those that defined the exclusion of its subjects.[84] The wide gap between prescription and practice suggests why the prescriptions were so insistently reiterated, updated and reapplied. Among those classified as European, there was little agreement on these prescriptions, which were contested, if not openly defied.

In 1884, legal access to European equivalent status in the Indies required a 'complete suitability [*geschiktheid*] for European society', defined as a belief in Christianity, fluency in spoken and written Dutch, and training in European morals and ideas.[85] In the absence of an upbringing in Europe, district authorities were charged with evaluating whether the concerned party was 'brought up in European surroundings as a European'.[86] But European equivalence was not granted simply on the display of a competence and comfort in European norms. It required that the candidate 'no longer feel at home' (*niet meer thuis voelt*) in native society and have already 'distanced' himself from his native being (*Inlander-zijn*). In short the candidate could neither identify nor retain inappropriate senses of belonging or longings for the milieu from which she or he came.[87] The mental states of potential citizens were at issue, not their material assets alone. Who were to be the arbitrators? Suitability to which European society and to which Europeans? The questions are disingenuous because the coding is clear: cultural competence, family form and a middle-class morality became the salient new criteria for marking subjects, nationals, citizens and different kinds of citizens in the nation-state. As European legal status and its equivalent became accessible to an ever broader population, the cultural criteria of privilege was more carefully defined. European women who subscribed to the social prescription of white endogamy were made the custodians of a new morality – not, as we shall see, those 'fictive' European women who rejected those norms.

Colonial practice contradicted the moral designations for European national and racial identity in blatant ways: which European morality was to be iconized? That embraced by those European men who cohabited with native women, became nativized and supported their offspring? Or the morality of European men who retained their cultural trappings as they lived with native women who bore métis children, then departed for Europe unencumbered when their contracts were done? Or was it the morality of colonial officials who barred the filing of paternity suits against European men by native women or the morality of those who argued for it on the grounds that it would hinder fraudulent acknowledgements and easy recognitions by lower-class European men? What can we make of the ruling on European equivalence for non-native residents that stipulated that candidates must be from regions or states that subscribed to a monogamous family law?[88] How did this speak to the thousands of Indisch Dutch men for whom concubinage was the most frequently chosen option? And finally, if national identity was, as often stated, 'an indescribable set of invisible bonds', what did it mean when a European woman upon marriage to a native man was legally reclassified to follow his nationality? As we shall see, these invisible bonds, in which women only had a conjugal share by proxy to their husbands, were those enjoyed by some but not all men. The paradox is that native women married to European men were charged with the upbringing of children, with the formative making of Dutch citizens, and with culturally encoding the markers of race. Colonial cultures created problematic contexts in which patriarchal principles and criteria for citizenship seemed to be at fundamental odds. At a time when European feminists were turning to motherhood as a claim to citizenship, this notion of 'mothers of citizens' meant something different in colonial politics, where definitions of proper motherhood served to clarify the blurred boundaries of nation and race.[89]

The mixed-marriage law of 1898

The mixed-marriage law of 1898 and the legal arguments which surrounded it are of special interest on several counts. Nowhere in the Dutch colonial record is the relationship between gender prescription, class membership and racial category so contentiously debated and so clearly defined; nowhere is the danger of certain kinds of mixing so directly linked to national image while references to race are denied.[90] This is a liberal discourse ostensibly about the protection of native (men's) rights and later viewed as the paragon of ethical intent to equalize and synchronize colonial and metropolitan law. But, as Willem Wertheim noted nearly forty years ago, it did far more to buttress racial distinctions than to break them down.[91]

Legal attention to mixed marriages was not new in the Indies but had never been formalized as it was to be now.[92] Mixed marriages had been regulated by government decree and church decretals soon after the East Indies Company established a settlement in Batavia in the early seventeenth century. The decree of 1617 forbidding marriages between Christian and non-Christian remained intact for over two hundred years. With the new Civil Code of 1848, the religious criteria were replaced with the ruling that marriage partners of European and native standing would both be subject to European law.

The legislation on mixed marriages prior to 1898 was designed to address one kind of union but not others. The 1848 ruling allowed European men already living in concubinage with non-Christian native women to legalize those unions and the children born from them. Although the civil law of 1848 was derived from the Napoleonic civil code, a dominant principle of it had been curiously ignored: that upon marriage a woman's legal status was made that of her husband. As Dutch jurists were to argue a half-century later, because mixed marriages had then been overwhelmingly between European men and native women, the latter's legal incorporation could be easily assumed. This, however, was no longer the case in the 1880s when Indies colonial officials noted two troubling phenomena: First, more women classified as European were choosing to marry non-European men; and second, concubinage continued to remain the domestic arrangement of choice over legal marriage.[93] Legal specialists argued that concubinage was a primary cause of Indo-European impoverishment and had to be discouraged. However, the mixed-marriage rulings, as they stood, were so complicated and costly that people continued to choose cohabitation over legal marriage. Perhaps more disturbing still, some European, Indo-European, and native women opted to retain their own legal standing (thereby protecting their own material assets and those they could bestow on their children), thus rejecting marriage altogether.[94]

Colonial lawyers were thus faced with a conundrum: how could they implement a ruling that would facilitate certain kinds of mixed marriages (over concubinage) and condemn others. Two basic premises were accepted on all sides: that the family was the bulwark of state authority and that the unity of the family could only be assured by its unity in law.[95] Thus, legitimate children could not be subject to one law and their father to another, nor could women hold native status while their husbands retained that of a European.[96] Given this agreement, there were two possible solutions: either the 'superior European standing' of either spouse would determine the legal status (and nationality) of the other; or, alternately, the patriarchal principle – that is, a woman follows the legal status of her husband (regardless of his origin) – would be applied. Principles of cultural and male supremacy seem to be opposed. Let us look at why they were not.

Those who argued that a European woman should retain her European standing in a mixed marriage did so on the grounds, among others, that European prestige would be seriously compromised. The liberal lawyer J. H. Abendanon cogently argued that European women would be placed in a 'highly unfavorable and insecure position'; by being subject to adat, she risked becoming no more than a concubine if her native husband took a second wife, as polygamy under Islamic law was not justification for divorce. Others pointed out that she would be subject to the penal code applied to those of native status. Should she commit a crime, she would be treated to 'humiliating physical and psychological punishment', for which her 'physical constitution' was unsuited. Her relegation to native status would thus cause an 'outrageous scandal', in the European community at large.[97]

The argument above rested on one central but contested assumption: that all women classified as European deserved the protection and privilege of European law. However, those who made the counter-case that the patriarchal principle be applied regardless of origin, argued that the quality of women with European standing was not the same. Although the state commission noted that mixed marriages between European women and native men were relatively few, it underlined their marked and 'steady increase among certain classes of the inhabitants'.[98] Such mixed marriages, all but unthinkable in 1848 but now on the rise among Indo-European and even full-blooded European women with native men, were attributed to the increasing impoverishment and declining welfare of these women on the one hand and of the 'intellectual and social development' among certain classes of native men on the other.[99] The latter issue, however, was rarely addressed because the gender hierarchy of the argument was contingent on assuming that women who made such conjugal choices were neither well-bred nor deserving of European standing.

One lawyer, Taco Henny, argued that the category, European, was a legal fiction not indicative of those who actually participated in the cultural and moral life of the European community and that the majority of women who made such choices were 'outwardly and inwardly indistinguishable from natives'. Because these women tended to be of lower-class origin or mixed racial descent, he held that they were already native in culture and inclination and needed no protection from that cultural milieu in which they rightly belonged. Similarly, their subjection to the native penal code was no reason for scandal because it was appropriate to their actual station. They were already so far removed from Dutch society proper that it would cause no alarm.

If Taco Henny's argument was not convincing enough, Pastor van Santen made the case in even bolder terms: 'The European woman who wants to enter into such a marriage has already sunk so deep socially and morally that it does not result in ruin, either in her own eyes or those of society. It merely serves to consolidate her situation.'[100] Such arguments rested on an interior distinction between *echte* Dutch women and those in whom 'very little European blood actually flowed in their veins' within the category of those classified as European. Pastor van Santen's claim that this latter group had already fallen from cultural and racial grace had its 'proof' in yet another observation: 'that if she was still European in thought and feeling, she would never take a step that was so clearly humiliating and debasing in the eyes of actual (*werkelijk*) European women'.[101] This reasoning (which won in the end) marshalled the patriarchal tenets of the civil code to exclude women of a certain class and cultural milieu from Dutch citizenship rights without directly invoking race in the legal argument.

But this gendered principle did more work still and could be justified on wider grounds. First, such legislation defined a 'true' European woman in accepted cultural terms: first, by her spousal choice, and, second, by her maternal sentiments. She was to demonstrate that she put her children's interests first by guarding their European standing, which would be lost to her future progeny if she married a non-European under the new law. As such, it strongly dissuaded 'true' European women from choosing to marry native men. This was its implicit and, according to some advocates, its explicit intent. In addition, it spoke on the behalf of well-to-do native men, arguing that they would otherwise lose their access to agricultural land and other privileges passed from fathers to sons under adat law.[102] Finally, the new legislation claimed to discourage concubinage, as native men could thus retain their customary rights and would not be tempted to live with Indo-European and 'full-blooded' European women outside of marriage. But perhaps most important, this appeal to patriarchy prevented the infiltration of increasing numbers of native men into the Dutch citizenry, particularly those of the middle classes, who were considered to have little to lose and much to gain by acquiring a Dutch nationality. Those who supported 'uplifting' native men to European status through marriage would in effect encourage marriages of convenience at the expense of both European women who were drawn to such unions and those who prided themselves on the cultural distinctions that defined them as European.[103] Here again, as in the fraudulent recognitions of métis children, at issue was the undesirability of an increase in 'the number of persons who would only be European in name'.[104]

In the end, the mixed-marriage ruling and the debates surrounding it were more an index than a cause of profound changes in thinking about sexual practice, national identity and colonial morality. Mixed marriages increased between native women and European men between 1900 and 1920. This was evident in the declining number of acknowledgements of children born out of wedlock and in an increased number of single European men who now married their *huishoudster* (housekeeper or sexual companion or both).[105] Condemnation of concubinage came simultaneously from several sources. The Pauperism Commission had provided new evidence that concubinage was producing an underclass of Indos that had to be curbed. By treating prostitution and the *huishoudster* system in the colonies as similar phenomena, the Nederlandschen Vrouwenbond (Dutch Women's Association) conflated the distinct options such arrangements afforded women and rallied against both.[106] The Sarekat Islam, one of the strongest native nationalist organizations, also campaigned against concubinage on religious grounds that may have discouraged some native women from such unions.[107] Still, in 1920 half the métis children of a European father and native mother were born outside of marriage. After 1925 the number of mixed marriages fell off again as the number of Dutch-born women coming to the Indies increased fourfold.

Hailed as exemplary liberal legislation, the mixed-marriage ruling was applied selectively on the basis of class, gender and race. By reinvoking the Napoleonic civil code, European men were assured that their 'invisible bonds' of nationality remained intact regardless of their legal partner. European women, on the other hand, were summarily (but temporarily) disenfranchised from their national community on the basis of conjugal choice alone.[108] Those mixed marriages which derived from earlier cohabitations between European men and native women were not the unions most in question, and jurists of different persuasions stated as much throughout the debate. These marriages were considered unproblematic on the assumption that a native woman would be grateful for, and proud of, her elevated European status and content with legal dependence on a European man. Were native women easily granted European legal standing and Dutch citizenship because there was no danger that they could or would fully exercise their rights? The point is never discussed because racial and gender privileges were in line.

But what about the next generation of métis? Although the new ruling effectively blocked the naturalization of native adult men through marriage, it granted a new generation of métis children a European standing by affixing their nationality to their father's. Would this generation be so assuredly cut from their mother's roots as well? The persistent vigilance with which concern for *omgeving*, upbringing, class and education were discussed in the 1920s and 1930s suggests that there were resounding doubts. The Netherlands Indies Eugenics Society designed studies to test whether children of Europeans born in the Indies might display different 'racial markers' than their parents.[109] Eugenicist logic consolidated discussions about national identity and cultural difference in a discourse of 'fitness' that specified the interior frontiers of the nation, reaffirming yet again that upbringing and parenting were critical in deciding who would be marked as a fictive compatriot or true citizen.

Although the race criterion was finally removed from the Indies constitution in 1918 under native nationalist pressure, debates over the psychological, physical and moral make-up of Indo-Europeans intensified in the 1920s and 1930s more than they had before. A 1936 doctoral dissertation at the University of Amsterdam could still 'explain the lack of energy' of Indo-Europeans by the influence of a sapping and warm, dank climate; by the bad influence of the 'energy-less Javanese race' on Indo-Europeans; and by the fact that 'halfbloods' were not descended from the 'average European' and the 'average Javanese'.[110] In the 1920s, the European-born Dutch population was visibly closing its ranks, creating new cultural boundaries while shoring up its old ones. Racial hate (*rassenhaat*) and representation were watchwords of the times. A renewed disdain for Indos permeated a discourse that heightened in the Depression as the nationalist movement grew stronger and as unemployed 'full-blooded' Europeans found 'roaming around' in native villages blurred with the ranks of the Indo poor. How the colonial state distinguished these two groups from one another and from 'natives' on issues of unemployment insurance and poor relief underscored how crucial these interior frontiers were to the strategies of the emerging welfare state.[111]

Indo-Europeans and the quest for a fatherland

The slippage between race and culture, as well as the intensified discussions of racial membership and national identity, were not invoked by the *echte-Europeesche* population alone. We have seen that the moral geography of the colonies had a metonymic quality. Despite the huge numbers of Europeans of mixed parentage and substantial economic means, the term Indo was usually reserved for that segment who were *verindische* (indianized) and poor. Less clear are the cultural, political and racial criteria by which those of mixed descent identified themselves. The contradictory and changing criteria used by the various segments of the Indo-European movement at the turn of the twentieth century highlight how contentious and politically contingent these deliberations were.

It is not accidental that the term Indo-European is difficult to define. In the Indies it applied to those of *mengbloeden* (mixed blood) of European and native origin, to Europeans born in the Indies of Dutch nationality and not of native origin, and to those *pur-sang* Europeans born elsewhere who referred to the Indies as a 'second fatherland'.[112] The semantics of mixing thus related to blood, place and belonging to different degrees and at different times. *Soeria Soemirat*, one of the earliest publications of the Indo-European constituency in the late 1890s, included among its members all Indies-born Europeans and took as its central goal the uplifting of the (Indo)-European poor. The Indisch Bond, formed in 1898, was led by an Indies-born European constituency that spoke for the Indo poor but whose numbers were rarely represented in their ranks. At the heart of both organizations was the push for an *Indisch vaderland*, contesting both the popular terms of Indonesian nationalism and the exclusionary practices of the Dutch-born (*totok*) society.[113]

The Indo-European movement never developed as a nationalist movement. As 'socially thin' as Benedict Anderson suggests its creole counterpart was in the Americas, it could neither enlist a popular constituency nor dissociate from its strong identification with the European-born Dutch elite. The Indisch movement often made its bids for political and economic power by invoking Eurasian racial superiority to inlanders while concurrently denying a racial criteria for judging their status *vis-à-vis* European-born Dutch. The subsequent effort in 1912 to form an Indische Partij (with the motto 'Indies for the Indiers') was stridently anti-government, with a platform that addressed native as well as poor Indo welfare. Despite an inclusionary rhetoric, its native and poor Indo constituency were categorically marginalized and could find no common political ground.[114] By 1919, when native nationalist mobilization was gaining strength, the need for a specifically Indo-Bond took on new urgency and meaning. As its founder argued, 'it would be a *class-verbond* (class-based association) to support the interests of the larger Indo-group'.[115] This organization, eventually called the Indo-Europeesch Verbond (IEV), with more than ten thousand members in 1924, continued to plead the cause of the Indo poor while remaining unequivocally loyal to the Dutch colonial state. This truncated version of a much more complicated story, nevertheless, illustrates the unsettling point that the poor Indo constituency never achieved a political voice. However large their numbers, they were silently rejected from the early Indonesian nationalist movement and could only make their demands based on claims to a cultural and racial alliance with those Dutch who ruled.[116]

Questions of cultural, racial and national identity were particularly charged around proposals for Indo-European agricultural settlements. This utopian project for white settler colonies peopled with those of mixed descent joined persons of widely disparate political persuasions in curious ways. In 1874 and 1902 state commissions on European pauperism had begun to explore the agricultural possibilities for the Indo poor. Their proposals focused on beggar colonies, self-sufficient rural confinements in which (Indo)European paupers would be housed, fed and kept out of sight. Other, more ambitious schemes advocated intensive horticultural and small-scale estates that would neither compete with native peasant production nor the agribusiness industry. These rural solutions to the mixed-blood problem, entertained in both the Indies and Indochina, were based on a common set of premises: that native blood ties would make them more easily acclimatized to tropical agriculture, while their European heritage would provide them with the reason and drive for success. Thus brawn and brains, tropical know-how and European science, and government assistance and private initiative were to come together to produce an economically self-sustaining, morally principled and loyal *volk*. The Indische Bond first, and the IEV later, made land rights and agricultural settlements for needy Indos one of its principal platforms. Conservative and fascist-linked organizations concerned with European unemployment in Holland and European prestige in the colonies also proposed a New Guinea settled by white people that would serve their imperial plan. As a province of a *Groter Nederland*, New Guinea might absorb an economically weak underclass in the metropole, alleviate Dutch unemployment and foster a settler colonialism in the Indies for continued rule.[117]

The vision of turning potential patricides into pastoral patriots never worked, but its discussion raised critical national issues for different constituencies. The state viewed the poor Indo population as déraciné, rootless and therefore dangerous. The Indisch movement clearly could not claim a fatherland without territorial rights and roots within it (since many Indo-Europeans had European standing, they could not own land). The movement's appeal to an *Indisch* nationalism lacked a proper mass-based constituency, a *volk* and a homeland to make its claims. For the conservative Vaderlandse Club, rural settler colonies in the 1930s were part of a wider effort to ward off a Japanese invasion while reducing overpopulation in The Netherlands. The Fatherlands' Club and the IEV joined in a short-lived alliance to support the settler schemes, to oppose the *ontblanking* (unwhitening) of the Indies and to attack the ethical policy that had fostered the increased entry of educated Javanese into subaltern civil service jobs. However, as the IEV became increasingly anti-Totok, their conflicting images of the future fatherland became difficult to deny.[118]

For the Indo-European movement, their *vaderland* was an Indisch fatherland independent of Holland. For the Indies fascists, who defined their task as the self purification of the nation (*zelfzuivering der natie*), their notion of the vaderland juxtaposed images of 'a tropical Netherlands', uniting The Netherlands and Indies into a single state.[119] Neither of these imaginings concurred with that of the native nationalists who were to oppose them both.

Rootlessness and cultural racism

With rootedness at the centre state of nationalist discourse, the notion of rootlessness captured a range of dangers about métissage.[120] Abandoned métis youths were generically viewed as vagrants in Indochina, as child delinquents in the Indies, as *de facto* stateless subversives without a *patrie*.[121] In times of economic crisis 'free-roaming European bastards' were rounded up for charity and goodwill in efforts to avert a racial disgrace. Liberal colonial projects spent decades creating a barrage of institutions to incorporate, inculcate, and insulate abandoned métis youths. But the image of rootlessness was not only applied to those who were abandoned.

In 1938, government officials in Hanoi conducted a colony-wide enquiry to monitor the physical and political movements of métis. The Resident of Tonkin recommended a comprehensive state-sponsored social rehabilitation programme to give métis youths the means to function as real *citoyens* on the argument that with 'French blood prevailing in their veins', they already 'manifested an instinctive attachment to France'.[122] But many French in Indochina must have been more equivocal about their instinctive patriotic attachments. The fear that métis might revert to their natural inclinations persisted, as did a continuing discourse on their susceptibility to the native milieu, where they might relapse to the immoral and subversive states of their mothers.

Fears of métissage were not confined to colonial locales. We need only read the 1942 treatise, *Les Métis*, of René Martial who combined his appointment on the faculty of medicine in Paris with eugenic research on the *anthrobiologie des races*. For him, métis were categorically persons of physical and mental deformity. He saw métis descent as a frequent cause both of birth defects in individuals and of the contaminated body politic of France. As he put it:

> Instability, the dominant characteristic of métis, . . . is contagious, it stands in opposition to the spirit of order and method, it generates indeterminable and futile discussion and paralyzes action. It is this state of mind that makes democracies fail that live with this chimera of racial equality, one of the most dangerous errors of our times, defended with piety by pseudo-French who have found in it a convenient means to insinuate themselves everywhere.[123]

That Martial's spirit continues to thrive in contemporary France in the rhetoric of Le Pen is not coincidental. The discourses on métissage in the early twentieth century and in Le Pen's rhetoric on immigrant foreigners today are both about external boundaries and interior frontiers. Both discourses are permeated with images of purity, contamination, infiltration and national decay. For both Martial and Le Pen, cultural identities refer to human natures and psychological propensities inimical to the identity of the French nation and a drain on the welfare state.[124]

On cultural hybridity and domestic subversions

These historically disparate discourses are striking in how similarly they encode métissage as a political danger predicated on the psychological liminality, mental instability and economic vulnerability of culturally hybrid minorities.[125] But could we not re-present these discourses by turning them on their heads, by unpacking what the weakness of métissage was supposed to entail? Recast, these discourses may be more about the fear of empowerment, not about marginality at all; about groups that straddled and disrupted cleanly marked social divides and whose diverse membership exposed the arbitrary logic by which the categories of control were made.[126] These discourses are not unlike those about Indische women that, in disparaging their impoverished and hybrid Dutch and non-European tastes, eclipsed the more compelling reality that they could 'sometimes pass between ethnic communities, cross lines drawn by color and caste and enter slots for which they had no birthright, depending on their alliance with men'.[127] The final clause is critical because through these varied sexual contracts citizenship rights were accorded and métis identities were contested and remade.[128] The management of sexuality, parenting and morality were at the heart of the late imperial project. Cohabitation, prostitution, and legally recognized mixed marriages slotted women, men, and their progeny differently on the social and moral landscape of colonial society. These sexual contracts were buttressed by pedagogic, medical and legal evaluations that shaped the boundaries of European membership and the interior frontiers of the colonial state.

Métissage was first a name and then made a thing. It was so heavily politicized because it threatened both to destabilize national identity and the Manichean categories of ruler and ruled. The cultural density of class, gender and national issues that it invoked converged in a grid of transgressions which tapped into metropolitan and colonial politics at the same time. The sexual affront that it represented challenged middle-class family order and racial frontiers, norms of childrearing and conjugal patriarchy, and made it increasingly difficult to distinguish between true nationals and their sullied, pseudo-compatriots. The issue of fraudulent recognition could be viewed in a similar light. Poor white men and native women who arranged legal recognition of their own children or those of others, defied the authority of the state by using the legal system to grant Dutch and French citizenship to a younger generation.[129]

The turn of the twentieth century represents one major break point in the nature of colonial morality and in national projects. In both the Indies and Indochina, a new humanitarian liberal concern for mass education and representation was coupled with newly recast social prescriptions for maintaining separatist and exclusionary cultural conventions regarding how, where and with whom European colonials should live. Virtually all of these differentiating practices were worked through a psychologizing and naturalizing impulse that embedded gender inequalities, sexual privilege, class priorities and racial superiority in a tangled political field. Colonial liberalism in its nationalist cast opened the possibilities of representation for some while it set out moral prescriptions and affixed psychological attributes which partially closed those possibilities down.

But the exclusionary strategies of the colonial state were not meted out to a passive population, nor is it clear that many of those who inhabited the borderlands of European colonial communities sought inclusion within them. At the core of the métis problem were cultural contestations of gender and class that made these 'laboratories of modernity' unwieldy sites of engineering.[130] The experiments were reworked by their subjects, not least of all by women who refused to give 'up' their children to charitable institutions for European training and by others who chose cohabitation (not concubinage) over marriage. Women and men who lived culturally hybrid lifestyles intercepted nationalist and racist visions. Without romanticizing their impoverishment, we might consider the possibility that their choices expressed a domestic subversion, a rejection of the terms of the civilizing mission. For those who did not adhere to European bourgeois prescripts, cultural hybridity may have affirmed their own new measures of civility.

Notes

1 Earlier versions of this chapter were presented at the American Anthropological Association meetings, 'Papers in Honor of Eric Wolf' in New Orleans, December 1990, and at the TNI Conference. 'The Decolonization of Imagination: The New Europe and Its Others', Amsterdam, May 1991. I thank Talal Asad, Val Daniel, Geoff Eley, Lawrence Hirschfeld, Barbara Laslett, Jeffrey Weeks, Luise White and fellows of the Histories of Sexuality Seminar at the Institute of the Humanities, the University of Michigan, for their comments.

2 Uday Mehta outlines some features of this relationship in 'Liberal Strategies of Exclusion', *Politics and Society*, 18:4 (1990), 427–54. He cogently argues for the more radical claim that the theoretical underpinnings of liberalism are exclusionary and cannot be explained as 'an episodic compromise with the practical constraints of implementation' (p. 429).

3 Cochinchine's European population increased only from 594 in 1864 to 3,000 by 1900 (Charles Meyer, *De Francais en Indochine, 1860–1910*, 70 (Paris: Hachette, 1985)). By 1914 only 149 planters qualified as electors in the Chamber of Agriculture of Tonkin and Annam; on Java alone there were several thousand (John Laffey, 'Racism in Tonkin before 1914', *French Colonial Studies*, 1 (1977), 65–81). In 1900 approximately 91,000 persons were classified as European in the Indies. As late as 1931 there were just under 10,500 French civilians in Indochina, when the Indies census counted 244,000 Europeans for the same year (see A. van Marle, 'De groep der Europeanen in Nederlands-Indie, iets over ontstaan en groei', *Indonesie*, 5:5 (1952), 490; and Gilles de Gante, *La population française au Tonkin entre 1931 et 1938*, 23 (Mémoire de Maitrise, Université de Provence, 1981).

4 See Jean Taylor's subtle gendered analysis of the mestizo features of colonial culture in The Netherlands Indies (*The Social World of Batavia* (Madison: University of Wisconsin Press, 1983)). The term *Indisch* is difficult to translate. According to Taylor, it is a cultural marker of a person who 'partook of Mestizo culture in marriage, practice, habit and loyalty' (p. xx). It is most often used in contrast to the life style and values of the Dutch *totok* population comprised of Hollanders born and bred in Europe who refused such cultural accommodations and retained a distinct distance from inlander (native) customs and social practice. Thus, for example, the European *blivjers* (those who stayed in the Indies) were commonly referred to as *Indisch* as opposed to *vertrekkers* (those Europeans who treated their residence in the Indies as a temporary assignment away from their native metropolitan homes).

5 See Martin Lewis, 'One Hundred Million Frenchmen: The "Assimilation" Theory in French Colonial Policy', *Comparative Studies in Society and History*, 3:4 (1961), 129–51. While the social positioning of Eurasians in India is often contrasted to that in the Indies, there are striking similarities in their changing and contradictory legal and social status in the late nineteenth century. See Mark Naidis, 'British Attitudes toward the Anglo-Indians', *South Atlantic Quarterly*, LXII:3 (Summer 1963), 407–22; and Noel Gist and Roy Wright, *Marginality and Identity: Anglo-Indians as a Racially-mixed Minority in India*, especially 7–20 (Leiden, 1973).

6 For an extended discussion of the politics of degeneracy and the eugenics of empire, see my 'Carnal Knowledge and Imperial Power: The Politics of Race and Sexual Morality in Colonial Asia', in *Gender at the Crossroads: Feminist*

Anthropology in the Post Modern Era, 51–101, ed. Micaela di Leonardo (University of California Press, 1991).

7 In the following section I draw on Etienne Balibar's discussion of this concept in 'Fichte et la Frontière Intérieure: A propos des *Discours à la nation allemande*', *Les Cahiers de Fontenay*, 58/59 (June 1990).

8 Fichte quoted in Balibar, 'Fichte et la Frontière Intérieure', 4.

9 See my 'Carnal Knowledge and Imperial Power' on métissage and contamination. Also see Andre-Pierre Taguieff's *La force du préjugé* (1987), in which he discusses 'la hantisse du métissage' and argues that the métis problem is not a question of mixed blood but a question of the indeterminate 'social identity' which métissage implies (p. 345).

10 This is not to suggest that the French and Dutch rejection of métis as a legal category followed the same trajectory or occurred in the same way. As I later show, the legal status of métis children with unknown parents was still a subject of French juridical debate in the 1930s in a discourse in which race and upbringing were offered as two alternative criteria for judging whether a métis child should be granted the rights of a *citoyen*. See Jacques Mazet, *La condition juridique des métis dans les possession françaises* (Paris: Domat-Montchresiten, 1932).

11 Paul Rich, *Race and Empire in British Politics* (Cambridge: Cambridge University Press, 1986), argues that the anti-black riots in Liverpool and Cardiff in 1919 represented 'the extension of rising colonial nationalism into the heart of the British metropolis itself at a time when nationalist ferment was being expressed in many parts of the empire' (p. 122).

12 The profusion of French juridical tracts in the 1930s debating whether métis should be made a separate legal category (distinct from European and *indigène*) and what were the political effects of doing so were forged in the tense environment in which Vietnamese nationalists were making their opposition most strongly felt. See David Marr's two important studies of the Vietnamese nationalist movements, *Vietnamese Anticolonialism, 1885–1925* (Berkeley: University of California Press, 1971) and *Vietnamese Tradition on Trial, 1920–1945* (Berkeley: University of California Press, 1981). It is noteworthy that Marr makes no reference to the métis problem (generally or as it related to citizenship, immigration and education) in either text.

13 This is not to suggest, however, that the battles for legal reform regarding, for example, paternity suits, illegitimate children and family law waged by jurists, feminists and religious organizations in The Netherlands and the Indies at the turn of the twentieth century were animated by the same political projects or fears; on the contrary, in the colonies, the social menace of illegitimate children, as we shall see, was not only about future criminals and prostitutes but also about mixed-blood criminals and prostitutes, about European paternity, and native mothers – and thus about the moral landscape of race and the protection of European men by the Dutch colonial state. For contrasting discourses on paternity suits in the Indies and Holland, compare Selma Sevenhuijsen's comprehensive study of this political debate (*De Orde van het Vaderschap: Politieke debutten over ongehuovd moedersc-hap, afstamming en huwelijk in Nederland 1870–1900* (Amsterdam: Stiching Beheer IISG, 1987)) to R. Kleyn's 'Onderzock naar het vaderschap' (*Het Recht in Nederlandsch-Indie*, 67 (1896), 130–50).

14 On the relationship between racial supremacy and new conceptions of British motherhood at the turn of the century, see Anna Davin's 'Imperialism and Motherhood' *History Workshop*, no. 5 (1978), 9–57, and Lucy Bland's ' "Guardians of the Race" or "Vampires upon the Nation's Health"?: Female Sexuality and Its Regulations in Early Twentieth-Century Britain', in *The Changing Experience of Women*, 373–88, eds Elizabeth Whitelegg, *et al.* (Oxford: Oxford University Press, 1982). On the European maternalist discourse of the emerging welfare

states, see Seth Koven and Sonya Michel's 'Womanly Duties: Maternalist Politics
and the Origins of the Welfare States in France, Germany, Great Britain, and the
United States, 1880–1920', *American Historical Review*, 95 (October 1990),
1076–108.

15 See Eugene Weber's *Peasants into Frenchmen*, 114 (Stanford: Stanford University
Press, 1976). Although Weber's argument that much of France's rural population
neither considered itself French nor embraced a national identity has been refuted
by some scholars, for my purposes his ancillary argument holds: debates over the
nature of French citizenship and identity were heavily contested at the time.

16 Weber, *Peasants into Frenchmen*, 110.

17 Raoul Girardet, *Le nationalisme français*, 30–1 (Paris: Seuil, 1983); and Robert
Nye, *Crime, Madness and Politics in Modern France: The Medical Concept of
National Decline*, 140 (Princeton: Princeton University Press, 1984).

18 See Pierre Nora, *Les Français d'Algerie* (Paris: R. Julliard, 1961).

19 French fertility rates began to decline in the late eighteenth century, much earlier
than in other European countries, but then decreased most sharply after 1881
(see Claire Goldberg Moses, *French Feminism in the 19th Century*, 20–4 (Bing-
hamton: SUNY, 1984)).

20 Thus, of the 200,000 '*Française d'Algerie*', more than half were of non-French
origin. Coupled with the 20,000 Parisian political undesirables deported there by
the Second Republic in 1851 (commonly referred to as '*les sans-travail*', '*les
révoltés*', '*les déracinés*'), the equivocal national loyalties of Algeria's French colonial population were reopened to question. See Nora's *Les Français d'Algerie*. Also
see Stephen Wilson's comprehensive study of French antisemitism at the turn of
the century, in which he suggests that violent cultural racism in the colonies
against Jews provided a 'model' for antisemitism at home (in *Ideology and Experience: Antisemitism in France at the Time of the Dreyfus Affair*, especially 230–42
(Teaneck: Fairleigh Dickinson University Press, 1982)).

21 See Ali de Regt's 'De vorming van een opvoedings-traditie: arbiederskinderen
rond 1900' in B. Kruithof, J. Nordman, Piet de Rooy, eds, *Geschiedenis van
opvoeding en onderwijs* (Nijmegen: Sun, 1982). On the relationship between the
development of the modern Dutch state and the new focus on family morality and
motherhood at the turn of the twentieth century, see Siep Stuurman's *Verzuiling,
Kapitalisme en Patriarchaat: aspecten van de ontwiddeling van de moderne staat in
Nederland* (1987). For France, see Jacques Donzelot's *The Policing of Families*
(New York: Pantheon, 1979) which traces state interventions in family life and
childrearing practices to a half-century earlier.

22 See I. Schoffer's 'Dutch "Expansion" and Indonesian Reactions: Some Dilemmas
of Modern Colonial Rule (1900–1942)', in H. Wesseling, ed. *Expansion and
Reaction*, 80 (Leiden: Leiden University Press, 1978); and Maarten Kuitenbrouwer's *The Netherlands and the Rise of Modern Imperialism: Colonies and
Foreign Policy, 1870–1902*, 220 (New York: Berg, 1991).

23 See Colin Bundy's 'Vagabond Hollanders and Runaway Englishmen: White Pov-
erty in the Cape before Poor Whiteism', in *Putting a Plough to the Ground:
Accumulation and Dispossession in Rural South Africa, 1850–1930*, 101–28,
William Beinart, Peter Delius, and Stanley Trapido (eds) (Johannesburg: Raven
Press, 1987). On the colonial state's concern about Dutch paupers in the Indies,
see *Rapport der Pauperisme-Commissie* (Batavia: Landsdrukkerij, 1902). I discuss
these issues at more length in 'A Sentimental Education: Native Servants and the
Cultivation of European Children in the Netherlands Indies' in *Fantasizing the
Feminine*, Laurie Sears (ed.), 1997, Durham: Duke University Press: 71–91.

24 See Kuitenbrouwer, *The Netherlands*, 223.

25 For The Netherlands, compulsory education was instituted only in 1900, about the
same time it was introduced to the Indies (see Jan Romein, *The Watershed of*

Two Eras: Europe in 1900, 278 (Middletown, CN: Wesleyan University Press, 1978)).

26 See T. H. Marshall, *Class, Citizenship and Social Development*, 81 (Westport, Conn.: Greenwood, 1963, reprint 1973).

27 See Gerard Sider, 'When Parrots Learn to Talk, and Why They Can't: Domination, Deception, and Self-Deception in Indian White Relations', *Comparative Studies in Society and History*, 27:1 (1987), 3–23.

28 See Mary Poovey's *Uneven Developments: The Ideological Work of Gender in Mid-Victorian England* (Chicago: Chicago University Press, 1988).

29 Benedict Anderson, *Imagined Communities*, 136 (London: Verso, 1983).

30 Archives d'Outre-Mer [hereafter AOM], Protectorat de l'Annam et du Tonkin, no. 1506, 17 December 1898.

31 See Archives d'Outre Mer, December 1898, no. 39127, Report from Monsieur E. Issaud, Procureur-Général to the Résident Superieure in Tonkon at Hanoi.

32 'Relations immorales qui ont pu exister entre le détenue et celui qui s'est declaré son père' (Archives d'Outre Mer, Fonds Amiraux, no. 1792, 12 December 1898).

33 AOM, Aix-en Provence, no. 1792, 12 December 1898. Report of M. Villemont, Procureur in Haiphong, to the Procureur-Général, Head of the Judicial Service in Hanoi.

34 According to the procureur-general, Raoul Abor, these fraudulent acknowledgements were threatening to submerge the French element by a deluge of naturalized natives (see Raoul Abor, *Des Reconnaisances Frauduleuses d'Enfants Naturels en Indochine*, 25 (Hanoi: Imprimerie Tonkinoise, 1917)).

35 George Mosse, *Nationalism and Sexuality* (Madison: University of Wisconsin Press, 1985).

36 John Boswell's *The Kindness of Strangers: The Abandonment of Children in Western Europe from Late Antiquity to the Renaissance* (New York: Pantheon, 1988). According to Boswell, this relinquishment might occur by 'leaving them somewhere, selling them, or legally consigning authority to some other person or institution' (p. 24). As we shall see, abandonment in colonial practice did not fit this definition at all.

37 See Jacques Donzelot's *The Policing of Families*, 29.

38 I do not use this term in the sense employed by Orlando Patterson with regard to slavery but to suggest the definitive exile from European society which abandonment implied:

39 AOM, Amiraux 7701, 1899. Statute of the 'Société de protection et d'éducation des Jeunes Métis Français de la Cochinchine et du Cambodge'.

40 AOM, no. 164, 11 May 1904 (my emphasis).

41 AOM, 13 November 1903.

42 Letter from the Administrative Resident in Bac-giang to the Résident Superieure in Hanoi.

43 AOM, Letter (no. 151) to the Governor-General in Hanoi from Monsieur Paris, the President of the Société de Protection et d'Education des Jeunes Métis Français abandonnés, 29 February 1904. This concern over the entrapment of European young women in the colonies coincides with the concurrent campaigns against the white slave trade in Europe (see Frank Mort, *Dangerous Sexualities: Medico-Moral Politics in England since 1830*, 126–7 (London: Routledge and Kegan Paul, 1987)).

44 For such recommendations, see A. Brou, 'Le métis franco annamite', *Revue Indochinois* (July 1907), 897–908; Douchet, *Métis et congaies d' Indochine* (Hanoi, 1928), Jacques Mazet, *La condition juridique des métis* (Paris, Domat Moneluestien, 1932); Philippe Gossard, *Études sur le métissage principalement en AOF* (Paris Les Presses Modernes, 1934).

45 Etats-Generaux du Feminisme, *Exposition Coloniale Internationale de Paris 1931, rapport général présenté pur le Gouverneur Général Olivier*, 139 (Paris: Imprimérie Nationale, 1931).

46 AOM, Amiraux 7701, *Report on Métis in the Dutch East Indies* (1901).

47 'Courte notice sur les métis d'Extreme Orient et en particulier sur ceux de l'Indochine', Firmin Jacques Montagne, AOM, Amiraux 1669 (1903), 1896–1909.

48 The fact that the issue of poor whites loomed large on a diverse number of colonial landscapes at this time, in part, may derive from the fact that white poverty itself was coming to be perceived in metropole and colony in new ways. In Calcutta nearly one-fourth of the Anglo-Indian community in the late nineteenth century was on poor relief (N. Gist and R. Wright, *Marginality and Identity: Anglo-Indians as a Racially Mixed Minority in India*, 16 (Leiden: Brill, 1973)). Colin Bundy argues for South Africa that white poverty was redefined 'as a social problem to be tackled by state action rather than as a phenomenon of individual failure to be assuaged by charity' (p. 104). In the Indies, this reassignment of poor relief from civic to state responsibility was hotly contested and never really made.

49 *Rapport der Pauperisme Commissie* (Batavia: Landsdrukkerij, 1902); *Uitkomsten der Pauperisme-Enquete: Algemeen Verslag* (Batavia: Landsdrukkerij, 1902); *Het Pauperisme onder de Europeanen in Nederlandsch-Indie*, Parts 3, 5 (Batavia: Landsdrukkerij, 1901); *Uitkomsten der Pauperisme-Enquete: Gewestelijke Verslagen* (Batavia: Landsdrukkerij, 1901); *De Staatsarmenzorg voor Europeanen in Nederlandsch Indie* (Batavia: Landsdrukkerij, 1901).

50 See Petrus Blumberger's *De Indo-Europeesche Beweging in Nederlandsch-Indie*, 26 (Haarlem: Tjeenk Willink, 1939).

51 See J. M. Coetzee, *White Writing: On the Culture of Letters in South Africa* (New Haven: Yale University Press, 1988), in which he argues that the British railed against Boer idleness precisely because they refused the possibility that an alternative, native milieu may have been preferred by some European men and have held a real attraction.

52 AOM, Archives Centrales de l'Indochine, nos. 9147, 9273, 7770, 4680.

53 *Encyclopedie van Nederlandsch-Indie* (1919), 367.

54 In 1900, an educational survey carried out in Dutch elementary schools in the Indies among 1,500 students found that only 29 per cent of those with European legal standing knew some Dutch and more than 40 per cent did not know any (Paul van der Veur, 'Cultural Aspects of the Eurasian Community in Indonesian Colonial Society' *Indonesia*, no. 6 (1968), 45.

55 See Dr I. J. Brugmans, *Geschiedenis van het onderwijs in Nederlandsch-Indie* (Batavia: Wolters, 1938).

56 See J. F. Kohlbrugge, 'Prostitutie in Nederlandsch-Indie', *Indisch Genootschap*, 19 February 1901, 26–8.

57 See n.a., 'Ons Pauperisme', *Mededeelingen der Vereeniging 'Soeriu Soemirat'*, no. 2 (1892), 8. One proof of the falsity of the claim was that these fathers often conferred upon these children 'repulsive and obscene' names frequently enough that a government ruling stipulated that no family name could be given that 'could humiliate the child' (G. H. Koster, 'Aangenomen Kinderen en Staatsblad Europeanen' *De Amsterdammer*, 15 July 1922).

58 Letter from the Administrative Resident in Bac-giang to the Resident Supérieure, Hanoi, AOM, no. 164, 11 May 1904.

59 See Jacques Mazet, *La Condition Juridique de Métis* (Paris: Domat-Montchrestien, 1932) and Douchet, *Métis et congnaies d'Indochine*.

60 Kohlbrugge, 'Prostitutie in Nederlandsch-Indie', 23.

61 See Linda Gordon's discussion of this issue for early twentieth-century America in *Heroes of Their Own Lives: The Politics and History of Family Violence* (New York: Vintage, 1988).

62 See Mazet, *La Condition Juridique de Métis*, 37, 42.

63 Questions about the legal status of métis and the political consequences of that decision were not confined to the French alone. The International Colonial Institute in Brussels created by Joseph Chailley-Bert in 1893 engaged this question in at least three of its international meetings in 1911, 1920, and 1924. See *Comptes Rendus de l'Institut Colonial International* (Bruxelles: Bibliothèque Coloniale Internationale, 1911, 1920, 1924).

64 Mazet, *La Condition Jurdique de Métis*, 114.

65 *Ibid.*, 80.

66 *Ibid.*, 90.

67 Statute of the 'Societé de protection des enfants métis', 18 May 1904, Article 37.

68 Similar debates occurred at the International Colonial Congress of 1889, in which scholars and administrators compared and contrasted pedagogic strategies for natives in the colonies to those for the peasants of France. See Martin Lewis, 'one Hundred Million Frenchmen: The "Assimilation" Theory in French Colonial Policy', *Comparative Studies in Society and History*, 3:4, 140.

69 J. Kohlbrugge, 'Het Indische kind en zijne karaktervorming', in *Blikken in het zielenleven van den Javaan en zijner overheerschers* (Leiden: Brill, 1907).

70 Michel Foucault's discussion of the historical shift from a 'symbolics of blood' to an 'analytics of sexuality' in the mid and late nineteenth century would be interesting to explore in this colonial context, where the mixed-blood problem invoked both of these principles in resolving issues of paternity and citizenship rights (*An Introduction*, vol. 1 of *The History of Sexuality*, especially 147–50 (New York: Pantheon Books, 1978)). Although a discussion of race and sexuality is notably absent from all but the very end of *The History of Sexuality*. Foucault once remarked that it was 'the fundamental part of the book', *Power/Knowledge: Selected Interviews and Other Writings, 1972–1977*, 222 (New York: Pantheon, 1980).

71 See, for example, the contributions of those in British cultural studies, such as by Stuart Hall and Paul Gilroy; also compare the discussion of nationalism and racism in France by Etienne Balibar, who does not mark cultural racism as a recent phenomenon but does argue for a new intensification of the force of cultural difference in marking the interior frontiers of the modern nation-state. See Etienne Balibar and Immanuel Wallerstein, *Race, Nation, Class: Ambiguous Identities* (New York: Verso, 1991).

72 Thus Paul Gilroy in *There Ain't No Black in the Union Jack*, 43 (London: Hutchinson, 1987), for example, argues that the 'novelty' of the new racism 'lies in the capacity to link discourses of patriotism, nationalism, xenophobia, Englishness, Britishness, militarism, and gender differences into a complex system which gives "race" its contemporary meaning. These themes combine to provide a definition of "race" in terms of culture and identity . . . "Race" differences are displayed in culture which is reproduced in educational institutions and, above all, in family life. Families are therefore not only the nation in microcosm, its key components, but act as the means to turn social processes into natural, instinctive ones.'

73 It is not coincidental that this is precisely the period in which George Stocking identifies a shift in the meaning of culture in the social sciences from its singular humanistic sense of refinement to the plural anthropological notion of cultures as shared values of specific human groups. Although Stocking argues that Franz Boas made the analytic leap from culture to cultures as an anti-racist response, it is clear that these two connotations joined to shape the exclusionary tenets of nationalist and racist projects (*Race, Culture, and Evolution: Essays in the History of Anthropology*, especially 200–4 (New York: Free Press, 1968)).

74 See Paul Rabinow's *French Modern: Norms and Forms of the Social Environment*,

especially 126–67 (Cambridge, MA: MIT Press, 1989), where he traces the effects of neo-Lamarckian thinking on colonial pacification policies. I am more concerned here with how this attention to milieu fixed the boundaries of the European community and identified threats to it. On the contaminating influences of milieu, see my 'Canal Knowledge and Imperial Power', 51–101.

75 The similarity to Pierre Bourdieu's notion of 'habitus' as a stylization of life, an unconsiously embodied set of rules of behaviour that engenders durable schemes of thought and perception, is striking. These colonial discussions of milieu denote not only a social ecology of acquired competencies but a psychological environment in which certain dispositions are promoted and affective sensibilities are shaped (Pierre Bourdieu, *Outline of a Theory of Practice* (Cambridge: Cambridge University Press, 1977), 82).

76 'In de beschaafd wereld, niemand zonder staatsverband mag zijn' (K. H. Beyen, *Het Nederlanderschap in verband met het international recht*, 'Utrecht, 1890'), quoted in J. A. Nederburgh, *Wet en Adat*, 83 (Batavia: Kolff and Co., 1898)). The word *staatsverband* literally means 'relationship to the state'. Nederburgh distinguishes it from nationality and defines it as 'the tie that exists between the state and each of its members, the membership of the state' (p. 91). Dutch scholars of colonial history say the term is rarely used but connotes citizenship.

77 *Ibid.*, 87–8.

78 *Ibid.*, 87.

79 See Willem Wertheim's incisive review of Professor R. D. Kollewijn's *Intergentiel Recht, Indonesie*, 19 (1956), 169–73. Nederburgh's name comes up in this critique of Kollewijn, whose liberal rhetoric and opposition to such conservatives as Nederburgh belied that fact that he praised the virtues of the Indies mixed-marriage legislation of 1898, despite the racist principles that underwrote it.

80 Nederburgh, *Wet en Adat*, 88.

81 *Ibid.*, 90.

82 Kooreman 1906.

83 *Ibid.*

84 See my 'Rethinking Colonial Categories: European Communities and the Boundaries of Rule', *Comparative Studies in Society and History*, 31:1 (1989), 134–61; and 'Carnal Knowledge and Imperial Power'.

85 W. E. van Mastenbroek, *De Historische Ontwikkeling van de Staatsrechtelijke Indeeling der Bevolking van Nederlandsch-Indie*. 70 (Wageningen: Veenam, 1934).

86 See W. F. Prins, 'De Bevolkingsgroepen in het Nederlandsch-Indische Recht' *Koloniale Studien*, 17 (1933), 652–88, especially 677.

87 *Ibid.*, 677; Van Marle, 'De groep der Europeanen in Nederlands' *Indonesie*, 5:2 (1951), 110.

88 See Mastenbroek, 87.

89 See Karen Offen's 'Depopulation, Nationalism and Feminism in Fin-de-Siècle France', *American Historical Review*, 89:3 (1984), 648–76.

90 The following discussion is based on several documents that I will abbreviate in referring to in the section below as follows: *Verslag van het Verhandelde in de Bijeenkomsten der Nederlandsch Indische Juristen-Vereeniging* on 25, 27, and 29 June 1887 in Batavia (hereafter, JV), 'Voldoet de wetgeving betreffende huwelijken tusschen personen behoorende tot de beide staatkundige categorien der Nederlandsch Indische bevolking (die der Europeanen en met hen, en die der Inlanders en met hen gelijkgestelden) aan de maatschappelijke behoefie? Zoo neen, welke wijzigingen zijn noodig?' (1887) (hereafter, VW); J. A. Nederburgh, *Gemengde Huwelijken, Staatsblad 1898, No. 158: Officiele Bescheiden met Eenige Aanteekeningen* (hereafter, GH).

91 Werthein, *Intergentiel Recht.*

92 The term mixed marriages (*gemengde huwelijken*) had two distinct but overlapping meanings in the Indies at the turn of the twentieth century. Common usage
defined it as referring to contracts between a man and a woman of different racial
origin; the state defined it as 'a marriage between persons who were subject to
different laws in The Netherlands Indies' with no reference to race. The distinction is significant for at least two reasons: (1) because the designations of legal
standing as inlander versus European cut across the racial spectrum, with generations of mixed bloods falling on different sides of this divide and (2) because
adat (customary) and Dutch law followed different rulings with respect to the
marriage contract, divorce, inheritance, and child custody.

93 Although the hierarchies of gender and race of Indies colonial society in part
account for the fact that in 1895 more than half of the European men in the
Indies still lived with native women outside of marriage, this may tell only one
part of the story. The juridical debates on legal reform of mixed marriages suggest that there were women who chose cohabitation over legal marriage. At the
very least, this suggests that concubinage may not have been an appropriate term
for some of these arrangements, nor does it necessarily reflect what options
women may have perceived in these arrangements.

94 W. F. Prins, 'De bevolkingsgroepen in het Nederlandsch-Indische recht', *Koloniale
Studien*, 17, 665. That some women chose cohabitation over legal mixed marriages is rarely addressed in the colonial or secondary literature on the assumption
that all forms of cohabitation could be subsumed by the term concubinage,
signalling the moral degradation of a 'kept woman' that the later term implies.
References in these legal debates to the fact that some women chose not to marry
suggests that this issue needs further investigation.

95 Nederburgh, *GH*, 17.

96 As the chairman of the commission poignantly illustrated, a woman with native
legal standing could be arrested for wearing European attire at the very moment
she emerged from the building in which she had just married a European. Nor
could a European man and his wife of native standing take the short boat trip
from Soerabaya to Madura without prior permission of the authorities since sea
passage for natives was forbidden by law (*JV*, 29–30).

97 Nederburgh, *GH*, 20.

98 *Ibid.*, 13.

99 *Ibid.*, 13.

100 *JV*, 39.

101 *Idem.*

102 *Ibid.*, 51.

103 *Ibid.*, 40. The arguments presented over the mixed-marriage ruling are much
more numerous and elaborate than this short account suggests. There were
indeed those such as Abendanon (the lawyer friend of Kartini), whose proposals
raised yet a whole different set of options than those offered in these accounts.
He argued that both man and woman should be given European status, except in
those cases in which a native man preferred to retain his rights under adat law.
Abendanon also singlehandedly countered the claim that any European woman
who chose to marry a native man was already debased, arguing that there were
many Dutch girls in The Netherlands for whom this was not the case. But these
arguments were incidental to the main thrust of the debate and had little sway in
the final analysis.

104 Nederburgh, *GM*, 64.

105 See A. van Marle's 'De Groep der Europeanen in Nederlands-Indie, iets over
ontstaan en groei,' *Indonesie*, 5:3 (1952), 322, 328. Van Marle suggests that the
much larger number of illiterate women of European standing in central Java and
the Moluccas compared to the rest of the Indies indicates that the number of

mixed marriages in these regions was particularly high (p. 330). But this was not the case everywhere. In East Java, European men acknowledged more of their métis children but continued to cohabit with the native mothers of their children outside of marriage (p. 495).

106 Mevrouw Douaire Klerck, *Eenige Beschouwingen over Oost-Indische Toestanden*, 3–19 (Amsterdam: Versluys, 1898).

107 S. S. J. Ratu-Langie, *Surekat Islam*, 21 (Baarn: Hollandia Drukkerij, 1913).

108 A woman who had contracted a mixed marriage could, upon divorce or death of her husband, declare her desire to reinstate her original nationality as long as she did so within a certain time. However, a native woman who married a European man and subsequently married and divorced a man of non-European status could not recoup her European status.

109 Ernest Rodenwalt, 'Eugenetische Problemen in Nederlandsch-Indie,' *Ons Nageslacht*, 1–8 (1928).

110 Johan Winsemius, *Nieuw-Guinee als kolonisatie-gebied voor Europeanen en van Indo-Europeanen*, 227 (Ph.D. Disser., Faculty of Medicine, University of Amsterdam, 1936).

111 Jacques van Doorn emphasizes the dualistic policy on poverty in the 1930s in 'Armoede en Dualistisch Beleid' (unpublished); I would refer to it as a three-tiered policy, not a dualistic one.

112 J. Th. Petrus Blumberger, *De Indo-Europesche Beweging in Nederlandsch-Indie*, 5 (Haarlem: Tjeenk Willink, 1939).

113 See Paul van der Veur's 'The Eurasians of Indonesia: A Problem and Challenge in Colonial History.' *Journal of Southeast Asian History*, 9:2 (September 1966), 191–207, and his 'Cultural Aspects of the Eurasian Community in Indonesian Colonial Society,' *Indonesia*, 6 (October 1968), 38–53.

114 On the various currents of Eurasian political activity, see Paul W. van der Veur's 'The Eurasians of Indonesia: A Problem and Challenge in Colonial History.' On the importance of Indo individuals in the early Malay press and nationalist movement, see Takashi Shiraishi's *An Age in Motion: Popular Radicalism in Java*, 1912–1926, especially 37, 58–59 (Ithaca: Cornell University Press, 1990). Neither account addresses the class differences within Eurasian groups and where their distinct allegiances lay.

115 Blumberger, *De Indo-Europeesche Beweging*, 50.

116 According to the historian, Rudolph Mrazek, the early silent rejection of the Indo-European community from the Indonesian nationalist project turned explicit under Soekarno in the mid-1920s, when Indo-Europeans were categorically barred from membership in nationalist political organizations. Mrazek suggests that this silence among Dutch-educated nationalist leaders on the Indo question should be understood as a response to their own cultural formation and identification as cultural hybrids themselves (personal communication).

117 See P. J. Drooglever's discussion of this failed effort in *De Vaderlandse Club*, 193–208 (Franeker: T. Wever, 1980).

118 P. J. Drooglever, *De Vaderlandse Club, 1929–1942: Totoks en de Indische Politiek*, 285 (Franeker: T. Wever, 1980).

119 *Verbond Nederland en Indie*, no. 3, September 1926, 3. In the late 1920s, this publication appended the subtitle to the name above of 'A Fascist Monthly.'

120 This issue of rootlessness is most subtly analyzed in contemporary contexts. Liisa Malkki explores the meanings attached to displacement and uprootedness in the national order of things ('National Geographic: The Rooting of Peoples and the Territorialization of National Identity among Scholars and Refugees,' *Cultural Anthropology* (1992). André-Pierre Taguieff examines Le Pen's nationalist rhetoric on the dangers of the rootlessness of immigrant workers in France. See Pierre-André Taguieff's excellent analysis of Le Pen's rhetoric in 'The Doctrine of

the National Front in France (1972–1989),' in *New Political Science*, no. 16/17, 29–70.

121 See A. Braconier, 'Het Pauperisme onder de in Ned. Oost-Indie levende Europeanen,' *Nederlandsch-Indie*, no. 1 (1917), 291–300, at 293.

122 Enquete sur Métissage, AOM, Amiraux 53.50.6.

123 René Martial, *Les Métis*, 58 (Paris: Flammation, 1942).

124 See Taguieff, 'The Doctrine of the National Front.'

125 On the recent British discourse on Britishness and the cultural threat of Islam to that identity, see Talal Asad's rich analysis in 'Multiculturalism and British Identity in the Wake of the Rushdie Affair.' *Politics and Society*, 18:4 (December 1990), 455–80.

126 Hazel Carby ('Lynching, Empire and Sexuality,' *Critical Inquiry*, 12:1 (1985), 262–77) argues that Afro-American women intellectuals at the turn of the century focused on the métis figure because it both enabled an exploration and expressed the relations between the races, because it demythologized concepts of pure blood and pure race while debunking any proposition of degeneracy through amalgamation. Such black women writers as Pauline Hopkins embraced the mulatto to counter the official script that miscegenation was not the innermost desire of the nonwhite peoples but the result of white rape (p. 274). In both the Indies and the United States at the same time, the figure of the Indo-mulatto looms large in both dominant and subaltern literary production, serving to convey strategic social dilemmas and political messages. It is not surprising, then, that the portrayal of the Indo in fiction was widely discussed in the Indies and metropolitan press by many more than those who were interested in literary style alone.

127 Taylor, *The Social World of Batavia*, 155.

128 Carole Pateman argues that the sexual contract is fundamental to the functioning of European civil society, in that the principle of patriarchal right defines the social contract between men, and the individual and citizen as male (*The Sexual Contract* (Stanford: Stanford University Press, 1988)).

129 I thank Luise White for pressing me to think out this point.

130 Gwendolyn Wright, 'Tradition in the Service of Modernity: Architecture and Urbanism in French Colonial Policy, 1900–1930,' *Journal of Modern History*, 59 (June 1987), 291–316, at 297.

2 Miscegenation, nation formation and cross-racial identifications in the early Francoist folkloric film musical

Jo Labanyi

In her introduction to an important collection of essays on regionalism in Latin America, Doris Sommer (1996) notes that the postmodern celebration of hybridity risks replicating the populist promotion of syncretism and miscegenation that has been central to much post-independence Latin American nationalist discourse, which set out to construct a seamless, unified national body via the assimilation of cultural and racial differences.[1] As Sommer stresses, our contemporary celebration of hybridity should not lose sight of the perceptions of the early twentieth-century Cuban ethnographer Fernando Ortiz, who coined the term 'transculturation' in order 'to distinguish the unresolvable, often violent tension among cultures in conflict from the neat resolutions of difference suggested by such ideal concepts . . . as syncretism, hybridity, or *mestizaje*' (Sommer 1996: 121–2). In insisting on the tensions between cultures – exemplified in the title of his *Cuban Counterpoint: Tobacco and Sugar* (1940) – Ortiz was rejecting the acculturation process through which the dominant culture procures social 'improvement' through the assimilation of subaltern cultural forms. In this chapter I explore the ways in which the early Franco regime used popular cinema to promote a totalitarian model of nationhood based, paradoxically, on miscegenation: a classic example of how hybridity can be invoked by those hostile to racial difference. I hope to show how, even in this totalitarian project, the signs of racial difference refuse to be elided.

The folkloric film musical which flourished in the early Franco period (known simply as the *folklórica* in Spanish) is a transparent case of the populist co-option of popular culture for the purposes of nation building; as such, it has been almost unanimously dismissed by later Spanish film directors and critics. Here the regime, always closer to Italian than to German fascism, was echoing Mussolini's belief in the cinema as a tool for indoctrinating the masses. It should be noted that the populist nature of fascist regimes gave them a better understanding of popular culture than was ever achieved (prior to the contemporary age of the mass media) by capitalist democracy, with its privileging of bourgeois cultural forms. For reasons that should become clear in the course of this chapter, popular culture was in the early Francoist folkloric musical represented largely by flamenco dance and song, performed by gypsy heroines whose gender and ethnic marking constructed them as subaltern. The romance format of these films culminates in the vast majority of cases with the betrothal of the gypsy heroine to a landowner, the 'nomadic' and marginal elements of the population thus being 'settled' and incorporated into a traditional property-owning system, naturalized by being based on the land. (In a small number of films, the gypsy heroine falls for a fellow gypsy, finally endowed with fame and fortune as a bullfighter, thus permitting the assimilation of both into society without the need for marriage across racial and class lines.) While these conservative plot resolutions do quite clearly represent the incorporation and thus elimination of difference, in practice the formulaic nature of the endings makes them bathetic. The appeal lies in the sparring and bargaining between racial, class and gender antagonists that takes place along the way, requiring the union to be postponed till the concluding moments. Indeed, the narrative always stops short of the actual marriage, perhaps indicating its unthinkability in real life but also leaving it out of the picture as not the main focus of the story. And there is never any talk (in a period of intense state pronatalist campaigns) of these cross-racial unions producing children, thereby transcending difference through its encapsulation in a single body. The resolution of difference thus remains a promise unrealized on screen. What particularly interests me about these films is that, despite their conservative plot resolutions, they were massively popular with the 1940s Spanish cinema-going public, and particularly with the lower classes and women: the two categories who most suffered from Francoist economic and moral repression. This implies that they allowed identifications that went against the grain of their overt message of the need to eliminate difference through the incorporation of the subaltern into dominant culture.

Before moving to the treatment of racial difference in these films, it is necessary to outline briefly the ideological roots of the Franco regime in Spanish colonial discourse. Like fascism elsewhere, Francoist rhetoric made abundant use of racial terminology, but Spain's different imperial trajectory gave this racial emphasis a very different inflection from the Nazi model – or indeed from British imperial discourse. Contrary to the British colonial model of commerce and exploitation, presupposing racial segregation, Spain's imperial expansion from 1492 had been based on conquest, settlement and conversion: that is, on enforced assimilation. The violence of the assimilation process bordered on, and in some places led to, genocide – but in the name of incorporation rather than exclusion. The different exclusionary process of systematic extermination that took place in Argentina occurred later in the nineteenth century, after independence from Spain and under strong British influence. Spanish colonial discourse was no less racist than its British counterpart but its belief in white superiority was articulated differently, in a way that allowed Spaniards – and post-independence Latin Americans – to convince themselves that they were not guilty of the racism that so visibly characterized the segregated societies of Britain's past or present empire.[2] Miscegenation was thus regarded as 'normal' or even, with the influence of Darwinist theory in the post-independence period, as a way of 'improving the stock', though in practice it was generally accepted only outside marriage and between white 'master' and female Indian or black, maintaining hierarchy. In reality, of course, this was a normalization of rape, resemanticized in Spanish colonial discourse as the myth of the white male generously donating his seed to the woman of colour and thereby founding a new hybrid race in which differences were transcended or redeemed. The use of religious terminology was frequent, for the Catholic practice of enforced conversion was the cultural model for this rhetorical justification of sexual violation. Such mass conversions coexisted with the Inquisition's practice – in Latin America as well as the metropolis – of burning heretics: in Spain, the prime target was Jews who, having accepted conversion to avoid expulsion in 1492, secretly maintained (or were suspected of maintaining) their religion. The practice of enforced conversion spawned as its corollary a paranoid fear of 'others' operating within the system. Nevertheless, the obsession with racial purity (*limpieza de sangre*) was primarily the expression of an intolerance of cultural difference; belief in the efficacy of conversion supposed that 'others' could and should be made 'the same'.[3]

This colonial model of miscegenation as a means of incorporating racial 'others' allowed the Spanish fascist intellectual Giménez Caballero, in his political tract *The Genius of Spain* (1932), to argue for the return of Don Juan as the Spanish 'Superman' or 'Messiah' who would subdue the (feminine) populace through sexual conquest, casting domination as love (and conversely casting love as domination). Giménez Caballero's blatantly sexual rhetoric (embarrassing to those used to the puritanism of British colonial discourse) proposes as national 'Saviour' a Great Inseminator who will redeem the wayward race, as the Spanish conquistadors had earlier done in the Americas, by planting in her his redemptive seed: the 'genius of Spain' is its virile, genital and (re)generative capacity.[4] Spanish fascist intellectuals generally distanced themselves from Hitler's exclusionary racial policies, instead arguing for a policy of racial incorporation on Mussolinian corporatist lines; Giménez Caballero even worked for the return to Spain of the Judeo-Spanish Diaspora. The appeal of such racial rhetoric in Spanish fascist discourse was, of course, that, in addition to constructing a blueprint of a seamless, unified nation, it kept alive nostalgia for an empire now lost and allowed the fantasy of a return to imperial glory. The imperialist rhetoric of early Francoism – mitigated after defeat of the Axis powers in 1945 in order to court US favour, but evident through to the early 1950s when US financial aid was finally secured – insisted on 'the glorious virtues of the Spanish race' rather than on racial purity. And the chief 'virtue of the Spanish race' (as the voice-over to numerous contemporary documentaries and newsreels makes clear) was its ability to assimilate other races, 'hispanicizing' even its Roman and Arab conquerors.

The Spanish fascist party Falange Española was only one of several extreme right-wing factions comprising Franco's Nationalist alliance. What bound all these factions together was an inability to accept the loss of Spain's last economically significant colonies (Cuba, Puerto Rico and the Philippines) in 1898 and a paranoid fear that growing local nationalisms (Catalonia, the Basque Country, Galicia) would lead to the break-up of the nation-state at home: the latter was seen as the logical extension of the former. Consequently the Nationalists' remedy to disaffection at home was the imposition of an imperial model of centralized rule; that is, the enforcement of cultural homogeneity through a process of internal colonization. It is no coincidence that Franco had made his military name as Commander of the Spanish Legion in Morocco, where Spain had attempted to compensate for loss of its American and Asian possessions through a (mostly disastrous) campaign of territorial expansion starting in the mid-nineteenth century.[5] Franco's Nationalist troops were notorious for their use of 'Moorish' soldiers in the Civil War, true to the Spanish colonial emphasis on incorporating the colonized; and during the war and its aftermath Franco appeared in public escorted by a dramatically attired escort of 'Moorish' horsemen. On winning the Civil War in 1939, Franco gave the 'army of occupation' (as it was called) the task of subordinating the Spanish regions and lower classes to central control in much the same way that he had previously used the Spanish Legion to subdue the Moroccan tribes.

It was only after 1939 that the heroines of the folkloric film musical became exclusively non-white: mixed-race Moroccan and mixed-race Cuban in two films set in colonial locations – *La canción de Aixa* (*Aixa's Song*, Rey 1939) and *Bambú*[6] (Sáenz de Heredia 1945) – and, in all the remaining films set in Spain, gypsy. Underdeveloped, largely rural Andalusia thus came to stand for the whole of Spain since, despite that fact that many gypsies had migrated to the urban centres in the north, Andalusia was traditionally seen as their 'natural habitat'. On the one hand, this concentration on Andalusian gypsy folklore represented a displacement of the politically charged local nationalisms of northeastern and northwestern Spain onto an area where regionalist sentiment remained largely confined to cultural forms of expression. But, more importantly, the use of Andalusian locations allowed the genre to serve as the basis of a model of nationhood constructed on colonial lines: eight centuries of Arab rule, as well as its significant gypsy population, had firmly implanted in the collective European (and Spanish) imaginary the idea that Andalusia was 'not quite European'. In other words, it was precisely Andalusia's 'foreignness' that enabled it to figure a concept of 'Spanishness' based, as in Spanish colonial discourse, on the incorporation of the racially alien. The high point of the folkloric musical genre in terms of popularity and quantity of output was the late 1940s, which also saw the production of a spate of films about missionaries which explicitly dramatized the incorporation of colonized subjects whether through miscegenation or conversion.[7]

One of the most striking features of the early Francoist folkloric film is the way in which the fetishistic camerawork and flamboyant performance style create an extraordinarily high degree of audience identification with the non-white (usually gypsy) heroine. (The necessarily subdued visual representation and pious comportment of the missionary genre's heroes condemned it to deserved oblivion; the audience identifications, if any, are with the native male whose bare torso is specularized by the camera, giving Spanish audiences under Francoist censorship a rare glimpse of naked flesh.) In all cases, the non-white heroine of the *folklórica* was played by a major star, whose name would routinely appear before the credits as the box-office draw; the male (usually white landowning) protagonists were played by relatively unknown actors, except in the small number of films where they too were gypsies, again ensuring that audience identifications were with the ethnically marked characters. However surprising this encouragement of audience identification with the non-white protagonists may seem, it is in a curious way logical given prevailing colonially based fantasies that national unification depended on the incorporation of racial 'others'. We have here something more complex than the ambivalent disavowal of racial difference which Bhabha (1994) has explored in British colonial discourse, whereby the colonizer's fetishization of the colonized subject's body is based on a simultaneous identification and repudiation. For the insistence in Spanish colonial discourse on the incorporation of the colonized via miscegenation gives identification itself the double function of disavowing (affirming/denying) racial difference: incorporation involves making part of the self that which is not part of the self. (The notion that, through miscegenation, the male colonizer makes the female colonial subject part of his body has the added advantage of cancelling out the biological fact that he enters her body.) My central argument in this chapter is that the folkloric musical's attempt to manage the threat of racial difference by creating a high degree of identification with it allows unorthodox pleasures to spectators belonging to groups categorized as 'other'.

As in all folkloric representations, the gypsy who appears in the early Francoist *folklórica* is an imaginary construct. Although the genre's gypsy characters stand for a floating population in need of settlement, in practice Spanish gypsies had long ceased to be nomads and even in rural Andalusia lived largely in cities where, unlike in the north, they had intermarried with other marginal elements of the local population to a considerable degree. As we shall see, many *folklóricas* are costume dramas set in the mid-nineteenth century: the period when the whole of the national territory was first brought under the control of an increasingly centralized state. One of the chief planks in this nation-formation process was the creation in 1844 of the Civil Guard as a paramilitary police force, subject to central control and positioned along the new radial road and railways network, entrusted among other things with the eradication of banditry and the policing of gypsies (seen as much the same thing). Gypsies thus became the embodiment of all outsiders who resist the law and refuse incorporation into a unified state: a process which of course turned them into outsiders in the first place, denying a more complex reality of partial integration (hybridization). As Timothy Mitchell (1994) stresses, the term *gitano* was applied loosely to members of the urban underclasses associated with gypsy culture (epitomized by flamenco dance and song) but not necessarily of gypsy origin – which, as Mitchell notes, is notoriously hard to pin down since non-ethnically constituted subcultures frequently take on pseudo-ethnic characteristics as a strategy for cultural survival. Mitchell observes that, while gypsy bands everywhere have tended to absorb other nomadic or marginal elements, this has been especially true in Spain, where 'gypsyness' eludes strict racial definition and is best seen as a subcultural lifestyle. That is, a form of cultural bricolage resulting from the traumatic displacements caused by urban modernity: first, through the ethnic chaos thrown up by the early modern trading centres (most importantly Seville, which channelled traffic to the New World); and later through capitalist modernization, producing mass migration to the cities. As Mitchell demonstrates, flamenco as we now know it developed as a performance art, syncretically mixing gypsy and other subcultural forms such as miners' songs, in the mid-nineteenth century when both *gitanos* (in the loose sense of the word) and the landowning patrons who paid them to perform converged in the newly expanding urban centres. The crucial importance of Mitchell's study is his demonstration that flamenco and the *gitanos* with whom it is linked are the hybrid products of urban modernity.

Mitchell is scathing about the 1920s avant-garde artists (Lorca and Falla) who, in true modernist spirit, attempted to turn flamenco into an elitist preserve by seeing it as an example of ethnically pure artistic primitivism (1994: 160–77). In fact, Lorca's and Falla's stance towards flamenco was complex: the famous flamenco competition they mounted in Granada in 1922 was a classic 'staging of the authentic', explicitly designed to save flamenco from a supposed imminent death – one thinks here of Michel de Certeau's description of folklore as 'the beauty of the dead' (1986: 119–36) – by restoring it to 'natural' (meaning ethnically pure) origins. As Mitchell points out, this was a defensive reaction against modern mass culture, where flamenco was thriving and adapting itself to modernity in various hybrid forms with no need for intellectuals to 'revive' it. On the other hand, Lorca's and Falla's incorporation of flamenco rhythms and gypsy motifs into their poetry and music was itself a conscious form of hybridization, based – as Papastergiadis notes with regard to Picasso's primitivism (1997: 263–4) – on an assimilation of the non-western in such a way that it becomes part of the western tradition while always exceeding it. Mitchell notes that the flamenco revival by 1950s Francoist intellectuals, who again attempted to fossilize it as an ethnically pure art form for the exclusive consumption of male connoisseurs, owed itself to the fact that Franco's victory in the Civil War had 'made Spain safe' for the landowning classes who were its patrons. One suspects that this 1950s flamenco 'revival' was also a reaction against the *folklórica*, which unashamedly co-opted flamenco dance and song – occasionally gesturing towards ethnic purism but mostly drawing on a hybrid music hall repertoire – for the purposes of modern mass entertainment.

Mitchell (1994: 9–14) also describes the attempt by leftist intellectuals under the Spanish Republic of 1931–6 to de-ethnicize flamenco by enlisting it, as an expression of class-consciousness, for the purposes of social protest. The folkloric film musical genre was first created, with the introduction of sound, under the Republic which sought to develop a national-popular cinema that would give a voice to the masses. As under early Francoism, the genre was conceived as part of a nation-formation project designed to incorporate marginal elements of the population, but in the Republic's case the goal was (in theory at least) the expression, and not elimination, of cultural difference. Under the Republic the heroines of the *folklórica* were not always gypsies, for class was the key issue. Thus *Nobleza baturra* (*Aragonese Peasant Nobility*, Rey 1935) is set in Aragon, recognizing regional difference and, although made for the conservative production company Cifesa, it proclaims its heroine's right to marry a landless peasant. *La hija de Juan Simón* (*The Gravedigger's Daughter*, Sáenz de Heredia 1935, produced by Buñuel for the left-wing production company Filmófono), deals with non-ethnically marked Andalusian victims of exploitation and injustice. Even when the heroine is a gypsy, social injustice remains the dominant theme, as in Rey's *Morena Clara* (1936, also for Cifesa), which is an overt denunciation of anti-gypsy prejudice: this film broke all previous Spanish box-office records, out-grossing even Hollywood movies. In rewriting class conflict as a miscegenation narrative, the early Francoist *folklórica* was disavowing the existence of class problems: one of the fantasies that Francoist discourse borrowed wholesale from fascism was that of an organic society transcending class divisions (the term 'class conflict' was banned by the censors in the 1940s). True to the double logic of the disavowal process, the ethnic marking of the female gypsy protagonist functions not only as a replacement for class difference but also as a reminder of it. In practice, such films would also inevitably have reminded 1940s Spanish spectators of their Republican predecessors, especially since the directors and female stars of many postwar *folklóricas*, up to 1946 at least, had made their names in the same genre under the Republic.

Although the genre's associations with the Republic helps to explain its popularity with those who were the Franco regime's main victims, there is not in practice a clear distinction between those films made before the war and those made at its end or after. The radical potential of the Republican *folklórica* is undercut by its melodramatic concentration on the female victim's point of view which, while producing audience identification with her, tends to produce a cathartic exaltation of suffering often indistinguishable from that propounded in early Francoist examples. And Florián Rey, the most successful director of folkloric musicals under the Republic, accepted an invitation to make German–Spanish co-productions in Nazi Berlin in 1938–9, as did another Spanish director, Benito Perojo, who had returned from Paris in the 1930s to work under the Republic, and who in 1939–40 went on to make Italian–Spanish co-productions at Cinecittà, the lavishly endowed film studios which Mussolini had himself inaugurated – to the slogan 'Cinema is the strongest weapon' – in 1937.

All of the films made in fascist Berlin and Rome by these directors were folkloric musicals, though those of Perojo were mostly slick urban comedies with a strong picaresque flavour, with trickster heroines who were working-class rather than gypsy. Rey was invited to Berlin because his wife and lead singer, Imperio Argentina, was one of Hitler's favourite actresses: Hitler told her in a private audience that he had seen her twenty-four times in *Nobleza baturra*. The appeal to Hitler of this melodrama of rural innocence slandered and rewarded makes clear the link between the *folklórica* and the Nazi exaltation of the *Volk*. It also makes clear the genre's debt to foreign views of Spain as Europe's exotic 'other'. The first film made in Berlin by Rey was a version of Mérimée's and Bizet's *Carmen*, titled *Carmen la de Triana* (1938): Rey had to overcome Goebbels's hostility to the idea of a film with a gypsy heroine. Given the Nazi emphasis on eliminating racial 'others', it is interesting that the film does not end, as in Mérimée's and Bizet's versions, with Don José killing Carmen but with her redemption, true to the Spanish fascist emphasis on incorporating racial 'others'. The first film made in Berlin by Perojo was a folkloric version of Beaumarchais's and Rossini's *The Barber of Seville*: although not specifically gypsy, it again constructs a foreigners' view of Andalusia as 'not quite European'. The Franco regime encouraged the export of Spanish films to Spanish America, particularly Mexico and Argentina which had large film industries, as a way of compensating for the loss of empire by continuing to exert cultural hegemony (what was called *hispanidad*). The most exportable commodity was the *folklórica*, catering to foreign stereotypes of 'Spanishness'. It was to break into the Spanish American market that the German–Spanish co-production company Hispano-Film-Produktion was set up in Berlin in 1937 in the first place. Several articles in early issues of the Falangist film magazine *Primer Plano* (founded in 1940) expressed concern about this mimicry of foreign images of Spanishness.

The second film made by Rey in Berlin, *La canción de Aixa* (*Aixa's Song*, 1939), again starring Imperio Argentina, was an orientalist fantasia set in Spanish Morocco, showing that the cultivation of the image of Spain as the West's oriental 'other' was linked for Spain, and no doubt also for Germany, to dreams of colonial expansion in North Africa. This film's complex dramatization of the superiority of Arab to European values problematizes the depiction of 'Spanishness', traditionally seen as not-quite-European while not-quite-Arab either. Bhabha (1994: 89) notes that the mimicry fundamental to colonial discourse construes difference as 'almost the same but not quite': the heroine of this film is a performer (a mimic) as well as mixed-race (almost the same but not quite). The romance plot here figures not the usual conquest of the non-white female by the white male, but the conquest of the mixed-race female (a cabaret singer who performs orientalist extravaganzas in a westernized cultural setting) by the indigenous male (an Arab prince who rejects europeanization, including western attitudes to marriage, contrasting with his decadent europeanized cousin, with whom Imperio Argentina is initially in love). Arab values here figure an extreme version of the patriarchal ethos propounded by early Francoism, but their exaltation requires spectators to identify with Arab culture and to reject European modernity represented in the film precisely by Spanish or Spanish-influenced characters. The film's critique of western decadence works against its depiction of colonial relations. The Arab prince who finally wins Imperio Argentina's heart rejects the supposed Arab code of male violence, upheld by his decadent cousin, because he has learnt the value of self-restraint from serving in the Spanish colonial army; in practice, this attempt to salvage Spanish colonial superiority leads to identification with a feminized, passive patriarch who refuses to act when goaded. The function of the film's musical numbers, as Imperio Argentina moves from orientalist spectacles mounted on a westernized cabaret stage to equally orientalist spectacles naturalized by their integration into the narrative's depiction of Arab palace life, is to make us identify with the Arab and feminine 'other'. For Imperio Argentina, this means a rejection of her paternal European (Spanish) inheritance for her maternal Arab roots. The split identifications embodied in Imperio Argentina's mixed-race role thus give way to total identification with the non-European, albeit represented from a western orientalist perspective.

Imperio Argentina also plays a mixed-race heroine in a later folkloric musical set in colonial Cuba, *Bambú* (José Luis Sáenz de Heredia 1945), explicitly linking the genre to an imperial model of nationhood (Cuba had since 1833 been categorized as a province of Spain). The Spanish male protagonist is an unsuccessful avant-garde composer who dies in the war against Cuban independence fighters. In his dying moments, he composes his masterpiece as a syncretic amalgam of the classical tradition and Afro-Caribbean dance and song, personnified by Imperio Argentina playing a mulatto carnival singer, who dies with him in a *Liebestod*: the glorious musical score is by Ernesto Halffter, the principal composer of the 1927 Generation that developed Falla's avant-grade musical 'primitivism'. As in many other *folklóricas* of the period, female song here stands as an expression of oral immediacy seen as more vital than male written culture. De Certeau has noted that ethnography eroticizes the 'savage' who offers the 'song of pure enunciation' waiting to be written down, and thus made intelligible, by the European observer: as he puts it, this 'pure enunciation' 'is senseless. It partakes of orgasm' (1988: 230). Thus in this film the miscegenation takes place not through sexual union but through musical procreation – the syncretic musical 'climax', filmed as a Busby-Berkeley-style extravaganza, is indeed orgasmic – injecting new life into the male European classical tradition. But at the same time Afro-Caribbean carnival, figured by a female, reveals the lack of vitality of European 'high' culture.

In those folkloric film musicals set in mid-nineteenth-century Spain, the parallel between the attempts of liberal governments from the 1850s through the 1880s to bring the regions under centralized control, and Francoist attempts to impose centralized state control in the 1940s, is clear. The theme of the need for national unification is dramatized through the stock plot of the female gypsy singer, brought up by bandits, falling for an army officer. The bandits in these films, who defy the army's attempts to bring the countryside under central state control, could not help but remind contemporary Spanish audiences of the rural guerrilla fighters who defied the Francoist army from the end of the Civil War till 1951, and who were referred to as 'bandits' in the notorious Banditry and Terrorism Decree of 1943. Rey's Berlin-made *Carmen la de Triana* stresses its gypsy heroine's links with banditry and makes her finally acknowledge the superior 'gentlemanliness' of the military, represented by her lover Don José, who dies saving the military from being blown up by the bandits. In *Estrella de Sierra Morena* (Ramón Torrado 1952), the heroine, brought up by bandits, turns out to be the daughter of the provincial governor, responsible for eradicating banditry, thus making possible her marriage to an army officer. This scenario is reversed in *La duquesa de Benamejí* (*The Duchess of Benamejí*, Luis Lucía 1949), whose male bandit singing lead wins the heart of a duchess and triumphs over the foppish, double-dealing representatives of the law. The political identifications here are entirely unorthodox, though in fact in all these costume dramas the bandits – apart from the exceptional traitor who proves the rule – are depicted as much more human than the military. This last film anticipates the gender reversal that would take place in the folkloric genre in the mid-1950s, as female musical stars were replaced by male singers, lower-class but not ethnically marked, whose success as urban performance artists habitually wins them a higher-class wife: a gender reversal which perhaps reflects the need to offer models of social mobility to an increasingly discontented male workforce. The result, however, is a loss of vitality since these male stars were singers but, unlike the genre's earlier female stars, not also dancers: while their representation in terms of the voice rather than the body in one sense constructs them as subjects rather than objects, it also produces an unappealingly static body language – increasingly masculinized in the course of the 1950s – which contrasts notably with the seductive physical exuberance allowed the non-white heroines who dominated the genre till around 1954. From 1957 the *folklórica* gave way to a new cabaret-based genre of film musical, offering a more modern, urban image of womanhood, in which the heroine – no longer ethnically marked – is however punished for public success through failure in love. From this point on, race disappeared as an issue in Spanish cinema till the mid-1990s.

The fact that the non-white heroines of the pre-1954 folkloric musical were both singers and dancers is important, for it gives them not only a bodily freedom of movement but also a verbal fluency articulated in their capacity for quick-witted popular repartee as well as song. In many films the non-white heroine's role is to voice the emotions repressed by her upper-class white male suitor; in the same way, the vitality of her performance as a dancer contrasts strikingly with his physical stiffness. Indeed, one of the genre's inherent flaws is the difficulty of understanding why its exuberant heroines should fall for such wooden males. The plot is not that of the seduction of the female by the male protagonist but the reverse; and it is without exception narrated from the seductive female's point of view. The audience is thus seduced by the female protagonist not because it sees her as the object of the desiring male's gaze but because it identifies with her position as seductress. It could be argued that this intense identification with the non-white heroine constructs spectators of both sexes as female; in the process they are also constructed, regardless of actual class affiliation, as members of an ethnic outgroup – one represented as infinitely more attractive than the stiff, repressed dominant classes. The gaze in these films resists analysis in terms of Laura Mulvey's notion of fetishism, whereby the inevitably masculine gaze objectifies the female star through its simultaneous denial and affirmation of sexual difference. More appropriate is Kaja Silverman's proposal that woman-as-spectacle can challenge and indeed exert power (1992: 125–56). Star theory too has shown that specularization can produce identification rather than objectification (Dyer 1979), and that spectators do not necessarily identify with characters of the same class, sex or race (Mayne 1993). The lack of star status and charisma of the male leads in these films (except when they are lower-class) may construct them as resolutely not exotic, but it also prevents any possible audience identification with the white landowning male, except inasmuch as he is the (inexplicable) object of the gypsy heroine's desire.

In several films, the Pygmalion theme of the attempt by a higher-class, white male to turn a female gypsy singer into a 'lady' is reversed as she sets about melting his educated restraint, teaching him the superiority of 'natural spontaneity'. In *Canelita en rama* (García Maroto 1942), the upper-class male re-educated by the gypsy heroine has been to university at Oxford: the 'spontaneous' female gypsy thus represents a positive 'Spanishness' which the upper-class white male has lost and needs to recover. This is, however, complicated by the fact that her 'natural spontaneity' makes her largely impervious to the convent boarding-school in northern Spain where she is sent to turn her into a 'lady'. A similar re-education of the male by the female also occurs in the one postwar Aragonese *folklórica*, *La Dolores* (1939), whose peasant heroine (Conchita Piquer) falls for an inhibited student and teaches him that he will 'learn more with a woman' than he will from books. On a surface level, the film is a typically fascist denigration of the intellectual in favour of an organic concept of *heimat* embodied in the peasant heroine; but what emerges in practice is that the middle-class hero is thick while the lower-class female is verbally quick-witted and active. Several 1940s folkloric film musicals were based on scripts or plays by José María Pemán, cousin of the founder of the Spanish fascist party and head of the Francoist Purification Committee that purged teachers and cultural workers at the end of the Civil War, implying that the genre's cult of the popular and of the feminine as the expression of emotion was the other side of the regime's anti-intellectualism. But the effect is to encourage audience identification with the lower-class, usually gypsy heroine.

Although the audience is invited to identify with the heroine's superior ability to express emotion, it is also invited to identify with the suffering expressed in her song, voicing her awareness of her racial and social inferiority which makes her unworthy of her upper-class suitor's love or leads him to treat her cruelly. Timothy Mitchell brilliantly describes flamenco as a psychodrama, enacted by members of the urban underclasses for their landowing playboy patrons, which provides cathartic release for dependency anxiety. One reason for the massive popularity of the *folklóricas* in early Francoist Spain is no doubt that it allowed the victims of Francoist repression a cathartic release from their own relations of dependency, while allowing members of the establishment the illusion of 'loving' (literally 'patronizing') the lower classes. But Mitchell notes that this culture of dependency, though based on collusion, offered the underclasses strategies for manipulating their patrons. A constituent feature of the *folklórica* genre is the gypsy heroine's ability to disarm and turn the tables on those who regard her as racially and socially inferior; indeed, in all these films she is a trickster figure. In *Estrella de Sierra Morena*, the heroine (played by the flamboyant Lola Flores whose reputation for sexual excess formed part of her star persona) wreaks massive havoc on polite society, tricking even the army officer she loves through her verbal quick-wittedness as well as her seductive powers. Many *folklóricas* hinge on their gypsy heroine giving the upper-class landowner who has abused her his come-uppance: in *Filigrana* (Luis Marquina 1949), Conchita Piquer, having become a successful performance artist and millionaire's widow, buys up the mansion of her erstwhile aristocratic seducer and throws him out on the street, leaving him to come slinking back to her in humiliation. This racial and class revenge is also a revenge by women on men. There is clearly an element of carnivalesque reversal here, allowing racial, class and gender inferiors their moment of cathartic release, even if the film's end reimposes hierarchy. Robert Stam has related carnival to the musical comedy, noting that the laughter it provokes appeals both to elitists who, like Nietzsche, seek a moment of transcendental release, and to those who, like Bakhtin, delight in popular, collective cultural forms. The heroines of the *folklórica* are characterized not only by their ability to voice suffering but also by their *alegría* (gaiety), as the dialogue frequently comments. This *alegría* can be seen not as the mindless escapism for which later Spanish film-makers and critics have condemned the genre but as a carnivalesque enactment of utopian pleasure. Needless to say, only those spectators who value popular culture will appreciate the subversive potential of the fun. Indeed, those intellectuals who have attempted to give flamenco the aura of high art, and who have also privileged male performers, have consistently stressed its tragic side, overlooking the fact that much of it is concerned with pleasure.

It could be said that the folkloric musical gives a more accurate picture of flamenco than that created by purist intellectuals, precisely because of its staginess and its frequent use of female protagonists who are performance artists hovering on the edge of prostitution and seduced by not always model landowners. Although a frequent motif is the superiority of emotion, embodied in the usually gypsy heroine, these films rarely gesture towards the authenticity which intellectuals have seen as the hallmark of flamenco: the performance style is self-consciously stagy, especially at moments of high emotional release. Indeed the use of stereotyped costume and *mise-en-scène*, frequently including mirrors, leads to an often explicit self-reflexivity. In their book on the Hollywood musical, Bruce Babington and Peter Evans note that its staginess makes it an inherently self-reflexive genre (1985: 5, 56, 162, 169). In 1950, Luis Lucía produced a pastiche *folklórica* with his French–Spanish co-production *El sueño de Andalucía (Dream of Andalusia)*, based on a French operetta and exploiting foreign cultural clichés of 'Spanishness' – and of 'Mexicanness' in the sequences set in Mexico – for comic effect. In a self-reflexive prologue, the film starts with its male singing star Luis Mariano, an exile who had made his name in operetta in France, reading the screenplay in Paris: as he reads out the stereotypical description of the Andalusian rural *mise-en-scène*, 'framed by cacti' etc., the opening scenes of the film appear on screen to his voice-over, which gradually fades out. At the film's climactic moment, as its hero is poised to triumph in Seville's bullring, the camera draws back to reveal the crew filming the scene in the Paris studio. The filming over, the actors set off for Seville to see the 'real thing', with a parodic newsreel voice-over announcing as they tour the city, 'This is the Giralda. Its main function is to appear in almost every Spanish film' etc., till we enter a studio set used earlier where the film's female star Carmen Sevilla appears at the window and the film-within-a-film threatens to start up again. This is one of the small number of films where the gypsy heroine (a dancer) achieves final union with her gypsy lover on his triumph as a bullfighter. Both protagonists are performers but the difference between performance and 'life' is blurred by the hero's tendency to burst into song throughout. Indeed, everyone in the Andalusian village that is the film's main location looks like a gypsy on a stage set, implying all Andalusians are gypsies but all of them are fake. Many *folklóricas* blur the distinction between songs sung as part of a stage performance embedded in the narrative, and songs which further the narrative as monologue, dialogue or commentary: in *El sueño de Andalucía*, the blurring is such that everything becomes a self-conscious performance. Richard Dyer (1993: 279) has proposed that the most subversive musicals are those which dissolve the distinction between musical numbers as escape and narrative as problems, for in such films 'the world of the narrative is also (already) utopian'. The racial 'otherness' of the genre's heroines places them in the 'other' world of utopia, where a freedom of expression and body movement is allowed that was denied Spanish audiences in the repressive 1940s. The very imaginary nature of the non-white, usually gypsy heroines embodied on screen by the genre's female stars enabled them to keep alive in their popular audiences a belief that a better world existed. Under conditions of political repression, fantasy can – up to a point – become a political weapon.

Terenci Moix (1993: 198) has told how contemporary Spanish male spectators of Luis Mariano's films would shout *maricón* ('fairy'), because his self-conscious acting style was seen as effeminate. The male singing leads of *El sueño de Andalucía* and of Lucía's similarly self-reflexive *La duquesa de Benamejí*, whose characters comment in verse dialogue on the traditional ballad they are enacting, are feminized by being cast in the role of seductive 'other' endowed with the ability to voice emotion. And, unlike the male stars of the mid-1950s *folklórica*, their free body movements – even though they are not dancers – contrast with the generally stiff male body language. But they are feminized men acting out stereotypically *macho* roles, just as the female stars perform stereotypically feminine roles with a swashbuckling gusto. The genre's explicit or implicit self-reflexivity subverts both masculine and feminine stereotypes by exposing them as a form of mimicry. The staginess of the representation of 'gypsyness' also constructs race as a form of mimicry. The early Francoist *folklórica* has in recent years enjoyed a revival with Spanish gay audiences, because of its camp exposure of the constructedness of gender roles. Self-reflexivity does not necessarily involve a critical stance; as Bhabha (1994) has shown, mimicry can be used as a strategy by the culturally colonized but its forms are imposed. The moments of racial, class and gender reversal in these folkloric musicals should not blind one to their conservative plots. But their self-conscious staginess at least makes the viewer aware that the fantasies of miscegenation being enacted on screen are just that: fantasies.

It is also worth noting that the stars, female and male, who played the role of racial 'other' in these films were not, as Spanish audiences knew, gypsies or, in *La canción de Aixa* and *Bambú*, mixed-race Moroccans or Cubans. A parallel can be drawn here with Hollywood blackface musical comedy, which allows a disavowal of racial difference by making it clear that the 'otherness' represented is only cosmetic. Mitchell (1994: 5, 45–7) points out that the ambivalent fetishization of the flamenco singer in Spanish cultural discourse echoes that of the jazz singer in the United States, so often mimicked in blackface. The mimicking by familiar white stars of non-white roles in the *folklórica* can be seen as an equivalent kind of 'whiteface': that is, a masquerade of racial difference. In some cases, even the Spanishness of these stars was open to question. As we have seen, Luis Mariano was brought up and made his career in France. Imperio Argentina's father was British and she first triumphed as a child star in Buenos Aires (hence her last name), later working in Paramount's Paris-based Joinville studios with (among others) Maurice Chevalier and Carlos Gardel. In the German version of *Carmen la de Triana*, the 'typically Spanish' characters were played by German actors, with the multilingual Imperio Argentina acting in German. The folkloric musicals made by Perojo at Cinecittà mixed Spanish and Italian actors. It is unlikely that this lack of concern with authenticity was a deliberate strategy to subvert the racial discourse of early Francoism. But the effect is to represent race as a form of mimicry, rather than as an inherent, biological category, and to permit identification with the fetishized images of racial 'otherness' on screen.

Michael Rogin (1996) has argued that Hollywood blackface, producing a split identification with a 'not quite other', allowed US audiences to come to terms with the white Jewish immigrants who mostly played blackface roles. The fetishization in early Francoist cinema of 'other-race' characters similarly uses race as a way of working through problems of class and gender whose existence was officially denied. As in Rogin's analysis of blackface, the emotional freedom of the racial 'other', associated with premodern pastoral,[8] is appropriated by white actors for white audiences, leaving actual racial 'others' literally and figuratively out of the picture. While noting important differences, Rogin draws suggestive parallels between the blackface minstrelsy tradition in nineteenth-century American popular theatre, which allowed white, mainly Irish, working-class immigrants to construct a national identity for themselves while excluding African-Americans, and the nineteenth-century exaltation of the *Volk* as the basis of nationhood by nineteenth-century European intellectuals who invented popular cultural traditions for their own purposes: the imaginary gypsy on which the folkloric film musical draws is, of course, central to this process.[9] Like Hollywood blackface minstrels, the non-white heroines played by the singing and dancing stars of early Francoist folkloric musicals are not enacting problems experienced by gypsies or mixed-race Cubans or Moroccans, but disavowing problems of white society.

Disavowal, however, is a dangerous double game. The use of white stars to play non-white roles ensured that Spanish audiences' identifications remained safely white. But it also facilitated identification with early Francoism's 'others'. No doubt the intention was to encourage spectators, of both sexes, to internalize the non-white heroine's surrender to dominant patriarchal culture. The use of feminized gypsy heroes was presumably a converse attempt to give *machismo* a seductive face. But in practice spectators find themselves identifying with gender, class and racial 'others' who, as the embodiment of dominant culture's lacks, are desired and courted by it. For those who ascribed to the repressive values of Francoism, this must have offered a temporary release from moral puritanism. For those who had themselves been made the 'others' of early Francoism, the spectacle on screen of stiff, repressed landowners succumbing to the charms of quick-witted, resourceful, hard-to-get 'other-race' heroines, or that of lithe, expressive 'other-race' heroes outshining or seducing their social superiors, must have provided a vicarious form of cultural revenge.

Notes

1 Her example is the Mexican post-revolutionary Minister of Education Vasconcelos's *The Cosmic Race* (1925); another paradigmatic example would be the Brazilian Gilberto Freyre's construction of a redemptive myth of miscegenation in *The Masters and the Slaves* (1934) (discussed by Papastergiadis in Werbner and Modood 1997: 260–2). Sommer has elsewhere (1991) examined the role played by nineteenth-century Latin American fiction in constructing fantasies of national unity via romantic love across racial and class divides.

2 Sommer (1996: 122) notes that race is 'an underdeveloped concern in Latin American studies'.

3 I am aware of the problems inherent in use of the term 'other', but precisely because of its problematic nature it adequately reflects the illusory social constructions of Francoist discourse, borrowed from Spanish colonial thought. Thus, in using the term, I am not suggesting a neat opposition between 'self' and 'other', but am describing the early Francoist attempt to construct such an opposition in order then to overcome it by incorporating that which had been placed safely outside. For this reason, I place the term in quotation marks. I have at other points in the chapter used the terms 'white' and 'non-white': these terms are, of course, also problematic in a southern European context since, although most Spaniards would regard themselves as 'white', southern Europeans are often seen as less white than northern Europeans.

4 Giménez Caballero's rhetoric of rape is discussed in Labanyi 1996.

5 Preston (1993: 16) quotes Franco as saying: 'Without Africa, I can scarcely explain myself to myself'.

6 Where, as here, the film's title consists in the heroine's name, I have not given a translation. My thanks to the Filmoteca Española in Madrid for making available to me a large number of the films discussed here.

7 These films are discussed, with the folkloric musical, in Labanyi 1997. My thanks to the editors of *Screen* for permitting me to include parts of this article here in revised form.

8 The blackface representation of male African-Americans as workshy and recalcitrant to the capitalist work ethic, noted by Rogin, is replicated in the *folklórica* by the representation of male gypsies, especially the minor, comic characters. Despite their caricaturesque depiction, the audience cannot help but empathize with their happy-go-lucky attitude to life. Blackface differs, however, from the folkloric musical in that it is largely male-centred, whereas the *folklórica* is massively woman-centred.

9 I take the phrase 'the imaginary gypsy' from Lou Charnon-Deutsch's forthcoming book *A History of the Imaginary Gypsy*, which covers Europe including Spain.

Bibliography

Babington, B. and Evans, P. W. (1985) *Blue Skies and Silver Linings: Aspects of the Hollywood Musical*, Manchester: Manchester University Press.

Bhabha, H. (1994) *The Location of Culture*, London and New York: Routledge.

De Certeau, M. (1986) *Heterologies: Discourse on the Other*, Manchester: Manchester University Press.

—— (1988) *The Writing of History*, New York: Columbia University Press.

Dyer, R. (1979) *Stars*, London: British Film Institute.

—— (1993) 'Entertainment and utopia', in S. During (ed.), *The Cultural Studies, Reader*, London and New York: Routledge.

Labanyi, J. (1996) 'Women, Asian hordes and the threat to the self in Giménez Caballero's *Genio de España*', *Bulletin of Hispanic Studies* (Liverpool), 73: 377–87.

—— (1997) 'Race, gender and disavowal in the Spanish cinema of the early Franco period: the missionary film and the folkloric musical', *Screen*, 38, 3: 215–31.

Mayne, J. (1993) *Cinema and Spectatorship*, London: Routledge.

Mitchell, T. (1994) *Flamenco Deep Song*, London and New Haven: Yale University Press.

Moix, T. (1993) *Suspiros de España*, Barcelona: Plaza & Janés.

Preston, P. (1993) *Franco*, London: HarperCollins.

Rogin, M. (1996) *Blackface, White Noise: Jewish Immigrants in the Hollywood Melting Pot*, Berkeley, Los Angeles and London: University of California Press.

Silverman, K. (1992) *Male Subjectivity at the Margins*, New York and London: Routledge.

Sommer, D. (1991) *Foundational Fictions: The National Romances of Latin America*, Berkeley, Los Angeles and London: University of California Press.

—— (1996) 'The places of history: regionalism revisited in Latin America', *Modern Language Quarterly*, 57, 2: 119–27.

Werbner, P. and Modood, T. (1997) *Debating Cultural Hybridity: Multi-cultural Identities and the Politics of Anti-racism*, London: Zed Books.

3   From miscegenation to hybridity: mixed relationships and mixed parentage in profile

Ann Phoenix and Charlie Owen

Racially mixed unions and mixed parentage are at the intersection of a number of theoretical and social policy debates because they highlight a range of racialised social relations and divisions. 'Mixed parentage' challenges binary, black–white, thinking and demonstrates some of the contestations that are constantly being waged around the terminology of 'race'. Since children of mixed parentage are more likely than white or black children to spend long periods in local authority care (Bebbington and Miles 1989), they illustrate most starkly the difficulties caused by the polarisation of debates on transracial adoption (Tizard and Phoenix 1993).

There is increasing recognition that people with one black parent and one white parent do not necessarily suffer from identity confusion because they are neither black nor white. Instead, new, 'mixed', identities have emerged (Tizard and Phoenix 1993).

This chapter first examines the social construction of black–white unions and mixed parentage as problematic. It then examines the demographic background which has, at least partly, provided the conditions of possibility for the emergence of 'mixed' identities. Finally, it uses some data from a study of the Social Identities of Young Londoners to demonstrate the complex ways in which young people of mixed parentage think about their racialised identities and how this contrasts with the simplistic ways in which they are often positioned by other people.

The construction of mixed parentage as problematic

The terms of colour

The construction of 'mixed parentage' as necessarily problematic can occur only when there is acceptance that there are clearly differentiated 'races' who are, in essence, necessarily polarised. The treatment of people in 'essentialist' ways has been much critiqued in feminist and cultural studies work as well as social science

First published, in B. Bernstein and J. Brannen (eds), *Children, Research and Policy* (London: Taylor & Francis, 1996).

literature for its obscuring of intra-group differences and commonalities between groups as well as its valorising of inter-group differences (Hall 1989; Brah 1992; 1996). Bipolar constructions of black and white have been responsible for notions that people can be 'between two cultures' or 'neither one colour nor the other' and denials that it is possible to have identities which are 'both/and', rather than 'either/or' (Collins 1990).

In Britain, and the USA, the conceptual polarisation of black people and white people has, historically, generally led to those of mixed parentage being included in the category now commonly called 'black'. It is indicative of the political nature of this categorisation that having one white parent has never been sufficient to permit inclusion as 'white', but having one black parent necessarily entailed classification as 'black'. Most states (at one time forty of fifty) in the USA enacted laws against racially mixed unions and marriages. Such laws were not declared unconstitutional until 1967 (Young 1995). Although the categories forbidden to marry in the various states were not consistent, all forbade marriage between black and white (Reuter 1931). Definitions of what constituted being black also varied, but, 'in practice – both legal and customary – anyone with *any* known African ancestry was deemed an African American, while only those without any trace of known African ancestry were called Whites' (Spickard 1992: 16). This is what became known as the 'one drop rule' or 'hypodescent'. Common sense would suggest that skin colour was the basis of the black–white differentiation, but some of those of mixed parentage could be lighter than some whites, but would still be classified as black (Spickard 1992). One edition of the *Oprah Winfrey* show (BBC2, Saturday 28 October 1995) vividly demonstrated this essentialist thinking: the featured guests were people living in the USA who had thought that they were white and who had been treated as white. Each had discovered that, in fact, they had black ancestry. They were then called 'black' and treated as black rather than as white. In some cases this included having to change schools – very much in line with the 'one drop' rule.

The binarism that underpinned the 'one drop rule' has 'sedimented into common sense'. Thus, it is not surprising that discussion on the *Oprah Winfrey* show reflected this old, but still pervasive, construction. Even some of the opposition to transracial adoption from black social workers and other black groups is based on the same principle as the 'one drop rule'. Arguments that people of mixed parentage have to recognise that, regardless of how they feel, they are black are based on a recognition that racism will differentiate them from white people. Yet such arguments construct black people and white people as cultural and visual opposites rather than either as part of a continuum or as united and/or differentiated by features other than 'race'. Instead of posing a challenge to racism or racialised discourses they (re)produce them, as in the following quotation from the black US magazine *Ebony*.

> Some biracial brothers and sisters might do well to heed advice from Lenny Kravitz [American rock star]. 'You don't have to deny the White side of you if you're mixed,' he says. 'Accept the blessing of having the advantage of two

cultures, but understand that you are Black. In this world, if you have one
spot of Black blood, you are *Black*. So get over it'.

(Norment 1995)

Although people with one black and one white parent have historically been
categorised as black, they have, simultaneously (and contradictorily), been identified as separate from both black and white people. The specific terms commonly
used to describe people of mixed, parentage, and sexual unions between black and
white people, tend to pathologise those who cannot easily be fitted into the
taken-for-granted racialised binary opposition. Thus, 'half-caste', 'mixed race',
'bi-racial', 'maroon', 'mulatto' (from mule) and 'métis' (French for mongrel dog)
all demonstrate essentialism and bipolar thinking. Many are also riven with
pathologising tones of impurity. In the same way, the terms mixed marriage;
intermarriage and 'miscegenation' (meaning 'interbreeding between races, especially sexual union of whites with Negroes', *Oxford Illustrated Dictionary*, 1980;
The Shorter Oxford English Dictionary, 1983) accept binary notions of 'race' and
have negative overtones. The ubiquitous nature of such terms is illustrated in the
work of the sociologist Fernando Henriques (1974). Henriques challenged
negative views of mixed marriages. Yet he called his book *Children of Caliban:
Miscegenation* and wrote about himself as a 'part of the process of miscegenation
that I have tried to describe' (p. 6).

Given the increasing numbers of people who are of mixed parentage and in
mixed relationships, it is not surprising that this is an area where terminology has
been contested. Although this contestation is perhaps less well known than was
the contestation over changing the term 'coloured' to 'black' in the 1960s and
1970s, many people now reject usage of terms such as 'mulatto', 'half-caste' and
'miscegenation'. In the USA, where 'Afro-American' has largely given way to
African-American, there is now widespread usage of the term 'bi-racial' to make
general reference to 'mixed parentage'. In Britain, Small (1986) has argued for
dropping the term 'mixed race' because it both accepts that there are 'races' and
denies blackness. He advocated use of the term 'mixed parentage' if 'black' would
not suffice. Yet, as with much of the terminology of 'race', terms to describe
'mixed parentage' are not satisfactory and, for that reason, are likely to continue
to change.

> What term adequately describes the relationship between a Black and a White
> parent? The term 'mixed race' is inappropriate because 'race' carries under-
> tones of biological inferiority and superiority. An alternative term needs to be
> found but we do not have one to offer. We use 'mixed parentage' but it too
> has racist undertones.
>
> Early Years Trainers Anti-Racist Network 1995: 11)

One reason for dissatisfaction with the term 'mixed parentage' to describe
those who have one black and one white parent is that it constructs an arbitrary
division between those of mixed parentage and others. Because the populations of

the world are almost all intermixed, most people have some mixed parentage (Small 1986). Indeed, because of slavery and colonial relationships, many more people are of mixed black–white ancestry than is generally accepted. May Optiz (1992) points out that, while 'Afro-German' is a new term and people of mixed black–white parentage in Germany are generally viewed as hated war babies, there has been a long history of mixed parentage as a result of Germany's colonial relationship with Cameroon, Tanzania and Namibia. Augustin Barbara makes similar points for France, while Peter Fryer (1984), Henriques (1974) and Visram (1986) document the long history of mixed relationships in Britain.

It is difficult to estimate the percentage of white British and US populations which have black ancestry, but it has been estimated that 70–80 per cent of all US black people have some white ancestry (Zack 1993). Some recent popular interest in the impact of mixed ancestry is demonstrated by the fact that the highly popular US *Oprah Winfrey* show has dedicated two programmes to white people who have black relatives and vice versa. One of these was also shown on British television (BBC 2, Saturday 28 October 1995).

In recent years, academics in cultural studies have produced terms which attempt to take on board the processual nature of ethnicity. Thus the terms 'hybridity' and 'hybridisation' are often used to denote the syncretism and plurality of racialised identities. Hall (1989) refers to 'the process of cultural *diaspora-ization*'. Such terms are not designed to refer particularly to people of mixed parentage, but they offer ways of thinking about ethnicity which include those of mixed parentage without pathologising them. It may seem paradoxical that the term 'hybridity' should be invested with positive connotations when 'miscegenation' is not. The dictionary definition of the term 'hybridity' is the condition of 'being produced by the interbreeding of two different species or varieties; mongrel; cross-bred; half-bred' (*Shorter Oxford English Dictionary*, 1983) as well as 'person of mixed nationality' (*Oxford Illustrated Dictionary*, 1980). Parker (1995) argues that the concept of hybridity 'is an uneasy biologistic metaphor for combination which can connote a state rather than a process ... The focus should be on specific processes of identity formation rather than subsuming them all into one state of hybridity' (Parker 1995: 26). Similarly, Young (1995: 27) argues that.

> There is an historical stemma between the cultural concepts of our own day and those of the past from which we tend to assume that we have distanced ourselves. We restate and rehearse them in the language and concepts that we use: every time a commentator uses the epithet 'full-blooded', for example, he or she repeats the distinction between those of pure and mixed race. Hybridity in particular shows the connections between the racial categories of the past and contemporary cultural discourse.

None the less, given that 'hybridity' is theorised as processes resulting from the combination of peoples and cultures, its use can be seen as part, however, unsatisfactory, of the process of reclamation of terms and contestation over meanings which was signalled by the change from 'coloured' to 'black'. The accounts of young people of mixed parentage interviewed in a study of the social identities of young Londoners and of people involved in racially mixed relationships can be said to demonstrate such a shift (Tizard and Phoenix 1993). Most of their discourses were not pathological constructions of 'miscegenation' and binary oppositions of 'neither one colour nor the other', but instead showed the beginnings of constructions of 'hybridity'.

In keeping with all racialised terms, the terminology of mixed relationships and mixed parentage thus demonstrates dynamism, contestation of power to define, and historical and geographical specificity.

> There are no terms that are 'right' forever more. Groups define and redefine themselves their sense of who they are culturally and politically as preferred terms change. Also within a group one person may like a term which another may not. We have to constantly pay attention to changing definitions and to the reasons why they are changed. People need to discover for themselves who they are and not have terms imposed on them.
>
> (Early Years Trainers Anti-Racist Network 1995: 11)

Opposition to 'racial mixing'

In countries with a colonial history, there has been (and continues to be) contradictory responses to racially mixed unions and children of mixed parentage. On the one hand, such unions have always existed where people of different colours and ethnicities have coexisted. On the other hand, there has long been a mainly negative orientation to unions between black and white people in countries such as Britain and the USA. In slavery and colonialism, mixed unions were often forced by white colonisers on colonised women (Spickard 1989). However, there always were some consensual unions. Yet, nineteenth-century white writers frequently denounced 'racial mixing' as indecent or unnatural. Such denouncements were obviously designed to dissuade readers from contemplating mixed unions:

> Who that has any sense or decency, can help being shocked at the familiar intercourse, which has gradually been gaining ground, and which has, at last, got a complete footing between the Negroes and the women of England? . . . but to accompany him *to the altar*, to become his wife, to breed English mulattoes, to stamp the mark of Cain upon her family and her country! Amongst white women, this disregard of decency, this defiance of the dictates of nature, this foul, this beastly propensity, is, I say it with sorrow and with shame, *peculiar to the English.*
>
> (Cobbett, *Cobbett's Weekly Political Register*, 16 June 1804. Quoted by Fryer (1984: 234–5)

There is some evidence on the extent of opposition to mixed marriages in modern Britain. For example, on a number of occasions between 1983 and 1991 the British Social Attitudes Survey has asked respondents if they would mind if a close relative married someone of *Asian* origin or of *West Indian* origin. About half of respondents said they would mind, either a lot or a little, although there has been a fall in the number who mind, from 54 per cent in 1983 to 43 per cent in 1991. (For more detail see Owen (in preparation).) In a poll conducted for *The Independent on Sunday* (7 July 1991), respondents were asked the extent to which they agreed or disagreed with the following statement: 'People should only marry people of their own ethnic group'. Among *white* respondents, 31 per cent said they agreed; 17 per cent of *black* respondents and 39 per cent of *Asian* respondents[1] also agreed.

More recently, the fact that there is still opposition to black–white relationships was brought home to a British public by media accounts of attacks on black men with white girlfriends (see, for example, *Daily Mail*, 19 October 1993; *The Guardian*, 10 June 1994; *The Sun*, 21 June 1994; *The Sun*, 23 September 1994).

While there has been a longstanding negative orientation to relationships between black and white people and the children from such unions, the nature of that negative orientation has shifted. There has been a shift from eugenic concerns with 'miscegenation' to liberal concerns with the welfare of the children born from such unions, i.e. to expressions of benevolent concerns about the children.

> Many people who are in almost all other respects very tolerant of coloured people defend their objection to mixed marriages on the grounds that the children of such marriages are bound to suffer.
>
> (Richmond 1961: 284)

> The prevailing view of mixed race children is that they have identity problems because of their ambiguous social position . . . the stereotype of the 'tortured misfit'.
>
> (Wilson 1987: 1–2)

Although this appears, at first sight, to be a benign shift, from concerns with miscegenation to liberal concerns, it is, in effect, also negative. This is because mixed relationships are still constructed as problematic. However, this apparently benevolent concern masks its deleterious effects in three related ways. First, it prevents charges of racism by deflecting attention from racist discourses onto children of mixed parentage as misfits. Second, it individualises the issue by shifting focus on to the problems of identity for the children produced from mixed unions. Finally, it constructs 'regimes of truth' (Foucault 1980) which are designed to lead to internal, individual regulation of mixed relationships since external controls are neither legal nor currently socially acceptable. Thus, since most parents do not have children with the intention of damaging them, the implication is that concerned, responsible parents should not produce children of mixed parentage. It thus warrants attempted deterrence of mixed relationships and intrusive comments to those who become parents of mixed-parentage children: 'In a society where our reluctance to become "involved" leaves tortured children at risk in their own homes and raped women lying in gutters, perfect strangers think they have the right to abuse you, or your partner or your child, because you have different skin colours' (Alibhai-Brown and Montague 1992: 4). Foreboding about the impact on children of being of mixed parentage arises from divergent political interests, since such fears are expressed by people who are positioned differently in relation to power and social control. Thus, some white people are concerned that mixed parentage involves a dilution of their 'race', while some black people are more concerned that it involves consorting with 'the enemy'. Yet, these positions coincide in discourses of concern for the welfare of children of mixed parentage in the same way that black people and white people sometimes apply the 'one drop rule' for different reasons. The construction of mixed parentage as a social problem represents a conflation of issues constructed as social problems. It is easier to impute causation of problems associated with minority status, discrimination and uncertainty about how to deal with those who do not fit into the artificially created binary division between black and white, to being of mixed parentage than to deal with these issues themselves.

While there has been strident opposition to 'racial mixing', it is possible to discern positive as well as negative themes in writing over the last sixty years. In 1937, for example, Stonequist argued in *The Marginal Man* that people of mixed parentage would almost inevitably experience a painful lack of belonging to either black or white groups. Mixed parentage was thus, according to Stonequist, inherently likely to cause negative experiences. By way of contrast, Park (1931), working in the same period, argued that there could be positive benefits of the marginality resulting from mixed parentage, in that the possessing of two cultures could make the marginal person a 'citizen of the world'. This conceptualisation of 'marginality' is, arguably, a forerunner of notions of 'hybridity', although current usage of the latter is intended to connote the forging of new cultures from syncretic blending and does not imply marginal existence.

Demographic trends: an example of contestation in practice

There are few demographic data available on people of mixed parentage. However those data available indicate that there is a growing number of people in 'racially' mixed relationships and big increases in number of people of mixed parentage. Thus, despite negative constructions of mixed parentage, many people are contesting the social proscription on crossing racialised boundaries. This section considers the demographic data on mixed parentage available in Britain. The demographic data provide the context within which it is possible to understand ideological and discursive shifts in regard to mixed parentage.

Prior to the 1991 Census, the main source of data on Britain's ethnic minority populations had been the Labour Force Survey (Owen 1993). The Census is now the main source, but it is very limited in the information it provides on mixed ethnic backgrounds. In fact, there is only one published table which includes any data on mixed parentage.

Census

The first British Census to include a question on ethnic group was 1991. The question went through extensive field trials, to get a wording that was both acceptable to those completing the Census form and usable by those who wanted the data:

> To be effective an ethnic classification has to be expressed both intelligibly and acceptably to all sections of the population: it has also to furnish information in the form in which it is needed . . . the various aims are not always compatible and . . . the final design has had to be a compromise between conflicting objectives.
>
> (Sillitoe and White 1992: 141)

The question that was finally used is shown in Figure 3.1.[2] The question is a mix of colour categories (*White* and *Black*) and geographical origins (e.g. *Indian, Chinese,* etc.), sometimes used in combination (e.g. *Black–Caribbean*). No simple classification could be entirely satisfactory, but this one does try to enumerate categories which reflect the important dimensions of discrimination in British society. The possibilities of ticking more than one box, or of having an explicit category of *Mixed* were both rejected. In the USA a race or ethnic question has been included on the census for many years. That question does not include a mixed category, but there is currently debate about whether to include such an option in the next census (Root 1996).

In the British Census people who ticked either of the *Black–Other* or *Any other*

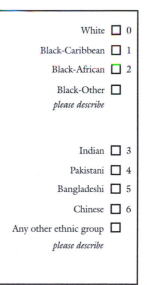

If the person is descended from more than one ethnic or racial group, please tick the group to which the person considers he/she belongs, or tick the 'Any other ethnic group' box and describe the person's ancestry in the space provided

Figure 3.1 Question on ethnic groups in the 1991 Census.

ethnic group boxes were asked to '*please describe*'. The answers given by those ticking *Black–Other* were assigned to eleven categories; those from the *Any other ethnic group* were assigned to a further seventeen categories. For all (but one) of the published Census tables, these categories were reassigned to larger groups.

Of the people who ticked one of these *other* boxes, some described themselves as of mixed or multiple ethnic origins. Table 3.1 shows the numbers involved: those who ticked the *Black–Other* or the *Any other ethnic group* boxes, but who otherwise gave similar answers, have been combined. It can be seen that altogether 228,504 people – out of a total enumerated of almost 55 million – identified themselves (or were identified by others in their household – e.g. by their parents) as being of mixed origin. Before going on to look at these mixed-parentage groups in more detail, we will first look at what data the Census has on mixed couples.

Mixed couples

There are no published tables on the ethnic groups of couples, but the Census Sample of Anonymised Records[3] does allow within-household analyses – including by ethnic group. For this chapter we have looked at the percentages with a *White* partner for each ethnic group. The results are shown in Table 3.2. (There were also 100 mixed couples where neither partner was *White*, but too few in any group for statistical analysis.) Over 99 per cent of *White* men and women living with a partner had a *White* partner. For the three *Black* groups, men were somewhat more likely to have a *White* partner than were women. More than a quarter of *Black–Caribbean* men living with a partner were living with a *White* partner, for *Black–Caribbean* women it was 14 per cent. For the *Black–Other* group, more than half the men and almost half the women who were living with a partner had a *White* partner. Clearly these mixed relationships are very common.

The percentages of relationships with *White* partners for the three South Asian groups were much lower. Of *Indian* men in couples, about 8 per cent had a *White* partner, 6 per cent of Pakistani men and 3 per cent of Bangladeshi men. The order was the same for women but the percentages were all lower. For the *Chinese* and

Table 3.1 Numbers identified as of mixed parentage in the Census and LFS

	Census		LFS	
	N	*%*	*N*	*%*
Black–White	54,569	0.099	570	0.126
Asian–White	61,874	0.113	591	0.131
Other mixed	112,061	0.204	1,192	0.264
Total	54,888,844		451,648	

Sources: Census 1991, Great Britain; LFS, 1989–91.

Table 3.2 Percentages of people in couples with a white partner

Ethnic group	Male		Female	
	N	%	N	%
White	125,128	99.5	125,128	99.3
Black–Caribbean	222	26.3	102	14.3
Black–African	48	17.5	41	15.8
Black–Other	74	51.0	63	43.8
Indian	133	7.7	70	4.3
Pakistani	41	5.6	9	1.3
Bangladeshi	7	3.2	0	0.0
Chinese	34	13.2	77	24.9
Other groups–Asian	54	15.1	143	32.2
Other groups–Other	215	51.2	138	39.2
Total	125,956	96.3	125,771	96.2

Source: Census 1991, Sample of Anonymised Records.

Other Groups–Other Asian the percentages were higher, and higher for women than for men: a quarter of *Chinese* women in couples were with a *White* partner. The final category, *Other Groups–Other*,[4] had a large percentage with *White* partners: over half the men and nearly 40 per cent of the women who were in couples had a *White* partner.

Mixed parentage in the Census

We have used data from the one published table that includes the full ethnic classification (OPCS/GRO(S) 1993: Table A) to look at those who were classified as mixed. There were 54,569 people identified as *Black–White*: this amounted to less than one tenth of 1 per cent of the population, or 994 persons per million. There were three *Black* groups distinguished by the Census question: these are *Black–Caribbean*, *Black–African* and *Black–Other*. However, this mixed category of *Black–White* combines all forms of black parentage.

There were 61,874 people identified as *Asian–White*: this is just over one tenth of 1 per cent, or, more precisely, 1,127 persons per million. The main Census classification includes five *Asian* categories: *Indian*, *Pakistani*, *Bangladeshi*, *Chinese* and *Other Groups–Other Asian*. The mixed group, *Asian–White*, includes all of these in their parentage. Given the relatively low number of relationships with *White* partners among the three South Asian groups, it is likely that the children in this group had parents who were either *Chinese* or from the so-called *Other Groups–Other Asian* group.

There was also a group of 3,776 people identified as *Mixed White*, but for all tables these were reassigned to *White* and are ignored here. Finally there is a group of 112,061 labelled as *Other Mixed*, approximately 0.2 per cent of the population or 2,042 persons per million.

Out of a total population for Great Britain of nearly 55 million, these three mixed groups – *Black–White, Asian–White* and *Other Mixed* – combined amount to less than half of 1 per cent. This may seem very small, but it does amount to 8 per cent of the ethnic minority population – i.e. of all those not classified as *White* in the Census. These three groups are the people who ticked one of the *Black–Other* or *Any other ethnic group* boxes (or had it ticked for them) and who wrote in something that could be constructed as mixed parentage. It cannot be known if the numbers would have been different if explicit *mixed* categories had been offered on the Census form, or if people had been allowed to tick more than one box. The wording of the question actually seems to encourage people of mixed parentage to identify with one of the main categories: *If the person is descended from more than one ethnic or racial group, please tick the group to which the person considers he/she belongs, or tick the 'Any other ethnic group' box and describe the person's ancestry in the space provided.*

It may seem surprising that *Black–White* is the smallest of the three mixed groups, as this is the group that draws most attention. However, some of the other sub-categories of the *Black–Other* group may include people of mixed ethnic origin, in particular the *Black Other: British* (58,106) and the *Black Other: Other Mixed* (50,668) sub-categories might include people who would have described themselves as mixed *Black–White* had that been offered as a choice. Nevertheless, it is interesting that the comparatively large *Asian–White* group receive much less attention – as does the even larger *Other Mixed* group.

The single Census table that shows the full classification, including the *mixed* categories, gives a population count – down to district level – but no other information, e.g. age, gender, class, household type, etc. However, the Labour Force Survey, which has included a question on ethnic group since 1979, does give more detail on mixed parentage.

The Labour Force Survey

The Labour Force Survey (LFS) is a national sample survey of private households. It collects interviews from around 60,000 households in Great Britain, annually prior to 1992 and quarterly since. Since 1979 the survey has included a question on ethnic origin. Respondents are shown a card and asked to say to which ethnic group they consider they belong. Prior to 1992 the ethnic groups distinguished in the list were: White, West Indian or Guyanese, Indian, Pakistani, Bangladeshi, Chinese, Arab, Mixed Origin and Other. If the respondents replied they were of Mixed or Other ethnic origin, the interviewer asked them to describe their ethnic origin in greater detail (Haskey 1990). From 1992 onwards the LFS has used the same question as the 1991 Census. For this chapter data for the three years 1989–91 will be considered.[5] This gives data from the same period as the Census, but is prior to the change of question, and so includes the explicit choice of *mixed* in the question.

Prior to 1992 the responses to the ethnic question for the LFS had been assigned by OPCS to thirty-six codes: twelve of these include *mixed* in their descriptions (plus *White Mixed*). This classification has more detail than the Census but, even with a sample size of almost half a million (obtained by combining three years), numbers in some categories are very small, and too small to give reliable data. For now, these groups have been combined to give three mixed categories, very similar to those in the Census. The numbers in the three categories are also shown in Table 3.1. In each case the proportion was higher for the LFS than for the Census. This suggests that people are more likely to describe themselves as mixed if that is one of the categories offered. In the USA, where there are numerous occasions on which people have to record racial and ethnic information, the fastest growing category has become 'other' and, according to the US Bureau of the Census, 'nearly a quarter million people "wrote in" a multiracial designator to the race question' (Root 1996: xvii).

As with the Census results, the *Black–White* mixed group is the smallest of the three, slightly smaller than the *Asian–White* group and considerably smaller than the *Other Mixed* group. The *Asian–White* group was made up of four LFS categories: *Indian–White* (252), *Pakistani–White* (79), *Bangladeshi–White* (15) and *Other Asian–White* (245), so that those of mixed South Asian and White origins comprise just over half the *Asian–White* group.

Age structure

Figure 3.2 shows the age structure of the three mixed ethnic groups. Each line shows the percentage of the groups within each five-year age band. For the total population there are approximately equal numbers of people in each age band, but these mixed ethnic groups clearly have a very young age structure: children younger than sixteen form 70 per cent of the *Black–White* group, 52 per cent of the *Asian–White* group and 56 per cent of the *Other Mixed* group, compared with 23 per cent in the total population. This indicates that the populations of mixed ethnicity are, on average, quite young, so that people of mixed parentage will form an increasing percentage of the population as they grow older. For example, whilst these three groups together account for 0.5 per cent of the population overall, they amount to 1.4 per cent of the population of children under the age of sixteen, and 1.8 per cent of under five.[6]

People of mixed ethnic background are much more likely to have been born in the UK than any other ethnic group except *White*. This partly reflects the young age structure, since only a minority of people who move to a different country are children. However, even amongst children the mixed-parentage groups are more likely to have been born in the UK than any of the other ethnic groups – except *White*.

Family structure

The rest of this discussion of demographic structure deals, just with the children aged under sixteen. For all three groups the majority of children are living with two parents, although not necessarily the biological parents. The percentages are

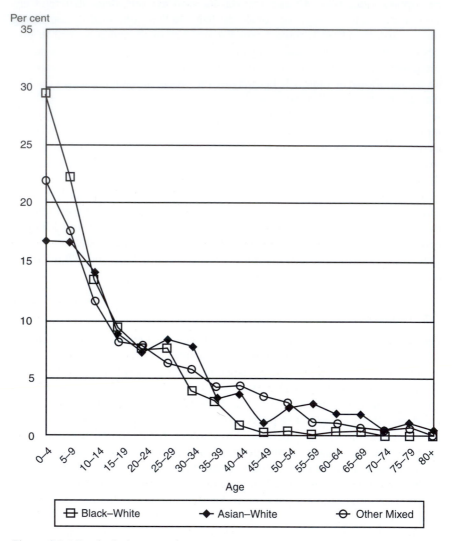

Figure 3.2 Mixed ethnic groups by age.

shown in Table 3.3, which also includes data on other ethnic groups for compara-tive purposes. For the *Black–White* group 53 per cent live with two adults acting as parents: this is a lot less than the percentage for *White* children (85 per cent) but a little higher than that for *Black* children (47 per cent). For the *Asian–White* group the percentage of children living with two parents is 82 per cent: this is slightly lower than the percentage for *White* children and 10 per cent below the percentage for *South Asian* children (93 per cent). For the *Other Mixed* group the percentage is 76 per cent: this is below the percentage for all groups except the *Black* group and the *Black–White* mixed group.

Table 3.3 Type of family unit for children aged under sixteen, by ethnic group

Ethnic group	Couple N	%	Lone parent Mother N	%	Father N	%	Total
White	73,369	84.5	12,305	14.2	1,152	1.3	86,826
Black	578	47.3	624	51.0	21	1.7	1,223
South Asian	4,014	92.7	293	6.8	24	0.6	4,331
Other	637	84.3	116	15.3	3	0.4	756
Black–White	202	53.2	173	45.5	5	1.3	380
Asian–White	250	83.1	51	16.9	0	0	301
Other mixed	426	62.3	244	35.7	14	2.0	684
Not stated	1,153	76.1	312	20.6	50	3.3	1,515
Total	80,629	84.0	144,118	14.7	1,269	1.3	96,016

Source: LFS, 1989–91.

Table 3.4 Percentage living with white parents

	White father N	%	White mother In couple N	%	Lone N	%	Total
Black–White	62	16.3	133	35.0	110	28.9	380
Asian–White	100	33.2	112	37.2	33	11.0	301
Other mixed	167	24.4	200	29.2	161	23.5	684

Source: LFS, 1989–91.

For all three groups of mixed-parentage children, more were living with a white mother than with a white father (see Table 3.4). The commonest family arrangement was to be living with a white mother in a couple. For the *Black–White* group, though, almost as many children lived with a lone white mother. This family type was uncommon for *Asian–White* children, more of whom lived with a white father than for the *Black–White* group. The *Other Mixed* group was least likely to be living with a white mother in a couple; they were between the *Black–White* and *Asian–White* groups in the percentages living with a lone white mother or with a white father.

Not all the children were living with a white parent. Overall 25 per cent of the *Black–White* group were not living with a white parent, 20 per cent of the *Asian–White* group and 26 per cent of the *Other Mixed* group. Of those not living with a white parent, many were living with at least one parent (or parent figure) who described themselves as *mixed*: this was true for 14 per cent of the *Black–White* group, 13 per cent of the *Asian–White* and 17 per cent of the *Other Mixed*.

Insider accounts from young people of mixed parentage

The demographic data demonstrate that people of mixed parentage constitute a small, but increasing, percentage of the British population. They are, however, a large percentage of the minority ethnic population. This fact, together with the greater numbers of younger than older people of mixed parentage, is important to the understanding of the context within which the identities of young people of mixed parentage are forged and expressed. The more people who are seen to fit into a particular group (ethnic, racialised or otherwise), the more likely it is that at least some will identify as part of that group and resist outsider classification of themselves (Root 1996).

The demographic data available makes clear that there are fewer people of *Black–White* parentage than of *Asian–White* parentage. This is not surprising, since there are twice as many people of Asian descent than of African (including African Caribbean) descent in Britain (3.4 per cent and 1.6 per cent respectively). Historically, *Asian–White* and *Black–White* mixed relationships were both frowned on:

> It would surprise many people to see how extensively these dark classes are tincturing the colour of the rising race of children in the lowest haunts of this locality: and many of the fallen females have a visible infusion of Asiatic and African blood in their veins. They form a peculiar class, but mingle freely with the others. It is an instance of depraved taste, that many of our fallen ones prefer devoting themselves entirely to the dark races of men, and some who are to them have infants by them.
>
> (*London City Mission Magazine*, August 1857: 217, quoted in Visram 1986: 62).

In the USA, there has been some interest in mixed parentage arising from relationships between people from a range of ethnic groups. However, in both the USA and in Britain more attention has been given to those born of black–white relationships (with black referring to people of African origin). In Britain, this is the 'racial/ethnic' group most likely to enter, and to stay for longer periods in, local authority care. Children of mixed parentage have also been central to considerations about 'transracial adoption'.

Transracial adoption: rehearsing the arguments

Over the last decade, there has been heated debate about the adoption and fostering of black children into white families. On the one hand, those in favour of transracial adoption argue that, if there is an insufficient supply of black (and, more recently, mixed) adoptive couples, black and mixed-parentage children should be placed with white parents rather than being left for long periods in institutions or foster care. Loving care in a family is argued to be children's primary psychological need while racial identity is less important in developmental terms.

It is often suggested that, for healthy psychological functioning, children and young people from minority ethnic groups need to have secure ethnic identities in order to develop 'positive identities', characterised by high levels of self-esteem (Phinney and Rosenthal 1992). This notion has been taken up by proponents of what has come to be known as 'same-race' adoption placements. Advocates of 'same-race' placements argue that black children brought up in white households may develop well in many ways, but will suffer from 'identity confusion', fail to develop a 'positive black identity' and be uncomfortable with black people. Furthermore, it is argued that white parents will be unable to pass on to black children the strategies they need in order to come to terms with and survive in a society where racism is common and where rejection by white people is likely. According to this argument transracial adoption is damaging to black children's identity development (Tizard and Phoenix 1994). Children of mixed parentage are not differentiated from those who are black by most proponents of this argument.

Both sides of the debate on transracial adoption thus draw on arguments about children's psychosocial development and, to some extent, both find support for their polarised views from the handful of studies that have been done on transracial adoption (see Bagley *et al.* 1993; McRoy and Hall 1996). There is, however, little research evidence with which to resolve this controversy (Kirton 1995), although, taken to the extreme, both sides of the debate have serious shortcomings. On the one hand, it is clear from the study of majority and minority ethnic children that 'race' and racism impinge on the lives of children who have not been adopted (Troyna and Hatcher 1992; Holmes 1995). There is, as yet, insufficient research evidence to indicate how continuous care from a loving white family affects, and is affected by, black and mixed-parentage children's experiences and racialised understandings. On the other hand, arguments that the adoption of black and mixed-parentage children by white parents will necessarily have a damaging effect on young people's 'positive black identity' rely on largely outdated theories of identity. There is no evidence, for example, that 'race' is privileged over gender or social class as social identities and it is now common for psychological approaches to view identities as plural rather than unitary and as dynamic rather than determined by particular characteristics. The challenge posed by new theories of identities is to explain how different identities intersect with each other.

This section uses data from a study of the racialised identities of mixed parentage (black–white) (58), black (101) and white (89) fourteen-to-eighteen-year-old young Londoners conducted by Barbara Tizard and Ann Phoenix. There were 152 young women and 96 young men in the sample. The sample was more middle-class than would have been expected by chance. If social class is assessed using fathers' occupational groupings, 50 per cent of the whole sample and 63 per cent of the mixed-parentage sample came from the middle classes. This percentage rises, if mothers' occupational groupings are used, to 66 per cent for the whole sample and 70 per cent for those of mixed parentage. Half the interviews lasted between an hour and an hour and a half. A quarter were longer and a quarter slightly shorter. See Tizard and Phoenix (1993) for fuller details of the sample and the study and Phoenix and Tizard (1996) for specific discussion of social class.

This study (referred to here as the 'Social Identities study') aimed to get a good understanding of the identities of non-adopted, non-clinical samples of young people in order to contribute to debates about transracial adoption and racialised identities. In order to avoid prejudging the issue of whether racial identities are necessarily different from other social identities or from more personal identities the study also focused on gender, social class and personal identities in addition to 'race'. However, given that transracial adoption was the starting point of the study, more attention was paid to issues of 'race'.

In attempting to understand the racialised identities of young people of mixed parentage, it is important to document the range of ways in which young people of mixed parentage think about themselves. This section of the chapter uses data from the study to demonstrate that many of the young people had the contradict-ory experiences of being treated on the one hand as if they are necessarily 'black' and, on the other, as if they are 'neither black nor white'. It argues that many of the young people had complex understandings of their racialised identities in which they used the terms of colour flexibly and shifted identifications over time and from context to context. This could mean that young people resisted using those terms the adults around them told them that they should use in describing themselves. As with all other identities, the diversity of mixed-parentage identities makes it untenable always to subsume those with one black and one white parent into the category 'black' (as would be suggested by the 'one drop principle', described above) or to assume that they constitute a unitary group.

Experiencing the legacy of 'one drop' thinking

In childhood, some of the sample of young people of mixed parentage reported that they came to recognise that other people found it difficult to accept that they had a white parent: 'People used to say I was adopted because my mother was white, and stuff . . . It was really horrible.' This reluctance to accept that they could have been born to their mothers is not because young children know or subscribe to the 'one-drop' thesis. In her study of how young children perceive race, Holmes (1995) found that US kindergarten children consider that children have to be the same colour as their parents unless children are adopted. Since, in Britain, children of mixed parentage are more likely to have white mothers than black mothers, this may explain why some children of mixed parentage were subjected to claims that they were adopted. Whatever the reason, however, it is one way in which young children of mixed parentage learn that they are more likely to be thought of as black than as white.

Young people of mixed parentage were sometimes surprised to find themselves subject to constructions of them as necessarily and only black. The following account, from a girl of mixed parentage, who goes to an almost exclusively white private school, makes painfully clear that 'one drop' thinking has left an identifi-able legacy. In her case, a close friend demonstrated an inability to conceive of people with one black and one white parent as having anything in common with white people of the same sex.

> Q. Have you ever discussed racism with your friends?
>
> A. Um I must admit actually it's not a subject that I often talk about with my friends. It doesn't really concern them. Or it does. I mean they're all sort of – you know, you know debate. You know they'll be sort of all for you know – racism is the most disgusting thing in their eyes, but – I remember arguing about um I was absolutely furious with my best friend who isn't any more really my best friend. But she said um, I said 'Who in school do you think I most look like? Which teacher would you say'? And she said um 'Mr –'. He's the only black teacher in the school. And I said 'Mr –?' And she said 'Well, yeah because you're black'. And . . . I said, 'I know, but I – that doesn't necessarily mean I look like him. And we had this really quite nasty argument about it. Well not really actually. It wasn't very long. It lasted about twenty or thirty seconds. She obviously thought I was grossly over-reacting, but I was extremely hurt because it just shows, it just shows underlying values that people have really about that and I . . . thought about it. It really hurt me, and I thought about it for a long time and I thought – well I mean I'm half white you know so it means that I should look just as much like someone white in the school than black, but no one else would see that. And maybe that's what people do think you know.

This example illustrates the intersection of 'race' with social class and school. The young woman's attendance at an expensive public school meant that she hardly saw anybody not from the white majority. Hence, her friend rarely had to think about issues of 'race' and ethnicity. At the same time, the respondent had nobody with whom she could feel that such issues could be discussed from an 'insider' perspective.

It is important to recognise that there are different reasons for the persistence of the 'one drop' notion. Those black people and social workers who produce arguments such as that described above are unlikely to consider that recognition of mixed parentage will dilute the purity of whiteness. Instead they are likely to be taking a pragmatic view based on recognition that people of mixed parentage are highly likely to be on the receiving end of racialised discrimination. Most of the young people of mixed parentage in the Social Identities study reported that they had experienced racialised discrimination. However, the argument that mixed-parentage people have to accept themselves as black and will, necessarily, be treated as black, ignores the fact that many children and young people of mixed parentage experience discrimination specific to their mixed parentage. Thus, many of the mixed-parentage young people in the Social Identities study were called names like 'peanut', 'yellow-belly', 'half-breed' and 'redskin' that were not used for black children (as well as racialised names to which black children reported that they were subjected). In addition, 20 per cent of them said that they were called racist names by black as well as by white people. This made a tiny minority of the mixed-parentage young people conscious of themselves whether they were with white or black people.

Both/and or either/or? Plural identities in practice

It is increasingly common for literature on mixed parentage to argue that people of mixed parentage must be allowed to assert their racialised identities in whichever ways they feel are most appropriate. In the USA, there is increasingly an assertion of mixed-parentage identities in the academic work of those who are themselves of mixed parentage (see, for example, the collection edited by Root, 1996). Root (1996) describes four of the ways in which it is possible to experience, negotiate and reconstruct the 'borders' between 'races': having *both* feet in *both* camps (as opposed to being 'between cultures'); practising 'situational ethnicity and situational race', i.e. changing identifications as the context shifts; 'border identity'; and locating in one 'camp' for an extended period of time. Collins (1990) argues for conceptualising identities as 'both/and'. Similarly, Parker (1995) styles this 'partial identification' and 'subjectivity of conditional belonging'. The emphasis in postmodern approaches on fluid, shifting and multiple identities is also potentially helpful in the conceptualisation of mixed-parentage identities.

How, then, did the young people interviewed in the Social Identities study think of their identities as young people of mixed parentage? Three related points are worth noting in relation to answering the question of whether or not they engaged in notions of 'one drop' thinking or thought of their racialised identities in more flexible, postmodern ways in which they were able to draw on a variety of constructions of identities.

1. '*If you've got one black parent, you must be black.*' Many of the young people recognised that they were expected by many to think of themselves as black. For a variety of specific reasons, some responded to this by identifying themselves as black while others rejected it.

2. *(Non-)dualist pluralism.* It was not uncommon for the young people to explain how they described themselves in different ways at different times and in different contexts. In this they appeared to have a range of ways in which they could individually express their racialised identities that could be said to be congruent with notions of postmodern plurality and flexibility. In expressing these identities, some seemed to accept, and others to reject, the dualism inherent in the treatment of 'black' and 'white' as oppositional categories. Gender and social class both differentiated the discourses of racialised identities used by the young people and the strategies available to them for dealing with 'race' and racism in different contexts (see Tizard and Phoenix 1993; Phoenix and Tizard 1996).

Those young people who rejected black–white dualism tended to do so by asserting that they were of mixed parentage and did not think of themselves in any other way. However, the experience of being 'different' whether with white or black people made some of the young people feel that they would like to be visibly either black or white. Since much literature on racial identity suggests that some young black children wish to be white, we asked the young people if they had ever wished to be another colour. Twenty-eight per cent of black young people, 14 per cent of white young people and 51 per cent of mixed-parentage young people said that they had, at some time, wished to be a different colour. The high percentage of young people of mixed parentage saying this generally said that they would have preferred to be either 'black' or 'white' rather than 'mixed' or 'half and half'. Mixed-parentage and black young people who had wanted to change their colour had generally wanted to do so earlier in life in order to avoid racial discrimination or name calling; in order not to 'be different' or to have the same hair as their white peers. Those young white people who wanted to do so tended to want to change colour later in life for reasons of style, youth culture or to look as if they were of mixed parentage (a look many found particularly attractive).

3. *Resisting outsider definitions and advice.* The young people found numerous ways in which to resist naming or identifying themselves in the ways suggested to them by parents or other people.

The issue of whether black parents make their children (black or mixed-parentage) proud to be black is one that is often assumed in debates on transracial adoption. In this study, black young people were much more likely than the other groups to report that they had been told by their parents to be proud to be black (66 per cent black; 40 per cent mixed parentage and 6 per cent white young people). In interpreting this, however, it is important to recognise that the young people's identities and ways of describing themselves were not simply the result of being told how to define themselves by their parents and others. It was quite clear that young people resisted advice that they did not want, either by simply not listening or by continuing to use the terms they chose. Such resistances indicated that 'professional', liberal discourses (from social workers, teachers, etc.) were part of the context in which young people asserted their own racialised discourses, sometimes in opposition.

Conclusions

Black–white unions and mixed parentage have both been socially constructed as problematic. The historical shift from concern with 'miscegenation' to concern about children of mixed parentage has not been unambiguously progressive. However, contestation about the terms in which to describe mixed relationships and mixed parentage helps to illuminate the different ways in which these categories have been constructed and resistance to dominant constructions from 'insiders'. The area of mixed relationships and mixed parentage is one where demography and social definitions can clearly be seen to intersect. The increasing number of mixed, black–white unions and people of mixed parentage, particularly young people, has been partly responsible for the emergence of insider-defined 'mixed' categories. These challenge the treatment of black and white racialised categories as binary opposites and the 'one drop' thesis that anybody with black ancestry is necessarily black.

Most of the young people interviewed in the Social Identities in Adolescence study identified as 'mixed' rather than 'black' or 'white'. Their accounts indicated that they had a range of ways in which they negotiated their racialised identities in different contexts and at different times. They indicated that the ways in which they constructed their identities had changed over time. It is likely, therefore, that the accounts they negotiated in their interviews will change over time. However, most of the young people were clear that they made their own decisions about whether to accept or reject the constructions their parents, teachers and friends attempted to persuade them to use.

Postscript 2000

This chapter is reprinted from *Children, Research and Policy* (Phoenix and Owen 1996), a selection of essays in honour of Barbara Tizard. The chapter was published in 1996, and much has changed since then, although much has stayed the same. The demographic increase in the number of people of mixed parentage has continued, and social recognition is reflected by the inclusion of a 'mixed' category in the 2001 Census, although hostility to mixed couples has continued to be expressed, sometimes violently.

The Office for National Statistics uses the Labour Force Survey to estimate the size of Britain's minority ethnic populations Schuman (1999), using data from the years 1995 to 1997, found that the population classified as 'mixed' had risen to 374,000, or 0.7 per cent of the population. This is still a small figure, but it represents 11 per cent of the minority ethnic population. Furthermore, the very young age profile, identified in the chapter, continues to be a feature of the mixed parentage population: more than half are children aged under fifteen, compared to 20 per cent in the total population. For this age group, children of mixed parentage represent 1.7 per cent of the total population and 19 per cent of the minority ethnic population. For the youngest group reported, children aged under five, children of mixed parentage make up 2.1 per cent of the total population and 21 per cent of the minority ethnic population. Whilst, of course, people of mixed parentage do not form a homogeneous group, mixed parentage itself has become a significant part of British demography.

This has been recognised in changes in the ethnic question for the 2001 Census. Unlike the 1991 Census, the 2001 Census includes a specific heading of 'Mixed', with four sub-headings: 'White and Black Caribbean', 'White and Black African', 'White and Asian' and 'Any other mixed background'. This change was, at least in part, in response to demand from within the group (Owen 2000).

In the years since the chapter was published many other pieces of work on mixed parentage have been published, including by people who are themselves of mixed parentage (e.g. McBride 1998; Ifekwunigwe 1999; Khan in preparation). There has also been a great deal of debate about how to refer to those of mixed parentage (see e.g. Goldstein 1999 and Phoenix 1999). This context, together with the demographic trends, has undoubtedly led to more acceptance that mixed parentage (however named) is an established and important social category. At the same time, there have continued to be racist attacks on mixed couples.

Acknowledgements

We should like to acknowledge the support of the Department of Health, who funded the *Social Identities in Adolescence* project described in this chapter, and of the ESRC, who funded the project *The Changing Social and Economic Circumstances of Families With Children* under their 'Understanding Social and Political Change' Initiative (Award L-303-35-3003), which included the demographic analyses in this chapter. We should also like to thank the schools and the young people themselves who took part in the research. Most of all, we should like to thank Barbara Tizard, who not only inspired the work reported in this chapter but has provided intellectual leadership and support to both of us over many years.

Notes

1 Data kindly made available by National Opinion Polls.
2 The question was not included in the Census form for Northern Ireland, so all figures in this section refer to Great Britain.
3 There are two Census SARs: a 2 per cent household sample and a 1 per cent individual sample, each chosen at random from the total population. The samples contain data on individuals in the population, but without identifying those individuals. They were introduced in the UK for the first time in 1991. The SARs make it possible to relate data on different people in the same household, such as couples or parents and children. In this chapter the 2 per cent household SAR has been used. For more detail see Marsh (1993). The data are Crown Copyright and have been made available through the Census Microdata Unit of the University of Manchester with the support of the ESRC/JISC/DENI.
4 This category includes all those who could not be assigned to one of the other nine Census ethnic group categories, including people who described themselves as North African or Arab. Most people of mixed parentage are included in this group. See OPCS/GRO(S) (1993).
5 Data for the LFS have been deposited at the ESRC Data Archive of the University of Essex by the Department of Employment, and are used here with permission. The data are Crown Copyright.
6 It might be that children are more likely to be described as of mixed ethnic origin by their parents than they are to so describe themselves when they are adult. This would account for the higher percentages for children. However this possibility is contradicted by the steady decline in the percentage with age, suggesting a real change rather than a change in reporting. It is possible that people become increasingly less likely to describe themselves as of mixed ethnic origin as they get older, but this seems less likely.

Bibliography

Alibhai-Brown, Y. and A. Montague (1992), *The Colour of Love: Mixed Race Relationships*. London, Virago.

Bagley, C., L. Young *et al.* (1993). *International and Transracial Adoptions*. Aldershot, Avebury.

Bebbington, A. and J. Miles (1989). 'The background of children who enter local authority care', *British Journal of Social Work*, 19, pp. 349–68.

Bernstein, B. and J. Brannen (eds) (1996). *Children, Research and Policy*. London: Taylor & Francis.

Brah, A. (1992). 'Difference, diversity and differentiation', in J. Donald and A. Rattansi (eds), *'Race', Culture and Difference*. London, Sage, pp. 126–45.

Brah, A. (1996). *Cartographies of Diaspora*. London, Routledge.

Collins, P. H. (1990). *Black Feminist Thought*. Cambridge, MA, Unwin Hyman.

Early Years Trainers Anti-Racist Network (1995). *The Best of Both Worlds . . . Celebrating Mixed Parentage*. London, EYTARN.

Foucault, M. (1980). *Power/Knowledge*. Brighton, Harvester.

Fryer, P. (1984). *Staying Power: The History of Black People in Britain*. London, Pluto Press.

Goldstein, B. P. (1999). 'Black, with a white parent, a positive and achievable identity', *British Journal of Social Work*, 29:2, pp. 285–301.

Hall, S. (1989). 'New ethnicities', in D. Morley and K.-H. Chen (eds), *Stuart Hall: Critical Dialogues in Cultural Studies*. London, Routledge, pp. 441–9.

Haskey, J. (1990). 'The ethnic minority populations of Great Britain: estimates by ethnic group and country of birth', *Population Trends*, 60, pp. 35–8.

Henriques, F. (1974). *Children of Caliban: Miscegenation*. London, Secker & Warburg.

Holmes, R. (1995). *How Young Children Perceive Race*. London, Sage.

Ifekwunigwe, J. (1999). *Scattered Belongings: Cultural Paradoxes of 'Race', Nation and Culture*. London, Routledge.

Kahn, Y. (in preparation). *Beyond Black or White: Mixed Race Britons*. London, Routledge.

Kirton, D. (1995). *'Race', Identity and the Politics of Adoption*. London, University of East London.

McBride, J. (1998). *The Color of Water: A Black Man's Tribute to His White Mother*. London, Bloomsbury.

McRoy, R. and C. I. Hall (1996). 'Transracial adoptions: in whose best interest?', in M. P. P. Root (ed.), *The Multiracial Experience: Racial Borders as the New Frontier*. Thousand Oaks, CA, Sage, pp. 63–78.

Marsh, C. (1993). 'The sample of anonymised records', in A. Dale and C. Marsh (eds), *The 1991 Census User's Guide*. London, HMSO, pp. 295–311.

Norment, L. (1995). 'Am I black, white or in between? Is there a plot to create a "colored" buffer race in America?', *Ebony* (August), pp. 108–12.

OPCS/GRO(S) (1993). *1991 Census: Ethnic Group and Country of Birth, Great Britain*. London, HMSO.

Opitz, M., K. Oguntoye *et al.* (eds), (1992). *Showing Our Colours: Afro-German Women Speak Out*. London, Open Letters.

Owen, C. (1993). 'Using the Labour Force Survey to estimate Britain's ethnic minority populations', *Population Trends*, 72, pp. 18–23.

Owen, C. (2000). 'Mixed race in official statistics', in M. Song and D. Parker (eds), *Rethinking Mixed Race*. London, Pluto.

Owen, C. (in preparation). 'British attitudes to mixed marriages'.

Park, R. E. (1931). 'Mentality of racial hybrids'. *American Journal of Sociology*, 36, pp. 534–51.

Parker, D. (1995). *Through Different Eyes*. Aldershot, Avebury.

Phinney, J. and D. Rosenthal (1992). 'Ethnic identity in adolescence: process, context and outcome', in G. Adams, T. Gullotta and R. Montemayor (eds), *Adolescent Identity Formation*. London, Sage, pp. 145–72.

Phoenix, A. (1999) '"Sensitive" to "race" and ethnicity? The intersection of social work, psychology and politics in transracial adoption practice', in D. Messer and F. Jones (eds), *Psychology and Social Care*. London, Jessica Kingsley.

Phoenix, A. and C. Owen (1996). 'From miscegenation to hybridity: mixed relationships and mixed parentage in profile', in B. Bernstein and J. Brannen (eds), *Children, Research and Policy*. London, Taylor & Francis, pp. 111–35.

Phoenix, A. and B. Tizard (1996). 'Thinking through class: the place of social class in the lives of young Londoners', *Feminism and Psychology*, 6.

Reuter, E. B. (1931). *Race Mixture: Studies in Intermarriage and Miscegenation*. New York, Whittlesey House.

Richmond, A. H. (1961). *The Colour Problem*. Harmondsworth, Penguin.

Root, M. P. P. (1996). 'A Bill of Rights for racially mixed people', in M. P. P. Root (ed.), *The Multiracial Experience: Racial Borders as the New Frontier*. Thousand Oaks, CA, Sage, pp. 3–14.

Schuman, J. (1999). 'The ethnic minority populations of Great Britain – latest estimates', *Population Trends*, 96, pp. 33–43.

Sillitoe, K. and P. H. White (1992). 'Ethnic Group and the British Census', *Journal of the Royal Statistical Society A*, 155, 1, pp. 141–63.

Small, J. (1986). 'Transracial placements: conflicts and contradictions', in S. Ahmed, J. Cheetham and J. Small (eds), *Social Work With Black Children and Their Families*. London, Batsford, pp. 81–99.

Spickard, P. R. (1989). *Mixed Blood: Intermarriage and Ethnic Identity in Twentieth-century America*. Madison, University of Wisconsin Press.

Spickard, P. R. (1992). 'The illogic of American racial categories', in M. P. P. Root (ed.), *Racially Mixed People in America*. Newbury Park, CA, Sage, pp. 12–23.

Stonequist, E. V. (1937). *The Marginal Man: A Study in Personality and Culture Conflict*. New York, Russell & Russell.

Tizard, B. and A. Phoenix (1993). *Black, White or Mixed Race?* London, Routledge.

Tizard, B. and A. Phoenix (1994). 'Black identity and transracial adoption', in I. Gaber and J. Aldridge (eds), *In the Best Interests of the Child*. London, Free Association Books, pp. 89–102.

Troyna, B. and R. Hatcher (1992). *Racism in Children's Lives: A Study of Mainly-white Primary Schools*. London, Routledge.

Visram, R. (1986). *Ayahs, Lascars and Princes: Indians in Britain 1700–1947*. London, Pluto Press.

Wilson, A. (1987). *Mixed Race Children: A Study of Identity*. London, Allen & Unwin.

Young, R. J. C. (1995). *Colonial Desire: Hybridity in Theory, Culture and Race*. London, Routledge.

Zack, N. (1993). *Race and Mixed Race*. Philadelphia, Temple University Press.

4 Welcome home: between two cultures and two colours

Amal Treacher

Eva Hoffman in *Lost in Translation* (1991) gives voice to her journey from Cracow to Vancouver, aged thirteen. For Hoffman's Polish Jewish family, the scars and fractures precipitated by this move caused profound dislocation. Hoffman speaks of Poland with full tones; the first section entitled 'Paradise', portrays a satisfying life before the unwelcome exile to the 'New World'. She muses thoughtfully on the 'nature' of language, emotional complexity, identity, feelings of belonging and marginalisation. The narrative moves back and forwards through a maze of emotional material in order to reach a more 'settled', 'satisfying' place and way of being. Hoffman confronts the difficulties of exile and the emotional consequences of having to leave that which is known and those who are loved. The book ends, however, with a new life in place. When I first read *Lost in Translation* I devoured it, grateful to discover that I was not alone; my explicit and implicit reliance on Hoffman's analysis will be apparent here.

I grew up in Cairo until the age of eleven. On my last visit there, in April 1998, my father and I were in the kitchen, familiar to me from childhood, and he turned towards me and said, with much affection, 'Welcome home'. Overwhelmed by the thickness of his emotion, feeling lost in an atmosphere resonating with the past, I withdrew and did not respond.

My parents met in London in the late 1940s. My father comes from an upper-middle-class, Muslim family and was in London studying for a doctorate. My mother comes from an English working-class family who were caretaking at the Egyptian Embassy at the time. She has a Jewish father but was brought up in a white Christian household. My mother went to Cairo, in the face of her family's ambivalent feelings, made a new life for herself, learnt Arabic and became a loved member of my father's family. They married in Cairo in 1952. My sister and I were born five years apart in the 1950s. I grew up surrounded by my extended family, playing with male cousins and gardening with my grandfather. I spoke Arabic and very little English, learnt the Qur'an and inhabited the noises, smells and life of an established district – Heliopolis.

This life was disrupted by my parents' acrimonious divorce. My mother, sister and myself moved into an apartment in the same district. When I was seven my father married a European, Coptic woman. Four years later my mother decided she needed to return home and the three of us came to London and endeavoured to build a new life. The only way my mother could create something anew was to forbid any contact with my father, refuse to allow us to speak Arabic or even to mention Egypt and our lives there. I later learnt that this was a repetition of my mother's early childhood experiences which were full of loss, absence and noisy silences which attempted to conceal a cupboard full of active skeletons. My mother married my step father, who has two sons, when I was nearly fifteen. During this time my sister and I were not allowed any contact with our father. He tried to find us but his attempts were blocked by my maternal family. In my mid-twenties I went to Cairo to find my father, my 'other' family, and, equally important, my 'lost' country.

This narrative of a life is about a web of people coming together, or not, across cultures, class, religion, colour, language and ethnicity. Interwoven through this narrative of cultural complexity, mixed-heritage identity is a more personal story of betrayal: a daughter who betrays her mother by going to find her father; a mother who betrays her daughter by refusing her access and knowledge; and a daughter who betrays her father by not loving or wanting him enough when she discovers he is not the father of her dreams.

I used my story, almost like a passport, to gain entry into a particular London middle-class sphere of people who, in my fantasy, were fascinated by it. Steedman (1986) has commented that the same narrative can be told in different tones and ways using humour, irony, courage, tragedy and struggle. I have used the full range. Until recently I told this narrative with confidence, ease and a sureness of touch which came from a knowledge that my audience was captive and caught up in the romance and adventure. My response, however, was divided. I was delighted to have a story that marked me out as special and through which I could declare I am not like you, while simultaneously I felt an unease and that something was wanting. This unease has become stronger. I now have a growing sense of alienation, of wanting to inhabit a more ordinary place. I want an identity which is not based on a family romance, feelings of loss, being at a loss, and one that, rather aggressively, asserts my difference from others.

I am attempting to explore issues of sameness/otherness, identification/distance, strangeness/recognition through this chapter while trying to bear in mind Kristeva's committed pleas in *Strangers to Ourselves* (1991). For Kristeva, a fuller humanity would be based on the recognition that we are all strangers and from that insight we can move towards treating strangers with more compassion and ease. Kristeva's arguments centre on the intractability of the unconscious, and due to the unknowability of the unconscious itself we are all 'strangers to ourselves'. We are all confronted continually and inevitability with the strangeness of the Other. This is part of the human condition, but for some of us the strangeness remains, and this is not just the strangeness of discovering another person's 'ineradicable strangeness' (Hoffman 1991: 189).

I have used my autobiography in this chapter, to explore aspects of a life which has been forged from a particular emotional complexity; and to edge towards speaking of an identity which has been built, in part, on dislocation and marginality so that I am often left feeling 'out of my skin'. These feelings and fantasies of dislocation arise from a move which resulted from my country of origin, and I am concerned with attempting to interweave the effects of that rupture through my experiences of being a mixed-heritage child. I want to move towards exploring the dynamics of skin colour on the formation of identity for the child whose parents are a different colour from one another and s/he in turn may be of a different colour to either of them; and how fantasies of skin colour and mixed-heritage relationships impact on and continue to form my identity as a woman and a human being. Above all, this chapter is an exploration of the way, to use an evocative phrase, that 'lived experience is shredded' (Bollas 1995: 142).

Lexicons of being

I am writing in the tongue of my mother, which is not my mother tongue. My unease that this voice cannot be theoretical enough lies alongside the feeling that this English cannot describe what I feel. It is not that I think it would be better expressed in Arabic (long forgotten in any case), it is a feeling that this language does not belong to me – it is the language I use, feel, think and dream in but it is not mine. My very utterances feel strange and stumbling. It is a resolute fantasy of mine that others use language more easily, that it trips off their tongue and they can canter with it; this capacity is not mine. I will always speak with a foreign tongue, with too careful an ear, in speech which is somehow constrained, and this produces an uneasy articulateness. To draw too quickly on the theoretical position that language is always alienating is to gloss over real differences in the relationship between and to language, words and feelings. For language also evokes and produces membranes of connections and associations which bind one person to another and to the community. As Hoffman argues, to lose a language which evokes attachments is also a loss of a living connection; it is not that the new language is empty but it does not have the same resonances and it requires effort to connect the sounds to interiority and to relationships with others (Hoffman 1991: 106–8).

The loss of a language is about the loss of much more than the spoken word and the knowledge of grammar and literature. It is also the loss of a language of childhood security in which tenderness, love, care and affection are expressed and relayed. For me the words of love and affection do not have the same resonances in English, they do not pull me into a tapestry of safety. The resonances of parental, more specifically fatherly, love are absent. This loss of a language, and the learning of another, was a process my mother undertook in moving to Cairo. She spoke to her daughters in the tongue of my father, which was not her mother tongue. She could not inhabit her new language with security. This lexicon of safety is also about placing oneself in a map of being and understanding the beings of others which is always by necessity in process. I learnt early of the losses that occur when memories are not kept alive, when they are not spoken of. It is the stuff of words which keep memories, feelings and atmospheres buoyant. This is not just a private affair, for we need the memories and speech of others to sustain our internal lives.

Fantasy is pervasive. The Kleinian view is that it accompanies all thought, emotion and perception. It gets in everywhere.[1] In mixed-heritage relationships and identity, fantasy is multilayered, it is a subtle web of social, cultural and personal responses. Part of the complexity stems from the child's need to develop a sense of him/herself as both the same and different from his/her parents in the first instance, and then within the wider family and peer group. The child cannot manage this emotional placing by him/herself and needs the security and help of his/her parents to be able to locate him/herself in this spectrum of identifications and differences. This of course is the challenge for us all.

There is, however, a specificity for the mixed-heritage child in terms of gaining an identity and being able to place him/herself within and separate from the parental dyad. On the whole, the child is a different colour from both of its parents, who in turn are a different colour from one another. As babies we gain our identity through touch, smell, looking and being looked at. We make sense of our world through our senses and gain our identity – slowly and messily – through what we perceive and how we are perceived. So how as inchoate babies do we make sense of skin colour and, more critically, the differences in colour? It is unclear whether babies recognise colour, and indeed I am sure they make sense of it only retrospectively. It gains meaning as signifying something alien and Other only through social and cultural meanings. I am not arguing that a baby seeing blackness or whiteness feels fear or alienation but, rather, I am asking what does it mean to a baby who is struggling to make sense of its world? It may mean something, nothing or a lot. Ken Wright argues pertinently, 'we are, [I] suppose, on dangerous ground when we start to speculate about an infant's experience; but if we do not allow ourselves to imagine and wonder about such things, we may well be closing the door to understanding elements of adult experience that are preverbal yet deeply important' (Wright 1991: 12). If smell, touch, sounds are the ways we internalise and become someone, it seems to me that there is no real reason why colour should not enter the picture.

I am here trying to explore issues and psychic processes which impact not only on self-esteem but also on our identities and our relationships with others. I am positing the view that we gain our identity, in part, through skin colour and make sense of the world through our skins, and this impacts on both a conscious and unconscious level.[2] I am in analysis with a white woman (her heritage is unclear and unknown). Some time ago I entered a session and saw we were both wearing black and grey. Unusually for me I spoke immediately and said, 'We are the same colour'. I then proceeded to tell a significant dream (relayed below) in detail and associated to it – freely. She linked my talking freely with my initial comment and offered the view that perhaps the only way I could tell her this dream was to make us the same colour. I then realised that in my visual imagination I had been changing both of us – making myself paler and her darker in order to find a subjective voice to express my fears and longings.

Fantasy enters language, visual identifications and our sense of self. We take in, moreover, not just parental fantasies but also social and cultural ones. Social myths operate powerfully against mixed-race relationships and these tend to centre on the mixing of blood. What we all know is that for a mix of blood to occur there has to be a mix of other fluids as well. The socially grounded myths are pervasive, they may be false but they operate in such a way that these myths structure our relationships with one another, and our relationships to ourselves. These myths have a social message and the strong injunction here is not to mix up categories, that 'pure' blood should not be mixed with the 'tainted' blood of the Other. It would be easy to dismiss these myths, toss them aside, if we did not, unfortunately, internalise them. In our family there were constant references to my sister and myself as having 'bad' blood – the blood of my father. When I was an adolescent with spots – in my vain memory no worse than any other adolescent's – my mother's response was to rush around the shops energetically buying 'blood-cleansing medicine'. I dutifully swallowed the stuff – anything to get rid of the spots – and swallowed the belief that I had bad blood. In contradiction to this I was bewildered and angry at these continual references to my blood, a view which, whether I like it or not, has been staggeringly difficult to shift. These myths have become part of my self-image and, while patently untrue as fact, they remain painfully operative at the level of psychic life.

These fantasies and feelings forge relationships with self and other. They are not free-floating or abstract. Indeed, they are both stubborn and subtle in that they are interwoven through my lack of, and persistent, desires. I will now relay the dream mentioned above. I dreamt I was in love and passionately desired a black man. We met my mother and stepfather who were outraged. We left them and went to enter a park but were prevented from doing so by a group of white, bulky, middle-aged men. In the rest of the dream I wandered about the park on my own, despairing, watching couples who were all white and young getting it together. This dream is about many things but it expresses clearly the cultural and internalised taboos. Further, it raises unconscious issues of desire and fantasy. I can only speculate here, but I wish to raise some issues for the mother/father/daughter triad in terms of sexuality and the oedipus complex. In my case, my Arab and dark-skinned father desired a white woman. My father speaks openly of the fact that part of my mother's and my stepmother's appeal is their Europeanness and the whiteness of their skin. He talks proudly of how when he lived in London he was teased for being more English than the English. The issue is further complicated by class, for my father married both women for their status as desirable European women and to prove his status within the upper/middle-class strata of Egyptian society. My mother married my father, in part, for his upper-classness. In my family history, my mother had an absent Jewish father and married a man from the Middle East. For both of them, the other was a route into status, desirability, social and emotional security.

It is into this complex that my sister and I forged our femininity. We have taken different paths: my sister into motherhood and a traditional femininity. Mine has been more ambiguous and fraught. It has involved a rejection of motherhood and rather ambivalent fantasies towards my body and feelings of desire. There are many layers that have to be unpicked to move towards an understanding of the emotional processes: mother/daughter, father/daughter, mother/father, mother/daughter/father. I can only attempt a speculative discussion of the possible dynamics.

The issue of skin colour, and the appreciation of difference of colour, is a crucial factor. It is from this base that other feelings and fantasies can flow. It is common-place within psychoanalytic theory to argue that the infant forms its relationship to the Other (mother) through the touch of the mother and through the mother's relationship to the skin of the infant. On this account, identity is formed, partly, through the relationship to skin, and provides the boundary between self and other. I am speculating that in some mother/daughter relation-ships if the mother cannot enjoy or desire, within the boundary of parental care, her daughter's body, it will be difficult for the daughter to relish her own desire and from that vantage point to view herself as desirable and desiring. In my mother's case this is complicated by her desire initially for a man darker than herself. My mother had contradictory desires for someone dark and for her daughters to be light. Similarly, my father desires women who are pale and has daughters who are not dark but not light either. I am raising here a point of discussion which centres on how my parents' desires for someone of a different colour from them impacts upon my femininity. Both my parents desired a colour which was different from their own colour, and was different from mine. My parents' fantasies and projections of the beautiful image was not fulfilled by myself, for both placed value and desirability on whiteness. My parents and myself are all embroiled in fantasies of the desired image and this is unfulfilled. These fantasies of desirability highlight a hidden racism, for they point to fantasies of hair, body shape, features. Time and time again, I find myself wishing I was paler, blonde and with 'finer' features. In contradiction, I envy women who are darker and invest them with fantasies. My feelings of envy and who I wish to be like change. It is out of this complex that I struggle to place myself and understand my parents and my own desires and passions.

Mixed feelings

In part, I can be impossible. People do not share my history and in the telling of it I long for them to have done so: Have you felt, experienced, thought, fantasised this? are the questions underpinning my narrative. I want other people to have been there, and to understand, and yet I have an equally compelling wish for people to realise that my story is unique. I wish for both, and it is in this contradic-tion that being difficult lies. If someone says, 'No, it is different', I grow angry. If someone says, 'Yes – I know what you mean', I wish to cling to my alienation as mine and mine alone. Between these paradoxical demands, I remain disap-pointed. This impossibility of satisfaction points to a dilemma which rests on how we understand and place ourselves and others as different and as similar.

Alongside, or interlinked with, these conflicting demands for absolute merger and/or complete aloneness lies the issue of my active and pervasive fantasy life. I have spent hours, nay years, of my life drifting through daydreams and fantasies, imagining what might have been. I have been lost and at a loss in a world which consists of what has been and an emotional retreat of 'if onlys'. At times, my past life, members of my Egyptian family – anything other than what was going on around me or had actuality – was all that existed. I was frozen, not just in the past but in a fantasy world which had very little life. I know full well the sapping activity of fantasy and that it takes away from a more fulfilling present. Paul Hoggett, following Winnicott (it is important to trace the lineage), explores how fantasy does not just fill up or enrich lives but actually destroys life (Hoggett 1992). He distinguishes between fantasy and imaginative activity to argue that fantasy erodes possibilities while imagination builds on what exists to produce a more creative life.

Christopher Bollas explores stringently that health is based on two major capacities: being able to move across temporal zones and being able to disseminate experience (Bollas 1995). These two interlinked capacities were for much of the time not available to me. I lived with the sheer constant effort of trying to understand, and gain knowledge of, how to behave and, perhaps most difficult of all, what and how much to feel. I often get this wrong – I feel shame when others are talking of 'guilt', believe that honour and family obligations are important at a time when others have different moral concerns. My tensions of being are awry – I am often over- or under-emotional. It is a relief when I am with someone who is not English, when I do not have to struggle with constraints imagined or not. Until recently, this effort has not been one of enrichment but rather one of survival. I am a keen observer. This has stood me in good stead, but often it has been a means of managing and of getting by. Similarly, I have often been in a space where the 'past is frozen in amber' (Hoffman 1991: 115) and this has not allowed me to flourish. I suspect that what is held in common among people who have had to move country, and from that rupture to build a new life, is a complex relationship to past and present. For, in contradiction to a frozenness in the past, I was also preoccupied with the strain of getting through the present. The past has not been a place from which I could rework memories, fantasies and feelings and thereby forge a present and a future.

Moreover, experiences cannot be disseminated. By this, following Bollas, I am pointing to the capacity to enable a movement from one thought to another, from one fantasy to a memory, from a feeling back to a thought. The psyche can exist, rather like time, frozen in a sterile paralysis. I am not here making a special claim for extraordinary emotional difficulties, for I am well aware that they exist for many. I am, however, trying to explore some of the experiences (or, ironically, lack of them) that can occur in the face of the trauma of moving across cultures, of losing languages, and all that has been known and inhabited. As Hoffman points out, 'underneath the detachment, aloofness, arrogance, [is] a cauldron of seething lost loves and places and a rage at the loss' (Hoffman 1991: 139). To this I would add my anger at the strain of having to fit in and my continual and pervasive feeling that I am not the right thing. I used to long for a less strenuous way of maintaining my identity, pride and place. This has become easier. The dilemma, which is perhaps more universal than I imagine, remains and this centres on 'how to bend without falling over' and how to reach 'an elastic balance' of being with others. My elastic identity could become easier still if people allowed me and others like me our specific difficulties and did not continually colonise the emotional terrain of marginality. These are tensions, however, for it involves the effort of identifying how one is the same and different to others in a struggle of finding a home and a secure place. It is a complex and fluid tapestry which should not be frozen in a theoretical framework or an emotional pinning down.

I find myself jealous of those who have not had to move country and home, and also at odds with others in terms of my thoughts and feelings about home and place. I know the problems of nationalism and agree that it is a dangerous senti- ment, for it destroys families, love, lives. It is an over-attachment to an idea and/ or a place which is romanticised. Above all, it destroys a knowledge of the truth that none of us belongs and that we all, with varying degrees of difficulty and pain, live on the margins. It destroys an identification that all of us have difficulty with, and feelings of despair, in relation to processes of belonging. But anti- nationalistic ideas deny this too, allowing one to retreat from the conflicts and dilemmas that exist in wishing to belong to a community or a nation.

As is well known, understandings of subjectivity in psychoanalytic object rela- tions focus attention on the gaining of identity through taking in, and relating to, another human being – in the first instance the primary caregiver.[3] On this preva- lent view people are objects that are internalised and constitute a person's inner world and their relationship to others. I would like to edge towards adding to this framework a view that we also internalise places, sounds, smells, external land- scapes – tangible objects and sensations – and these are internalised. Thus, tan- gible and intangible objects and sensations also constitute a person's identity for they get internalised and form a person's sense of self and relationship to the external world. We become, not just through relating to other people but also through relating to actual objects. I have internalised sounds, smells, sights which I turn to at various moments and at other moments they arise unbidden in my experiences of daily life. I cannot for example hear the sounds of the call for prayer, or smell a mango, or remember times on the balcony in Heliopolis with- out a whole welter of feelings, memories and fantasies.

Within some aspects of contemporary cultural theory there is a tendency to theorise these feelings and fantasies as the wish to return to a place which has never existed. Further, drawing on psychoanalytic theorisings these yearnings are conceptualised as a wish to return to a fantasised moment of plenitude with the mother (Hall 1992). While not disputing the central insights of these arguments, I wish to question two issues here. First, the different relationship to a place if one has lived there, and second, as adults we wish to return or stay from both sides of the oedipal divide. There is a continent of difference between wishing to 'return' to a place one has never lived in or even visited and wishing to return to a known place. The fantasies and emotions embedded in this wish are different to those wishes involving somewhere one has lived before when one has had to forge a home in a new place. They are not the same social or emotional processes and we cannot theoretically, or from our own experience, collapse the two fantasies as if they involve the same dynamics. I am making a plea here for the impact of actual experience on fantasy and desire and the difference this makes to how one makes a home and how one integrates two or more places within the heart and psyche.

There are important theoretical shifts which place the formation of subjectivity earlier and a crucial shift has occurred from an emphasis on oedipal relationships to pre-oedipal ones – from an emphasis on father to a preoccupation with mother.[4] This turn has produced crucial understandings, and here I wish to make a plea that we attempt to hold both the oedipal and pre-oedipal in mind. For we experience living, others, places, ourselves not just pre-oedipally in fantasies of no-difference or a wish to continually return to the mother of plenitude. We do so with a knowledge of difference, with experiences of boundary, limits, and on the whole, even if reluctantly, a knowledge of the reality principle. Bollas in 'Why Oedipus' (1993) argues that through the oedipus complex two crucial processes occur: the child shifts from being in a dilemma (a dyad) to being in a complex (a triad), and interlinked with this the child recognises that life is complex.

This knowledge of the complexity of living, of other and one's own passions and feelings, profoundly influences experiences and fantasies. This knowledge of complexity of oneself and others includes the knowledge of contradictory fantasies and wishes. In a marvellous essay on *The Wizard of Oz* (MGM 1939) Salman Rushdie wishes poignantly for a good pair of ruby slippers which can help one to reach a better place. Rushdie points to the yearning in Judy Garland's voice as she sings 'Over the Rainbow', and comments 'what she expresses here, what she embodies with the purity of an archetype, is the human dream of leaving, a dream at least as powerful as its countervailing dream of roots' (Rushdie 1992: 23). So perhaps whatever our histories of diaspora we all inhabit contradictory wishes and impulses: longings to be elsewhere and yearnings to be home. I have wished to be in Cairo and I have wished never to return there. Similarly, I have wished to have no home other than London and also wished wholeheartedly to live anywhere but here.

Alongside these contradictory yearnings the picture would not be complete if I did not talk about refusal. For it is true that I have at times lived a life full of fantasy and refused the present and simultaneously I have also refused all that is Egyptian, my past life there and any wish to visit. Alongside all this loss and absence is my stubbornness – a stubbornness which has refused to be anywhere at all. It is not that that is a truer state or that longing and yearning are more real emotions. I am edging towards drawing out ambivalences. It has at times been a relief to have left Cairo. To have left behind attachments which can be overbearing and a family life which can be imprisoning in its demands and obligations. To have left a country whose economic structure is devastating in its divide between the rich and poor and where the levels of poverty beggars belief. It is a relief to have a life which can be freer and more mobile and which does not constrain me as a woman. All of this refusal and relief lies alongside the wish to be there, to return and above all that we had never left.

Minding the gulf

I do not wish to apportion blame or responsibility. I do not in that way wish to refuse knowledge of parental pain, difficulties or, in a different register, cultural conflicts which abound for those from a different place. I wish to struggle with the conflicts, meanings and complexities and to appreciate past and present. The emotional task would centre, in part, on the capacity to stand in a place of indifference and to be able to remember and to forget. It is out of our precarious and precious memories that we are partly made, that we can hold on to good things, and that we become good things. These memories cannot be shared for any of us, but there is a difference between shared childhoods within a common culture and those lives that were made in different place. It is all too easy to dismiss these yearnings for a communality of experience as nostalgic or regressive, for nostalgia can also be an expression of and a wish for a good relationship to the past and, as Foucault argues, nostalgia can be a good and necessary feeling as long as it is not based on aggression or contempt for the present (Foucault 1988: 12).

It has become commonplace to argue that the story of exile is the story of the twentieth century and of the postmodern condition; indeed, the byline on Hoffman's book reads, 'this is a story about us all'. It is not. Most people do not have to begin again in the most profound way imaginable – do not have to learn a new language to dream in and to express experiences, thoughts and feelings. This rupture is not shared, for most people have not been 'cast adrift in incomprehensible space' (Hoffman 1991: 104). I am not talking about a loss of a romantic past, of an imagined wholeness, but actual losses of scenes, family, friends, that which makes up and is a life – internal and external landscapes. For, as Rose argues, talk of the 'postmodern predicament – belonging everywhere and nowhere at the same time – has never felt quite right. There is something about this vision of free-wheeling identity which seems bereft of history and of passion' (Rose 1998: 2).

It is tempting, theoretically and emotionally, to dismiss these yearnings as a wish to return to somewhere elsewhere – a regressive space which is located in fantasy. We need to tread carefully, for these yearnings are part of an emotional quagmire which is full of tensions pulling in every direction. This texture of a life, the tugs between past and present, here and elsewhere, must also be directed towards a future. To move towards an analysis of a life is to confront the shredded and multi-layered nature of experience, fantasies and feelings. It is, to state the banal and the obvious, a continual confrontation with conscious and unconscious contradictions. Place and home in this article can be read as important issues in their own right and as standing in for emotional states of belonging, security and movement. Indeed, 'there's no place like home' in that there is no place like it *and* it does not exist. Embedded in a cosy homily are truths about home as a place, a psychic necessity and a metaphor.

John Forrestor argues that a purpose of psychoanalysis is to restore to metaphors their metaphoricity, so that metaphors and words can convey and carry meaning (Forrester 1997: 58). It is in recognising the importance of metaphor as that which can convey psychic actuality, meaning and hope that we can reach a different theoretical and emotional place based on Hoggett's plea for imaginative living and Bollas's understandings of emotional complexity. We all, in different ways and from different positions, struggle to make better homes for ourselves and others. For, as Rushdie argues,

> so Oz finally became home; the imagined world became the actual world, as it does for us all, because the truth is that once we have left our childhood places and started out to make up our lives, armed only with what we have and are, we understand that the real secret of the ruby slippers is not that 'there's no place like home', but rather that there is no longer any such place as home: except, of course, for the home we make, or the homes that are made for us, in Oz: which is anywhere, and everywhere, except the place from which we began.
>
> (Rushdie 1992: 57)

In other words, all of us have to engage in forging a life and a place which can carry and convey the complexity of meanings and lived experience. Perhaps now I can respond to my father's 'welcome home' with more grace and gratitude, based on a knowledge of two places which are not divided, yet are separate and held together.

Acknowledgements

I am grateful to Mrs Sally Weintrobe for her careful and incisive thoughtfulness. I would also like to thank my parents for giving me much more than this article indicates.

Notes

1 Within Kleinian theory phantasy is defined as the mental expression of instincts and is presumed to exist from the beginning of life. It expresses and organises mental life and the primitive relationships to caregivers which at the beginning are perceived as part-objects, and as the infant struggles for maturity these are experienced and felt more as whole objects. See R. Hinshelwood's *A Dictionary of Kleinian Thought*, London: Free Association Books, 1991, for exemplary elucidation of this psycho-analytic framework.

2 Within object relations psychoanalytic theory, skin is theorised as the most prominent element in very early life. The relationship to the skin of self and other forms our first experiences and is embued with fantasy life. See D. Pines, *A Woman's Unconscious Use of Her Body*, London: Virago, and E. Bick, 1993, 'The experience of the skin in the early object-relations', *International Journal of Psychoanalysis*, 49(1968): 484–6.

3 The object relations framework is dominant within the British psychoanalytic schools. It is based on a view that from the beginning of life the infant is orientated to, and formed by, its relationships with others. The wish for relationships with others structures our distinctive pattern of being with self and other, and importantly mental functioning becomes more complex and differentiated through

maturity. See the work of W. Fairbairn, *Psychoanalytic Studies of the Personality*, London: Routledge & Kegan Paul, 1952; M. Klein, *Envy and Gratitude*, London: Hogarth Press, 1975; D. Winnicott, *Playing and Reality*, London: Tavistock/ Routledge 1991.

4 The shift of emphasis to the pre-oedipal relationship between mother and infant is an important aspect of the object relations understandings. It places emphasis as indicated above on early life and its continual presence throughout adult life.

Bibliography

Bollas, C., 1993, 'Why Oedipus', in *Being a Character*, London: Routledge.

—— 1995, 'The Functions of History', in *Cracking Up*, London: Routledge.

Forrester, J., 1997, 'On holding as a metaphor: Winnicott and the figure of St Christopher', in V. Richards with G. Wilce (eds), *Fathers, Families, and the Outside World*, London: Karnac Books.

Foucault, M., 1988, 'Interview with R. Martin: Truth Power, Self', in L. H. Martin *et al.*, (eds), *Technologies of the self*, London: Tavistock Publications.

Hall, S., 1992, 'New Ethnicities', in J. Donald and A. Rattansi (eds), *'Race', Culture and Difference*, London: Sage.

Hoffman, E., 1991, *Lost in Translation*, London: Minerva.

Hoggett, P., 1992, *Partisans in an Uncertain World: The Psychoanalysis of Engagement*, London: Free Association Books.

Kristeva, J., 1991, *Strangers to Ourselves*, New York: Columbia University Press.

Rose, J., 1998, *States of Fantasy*, Oxford: Oxford University Press.

Rushdie, S., 1992, *The Wizard of Oz*, London: British Film Institute.

Steedman, C., 1986, *Landscape for a Good Woman*, London: Virago.

Wright, K., 1991, *Vision and Separation*, London: Free Association Books.

Part II

Engineering the future: genetic cartographies and the discourse of science

5   Deanimations: maps and portraits of life itself[1]

Donna Haraway

Get a Life! SimLife, the genetic playground, allows you to build ecosystems from the ground up and give life to creatures from the depths of your imagination . . . It's up to you to keep your species off the endangered list! Give life to different species in the Biology Lab and customize their look with the icon editor.

(Advertisement in *Science News* 142, 20 (14 November 1992): 322)

Creation science

The user manual for the Maxis computer game *SimLife* opens with the words of Supreme Court Chief Justice Oliver Wendell Holmes, 'All life is an experiment'.[2] That grounding juridical point is equally the foundation of this chapter on the comedic portraiture and cartography of 'life itself'. My focus is on advertising, joking, and gaming dimensions of genetic portraiture and mapping. These contemporary practices have taproots into the geometric matrices of spatialization and individualization constructed in early modern Europe. The matrices emerged from the instrumental, epistemological, and aesthetic innovations of perspectivism, which became prominent in the narrative time called the Renaissance. 'Perspectivism conceives of the world from the standpoint of the "seeing eye" of the individual. It emphasizes the science of optics and the ability of the individual to represent what he or she sees as in some sense "truthful", compared to superimposed truths of mythology or religion'.[3] Perspectivism engages types of troping that their practitioners find hard to acknowledge. I want to *spelunk* through the taproots of spatialization and individualization to see how the carbon-silicon-fused flesh of technoscientific bodies at the end of the second Christian millennium get their semiotic trace nutrients.

In Maxis games, as in life itself, map making is world making. Inside the persistent Cartesian grid conventions of cyber-spatializations, the games encourage their users to see themselves as scientists within narratives of exploration, creation, discovery, imagination, and intervention. Learning data-recording practices, experimental protocols, and world design is seamlessly part of becoming a normal subject in technoscience. Cartographic practice is learning to make projections that shape worlds in particular ways for various purposes.

The Maxis games invite an equation with Christian readings of the creation discourse in Genesis. *The SimEarth Bible* is the title of that game's strategy book. The *Bible*'s introduction tells the reader that SimEarth is 'a laboratory on a disk for curious people to experiment with'.[4] The author is frankly Christian in his theistic beliefs about evolution, but the game and the strategy manual are deeply enmeshed in 'Judeo-Christian' mimesis – i.e., Christian salvation history – even in totally secular interpretations. So too is the perspectivism, which was critical to the history of Western early modern and Renaissance art and map making, enabled by a 'Judeo-Christian' point of view. And what was 'point of view' before the implosion of biologics and informatics has become, since that impaction in narrative and material spacetime, 'pov'. Pov is the cyberspace version of secularized creation science's optical practice.

This respectable creation science is not about opposition to biological evolution or promotion of divine special creation. The creation science of the Maxis games, and of much of contemporary technoscience, including molecular biology, genetic engineering, and biotechnology, is resolutely up to the minute in leading-edge science. The secular creationism is intrinsic to the narratives, technologies, epistemologies, controversies, subject positions, and anxieties. 'Give life to different species in the Biology Lab and customize their look with the icon editor' urges the *SimLife* advertisement. This is a kind of paint-by-bit game that fills portrait galleries in the cyber-genealogies of life itself. Getting into the spirit, I call the narrative software of my essay 'Sim-Renaissance™'. I am interested in the official versions of scientific creationism in life worlds after the implosion of informatics and biologics.

My point of view in this examination of perspective technologies is that of the chief actor and point of origin in the drama of life itself – the gene. This slant gives me a curious vertigo that I blame on the godlike perspective of any autotelic entity. The gene is the subject of the portraits and maps of life itself in the terminal narrative technology proper to the end of the second millennium. Sociobiologist Richard Dawkins, an inspiration for the Maxis game makers, explained that the body is merely the gene's way to make more copies of itself, in a sense, to contemplate its own image. 'Evolution is the external and visible manifestation of the differential survival of alternative *replicators*. Genes are replicators; organisms and groups of organisms . . . are *vehicles* in which replicators travel about'.[5] Mere living flesh is derivative; the gene is the alpha and omega of the secular salvation drama of life itself. Faced with this barely secular Christian Platonism, I am consumed with curiosity about the regions where the lively subject becomes the undead thing.

Life itself

Following the rules of the game, I mutate the term 'life itself' from Sarah Franklin.[6] The instrumentalization of life proceeds by means of cultural practices – sociopolitical, epistemological, and technical. Informed by Foucault on biopower and the history of the concept of life, Franklin analyses how nature

becomes biology becomes genetics, and the whole is instrumentalized in particular forms.[7] 'Life, materialized as information and signified by the gene, displaces
'Nature', pre-eminently embodied in and signified by old-fashioned organisms.
From the point of view of the Gene, a self-replicating auto-generator, 'the whole
is not the sum of its parts, [but] the parts summarize the whole'.[8] Rather, within
the organic and synthetic databases that are the flesh of life itself, genes are not
really *parts* at all. They are another *kind* of thing, a thing-in-itself where no trope
can be admitted. The genome, the totality of genes in an organism, is not a whole
in the traditional, 'natural' sense, but a congeries of entities that are themselves
autotelic and self-referential. In this view, genes are things-in-themselves, outside
the lively economies of troping. To be outside the economy of troping is to be
outside finitude, mortality, and difference, to be in the realm of pure being, to be
One, where the word is itself.

In the game of life itself, '[i]t's up to you to keep your species off the
endangered list!' Fetishism has never been more fun, as undead substitutes and
surrogates proliferate. But fetishism comes in more than one flavour. Nature
known and remade as Life through cultural practice figured as technique within
specific proprietary circulations is critical to Franklin's and my spliced argument. I
hope Marx would recognize his illegitimate daughters, who, in the ongoing comedy of epistemophilia, only mimic their putative father in a pursuit of undead
things into their lively matrices. Marx, of course, taught us about the fetishism of
commodities. Commodity fetishism is a specific kind of reification of historical
human interactions with each other and with an unquiet multitude of non-
humans, which are called nature in Western conventions. In the circulation of
commodities within capitalism, these interactions appear in the form of, and are
mistaken for, things. In proprietary guise, genes displace not only organisms, but
people and non-humans of many kinds, as generators of liveliness. Ask any biodiversity lawyer whether genes are sources of 'value' these days, and the structure
of commodity fetishism will come clear.

Fetishism of the map

However, I am interested in another, obliquely related flavour of reification that
transmutes material, contingent, human, and non-human liveliness into maps of
life itself and then mistakes the map and its reified entities for the bumptious, non-
literal world. I am interested in the kinds of fetishism proper to worlds without
tropes, to literal worlds, to genes as autotelic entities. Geographical maps are
embodiments of multifaceted historical practices among specific humans and
non-humans. Those practices constitute spatiotemporal worlds; that is, maps are
both instruments and signifiers of spatialization. Geographical maps can, but
need not, be fetishes in the sense of appearing to be non-tropic, metaphor-free
representations of previously existing 'real' properties of a world that are waiting
patiently to be plotted. Instead, maps are models of worlds crafted through and
for specific practices of intervening and ways of life.

In Greek, *trópos* is a turn or a swerve; tropes mark the non-literal quality of being and of language. Fetishes – themselves 'substitutes', that is, tropes of a special kind – produce a characteristic 'mistake'; fetishes obscure the constitutive tropic nature of themselves and of worlds. Fetishes literalize and so induce an elementary material and cognitive error. Fetishes make things seem clear and under control. Technique and science appear to be about accuracy, freedom from bias, good faith, and time and money to get on with the job, not about material semiotic troping and so building certain kinds of worlds rather than others. Fetishized maps appear to be about things-in-themselves; non-fetishized maps index cartographies of struggle,[9] or more broadly, cartographies of non-innocent practice, where everything does not always have to be a struggle.

The history of cartography can look like a history of figure-free science and technique, not like a history of 'troping', in the sense of worlds swerving and mutating through material cultural practice, where all of the actors are not human. Accuracy can appear to be a question of technique, and to have nothing to do with inherently non-literal tropes. Such a 'real' world that pre-exists practice and discourse seems to be merely a container for the lively activities of humans and non-humans. Spatialization as a never-ending, power-laced process engaged by a motley array of beings can be fetishized as a series of maps whose grids non-tropically locate naturally bounded bodies (land, people, resources – and genes) inside 'absolute' dimensions like space and time. The maps are fetishes in so far as they enable a specific kind of mistake that turns process into non-tropic, real, literal things inside containers.

People who work with maps as fetishes do not realize they are troping in a specific way. This 'mistake' has powerful effects on the formation of subjects and objects. Such people might well know explicitly that map making is essential to enclosing entities (land, minerals, populations, etc.) and readying them for further exploration, specification, sale, contract, protection, or management. These practices could be understood as potentially controversial and full of desires and purposes, but the maps themselves would seem to be a reliable foundation, free of troping, guaranteed by the purity of number and quantification, outside of yearning and stuttering. Questions of 'value', that is, tropes, could be understood to pertain to decisions to learn to make certain kinds of maps and to influence the purposes to which charts would be put. But the map making itself, and the maps themselves, would inhabit a semiotic domain like the high-energy physicists' 'culture of no culture',[10] the world of the non-tropic, the space of clarity and uncontaminated referentiality, the kingdom of rationality. That kind of clarity and referentiality are god tricks. Inside the god trick, the maps could only be better or worse, accurate or not; but they could not be *themselves* instruments for and sediments of troping. From the point of view of fetishists, maps – and scientific objects in general – are purely technical and representational, rooted in processes of potentially bias-free discovery and non-tropic naming. They would say: 'Scientific maps could not be fetishes; fetishes are for perverts and primitives. Scientific people are committed to clarity; they are not fetishists mired in error. My gene map is a non-tropic representation of reality, i.e., of genes themselves.' Such is the structure of denial in technoscientific fetishism.[11]

That is how the mistake works. Perhaps worst of all, while denying denial in a recursive avoidance of the trope – and so unconscious – tissue of all knowledge, fetishists mislocate 'error'. Scientific fetishists place error in the admittedly irreducibly tropic zones of 'culture', where primitives, perverts, and other lay people live, and not in the fetishists' constitutional inability to recognize the trope that denies its own status as figure. In my view, contingency, finitude, and difference – but not 'error' – inhere in irremediably tropic, secular liveliness. Error and denial inhere in reverent literalness. Error inheres in the literalness of 'life itself', rather than in the unapologetic swerving of liveliness and worldly bodies-in-the-making. Life itself is the psychic, cognitive, and material terrain of fetishism. By contrast, liveliness is open to the possibility of situated knowledges, including technoscientific knowledges.

Corporealization and genetic fetishism

Gene mapping is a particular kind of spatialization of the body, perhaps better called 'corporealization'. If commodity fetishism is the kind of mistaken self-identity endemic to capital accumulation, and liberalization of the categories is the form of self-invisible circulatory sclerosis in important areas of scientific epistemology, what flavour of fetishism is peculiar to the history of corporealization in the material and mythic times of Life Itself? The goal of the question is to ferret out how relations and practices get mistaken for non-tropic things-in-themselves in ways that matter to the chances for liveliness of humans and nonhumans.

To sort out analogies and disanalogies, let us return briefly to commodity fetishism. The Hungarian Marxist philosopher Georg Lukács defined this kind of reification as follows: 'Its basis is that a relation between people takes on the character of a thing and thus acquires a "phantom objectivity," an autonomy that seems so strictly rational and all-embracing as to conceal every trace of its fundamental nature: the relation between people.'[12] Marx defined commodity fetishism as 'the objective appearance of the social characteristics of labour'.[13] Corporealization, however, is not reducible to capitalization or commodification.

I define corporealization as the interactions of humans and non-humans in the distributed, heterogeneous work processes of technoscience. The non-humans are both those made by humans, e.g., machines and other tools, and those occurring independently of human manufacture. The work processes result in specific material-semiotic bodies – or natural-technical objects of knowledge and practice – such as cells, molecules, genes, organisms, viruses, or ecosystems. The work processes make humans into particular kinds of subjects, called scientists. The bodies are 'real', and nothing about corporealization is 'merely' fiction. But corporealization is tropic and historically specific at every layer of its tissues.

Cells, organisms, and genes are not 'discovered' in a vulgar realist sense; but they are not made up. Technoscientific bodies, such as the biomedical organism, are the nodes that congeal from interactions, where all the actors are not human, not self-identical, not 'us'. The world takes shape in specific ways, and cannot take shape just any way; corporealization is contingent, physical, tropic, historical, interactional. Corporealization involves institutions, narratives, legal structures, power-differentiated human labour, and much more. The processes 'inside' bodies – like the cascades of action that constitute an organism or that constitute the play of genes and other entities that make up a cell – are interactions, not frozen things. A world like 'gene' specifies a multifaceted set of interactions among people and non-humans in historically contingent, practical, knowledge-making work. A gene is not a thing, much less a 'master molecule' or a self-contained code; instead, the term 'gene' signifies a node of durable action where many actors, human and non-human, meet.

Commodity fetishism was defined so that only humans were the real actors, whose *social* relationality was obscured in the reified commodity form. But 'corporeal fetishism', or more specifically gene fetishism, is about mistaking *heterogeneous* relationality for a fixed, seemingly objective thing. Strong objectivity in Sandra Harding's terms[14] and situated knowledges in my terms are lost in the pseudo-objectivity of gene fetishism, or in any kind of corporeal fetishism that denies the ongoing action and work that it takes to sustain technoscientific material-semiotic bodies in the world. The gene as fetish is a phantom object, like and unlike the commodity. Gene fetishism involves 'forgetting' that bodies are nodes in webs of interactions, forgetting the tropic quality of all knowledge claims. My claim about situated knowledges and gene fetishism can itself become fixed and dogmatic and seem to stand for and by itself, outside of the articulations that make the claim sensible. That is, when the stuttering and swerving are left out, a process philosophy can be just as fetishistic as a reductionist one. Both scientists and non-scientists can be gene fetishists; and US culture in and out of laboratories is rife with signs of such fetishism, as well as of resistance to it.

With a little help from Marx, Freud, and Whitehead, let me precipitate from the preceding pages what has been left in solution until now; i.e., the intertwining triple strands – economic, psychoanalytic, and philosophical – in the gene fetishism that corporealizes 'life itself' through its symptomatic practices in molecular genetics and biotechnology, for example in the Human Genome Project (medicine), biodiversity gene prospecting (environmentalism and industry), and transgenics (agriculture and pharmaceuticals). I do not mean that scientists or others in these areas necessarily practise gene fetishism. Corporealization need not be fetishized, need not inhabit the culture of no culture and the nature of no nature. Under widespread epistemological, cultural, psychological, and political economic conditions, however, fetishism is a common syndrome in technoscientific practice.

It takes little imagination to trace commodity fetishism in the transnational market circulations where genes, those 24-carat-gold macromolecular things-in-themselves, seem to be themselves the source of value. This kind of gene fetishism rests on the denial of all the natural-social articulations and agentic relationships among researchers, farmers, factory workers, patients, policy makers, molecules, model organisms, machines, forests, seeds, financial instruments, computers, and much else that bring 'genes' into material-semiotic being. There is nothing exceptional about genetic commodity fetishism, where focus on the realm of exchange hides the realm of production. The only amendment I made to Marx was to remember all the non-human actors too.[15] The gene is objectified in and through all of its naturalsocial (one word) articulations; and there is nothing amiss in that. Such objectification is the stuff of real worlds. But the gene is fetishized when it seems to be itself the source of value; and those kinds of fetish-objects are the stuff of complex mistakes, denials, and disavowals.[16]

The hardest argument for me to make is that there is a psychoanalytic quality to gene fetishism, at least in cultural, if not in personal psychodynamic, terms; but I am driven to this extreme by the evidence. According to Freud, a fetish is an object or part of the body used in achieving libidinal satisfaction. In the classical psychoanalytic story about the fear of castration and masculine subject development, fetishism concerns a special kind of balancing act between knowledge and belief. The fetishist-in-the-making, who must be a boy for the plot to work, at a critical moment sees that the mother has no penis, but cannot face that fact because of the terrible ensuing anxiety about the possibility of his own castration. The youngster has three choices – become a homosexual and have nothing to do with the terrifying castrated beings called women, get over it in the recommended Oedipal way, or provide a usable penis-substitute (a fetish) to stand in as the object of libidinal desire. The fetishist knows and does not know that the fetish is not what it must be to allay the anxiety of the all-too-castratable subject.

For Freud, the penis-substitute is the objectification inherent in a process of disavowal of the mother's (real) castration. The fetish is a defense strategy. 'To put it plainly: the fetish is a substitute for the woman's (mother's) phallus which the little boy once believed in and does not wish to forego – we know why.'[17] Or, as Laura Mulvey put it, 'Fetishism, broadly speaking, involves the attribution of self-sufficiency and autonomous powers to a manifestly "man" derived object . . . The fetish, however, is haunted by the fragility of the mechanisms that sustain it . . . Knowledge hovers implacably in the wings of consciousness.'[18] The fetishist is not psychotic; he 'knows' that his surrogate is just that. Yet, he is uniquely invested in his power object. The fetishist, aware he has a substitute, still believes in – and experiences – its potency; he is captivated by the reality effect produced by the image, which itself mimes his fear and desire.

Since technoscience is, among other things, about inhabiting stories, Freud's account of fetishism casts light on an aspect of the fixations and disavowals necessary to belief in 'life itself'. Life itself depends on the erasure of the apparatuses of production and articulatory relationships that make up all objects of attention, including genes; it relies as well as on denial of fears and desires in technoscience. Disavowal and denial seem hard to avoid in the subject formation of successful molecular geneticists, where reality must be seen to endorse the specific practices of intervention built into knowledge claims.

The odd balancing act of belief and knowledge that is diagnostic of fetishism, along with the related cascade of mimetic copying practices that accompany fascination with images, is evident in biotechnological artefacts – including textbooks, advertisements, editorials, research reports, conference titles and more. Belief in the self-sufficiency of genes as 'master molecules', or as the material basis of life itself, or as the code of codes, not only persists, but dominates in libidinal, instrumental-experimental, explanatory, literary, economic, and political behaviour in the face of the knowledge that genes are never alone, are always part of an interfactional system. That system at a minimum includes the proteinaceous architecture and enzymes of the cell as the unit of structure and function, and also the whole apparatus of knowledge production that concretizes (objectifies) inter-actions in the historically specific form of 'genes' and 'gnomes'. There is no such thing as disarticulated information – in organisms, computers, phone lines, equa-tions, or anywhere else. As the biologist Richard Lewontin put it, 'First, DNA is not self-reproducing, second, it makes nothing, and third, organisms are not determined by it.'[19] This knowledge is entirely orthodox in biology, a fact that makes 'selfish gene' or 'master molecule' discourse symptomatic of something amiss at a level that might as well be called 'unconscious'.

But if I am to invoke Freud's story, I need a particular kind of balancing act between belief and knowledge, one involving a threat to potency and wholeness at critical moments of subject formation. Can gene fetishism be constructed to involve that kind of dynamic? Leaving aside individual psychosexual dynamics and focusing on the social-historical subject of genetic knowledge, I think that such an account makes rough sense, at least analogically. But first, I have to rearrange Freud's account to dispute what he thought was simply true about possession of the 'phallus', that signifier of creative wholeness and power. Freud thought women really did not have it; that was the plain fact the fetishist could not face. I rely on feminism to insist on a stronger objective claim, namely that women are whole, potent, and 'uncastrated'. Wholeness here means inside articulations, never reducing to a thing-in-itself, in sacred, secular, or psychoanalytic terms. Freud got it wrong, even while he got much of the symbolic structure right in male-dominant conditions. Freud, and a few other good men (and women), confused the penis and the phallus after all.

My correction is necessary to make the analogy to gene fetishism. Organisms are 'whole' in a specific, non-mystical sense; i.e., organisms are nodes in webs of dynamic articulations. Neither organisms nor their constituents are things-in-themselves. Sacred or secular, all autotelic entities are defences, alibis, excuses, substitutes – dodges from the complexity of material-semiotic objectifications and apparatuses of corporeal production. In my story, the gene fetishist 'knows' that DNA, or life itself, is a surrogate, or at best a simplification that readily degener-ates into a false idol. The substitute, life itself, is a defence for the fetishist, who is deeply invested in the switch, against the knowledge of the actual complexity and embeddedness of all objects, including genes. The fetishist ends up believing in the code of codes, the book of life, and even the search for the grail. Only half jokingly, I see the molecular biological fetishist to be enthralled by a phallus-substitute, a mere 'penis' called the gene, which defends the cowardly subject from the too-scary sight of the relentless material-semiotic articulations of bio-logical reality, not to mention the sight of the wider horizons leading to the real in technoscience. Perhaps acknowledging that '[f]irst, DNA is not self-reproducing, second, it makes nothing, and third, organisms are not determined by it' is too threatening to all the investments, libidinal and otherwise, at stake in the material-semiotic worlds of molecular genetics these days. So the fetishist sees the gene itself in all the gels, blots, and printouts in the lab, and 'forgets' the natural-technical processes that produce the gene and genome as consensus objects in the real world. The fetishist's balancing act of knowledge and belief is still running in the theatre of technoscience.

The third strand in my helical spiral of gene fetishism is spun out of what Whitehead called the 'fallacy of misplaced concreteness'[20] Growing out of his examination of the still astonishing concatenation of theoretical, mathematical, and experimental developments that mark the European seventeenth century as 'The Century of Genius', Whitehead foregrounded the importance to the history of Western natural science of two principles: (1) simple location in space-time, and (2) substances with qualities, especially primary qualities defined by their yielding to numerical, quantitative analysis. These were the fundamental commitments embedded in seventeenth-century and subsequent Western practices of spatialization, including cartography, and the role of these principles in the history of philosophical and scientific mechanism is not news. Whitehead wrote in 1925, when mechanism, the wave-particle duality, the principle of continuity, and simple location had been under fruitful erosion in physics for decades. These dated conventionally from Maxwell's mid-nineteenth-century equations founding electromagnetic field theory and continuing with the developments in quantum physics in the 1920s and 1930s, and were tied to work by both Niels Bohr in wave mechanics and Albert Einstein on the light quantum, among other critical transformations of physical theory.

Whitehead had no quarrel with the utility of the notion of simple location and the attention to primary qualities of simple substances – unless these abstract logical constructions were mistaken for 'the concrete'. Albeit expressed in his own arcane terminology, 'the concrete' had a precise meaning for Whitehead, related to his approach to 'an actual entity as a concrescence of prehensions'. Stressing the processual nature of reality, he called actual entities actual occasions. Objectifications had to do with the way 'the potentiality of one actual entity is realized in another actual entity'.[21] Prehensions could be physical or conceptual, but such articulations, or reachings into each other in the tissues of the world, constituted the most basic processes for Whitehead. I ally with Whitehead's analysis to highlight the ways that gene fetishists mistake the abstraction of the gene for the concrete entities and 'occasions' that make up the biological world.

So, gene fetishism is compounded of a political economic *denial* that holds commodities to be sources of their own value, while obscuring the socio-technical relations among humans and between humans and nonhumans that generate both objects and value; a *disavowal*, suggested by psychoanalytic theory, that substitutes the master molecule for a more adequate representation of units or nexuses of biological structure, function, development, evolution, and reproduction; and a philosophical-cognitive *error* that mistakes potent abstractions for concrete entities, which themselves are ongoing events. Fetishists are multiply invested in all of these substitutions. The irony is that gene fetishism involves such elaborate surrogacy, swerving, and substitution, when the gene as the guarantor of life itself is supposed to signify an autotelic thing in itself, the code of codes. Never has avoidance of acknowledging the relentless tropic nature of living and signifying involved such wonderful figuration, where the gene collects up the people in the materialized dream of life itself.

Inside and outside laboratories, genetic fetishism is contested, replicated, ironized, indulged, disrupted, consolidated, examined. Gene fetishists 'forget' that the gene and gene maps are ways of enclosing the commons of the body – of corporealizing – in specific ways, which, among other things, often write commodity fetishism into the program of biology. I would like to savour the anxious humour of a series of scientific cartoons and advertisements about the gene in order to see how joking practice works where gene fetishism prevails. We move from Maxis's *SimLife* to maps and portraits of the genome itself.

Genome

My reading of comic portraiture and cartography – the story of life itself – picks up after the implosion of informatics and biologics, especially in genetics, since the 1970s. Still absent from Webster's 1993 unabridged dictionary, *genome* progressively signifies a historically new entity engendered by the productive identity crisis of nature and culture. The cultural productions of the genome produce a category crisis, a generic conundrum in which proliferating ambiguities and chimeras animate the action in science, entertainment, domestic life, fashion, religion, and business. The pollution works both ways: culture is as mouse-eaten as nature is by the gnawings of the mixed and matched, edited and engineered, programmed and debugged genome.

A 1991 residential seminar at the University of California Humanities Research Center spent considerable time on the Human Genome Project. One philosopher in the seminar put his finger on potent double meanings when he understood the science studies scholars, who suggested the term 'the cultural productions of the genome' as the title for a conference, to be referring to musical, artistic, educational, and similar 'cultural productions' emerging from popularization of science. The science studies professionals meant, rather, that the genome was radically 'culturally' produced, and no less 'natural' for all that. The gene was the result of the work of construction at every level of its very real being; it was constitutively artefactual. 'Technoscience is cultural practice' might be the slogan for mice, scientists, and science analysts.

Attending to how the permeable boundary between science and comedy works in relation to the genome – and at the risk of giving comfort to those who still think the cultural production of the genome means its popularization – I pursue my story literally by reading the comics. My structuring text is a family of images, all cartoon advertisements for lab equipment drawn by Wally Neibart and published in *Science* magazine in the early 1990s (see Figures 5.1 and 5.2). I am reminded of David Harvey's observation that advertising is the official art of capitalism.[22] Advertising also captures the paradigmatic qualities of democracy in

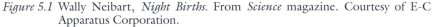
Figure 5.1 Wally Neibart, *Night Births*. From *Science* magazine. Courtesy of E-C Apparatus Corporation.

Figure 5.2 Wally Neibart, *Portraits of Man*. From *Science* magazine. Courtesy of E-C Apparatus Corporation.

the narratives of life itself. Finally, advertising and the creation of value are close twins in the New World Order, Inc. The cartoons explicitly play with creation, art, commerce, and democracy.

The Neibart cartoons suggest who 'we', reconstituted as subjects in the practices of the Human Genome Project, are called to be in this hyper-humanist discourse: Man™. This is man with property in himself in the historically specific sense proper to the New World Order, Inc. Following an ethical and method-ological principle for science studies that I adopted many years ago, I will critically analyse, or 'deconstruct', only that which I love and only that in which I am deeply implicated. This commitment is part of a project to excavate something like a technoscientific unconscious, the processes of formation of the technoscientific subject, and the reproduction of this subject's structures of pleasure and anxiety. Those who recognize themselves in these webs of love, implication, and excav-ation are the 'we' who surf the Net in the sacred/secular quest rhetoric of technoscience.

Interpellated into its stories, I am in love with Neibart's comic craft. His car-toons are at least as much interrogations of gene fetishism as they are sales pitches. His cartoons depend on a savvy use of visual and verbal tropes. In his wonderful cartoon image advertising an electrophoresis system, a middle-aged, white, bedroom-slippered and labcoat-clad man cradles a baby monkey wearing a diaper (Figure 5.1).[23] Addressing an audience outside the frame of the ad, the scientist holds up a gel with nice protein fragment separation, generated by the passage of charged molecules of various sizes through an electrical field. The gel is part of a closely related family of macromolecular inscriptions, which include the DNA polynucleotide separation gels, whose images are familiar icons of the genome project. In my reading of this ad, the protein fragment gel metonymically stands in for the totality of artefacts and practices in molecular biology and molecular genetics. These artefacts and practices are the components of the apparatus of bodily production in biotechnology's materializing narrative. My metonymic substitution is warranted by the dominant molecular genetic story that still over-whelmingly leads unidirectionally from DNA (the genes), through RNA, to pro-tein (the end product). In a serious and persistent joke on themselves, the kind of joke that affirms what it laughs at, molecular biologists early labelled this story the Central Dogma of molecular genetics. The Central Dogma has been amended over the years to accommodate some reverse action, in which information flows from RNA to DNA. 'Reverse transcriptase' was the first enzyme identified in the study of this 'backward' flow. RNA viruses engage in such shenanigans all the time. HIV is such a virus, and the first (briefly) effective drugs used to treat people with AIDS inhibit the virus's reverse transcriptase, which reads the information in the viral genetic material, made of RNA, into the host cell's DNA. Even while marking other possibilities, the enzyme's very name highlights the normal orien-tation for control and structural determination in higher life forms. And even in the reverse form, Genes 'R' Us. This is the Central Dogma of the story of Life Itself.

In the Neibart cartoon, while the scientist speaks to us, drawing us into the story, the monkey's baby bottle is warming in the well of the electrophoresis apparatus. The temperature monitor for the system reads a reassuringly physiological 37 degrees Celsius, and the clock reads 12:05. The time is five minutes past midnight, the time of strange night births, the time for the undead to wander, and the first minutes after a nuclear holocaust. Remember the clock that the *Bulletin of Atomic Scientists* used to keep time in the Cold War; for many years it seemed that the hands advanced relentlessly toward midnight. As Keller argued persuasively, the bomb and the gene have been choreographed in the last half of the twentieth century in a dance that intertwines physics and biology in their quest to reveal 'secrets of life and secrets of death.'[24]

In the electrophoresis system ad, Neibart's image suggests a reassuring family drama, not the technowar apocalypse of secular Christian monotheism, nor the Frankenstein story of the unnatural and disowned monster. But I am not reassured: all the conventional rhetorical details of the masculinist, humanist story of man's autonomous self-birthing structure the ad's narrative. The time, the cross-species baby, the scientist father, his age, his race, the absence of women, the appropriation of the maternal function by the equipment and by the scientist: all converge to suggest the conventional tale of the second birth that produces Man. It's not 'Three Men and a Baby' here, but 'A Scientist, a Machine, and a Monkey'. The technoscientific family is a cyborg nuclear unit. As biologist – and parent – Scott Gilbert insisted when he saw the ad, missing from this lab scene are the post-docs and graduate students, with their babies, who might really be there after midnight. Both monkey and molecular inscription stand in for the absent human product issuing from the reproductive practices of the molecular biology laboratory. The furry baby primate and the glossy gel are tropes that work by part-for-whole substitution or by surrogacy. The child produced by this lab's apparatus of bodily production, this knowledge-producing technology, this writing practice for materializing the text of life, is – in fruitful ambiguity – the monkey, the protein gel (metonym for man), and those interpellated into the drama, that is, us, the constituency for E-C Apparatus Corporation's genetic inscription technology.

I over-read, naturally; I joke; I suggest a paranoid reading practice. I mistake a funny cartoon, one I like immensely, for the serious business of real science, which surely has nothing to do with such popular misconceptions. But jokes are my way of working, my nibbling at the edges of the respectable and reassuring in technosciences and in science studies. This nervous, symptomatic, joking method is intended to locate the reader and the argument on an edge. On either side is a lie: on the one hand, the official discourses of technoscience and its apologists; on the other, the fictions of conspiracy fabulated by all those labeled 'outsider' to scientific rationality and its marvellous projects, magical messages, and very conventional stories.

My interest is relentlessly in images and stories and in the worlds, actors, inhabitants, and trajectories they make possible. In the biotechnological discourse of the Human Genome Project, the human is produced in a historical form, which enables and constrains certain forms of life rather than others. The technological products of the several genome projects are cultural actors in every sense.

Portrait™

A second Wally Neibart cartoon for a *Science* ad makes an aspect of this point beautifully – literally (Figure 5.2). Evoking the world of (high) art, this ad puns on science as (high) cultural production. That should not prevent the analyst from conducting another, quasi-ethnographic sort of 'cultural' analysis. I think Neibart subtly invites a critical reading; he is laughing *at* gene fetishism, as well as using it. Our same balding, middle-aged, white, male scientist – this time dressed in a double-breasted blue blazer, striped shirt, and slacks – is bragging about his latest acquisition to a rapt, younger, business-suit-clad, white man with a full head of hair. They get as close to power dressing as biologists, still new to the corporate world, seem to manage. The two affluent-looking gentlemen are talking in front of three paintings in an art museum. (We assume they are in an art museum – that is, if the *Mona Lisa* has not been relocated as a result of the accumulated wealth of the truly Big Men in informatics and biologics. After all, in 1994 William H. Gates, chairman and founder of Microsoft, purchased a Leonardo da Vinci notebook, *Codex Hammer*, for a record $30.8 million in a manuscript auction.)[25]

Neibart's three paradigmatic portraits of man on display are not of male human beings, nor should they be. The self-reproducing mimesis in screen projections works through spectacularized difference. One painting in Neibart's ad is da Vinci's *Mona Lisa*; the second is Pablo Picasso's *Woman with Loaves* (1906); the third, gilt-framed like the others, is a superb DNA sequence autoradiograph on a gel. The Italian Renaissance and modernist paintings are signs of the culture of Western humanism, which, in kinship with the Scientific Revolution, is narratively at the foundations of modernity and its sense of rationality, progress, and beauty – not to mention its class location in the rising bourgeoisie, whose fate was tied progressively to science and technology. Like the humanist paintings, the sequence autoradiograph is a self-portrait of man in a particular historical form. Like the humanist paintings, the DNA gel is about instrumentation, framing, angle of vision, lighting, colour, new forms of authorship, and new forms of patronage. Preserved in gene banks and catalogued in databases, genetic portraits are collected in institutions that are like art museums in both signifying and effecting specific forms of national, epistemological, aesthetic, moral, and financial power and prestige. The potent ambiguities of biotechnological, genetic, financial, electrical, and career power are explicitly punned in the ad: 'I acquired this sequence with my EC650 power supply.' The E-C Apparatus Corporation offers 'the state-of-the-art in Power Supplies' – in this case, a constant power supply device.

The unique precision and beauty of original art become replicable, everyday experiences through the power of technoscience in proprietary networks. The modernist opposition between copies and originals – played out forcefully in the art market – is erased by the transnational postmodern power of genetic identification and replication in both bodies and labs. Biotechnological mimesis mutates the modernist anxiety about authenticity. 'Classic sequence autoradiographs are everyday work for E-C Electrophoresis Power Supplies.' No longer oxymoronically, the ad's text promises unlimited choice, classical originality, eighteen unique models, and replicability. At every stage of genome production, in evolutionary and laboratory time, database management and error reduction in replication take the place of anxiety about originality.

But a calmed opposition between copy and original does not for a minute subvert proprietary and authorial relations to the desirable portrait in all its endless versions, although the subjects of authorial discourse have mutated, or at least proliferated. Just as I am careful to credit Neibart and seek copyright releases, E-C is careful to confirm authorial and property relations of the beautiful, framed DNA sequence autoradiograph, which is reproduced in the ad 'courtesy of the U.S. Biochemical Corporation using Sequenase™ and an E-C Power Supply'.[26] E-C used the molecular portrait of man with permission, just as I must, in the escalating practices of ownership in technoscience, where intellectual and bodily property become synonymous. The 'great artist' of the technohumanist portrait is a consortium of human and non-human actants: a commercially available enzyme, a biotech corporation, and a power supply device. Like the art portraiture, the scientific portrait of man as gel and database signifies genius, originality, identity, the self, distinction, unity, and biography. In eminently collectible form, the gel displays difference and identity exhaustively and precisely. Human beings are collected up into their paradigmatic portrait. No wonder aesthetic pleasure is the reward. The autoradiograph reveals the secrets of human nature. Intense narrative and visual pleasure are intrinsic to this technoscientific apparatus, as it is to others, which none the less try to ensure that their productions can only be officially or 'scientifically' discussed in terms of epistemological and technological facticity and non-tropic reality. Genes *are* us, we are told through myriad 'cultural' media, from DNA treated with reagents like Sequenase™ and run on gels, to property laws in both publishing and biotechnology. Narrative and visual pleasure can be acknowledged only in the symptomatic practices of jokes and puns. Displayed as 'high science' explicit 'knowledge' must seem free of story and figure. Such technohumanist portraiture is what guarantees man's second birth into the light and airy regions of mind. This is the structure of pleasure in gene fetishism.

The strong bonding of biotechnology with the Renaissance, and especially with Leonardo da Vinci, demands further dissection. Commenting on the potent mix of technique, ways of seeing, and patronage, a venture capitalist from Kleiner Perkins Caufield & Byers summed up the matter when he observed that biotechnology has been 'for human biology what the Italian Renaissance was for art'.[27] Leonardo, in particular, has been appropriated for stories of origin, vision and its tools, scientific humanism, technical progress, and universal extension. I am especially interested in the technoscientific preoccupation with Leonardo and his brethren in the 'degraded' contexts of business self-representation, advertising inside the scientific community, science news illustration, conference brochure graphics, science popularization, magazine cover art, and comic humour.

Consider Du Pont's remarkable ad that begins, 'Smile! Renaissance™ non-rad DNA labeling kits give you reproducible results, not high backgrounds'.[28] The text occurs underneath a colour reproduction of Andy Warhol's giant (9′2″ × 7′ 10½″) 1963 photo-silkscreen, in ink and synthetic polymer paint, that 'clones' the *Mona Lisa*. Filling in a grid of five *Mona Lisa's* across and six down, Warhol's multiplied version is entitled *Thirty Are Better Than One*. In Warhol's and Du Pont's versions, the paradigmatic, enigmatically smiling lady is replicated in a potentially endless clone matrix. Without attribution, Du Pont replicates Warhol replicates da Vinci replicates the lady herself. And Renaissance™ gets top billing as the real artist *because* it facilitates replicability. But how could Warhol, of all artists, object to his work being anonymously appropriated for commodity marketing under the sign of 'debased' high art and high science enterprised up? In the Du Pont ad, the only mark of intellectual property is – in a comic, recursive self-parody – Renaissance™. The mythic chronotope itself bears the trademark of the transnational biotechnology corporation. Recursively, the brand marks detection and labelling tools, for the code of codes, for life itself.

In the company of genes

The company the gene keeps is definitely upscale. Fetishes come in matched sets. Master molecule of the Central Dogma and its heresies, the gene affiliates with the other power objects of technoscience's knowledge production: neuro-imaging, artificial intelligence, artificial life, high-gloss entertainment, high technology, high expectations. The ten-part series, 'science in the 90s', which ran from 5 January to 8 May 1990, gives a broad sense of what counts as cutting-edge technoscience for the news writers and editors of *Science*. The excitement came from high tech/high science, including neuroscience, computing and information sciences, and molecular genetics. The boring and discouraging notes came from (very brief) consideration of ongoing racial and sexual 'imbalance' in who does technoscience and the troubles that arise when 'politics' gets into a scientist's career.

The chief power sharer in the gene's new world community is the nervous system. Even the *UNESCO Courier* carries the news that links mind and origins, neuron and gene, at the helm of life itself: 'No one would deny that, within the highly organized framework of a human being, two "master elements" account for most of our characteristics – our genes and our neurons. Furthermore, the nature of the dialogue between our genes and our neurons is a central problem of biology'[29]

Every autumn since 1990, *Science*, the magazine of the American Association for the Advancement of Science, has put out a special issue updating its readers on progress in genome mapping, and especially in the Human Genome Project. The table of contents of the first special issue highlights the tight coupling of genetic and nervous systems in the discourse of millennial science.[30] Citing a recent example of homicidal mania, *Science* editor Daniel Koshland, Jr, introduced the issue with the argument that hope for the mentally ill – and for society – lies in neuroscience and genetics. Necessary to the diagrams of life itself, the tie to informatics is explicit: 'The irrational output of a faulty brain is like the faulty wiring of a computer, in which failure is caused not by the information fed into the computer, but by incorrect processing of that information after it enters the black box.'[31] In addition to the articles on the genome project and the map insert, the issue contains a research news piece called 'The High Culture of Neuroscience' and eight reports from neurobiology, spanning the range from molecular manipulation of ion channels, to a study of primate behaviour, to a psychological assessment of human twins reared apart.

Located in the potent zones where molecular genetics and neurobiology ideologically converge, this last study on twins reared apart lists as its first author Thomas Bouchard, a former student of Arthur Jensen. Jensen promoted the idea of the linkage of genetic inheritance, IQ, and race in his famous 1969 *Harvard Educational Review* article. The special gene map issue of *Science* was the first major professional journal to publish Bouchard's controversial work, which ascribes most aspects of personality and behaviour to genes. Many of Bouchard's papers had been rejected through peer review, but he brought his message successfully to the popular media. Following *Science*'s publication, Bouchard's ideas gained authority and prominence in public debates about genetics and behaviour.[32]

Cartography, the high science of the Age of Exploration, tropically organizes the first *Science* gene map issue, from the design of its cover to the content of its prose. Collectively labelled 'The Human Map', the cover is a collage of mapping icons – including a Renaissance anatomical human dissection by Vesalius, a Mendelian genetic-cross map superimposed on the great scientist's facial profile, a radioactively labelled region of metaphase chromosomes, a linkage map and bit of a sequence data rendered by the cartographical conventions that have emerged in the genome projects, a flow diagram through the outline of a mouse body, and a computer-generated coloured-cell map of an unidentified abstract territory. The cover design is explained inside: 'Just as the ancient navigators depended on maps and charts to explore the unknown, investigators today are building maps and charts with which to explore new scientific frontiers.'[33]

The reference to the Renaissance cartographers, a common rhetorical device in genome discourse, is not idle. Genomics 'globalizes' in specific ways. Species being is materially and semiotically produced in gene mapping practices, just as particular kinds of space and humanity were the fruit of earlier material-semiotic enclosures. Traffic in bodies and meanings is equally at stake. The orthodox stories of the Renaissance and early modern Europe are useful to my narrative of genome mapping as a process of bodily spatialization akin to enclosing the commons in land, through institutions of alienable property, and in authorship, through institutions of copyright. Harvey points out that the introduction of the Ptolemaic map into Florence from Alexandria in 1400 gave Europeans the critical means to see the world as a global unity.[34] The Ptolemaic map and its offspring were the air pumps of scientific geography, embedded in material, literary, and social technologies that made the 'global' a mobile European reality. '[M]athematical principles could be applied, as in optics, to the whole problem of representing the globe on a flat surface. As a result it seemed as if space, though infinite, was conquerable and containable for purposes of human occupancy and action.'[35] The elaboration of perspective techniques in mid-fifteenth-century Florentine art was entwined with the construction of individualism and perspectivism critical to modern spaces and selves. The sixteenth-century Flemish cartographer Gerardus Mercator, after whom a biotechnological corporation is named, crafted projections of the globe geared to navigation on the high seas in a period of intense world exploration by Europeans. All of these practices constituted a major reworking of conceptions of space, time, and person. And all of these practices are in the family tree of genetic mapping, which is a distributed, located practice enabling certain sorts of power-charged global unity. No wonder Mercator's grids and projections line the scientific unconscious of biotechnology researchers and advertisers.

Bruno Latour illuminates the mobilization of worlds through mapping practices.[36] Cartography is perhaps the chief tool-metaphor of technoscience. 'Mapping Terra Incognita (*Humani Corporis*)', the news story toward the less technical front of *Science*'s first special issue on the genome project, has all of the expected allusions to Vesalius's Renaissance anatomy.[37] This kind of ubiquitous new-world imagery, like the extended propaganda for cybernetics in the United States in the 1950s and 1960s, indicates a 'distributed passage point', through which many popular and technical projects get loosely associated with the high gloss of molecular biology and biotechnology.[38] The second article on genome mapping in the special issue, 'Mapping the Human Genome: Current Status', charts another kind of intersection, one Latour called an 'obligatory passage point'.[39] This node represents the fruit of the mobilization of resources and the forging of alliances among machines, people, and other entities that force others to pass through *here*, and nowhere else. The sociotechnical achievements of molecular biology are a node through which many *must* pass: paleoanthropologists who wish to resolve evolutionary arguments, physicians who wish to diagnose and treat disease, developmental biologists who seek resolution of their questions, ideologists who proclaim legitimation for or exemplary condemnation of technoscience. Molecular biology does not just claim to be able to decode the master molecule; it installs the tollbooths for a great deal of collateral traffic through nature.

The human genome map inserted into the special issue of *Science* in 1990 inaugurated the practice of annually giving each subscriber-member of the AAAS a personal copy of the most up-to-date chart available. The practice reverberates with *National Geographic*'s presentation to subscribers of the new Robinson projection map of the globe in its January 1988 issue, which featured on the front cover the holographic portrait of the endangered planet earth at the dawn of the decade to save man's home world. (A holographic ad for McDonald's, with appropriate words from the transnational fast food chain's founder, graced the back cover.) Just as all subscribers to *National Geographic* are automatically members of a scientific society, and so patrons of research, all subscribers to *Science* are members of the AAAS and share symbolically in its ideological and material privileges. As subscribers, 'we' are the constituents of technoscience, a mapping practice of the highest order. With more than 150,000 subscribers, *Science* reaches about three times the number as does *Nature*, its British sibling and nearest world-class competitor. *National Geographic* reaches millions.

In a mid-1990s ad for DNA-cutting enzymes, New England Biolabs invokes the imploded global bodies materialized by both *National Geographic* and by the Human Genome Project (Figure 5.3). The oxymoronic Global Native embodies the Global Gene, literally. Difference is mapped and enclosed; art, science, and business join in the dance. From the left side of the page, against a black background, the body of a beautiful young woman with generically (and oxymoronically) 'indigenous' facial features flows forward. Her body *is* the mapped terrain globe, shaped to her lovely female contours; she is its soul. Of the earth, she moves through it as both its spirit and flesh. Arms raised in a dance gesture, the native woman is clothed with the tissue of the mapped planet, which billows into a semicircle continuous with her figure. Marked off by its geometric co-ordinates, the projection map shows the bulge of west Africa and the Atlantic Ocean. The seas are dotted with the great sailing cutter ships of Europe's age of exploration and marked with the fabulous Latin names bestowed by the navigators' culture. The map-woman is an animated Mercator projection.

The earth is both the woman's body and her dress, and the colour-enhanced regions highlighting the beige tones of the swirling hemispherical corpus/fabric are like style elements in a United Colors of Benetton celebration of global multiculturalism. To remember the slave trade and the middle passage across the region of the world shown on this lovely map seems petty. The woman-earth's body confronts text at the midline of the page: 'Mapping the Human Genome'. The earth and the genome are one, joined in the trope of the technoscientific map. 'Advanced by a diverse range of 8-base Cutters', the new cartography will be enabled by New England Biolab's restriction enzymes. Map, women, earth, goddess, science, body, inscription, technology, life, the native: all are collected in an aestheticized image like a Navaho sand painting that places the holy people inside the four sacred mountains. Who said master narratives, universalism, and holism were dead in the New World Order's extended networks? Advanced by the code-analyzing restriction enzymes given by the globalized history of race and gender, naturalization has never been more florid. I doubt that is what New England Biolabs meant to signify in its ad, which promised 'exceptional purity and unmatched value essential for success in your genomic research'.

In short, biotechnology, in general, and the Human Genome Project, in particular, aim high. No wonder the Human Genome Project's apologists called it biology's equivalent to putting a man on the moon. Where else could he go with all that thrust? The Human Genome Project is discursively produced as 'one small step . . .' At this origin, this new frontier, man's footprints are radioactive traces in a gel; at the dawn of hominization, the prints were made in volcanic dust at

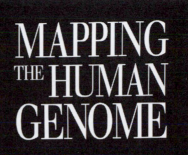

Figure 5.3 Global Native. Courtesy of New England BioLabs.

Laetoli in Ethiopia; at the dawn of the space age, a white man, acting as surrogate for mankind, walked in moon dust. All of these technoscientific travel narratives are about freedom, the free world, democracy, and, inevitably, the free market.

Representation, recursion, and the comic

Under the signifiers of freedom and democracy, a third Neibart cartoon (not illustrated here) completes this comic essay's catalogue of the savvy artist's potent jokes. Two senior white male scientists in business suits, one the same successful fellow who acquired the techno-humanist portrait of man in the form of a DNA separation gel, stand with their hands clenched above their heads in the sign of victory on a stage above a cheering mob at a political convention. The figures in the crowd wave the red, white, and blue banners inscribed with the names of their constituencies: DNA, protein, AGTC, RNA, PCR, and all the other molecular actors in the genomic drama. 'With 90% of the vote already in, it is a landslide' for the E-C Apparatus Corporation's power supply. The joke makes the concretized entities of the biotechnological laboratory into the voters in the democracy of science. The molecules and processes – themselves the feat of the scientists in the productive drama of the laboratory – are the actors with a vengeance. The sedimented feats of technoscientific virtuosity authorize their ventriloquists under the sign of freedom and choice. This is material subject construction, Oedipal and not.

Jokingly ironized in the Neibart cartoon, this scene is also gene fetishism at its most literal. Literary, social, and material technologies converge to make the objects speak, just as Shapin and Schaffer showed us in the story of Robert Boyle's air pump.[40] In the culture of no culture conjugated with the nature of no nature, the objects speak with a withering directness.

It is not new to link the stories of science and democracy, any more than it is new to link science, genius, and art, or to link strange night births and manly scientific creations. But the interlocking family of narratives in the contemporary US technoscientific drama is stunning. The Neibart cartoon must be read in the context of *Science 85*'s cover of a decade ago, 'The American Revolution'. The magazine cover featured the chip and the gene, figured, as always, as the double helix, against the colours of red, white, and blue, signifying the New World Order, Inc., of nature 'enterprised up',[41] where free trade and freedom implode. This warped field is where, to misquote the Supreme Court Chief Justice, 'Life Itself is always an experiment'. It is also a venture in marketing.

What are advertisements in technoscience doing? Do the ads in magazines like *Science* matter, and if so, how? Can I make a case for reading these materials as even gently ironic, rather than celebratory and instrumental in strengthening gene fetishism? Is anxious humour enough to force the trope into the open and disrupt literalism? Who besides me is anxiously laughing or crying at these ads? I do not know enough about how ad designers in technoscience produce their work, how graphic artists' views do and do not converge with scientists' or corporate managers' discourse, or how readers appropriate and rework ad images and text. I do know that the ads are more than pretty designs and helpful information. They are part of the visual culture that makes the gene fetish – and the epistemology of the gene fetishist – so productive.

Although many of the ads contain considerable technical information, I do not think a strong case can be made for seeing these ads principally as sales strategies. The companies that supply the key equipment and products to biological and engineering labs have more effective mechanisms for informing and servicing clients. Company and product name recognition is enhanced, and I would not argue against modest functionalist economic readings of such ads. Urged to learn more about potentially powerful tools, readers get toll-free phone numbers and reader-response cards for ordering catalogues.

More significantly, the readers of these ads taste the pleasures of narrative and figuration, of recognizing stories and images of which one is part. Advertising is not just the official art of capitalism; it is also a master teacher of history and theology in postmodernity. The debates about historical and literary canons should be taking place in graphic artists' studios in corporations, as well as in classrooms. The ads draw from and contribute to a narrative and visual world that activates the unconscious mechanisms that issue in the possibility of a joke. The joke is a sign of successful interpellation, of finding oneself constituted as a subject of knowledge and power in these regions of sociotechnical space. Whoever is inside that joke is inside the materialized narrative fields of technoscience, where, in the words of a recent Du Pont ad, 'better things for better living come to life'. These ads work by interpellation, by calling an audience into the story, more than by informing instrumentally rational market or laboratory behaviour. Such interpellation is the precondition of any subsequent rationality, in epistemology or in other such duplicitous free markets. In the Book of Life Itself, fetishism in all its flavours is comic to the end.

Finally, the Neibart cartoons draw on the comic in quite another sense than 'funny'. In the literary analysis of the comic mode in drama, 'comic' means reconciled, in harmony, secure in the confidence of the restoration of the normal and non-contradictory. Shakespeare's comedies are not funny; rather, their endings restore the normal and harmonious, often through the ceremonies of marriage, through which opposites are brought together. The comic does not recognize any contradictions that cannot be resolved, any tragedy or disaster that cannot be healed. The comic mode in technoscience is reassuring in just this way.[42] For those who would reassure us, the comic is just the right mode for approaching the end of the second Christian millennium.

Edgy and nervous, I must end by jokingly repeating myself in a comic recursion that restores few harmonies. In a Sydney Harris cartoon in *Science*, a white male researcher in a lab-coat reads to a white female scientist, similarly dressed, surrounded by their experimental animals and equipment, 'Here it is in Genesis: "He took one of Adam's ribs and made the rib into a woman." Cloning, if I ever heard it'[43] Woman™ cultured from the osteoblasts of Man™: this Genesis replicates salvation history compulsively, repeating *in saecula saeculorum* 'a few words about reproduction from an acknowledged leader in the field'.[44]

Figuring the implosion of informatics and biologics, this bastard scriptural quotation comes from a Logic General Corporation ad for a 1980s software duplication system. In the foreground, under the earth-sun logo of Logic General, a biological white rabbit has her paws on the grid of a computer keyboard. The long-eared rodent is a cultural sign of fecundity, and 'breeding like rabbits' is a popular figure of speech. But Logic General's hare, a brand of technoscientific Easter Bunny, evokes the pregnancy-test rodent famous in the history of reproductive medicine. Looking into the screen of a video display terminal, the organic rabbit faces its computer-generated image, who locks its cybergaze with the ad's reader. In her natural electronic habitat, the virtual rabbit is on a grid that insists on the world as a game played on a chess-like board, or Cartesian grid, made up of a square array of floppy disks. The disks constitute a kind of Mercator™ projection at the end of the second Christian millennium. The replication-test bunny is a player in *SimLife*. Remember the game ad's version of the injunction to be fruitful and multiply: 'Give life to different species in the lab and customize their look with the icon editor.'

Both the pregnancy-test and replication-test rabbits in the Logic General ad are cyborgs – compounds of the organic, technical, mythic, textual, economic, and political. They call us, interpellate us, into a world in which we are reconstituted as technoscientific subjects. Inserted into the matrices of technoscientific maps, we may or may not wish to take shape there. But, literate in the material-semiotic practices proper to the technical-mythic territories of the laboratory, we have little choice. We inhabit these narratives, and they inhabit us. The figures and the stories of these places haunt us, literally. The reproductive stakes in Logic General's text – and in all the tropic, materializing action of the laboratory – are future life forms and ways of life for humans and unhumans. The genome map is about cartographies of struggle – against gene fetishism and for livable technoscientific corporealizations.

Notes

1 Thanks especially to Sarah Franklin, Helen Watson-Verran, Caroline Jones, Peter Galison, and Bruno Latour. The uncut essay appears in my book, *Modest_Witness @Second_Millennium. Female-Man©_Meets_OncoMouse™* (New York: Routledge, 1996).
2 Michael Bremer, *SimLife User Manual* (Orinda, Cal.: Maxis, Bremer, 1992), p. 9.
3 David Harvey, *The Condition of Postmodernity* (Oxford: Basil Blackwell, 1989), p. 245.
4 Johnny L. Wilson, *The SimEarth Bible* (Berkeley: McGraw Hill, 1991), p. xviii.
5 Richard Dawkins, *The Extended Phenotype* (London: Oxford University Press, 1982), p. 82. On the gene as a sacralized object in US culture, see Dorothy Nelkin and M. Susan Lindee, *The DNA Mystique* (New York: Freeman, 1995), pp. 38–57.
6 Sarah Franklin, 'Life Itself' 9 June 1993, Center for Cultural Values, Lancaster University. See also Sarah Franklin, 'Life', in *Encyclopedia of Bioethics* (New York: Macmillan, forthcoming) and 'Romancing the Helix', in *Romance Revisited*, ed. L. Pearce and J. Stacey (London: Falmer Press, 1995), pp. 63–7.
7 Michel Foucault, *The Order of Things* (New York: Pantheon, 1971); and *The*

History of Sexuality, vol. 1, trans. Robert Hurley (New York: Pantheon, 1978). Barbara Duden, *Disembodying Women* (Cambridge, Mass.: Harvard University Press, 1993).

8 Franklin, 'Romancing the Helix', p. 67.

9 Chandra Talpade Mohanty, 'Cartographies of Struggle', in *Third World Women and the Politics of Feminism*, ed. C. Mohanty, A. Russo, and L. Torres (Bloomington: Indiana University Press, 1991).

10 Sharon Traweek, *Beamtimes and Lifetimes* (Cambridge, Mass.: Harvard University Press, 1988), p. 162.

11 See Helen Watson-Verran, 'Re-negotiating What's Natural', Society for Social Studies of Science, 12–15 October 1994, New Orleans, for analysis of how both admitted and denied tropes work within knowledge systems developed by European and aboriginal Australians in contending for land possession. Communication in power-laced practical circumstances makes the work of codification, situating, and mobilization of categories explicit for all parties, changing everybody and everything in the process, including the categories. This kind of articulation precludes fetishism – nothing gets to be self-identical. The maps and the facts turn out to be tropic to the core and *therefore* part of knowledge practices. This analysis is important for understanding knowledge production in general, including natural science.

12 Georg Lukács, *History and Class Consciousness*, trans. Rodney Livingstone (Cambridge, Mass.: MIT Press, 1971), p. 83.

13 Karl Marx, *Capital*, vol. 1, trans. Ben Fowkes (New York: Random House, 1976), p. 176.

14 Sandra Harding, *Whose Science? Whose Knowledge?* (Ithaca: Cornell University Press, 1991).

15 See Michael Flower and Deborah Heath, 'Anatomo-Politics: Mapping the Human Genome Project', *Culture, Medicine and Psychiatry* 17 (1993): 27–41, for the semiotic-material negotiations solidifying the 'consensus DNA sequence' that instantiates 'the' human genome.

16 The word 'fetish' is rooted in a mistake and disavowal of the colonialist and racist kind, one shared by both Marx and Freud, in which 'Westerners' averred that 'Primitives' mistook objects to be the real embodiment or habitation of magical spirits and power. Fetishism, these rational observers claimed, was a kind of misplaced concreteness that depended on 'Primitives' lower powers of abstract reasoning and inferior forms of religious faith. 'Primitive' fetishes were about 'magical thinking'; i.e. they were about the potency of wishes, where the desire was mistaken for the presence of its referent. Anthropologists discarded this doctrine of fetishism, but the racialized meaning, connoting the underdeveloped, irrational, and pathological, persists in many domains. The irony of the doctrine of 'primitive' fetishes is that, if one follows Whitehead's explanation of the 'fallacy of misplaced concreteness' that comes from the belief in simple location, relation-and observer-free pre-existing objects, and a metaphysics of substantives with primary and secondary qualities, then the children of the Scientific Revolution are the world's first and maybe only serious fetishists, whose most extraordinary abstractions are taken to be reality itself. See A. N. Whitehead, *Science and the Modern World* (New York: Mentor, 1948, orig. 1925), pp. 41–56.

17 Sigmund Freud, 'Fetishism', in *Sexuality and the Psychology of Love*, ed. P. Rieff (New York: Collier, 1963, orig. 1927), p. 205.

18 Laura Mulvey, 'Some Thoughts on Theories of Fetishism in the Context of Contemporary Culture', *October* 65 (Summer 1993): 3–20, p. 7.

19 Richard Lewontin, 'The Dream of the Human Genome', *New York Review of Books* (28 May 1992): 31–40, p. 33.

20 Whitehead, *Science and the Modern World*, p. 52.

21 A. N. Whitehead, *Process and Reality* (New York: Free Press, [1929] 1969, p. 28.

22 Harvey, *Condition of Postmodernity*, p. 63.

23 *Science* (1 February 1991): back cover.

24 Evelyn Fox Keller, *Secrets of Life, Secrets of Death* (New York: Routledge, 1992), pp. 39–55.

25 Carol Vogel, 'Leonardo Notebook Sells for $30.8 Million', *New York Times* (12 November 1994): A1, A11.

26 Sequenase™, a DNA polymerase used in sequence analysis, is marketed in versions, for example, Sequenase Version 1.0 or 2.0, like software, such as Microsoft Word 5.0 – another signifier of the bond between informatics and genomics.

27 Joan O'C. Hamilton, 'Biotech: An Industry Crowded with Players Faces an Ugly Reckoning', *Business Week* (26 September 1994): 84–90, p. 85.

28 *Science* 18, 1 (1995): 77. A non-radioactive DNA-detection tool from Boehringer Mannheim is called Genius™ System, with the slogan 'leaving the limits behind'. An ad in *Biotechniques* 17, 3 (1994): 511, links the Genius™ System protocols with the toe pads of a tree frog, 'allowing it to perform the most sensitive maneuvers . . . in pursuit of insect prey'. The company offers natural design, delicacy, transcendence, and genius. Who could want more?

29 François Gros, 'The Changing Face of the Life Sciences', *UNESCO Courier* (1988): 7.

30 *Science* 250 (12 October 1990).

31 Daniel Koshland, Jr, 'The Rational Approach to the Irrational' *Science* 250 (12 October 1990): 189.

32 Nelkin and Lindee, *DNA Mystique*, pp. 81–2. Thomas J. Bouchard, Jr, D. T. Lykken, M. McGue, N. L. Segal, and A. Tellegen, 'Sources of Human Psychological Differences: The Minnesota Studies of Twins Reared Apart', *Science* 250 (12 October 1990): 223–8. Arthur Jensen, 'How Much Can We Boost IQ and Scholastic Achievement?', *Harvard Educational Review* 39 (Winter 1969): 1–123.

33 *Science* 250 (12 October 1990): 185.

34 Harvey, *Condition of Postmodernity*, pp. 244–52.

35 *Ibid.*, p. 246.

36 Bruno Latour, *Science in Action* (Cambridge, Mass.: Harvard University Press, 1987), pp. 215–57.

37 Barbara Culliton, 'Mapping *Terra Incognita* (*Humani Corporis*)', *Science* 250 (12 October 1990): 210–12.

38 Geoff Bowker, 'How to Be Universal: Some Cybernetic Strategies', *Social Studies of Science* 23 (1993): 107–27.

39 Latour, *Science in Action*, p. 245. J. C. Stephens, M. L. Cavanaugh, M. I. Gradie, M. L. Mador, and K. K. Kidd, 'Mapping the Human Genome: Current Status', *Science* 250 (12 October 1990): 237–44.

40 Steven Shapin and Simon Schaffer, *Leviathan and the Air-Pump: Hobbes, Boyle, and the Experimental Life* (Princeton: Princeton University Press, 1985).

41 Marilyn Strathern, *Reproducing the Future* (New York: Routledge, 1992), p. 39.

42 See Sharon Helsel, 'The Comic Reason of Herman Kahn' (Ph.D. dissertation, History of Consciousness Board, University of California at Santa Cruz, 1993).

43 *Science* 251 (1 March 1991): 1050.

44 *Science* (1 May 1983), Logic General Corporation advertisement.

6 Reading genes/writing nation: Reith, 'race' and the writings of geneticist Steve Jones

Deborah Lynn Steinberg

The era of genetic engineering capabilities is now entering its fourth decade. By now, the gene has emerged as perhaps the quintessential icon of both scientific progress and popular imagination. Since 1970, new developments in recombinant DNA technology have appeared at a staggering pace, heralding radical transformations in medical, industrial and agricultural practices and in common-sense understandings of disease, kinship and identity.[1] The gene itself has become, at once, a dominant cultural referent for processes of social and biological reproduction and a key cultural metaphor for the re-articulation of 'race', nation and otherwise imagined bodies and communities.[2] Indeed, the entry of the language of genes into popular discourse has crossed most representational genres from documentary reportage to science fiction, from textbook to comic strip, from metaphor to gag.[3] An emergent strand of critical writing about the interrelationships of professional and popular spheres of scientific common sense has emphasised the narrative character both of scientific discourse and of the role of the scientist as author in both contexts.[4] Indeed, an examination of moments of popularisation with respect to particular scientific enterprises can reveal the ways in which the social relations and conceptual trajectories of scientific cultures shape and are shaped by broader popular discourses.[5]

This chapter will provide an examination of one such moment of nexus between professional and popular sensibilities surrounding the science of genetics. Through a close textual analysis of the 1991 Reith Lectures – entitled *The Language of the Genes* and delivered by Steve Jones, then Reader (now Professor) in Genetics at University College London – this chapter will consider the textual economies, narrative and metaphoric, through which the science of genetics is translated for a popular, albeit elite, audience. I am particularly interested in the use of the metaphor of 'language' for the ways in which it would seem to democratise the expert conceptual terrains of science and to invite a familiar, communicative relationship with the non-scientific reader. Additionally, the languages of literacy – of reading and writing genes; the conceptualisation of genes as reproductive and metamorphic bodies; and the narrative conventions through which genes are envisioned, on the one hand, as the dominant discursive consituents of 'race' and 'nation', while, on the other, they are disclaimed for racism and nationalism – will be semiotically traced in the imagined pasts and futures that constitute Jones's vision of genetic science.

Specifically, the chapter begins with a brief examination of the British Broadcasting Corporation, the immediate context for the Reith Lectures slot, and considers the role of both in the production of a particular, if contradictory, version of British nation. Against this backdrop, Jones's lectures are considered for the ways which these notions of Britishness mediate the representation of genes, genetic science and Jones himself as geneticist. Discussion in this context will, as noted above, focus in particular on metaphors of language and literacy. Finally, the analysis will turn to the textual and subtextual motifs surrounding 'race' and 'nation' as articulated through Jones's claims for an anti-racist genetics.

The 'best of British': British broadcasting, the Reith Lectures and the production of nation

Steve Jones's Reith Lectures were broadcast over BBC Radio 4 over a five-week period in the autumn of 1991.[6] These lectures were significant for a number of reasons. First, they constituted a formative moment in the contemporary dispersal of genetic discourse into wider cultural common sense in Britain. Not only did they herald in their small way (as the Hollywood film *Jurassic Park* would do on a grand scale) what would become a vertiable genetification of popular vernacular, but, unlike *Jurassic Park*, they offered a version of genetics peculiarly inflected with a notional Britishness. They also launched Jones himself as a mass media 'star' of sorts, the new populist translator of the arcane 'languages of the gene' who would not only cross cultures from laboratory to lay, but cross genres from the high-brow of coffee-table science books to the 'low' of an automobile advert on television. Third, the lectures foregrounded a number of thematic trajectories and tensions that have come to pervade debates within genetic science itself and the project of its popularisation. These include contestatory imaginaries, dystopian and utopian, that have widely characterised speculations about the potential impact and futures of genetics.

The immediate context of Jones's lectures has particular pertinence for the meanings accruing to them. As part of a tradition of such talks, going back to the inception of the BBC, both Jones's performance as Reith Lecturer and the subject matter of his lectures necessarily draw on and reinvest in the historical currency of British broadcasting with its postwar (First World War), post-Victorian and incipiently post-imperial agenda of, on the one hand, paternalistic moral uplift and public service (the education of the poor towards its 'better British self'), and on the other, public interest and social responsibility (the promotion of a more democratic society).[7]

The talks tradition, beginning with the National Lectures in 1928, later becoming the Reith Lectures, perhaps best encapsulate the 'high culture' version of Britishness espoused in the British broadcasting tradition.[8] The talks format, and the National Lectures in particular, were, as Scannell and Cardiff write, 'designed to hold the blue ribbon of broadcasting and to provide, on two or three occasions in the year, for the discussion of issues of major importance and the interpretation of new knowledge by men of distinction in the world of scholarship and affairs' (1981: 182). The intrinsically classed and gendered (and implicitly racialised) paternalism implied in the National Lectures remit where professional intellectuals, particularly those of a liberal persuasion, bring high culture to the public, formed the direct model for the Reith Lectures[9] (and its long line of almost exclusively white, male and middle-class Lecturers).[10]

With Jones's *The Language of the Genes*, the particular connotations of Britishness and intellectual elitism invested in the Reith Lectures, and in the Reithian tradition more broadly, are thus implicitly constitutive both of Jones's own profile as, ostensibly the educated 'better self' of Britain and that of the object of his expertise – genetics. In this context, Jones's Lectures were a key moment of transition for both the science and the scientist in a number of respects. First, the Lectures provided a moment where an exclusive professional discourse was (re)articulated as a popular narration and where a seemingly unassuming man of science became, of sorts, a star. Jones's own self-effacing presentation as a rather eccentric snail geneticist[11] who sat all day watching snails or sequencing proteins seemed resonant of a particular version of quaint, safe, even charmingly gauche masculinity popularly embodied as the unassuming yet genius and very British boffin. Second, as science repackaged for the people, Jones's translation of the arcane languages and practices of genetics promised both access to and popular ownership of the privileged terrain of bodies (of knowledge and of knowers) that matter.[12] In this context, the constitution of preferred audience was clearly aspirationally located in middle-class (perhaps even upper-middle-class), professional England. Finally, the resonances of these particular versions of Britishness subliminally associated genetic science with the putative qualities of legitimacy, social responsibility, moral and educative uplift and just paternalism connoted by the Reithian tradition itself. Genetics, in other words, became in this moment, if not transformed into, then at least implicated in a mutually validating project of nation (for example, as a national resource) as well as of expertise.

Received pronunciations: genes and the language of language

> [In] its programmes and policies, [the BBC] set out to *address* the nation it had so constructed and then become its 'Voice' . . . The whole gamut of 'national voices' was reflected back to the nation through the medium of the sound waves. Yet the Standard Voice – the 'received' accent, pronunciation, tonal pitch of the 'BBC voice' – circumscribed and *placed* them all. This was *not*, of course, 'Cockney' or 'Scouse' or even, quite, 'Oxbridge'. It was a variant synthesis of the educated, middle-class speech of the Home Counties.
>
> (Hall 1982: 33, original emphasis)

Given the historical (indeed almost cliché) centrality of 'received pronunciation'[13] to the BBC's construction of Britishness, the language and literacy metaphors that permeate Jones's *pronunciations* about genes take on a particular resonance. They become at once a familiar touchstone through which the broadcasting public may aspirationally identify themselves in the articulations of expert culture and agency and an ostensible invitation into the democratisation of science such metaphors seem to herald.

Genes and the metaphor(s) of language

As the title of the Lecture series suggests, the notion of genes *as* a language constitutes the framing metaphor for his Jones's consideration of the cultural significance of genetic science. In the very first lecture, entitled 'A Message from Our Ancestors', there is a direct attribution both linguistic and narrative functions to genes:

> Genetics is a language, a set of instructions passed from generation to generation. It has a vocabulary – the genes themselves, a grammar – the way in which the inherited information is arranged, and a literature – the thousands of instructions needed to make a human being.
>
> (1991: 4)

> Our understanding about our place in nature has been transformed by the new ability to read inherited messages from the past.
>
> (1991: 2)

> We can use [genes] to piece together a picture of human history more complete than from any other source.
>
> (1991: 3)

The gene thus emerges as a structural singularity, an embodied enscription of both meaning, in the historical sense, and function in the material sense. The ascription of a narrative property to the gene is implicit in the language metaphor (and graphic in the 'history' metaphor) with their connotations of recording, of purposeful communication ('messages' are 'passed'; 'instructions' are 'pictures more complete than from any other source'). In this formulation, the genetic scientist as reader, decodes, though significantly does not produce, is a recipient rather than mediator of meanings construed as already embedded, already intact in the structure of human (and, by implication, other species') biology. A number of interesting implications accrue to this notion of genes. First is the double movement of the notion of a language of nature. On the one hand, genes are constituted in terms of authorship, the agency of meaning production located as biological essence. At the same time, language is similarly essentialised in structuralist, positivistic terms. The denotative properties, of genes as words, their 'truths' as it were, emerge as twin certainties. Indeed, these certainties include 'errors in the message, genetic abnormalities' which are taken to represent 'sometimes . . . the only clues of shared descent' (1991: 3).

Genes and the metaphor of text

A second and similar set of implications accrues to the construction of genes as texts. As suggested in an earlier passage quoted above, one of the guiding claims of the Lectures is that genes encode an historical record more accurate than from any other source. Indeed, Jones periodically dismisses the fields of psychology, education and history, for their purportedly incomplete, inaccurate or ill-intentioned explanations of identities, societies and migrations. In his discussion of scientific racisms and the eugenics movement, for example, Jones begins by identifying the role of biology as a science in the service of prejudice (1991: 45), but then displaces this history onto anthropology (and at other points, psychology and education), which not only 'waited years in trying to sort out divisions into which people could be classified [thus illustrating that] it is only a tiny step from classifying people to judging them' (1991: 47). Biology, however, is recuperated with the assertion that it has now broken 'the ties between the genetics and politics of race' (1991: 48). How it is that anthropology's misguided taxonomy of 'imaginary pure races' (1991: 47) is not replicated in contemporary genetic taxonomies, Jones does not explain. One is left with the implication (and at times the explicit assertion as discussed below) that contemporary genetics, because of its purportedly unprecedented accuracy, is an antidote to the excesses that accrued to its not-really-scientific past.

In this context, the gene appears to represent a peculiar elision of narrative and nature. On the one hand, history (as a set of social/cultural practices) is understood literally to *write* genes. Yet at the same time, genes are taken not only to materially *enscribe* historical events, but indeed as superordinate *narrational* records of culture, identity and meaning.

> Sometimes history itself is a clue as to where to start. Alex Haley, in his book *Roots*, used documents on the slave trade to try to find his African ancestors. He found only one, Kunta Kinte by name, who had been taken as a slave from the Gambia in 1767. The patterns of genetic diversity in today's black Americans could have told him much more . . . Alex Haley, by comparing his genes with those from different African countries, might have learned much more about his ancestors than he could from the written records.
>
> (1991: 7–8)

Jones's invocation of *Roots* as illustrative of the limits of social history and potentiality of genetics takes the textual metaphor to a number of disturbing conclusions. First is that genes enscribe a precise taxonomy of racial/ethinc origins. Here racial, ethnic and national identities elide, emerging as definitive homogeneities – i.e. the putative Gambian gene. Second is the positivist notion that genetic profiling not only (accurately) traces racial, ethnic and national migrations but that these tracings are meaningful, indeed more meaningful, when they are stripped of political and economic context (as described in the documentations of the slave trade). Thus while historical records may suggest the locus of significant genes, the 'real', objective and unadulterated story resides in biology. Historians (like anthropologists) produce imagined communities and identities, while geneticists discern their truths. Here we have the apotheosis of reductive history, scientifically rendered. A DNA map could have saved Alex Haley the trip.

This positivist investment in the precision of genetic profiling, premised as it is on a denial of interpretive agency on the part of the geneticist, seems utterly to dismiss historical contingency, ambiguity and complexity. As with the *Roots* example, most of the lectures are preoccupied with migrations, but only as movements of populations, with the political exigencies of those movements (invasion, colonial occupation and underdevelopment, civil war) euphemised or ignored. Thus the 'roots' and routes of nation and identity become stripped to discrete, reified biological traits constituted as emblematic of such differences: the 'Hapsburg lip' of European Royalty (1991: 3); Gambian DNA that codes for 'sickle-cell' (1991: 8); Kenyans' long legs (1991: 23). In textual terms, the 'reading' of genes as *documentary* evidence interprets, essentialises and narrates social history as (a functional effect of) evolutionary biology.

Genes and the metaphor(s) of literacy

Literacy, the ability to read and write, has, I would suggest, connotations of the chief values associated with a democratic society: freedom of expression, self- and communal empowerment, full citizenship. These connotations accrue in no small part from the historical centrality of education to both progressive liberal and revolutionary movements for social liberation. Struggles for education have been central, for example, to anti-oppressive struggles for freedom, for citizenship, for equality.[14] Similarly, as many commentators have argued,[15] the complex classed, gendered and racialised relations of expertise revolve, in part, around the politics of access to the languages and texts of professionals. The marginalisation of women in (or their exclusion from) scientific professions, for example, has been underpinned by the marginalisation or exclusion of girls and women from science education (Whitelegg 1992).[16] Finally, literacy and the lack thereof are deeply embedded in the constitution of national identity in at least two key respects: first, as a condition of access to or marginalisation from citizenship; and second, as a matrix through which the notional histories, boundaries and exclusionary unities of nationhood are written, read and *materialised* (Butler 1993).[17] The authorship of nation, the constitution of its preferred memberships (and the preferred readings thereof), are thus embedded in unequal conditions of access to the hegemonic (very often expert) languages, the literal and figurative passwords, of legitimate(d) national identity.

On the one hand, Jones's framing genes and genetics through metaphors of language, text, reading and writing can be said to invoke the liberatory connotations of literacy. Indeed, resonant with the Reithian educational remit, the Lectures represent a not insignificant effort to open the linguistic borders between science and 'the people'. It is not often, after all, that scientists take on an explicitly educative role through popular culture or demonstrate a sense of professional accountability to those outside their circles. At the same time, the use of the languages of literacy in this context raise significant questions about the extent to which they represent a substantive challenge to the exclusionary relations of expertise. When Jones tells us what he reads of genes, in other words, he does not confer upon us the ability to read them ourselves. The putative 'language of the genes', notwithstanding its conscription into familiar analogies or popular mythologies, is premised on the language of *genetics* – an expert discourse; a terrain of conceptual authority and empirical application effectively closed to those who have won no legitimate right of trespass. The notion of 'reading genes' is a metaphor which both refers to and obscures the mechanics of the 'reading' process – those complex feats of biochemistry, micro- and IT engineering that constitute the laboratory protocols of recombinant DNA science. However user-friendly it may sound, 'reading' genes is not like reading.

Similarly, the metaphor of writing, although taken up only marginally in the Lectures, is none the less implicitly and inextricably linked to a notion of reading. In this context, the power to 'read' genes is, in part, embedded in the power to manipulate them; to, in effect, 're write' the organism – the substantive meaning of *recombinant* DNA techniques.[18] Here too, *editorial* decisions about which genes are meaningful, which genes can or should be mapped, cut, copied or pasted, which should be deleted are predicated on the gendered, classed and racialised closures and institutionalised dependencies that shore up the boundaries of professional expertise, authority and authorship. The effective closures of the genetics reading/writing community have particular implications for Jones's claims for socio- or historo-genetics. For example, even as genetics is defined by its exclusivity, so too is the historical record ostensibly produced through the 'reading' of genes.[19] Genetics rarefies rather than democratises the journey for 'roots': fostering increasing dependencies of a wider public on professional readers; intensifying, albeit in potentially restructured forms, the multiple social divisions organised around scientific expertise. In its effective reinvestment in universalising explanations of social formations and historical movements *as 'nature'* moreover, it reduces rather than expands what is constituted as meaningful and who may be considered legitimate meaning-makers.

Articulated tensions: reading genes/writing (anti)racism

The tensions in Jones's Lectures surrounding the representational economies of language and literacy inform a similarly ambivalent evaluation of the relationship of genes to questions of race/ism and nation. As I shall discuss below, two rather contradictory currents shape the text in these respects proposing on the one hand a genetics that mitigates against racism and on the other a science continuing in the service of racial and national taxonomisation.

Re-mapping anatomical geographies

Jones proposes genetics as antidote to racism in two key respects, both of which, he argues, represent significant breaks from the past 'grim' relationship between science and racism (Jones 1991: 46). First is the claim that genetics challenges and puts paid to the notion of biologically discrete races, a notion which Jones views as the basis of racism:

> Genetics has at last given us a way of testing the pure race theory.
>
> (1991: 49)

> Individuals – not nations and not races – are the main repository for genes whose function is known. The idea that humanity is divided up into a series of distinct groups is quite wrong. The ancient private homeland in the Caucasus – the cradle of the white race – was just a myth.
>
> (1991: 51)

> Even forty years ago, racial stereotypes of the most predictable kind were the norm among psychologists. They were the last remnant of the idea of racial type, a view which biologists had abandoned long before.
>
> (1991: 52)

Science, in this construction, emerges ambivalently: on the one hand as implicated in (but in a lesser way) such common senses of racial difference yet, on the other hand, as a counter-hegemonic discourse which now, thanks to developments in genetics, has the tools to reveal the erroneous and unscientific foundations of racial discrimination. In this context, Jones points out that 'race' itself is an unstable category with historically shifting notions of the boundaries understood to constitute a racial identity or characteristic. Jones points up skin colour in particular as an historically contested marker of race (1991: 46) Genetics, he argues, empirically destabilises racial categories, having the capacity both to reveal *individuals* rather than groups as the repository of biological difference(s) and thus, to, disassociate (the taxonomisation of) *traits* from (the construction of) identity. This, in turn, has implications for the relationship between 'race' and racism:

> Other creatures vary much more from place to place [than humans] . . . The genetic differences between the snail populations of two Pyrenean valleys are much greater than that between Australian aboriginals and ourselves. The difference between the highland and the lowland populations of the mountain gorilla a few miles apart in central Africa is more than that between any two human groups. If you are a snail or a mountain gorilla, it makes good biological sense to be a racist; but if you're not, you have to accept the fact that humans are a tediously uniform species.
>
> (1991: 51)

Although this passage is written in a rather tongue-in-cheek vein, the implication that racism *legitimately* accrues from racial differences which can be validated empirically is nevertheless inescapable. Racism is wrong when/because there is just not enough 'real' difference to justify it. Genetics then becomes a tool to remedy the injustices caused by illegitimate racial categorisation, as opposed to biological categorisation *per se*. There is clearly a mixed message here: for if genetics reveals 'real' differences and these differences can be taxonomically mapped, then what is implied is not a rejection but a reconstitution of 'race' – the grounds, in other words, for a 'new racism'.[20]

Thus, at the same time that Jones appears to reject 'race' as a meaningful category, it re-emerges, threading through the text in an uneasy counter-motif. Race, for example, is a key analogy through which Jones explains the mechanisms of genetic inheritance.[21] References, as noted earlier, to royal pedigrees and to racial or ethnically based taxonomies of disease[22] or physical traits recuperate the very foundationalist notions of human difference that Jones disclaims for contemporary genetics. So too do characteristic elisions of racial and national identity that permeate the text:

> We, the British, contain more hunting genes than do, say, the Greeks, who had rolled over the earlier economy and absorbed its genes long before.
>
> (1991: 41)

> Throughout modern Europe, we can see patches of genes which reflect the successes and failures of nations and economies long gone . . . today's southern Italians and Sicilians are still genetically distinct from their compatriots in the north.
>
> (1991: 41)

> A genetic map of Europe shows that most language boundaries are in fact regions of genetic change. In Wales, there are genetic differences between Welsh and English speakers.
>
> (1991: 42)

> Genes persist far longer and can tell us much more about the past [than language] . . . We see this in the Etruscans [whose language and culture are now extinct].
>
> (1991: 43)

> We can use genes to make a family tree of human kind, and to reconstruct the relationships of the peoples of the world. Africans as a group are on a branch of the human family which split off from the others rather early on, and most of the rest of us are more closely related to each other than we are to the populations so far tested in Africa.
>
> (1991: 52)

These passages represent a distinctively corporealised/reified – i.e. *racialised* – notion of nation embedded in genetic profiles, its multicultural constituencies obscured, mapped out instead as discrete homogeneities (*the* English, *the* Welsh, *the* southern Italians). Indeed, as with the Etruscan example, genes are understood to encode national identity even where its usual cultural markers (e.g. language) are 'extinct'. The representation, furthermore, of Africans as a branch of humanity 'split off' from 'the rest of us' not only connotatively elides Africa a nation with African as black race (even as 'English' evokes 'white') but resonates colonial and eugenic notions of racial hierarchy.[23] Such implications are reinforced through discussions, elsewhere in the lectures, of 'modern primitive' cultures like the Yanomamo tribe of South America among whom '[r]ape, murder and theft are common' (p. 37) or India, putative home of sex selection practices where 'being female is often seen as a genetic disease' (1991: 58) as the repository of uncivilised, hyper-patriarchal values and practices[24] (but which nevertheless, or indeed because of this, may carry edifying messages about 'ourselves').

Rereading genetics after eugenics

The subtextual (and perhaps uncalculated) mobilisation of the racist common senses of colonial discourse inform similar contradictions in Jones's second, and related, claim for a remedial genetics revolving specifically around the question of eugenics.

> Much of the story of the genetics of race – a field promoted by some of the most eminent scientists of their day – turns out to have been prejudice dressed up as science, a classic example of the way that biology should not be used to help us understand ourselves. Most geneticists are genuinely ashamed of the early history of their subject and make every effort to distance themselves from it.
>
> (1991: 54)

Jones argues that contemporary genetics breaks from its early history in two key respects. First, as previously noted, Jones makes the sustained claim that contemporary genetics deals no longer in imaginary traits but in empirical realities: '[eugenics'] disgrace was made more complete by simple errors: the genes involved often did not exist outside the doctor's imagination' (1991: 57). This would seem to square uneasily, at the very least, with the association, elsewhere in the Lectures, of genetics with notional constructions of racial/national traits and heritage. Second, Jones argues that geneticists are no longer interested in the grand project of eugenic social engineering. He states, for example:

> We now have the answers to many of the genetical questions which obsessed the eugenics movement. However, there has been an odd shift in attitude: modern geneticists scarcely involve themselves with what their work implies for the future of humanity. They feel responsible to people rather than to populations, to individuals rather than to posterity.
>
> (1991: 57)

No serious scientist now has the slightest interest in reproducing a genetically planned society.

(1991: 58)

It is not clear how the individualisation of genetic selection obviates eugenics, particularly if contemporary genetics has 'given us the answers to many of the genetical questions which obsessed the eugenics movement'. Indeed, it can be argued that an increasingly common-sense ethos of reproductive screening might obviate the need for eugenic masters or grand plans. Nor is it clear how a more localised focus for genetic science eschews the quality of 'planning'. Clearly its applications do not operate in an institutional/conceptual vacuum. Jones, moreover, states that 'moral problems about the quality of people and whether we can, or should, make choices based on genes' (1991: 58) inevitably accrue from genetic screening. Yet this effective acknowledgement of a shared institutional ethos between past and present genetics is nevertheless dismissed in a double-edged recuperation of scientific agency. For Jones interprets the 'disgrace' of early genetics as a consequence of the prejudicial, hubristic and unrealistic intentionalities of (bad) scientists. In this context, and in a stunning contrast to Jones's own use of such grand narratives, contemporary scientists are construed to be no longer dangerous utopian visionaries but benign and modest practitioners invested in tracing lost histories and preventing disease, both quests now (properly) dislocated from questions of morality or politics. Jones concludes:

Fictional Utopias nearly all seem to evolve in roughly the same way. A master race imposes its will on lesser breeds, only to meet its doom because of its own biological failings . . . Evolution always builds on its weaknesses, rather than making a fresh start. It is this lack of a grand plan which has made life so adaptable, and humans – the greatest opportunists of all – so successful.

(1991: 61)

Jones's analogy argues for a genetics redeemed of its past 'failings', a eugenics purified of its previous obsessions and grandiosity, a progress and language, at last, restored to nature. Genetics, in other words, relocated to the putatively benign neutrality of natural selection, is thus seen to be rescued from ideology and its attendant bad intentionalities.

Conclusion

As it became possible to look to 'nature' for explanations for human society and character, so too was Darwin's loan 'read back', as Strathern describes it, enabling nature to become subject to visions of social improvement. This traffic . . . much as it has informed the Euro-American imagination more broadly . . . has specific roots in England where the national culture has long been formed in relation to the zig-zagging repeat of analogies linking nature, progress and society.

(Franklin 1997: 99)

As I have traced throughout this chapter, Jones's use of metaphors of language and literacy and his claims for an anti-racist genetics produce a seductive image of a science harnessing nature in the service of democracy and social progress. There is a distinct (if limited) register of popularisation, an apparently alternative (non-programmatic) programme of liberal social improvement, a promised breaking of links with a dubious past except in so far as lessons that have been learnt to the better. Yet on closer inspection, we find a science proposed as an antidote for problems in which it remains foundationally embedded. The apparent democratising tendencies of the Lectures are revealed as compromised, even duplicitous, effectively masking rather than challenging the institutional closures of expert agency. The claims for an anti-racist genetics, however well intentioned, emerge as little better than a rhetorical exercise, window dressing, a contradiction in terms as the foundationalist, patriarchal notions of race and nation which Jones appears to dismiss are immediately reinscribed. Finally, Jones's casting of contemporary genetics as a science no longer tainted by ideology or grandiose intentionalities constitutes an extraordinary denial of the putatively alternative ideological underpinnings of his own readings of genes and of the power relations accruing to his claims for genetic literacy.

The profound tensions characterising Jones's Lectures raise difficult questions about the limitations and potentialities that might constitute genetic science, whatever version is pursued. Can there be a genetics divorced from its own history? If the conceptualisation of genes is intrinsically embedded in foundationalist epistemology and ontological taxonomies (conventionally constituted, for example, as classed/gendered/racial/ethnic/national identities), how can an anti-racist/anti-oppressive genetics be possible? To paraphrase Illich (1976), how can the progressive genetification of life not produce a cultural iatrogenesis that exacerbates existing inequalities or creates unprecedented dependencies? Finally, does a liberal standpoint intrinsically support the totalitarian tendencies of scientific progress even as it promises to recuperate them for a better world?

Notes

1 See for example, Cook-Deegan 1994; Jones 1996; Kitcher 1996.
2 See Steinberg (2000) for further discussion on genes, narrative and embodiment.
3 This emergence of the gene as popular vernacular is evident in the by now ubiquitous reportage of gene-discovery stories (from gay genes to genes for anorexia), transgenic animal inventions (from Dolly the cloned sheep to transgenic pigs for transplant organs) and feats of forensic justice achieved through DNA fingerprinting. Similarly, genetic science has become an entrenched motif across genres of science fiction (from *Jurassic Park* to *The X Files*). Indeed, *The X Files* in particular has taken up the theme of 'mutant' genes as its dominant metaphor of 'alienness'

and its narrative problematisations of nations of nation, identity, science and 'truth'.

4 See for example, Jordanova (1986); Haraway (1992).

5 For an extended discussion of this point, see Steinberg (2000).

6 The lectures were broadcast on BBC Radio 4, Wednesday evenings from 13 November to 18 December 1991 and repeated on BBC Radio 3 on Saturdays, 16 November to 21 December 1991.

7 For further discussion see: Scannell and Cardiff (1981); Hall (1982); MacCabe and Stewart (1986); Scannell (1990).

8 The British Broadcasting Corporation, incorporated in 1922, was founded on the twin, and highly contradictory, principles of paternalism and democratisation. Named for its first director John Reith, the Reithian tradition of British broadcasting was styled as a veritable cultural dictatorship. It was to be an institutional arbiter and elevator of tastes, standards and audience needs aimed to cultivate 'the best of British' culture. At the same time, through its role as a public utility, the BBC was intended to make a contribution to an informed, educated public and a more participatory society. Indeed, Scannell (1990) has argued that the central organising contradiction of the BBC derives from two histories: on the one hand, a Victorian middle-class notion of 'public service'; and on the other, a notion of public 'interest' which had developed out of democratic political struggle. The notion of 'service', Scannell explains, articulates a 'Victorian reforming ideal of service . . . animated by a sense of moral purpose and of social duty on behalf of the community, aimed particularly at those [deemed] most in need of reform – the lower classes' (p. 22). In the context of broadcasting, reform focused on paternalistic assessments of the educational and cultural needs of the poor and reflected a concern for 'social unity mingled with national pride' (p. 23), thus linking culture with nationalism. By contrast, the notion of public interest is grounded in struggles for political and civil rights – free speech, public assembly, the right to vote. This translated into the Reithian committment to the development of mass democracy through broadcasting. Thus the BBC was thus constituted, as Hall (1982) has noted, as an agency for the promotion as well as the containment of democracy. In this context, hegemonic struggles over definitions of culture and national identity were imbued with the classed, gendered and racialised inequalities embedded in British society.

9 They also set the tone for and other talks slots, both on radio and television. For example, the 'David Dimbleby Lecture' broadcast on television in November 1997 follows in this tradition.

10 Indeed, the centrality of both liberalism and Britishness to the slot emerged pointedly in the minor furore, particularly in the *Daily Mail* tabloid, that surrounded the invitation of Patricia J. Williams to perform as Reith Lecturer in 1997. That Williams was clearly perceived as neither a 'fit' nor a 'fitting' choice accrued not only to the drawing-room masculinity and whiteness of the Reithian heritage but also to the liberal politics which have historically characterised previous lecturers. Williams is not only an African-American woman but an American lawyer (evidently not perceived as a suitably elevated and respectable occupation) who not only is not a liberal but indeed has a radical critique of precisely the white liberal political agenda of the Reithian heritage.

11 In an interview on Radio 4 the week preceding the delivery of his first lecture, Jones made jokes about a life of snail-watching.

12 I have drawn here on the multiple meanings suggested by Judith Butler (1993) in her book of the same name.

13 Interestingly, it can be argued that the standardised BBC accent has had something of a demise in recent years, with regional accents (though clearly biased toward the southern, middle class) somewhat more in evidence. Whether this

represents a significant challenge to earlier versions of national identity projected through a particular accent is, however, debatable.

14 See, for example, Friere 1970; hooks (1982); King (1986).

15 See, for example, Friedson (1970); McNeil (1987); Witz (1992).

16 Margaret Lowe Benston (1992) argues that patriarchal relations of technology accrue from and reinvest in the lack or denial of literacy to women in the languages of technology.

17 I refer here to the triple meaning of Judith Butler's use of the term 'matter': matter as both noun and transitive verb – that which is material, that which is *made* material or *materialised*, and that which *matters*.

18 The creation of hybrid organisms, the 'supermouse' (a mouse with the 'gene for' human growth hormone), for example, or the 'geep' (a genetically engineered combination of sheep and goat), are high-profile examples of 'rewriting' practices carried out by genetic researchers. However, the biochemistry applied to disaggregate the genetic material of a cell, to clone particular material in culture and to isolate functions can also be construed as an *editorial* process combining the intertwined protocols of 'reading' and 'writing' as active *recombinant* interventions.

19 This is not to suggest that the authorship of written histories is not also boundaried by relations of literacy and expertise. However, there is a potential, however latent, to democratise the conventions readership and authorship which patently does not accrue to recombinant genetics and the authorial and readerly practices that constitutes contemporary genetic 'literacy'.

20 Martin Barker (1981) makes a comparable point about the 'new racism' of contemporary sociobiology and ethology, sciences which have eschewed 'dated' and conventional languages of racial hierarchy in favour of a discourse of 'ways of life', human tendencies to form exclusive and biological dispositions towards xenophobia. Jones, in common with the assumptions of these new sociobiological and ethological discourses, explains racism chiefly as a function of racial heirarchisation.

21 In explaining the mechanisms of matrilineal inheritance Jones writes: '[s]perm contribute very few mitochondria when they fertilise an egg so, like Jewishness, this DNA is passed through the female line. It contains the history of the world's women, with almost no male interference' (p. 8). Here, then, we see a characteristic elision of biological mechanisms with social history. Jewishness is quite extraordinarily constituted here both as a genetic trait and part of a more or less pure history of femaleness. The putative 'pure' biologies of fe/maleness, in turn, equate with their apparently unified and separate histories.

22 Tay Sachs, for example, as a European Jewish trait; sickle cell as an African trait and so on.

23 At other moments, this discourse is quite graphic, as in Jones's representation, in characteristic (hetero) sexist colonial/anthropological vein, of the Yanomamo:

> We can get some idea what life was like by looking at modern tribal peoples . . . The Yanomamo Indians of South America . . . call themselves 'the fierce people', with good reason. The commonest cause of death is violence . . . [they] exist in a series of small bands. These are in constant conflict. Rape, murder and theft are common.
>
> Social Systems based on hunting and gathering – as all were for 90% of human history – may have been like this. It is dangerous to make too much of what one tribal culture like the Yanomamo does. Others – such as the Bushmen – are far better behaved. (Jones 1991: 36–7)

24 Jones contrasts this with Britain and 'most Western Countries' where he imagines

that 'Most people would . . . see the possibility of terminating a pregnancy just because it is the wrong sex as being ethically unacceptable' (p. 59). While Jones in fact does not reject sex selection on health grounds, he does suggest that 'most people' might be more prepared to accept sex-preselection (separation of x and y sperm, rather than abortion of 'wrong' sex foetuses, India is nevertheless invoked as an example of the unacceptable version of sex selection, while its more 'ethically' justifiable use is suggestively located in Britain and 'most Western Countries' (Jones 1991: 58). Later in the lecture, Jones invokes the Indian village as an iconographic site of backwardness characterised by remoteness and therefore 'inbreeding'. This he contrasts, in rather utopian vein, to the process of population mixing through which both biological and therefore cultural differences (e.g. between England and Scotland) will be 'even[ed] out' (p. 65), thus minimising the chances of recessive illness. Here Jones characteristically elides genetic and cultural differences, disease and identity.

Bibliography

Barker, Martin. 1981. *The New Racism: Conservatives and the Ideology of the Tribe.* London: Junction Books.

Benston, Margaret Lowe. 1992. 'Women's Voices/Men's Voices: Technology as a Language' in Gill Kirkup and Laurie Smith Keller (eds), *Inventing Women: Science, Technology and Gender.* London: Polity, pp. 33–41.

British Broadcasting Corporation (BBC). 1993. 'Producers' Guidelines' in John Corner and Sylvia Harvey (eds), *Television Times: A Reader.* London: Arnold, pp. 246–52.

Butler, Judith. 1993. *Bodies that Matter: On the Discursive Limits of 'Sex'.* New York: Routledge.

CIBA Foundation (ed.). 1986. *Human Embryo Research: Yes or No?* London: Tavistock.

—— 1996. *Genetics of Criminal and Antisocial Behaviour (Symposium 194).* Chichester: John Wiley & Sons.

Clarke, Angus (ed.). 1994. *Genetic Counselling: Practice and Principles.* London: Routledge.

Clarke, Cyril A. 1987. *Human Genetics and Medicine* (Third Edition). London: Edward Arnold.

Colls, Robert and Philip Dodd. 1986. *Englishness: Politics and Culture 1880–1920.* London: Croom Helm.

Cook-Deegan, Robert. 1994. *The Gene Wars: Science, Politics, and the Human Genome.* New York: W. W. Norton & Company.

Corner, John and Sylvia Harvey (eds). 1993. *Television Times: A Reader.* London: Arnold.

Curran, James and Jean Seaton. 1988. *Power Without Responsibility: The Press and Broadcasting in Britain* (Third Edition). London: Routledge.

Doyle, Brian. 1986. 'The Invention of English' in Robert Colls and Philip Dodd (eds), *Englishness: Politics and Culture 1880–1920.* London: Croom Helm.

Franklin, Sarah. 1997. *Embodied Progress: A Cultural Account of Assisted Conception.* London: Routledge.

Freire, Paulo. 1970. *Pedagogy of the Oppressed.* New York: Seabury.

Friedson, Eliot. 1970. *Profession of Medicine: A Study of the Sociology of Applied Knowledge.* New York: Dodd, Mead.

Goodwin, Andrew and Garry Whannel (eds). 1990. *Understanding Television*. London: Routledge.

Graddol, David, Dick Leith and Joan Swann (eds). 1996. *English: History, Diversity and Change*. London: Routledge/Open University.

Hall, Stuart. 1982. 'Culture and the State' (Unit 28) of *The State and Popular Culture* (Block 7) of *Popular Culture* (Open University Course U203). Milton Keynes: Open University Press (Division of the Open University).

Haraway, Donna. 1992. *Primate Visions: Gender, Race and Nature in the World of Modern Science*. London: Verso.

Harding, Sandra (ed.). 1993. *The 'Racial' Economy of Science: Toward a Democratic Future*. Bloomington: Indiana University Press.

Hodson, Anna. 1992. *Essential Genetics*. London: Bloomsbury.

hooks, bell. 1982. *Ain't I a Woman: Black Women and Feminism*. London: Pluto.

Hubbard, Ruth and Elijah Wald. 1993. *Exploding the Gene Myth: How Genetic Information is Produced and Manipulated by Scientists, Physicians, Employers, Insurance Companies, Educators and Law Enforcers*. Boston: Beacon Press.

Illich, Ivan. 1976 (1985 edition). *Limits to Medicine; Medical Nemesis – The Expropriation of Health*. Harmondsworth: Penguin.

Jones, Dr Steve. 1991. *The Language of the Genes (The 1991 Reith Lectures)*. Transcripts. London: BBC Radio, Science Unit.

—— 1993. *The Language of the Genes*. London: Flamingo.

—— 1996. *In the Blood: God, Genes and Destiny*. London: Harper.

Jordanova, Ludmilla (ed.). 1986. *Languages of Nature: Critical Essays on Science and Literature*. London: Free Association Books.

King Jr, Martin Luther (James Melvin Washington ed.) 1986. *I Have a Dream: Writings and Speeches that Changed the World*. San Francisco: HarperCollins.

Kirkup, Gill and Laurie Smith Keller. 1992. *Inventing Women: Science, Technology and Gender*. London: Polity.

Kitcher, Philip. 1996. *The Lives to Come: The Genetic Revolution and Human Possibilities*. London: Penguin.

MacCabe, Colin and Olivia Stewart (eds). 1986. *The BBC and Public Service Broadcasting*. Manchester: Manchester University Press.

McNeil, Maureen. 1987. *Gender and Expertise*. London: Free Association Books.

Scannell, Paddy. 1990. 'Public Service Broadcasting: the History of a Concept' in Andrew Goodwin and Garry Whannel (eds), *Understanding Television*. London: Routledge, pp. 11–29.

Scannell, Paddy and David Cardiff. 1981. 'Serving the Nation: Public Service Broadcasting Before the War' in Bernard Wites, Tony Bennett and Graham Martin, *Popular Culture: Past and Present*. Milton Keynes: Open University Press, pp. 161–87.

Schiebinger, Londa. 1993. *Nature's Body: Gender in the Making of Modern Science*. Boston: Beacon Press.

Spanier, Bonnie B. 1995. *Im/Partial Science: Gender Ideology in Molecular Biology*. Bloomington: Indiana University Press.

Steinberg, Deborah Lynn. 1999. 'Pedagogic Panic or Deconstructive Dilemma? Gay Genes in the Popular Press' in Debbie Epstein, and Jim Sears (eds), *Dangerous Knowing: Sexualities and the Meta-narrative*. London: Cassell.

—— 2000. 'Recombinant Bodies: Corporeal Cartographies of the Gene' in Simon Williams *et al.* (eds), *Theorising Medicine and Health*. London: Sage.

Stepan, Nancy Leys. 1993. 'Race and Gender: The Role of Analogy in Science' in

Sandra Harding (ed.), *The 'Racial' Economy of Science: Toward a Democratic Future*. Indiana: Indiana University Press, pp. 359–76.

Terry, Jennifer and Jaqueline Urla (eds). 1995. *Deviant Bodies*. Bloomington: Indiana University Press.

Whitelegg, Liz. 1992. 'Girls in Science Education: of Rice and Fruit Trees' in Gill Kirkup and Laurie Smith Keller (eds), *Inventing Women: Science, Technology and Gender*. London: Polity, pp. 178–87.

Wites, Bernard, Tony Bennett and Graham Martin. 1981. *Popular Culture: Past and Present*. Milton Keynes: Open University Press.

Witz, Anne. 1992. *Professions and Patriarchy*. London: Routledge.

7 Hybridity's discontents: rereading science and 'race'

Lola Young

Hybrid histories

There are significant numbers of white people who explicitly reject the possibility of cultural hybridity, even while they unconsciously engage with it on a day-to-day basis, experiencing and living through many hybrid moments. Some are attracted to a rhetoric which espouses nationalism, essentialism and the physical, moral and intellectual superiority of their 'race'. There is a substantial literature which describes and analyses, historically and in contemporary times, aspects of white people's theories of 'race' and racism (Stepan 1982; Gilman 1985; Harding 1993; Gould 1981; Frankenberg 1993): I want to indicate here some of the ways in which a sense of 'racial pride' is being reinforced by the construction of similar theories by certain black scholars for black people. This in turn raises issues regarding the explicit or implicit rejection of notions of hybridity by black people as well.

In this chapter, I will suggest some of the ways in which hybridity as a concept is inherently problematic, particularly with regard to its genesis in nineteenth-century scientific racism and its metaphorical displacement in the discourse of human 'race' or 'species'-mixing. Through the analysis of two texts in the canon of literature which promote the alleged attributes of melanin – *The Isis Papers: The Keys to the Colors* by Dr Frances Cress Welsing, and Carol Barnes's *Melanin: The Chemical Key to Black Greatness* – which may be seen as in an antithetical relationship to contemporary discourses on hybridity and the heterogeneity of black subjectivity, I will argue that the methodologies of these contemporary narratives, whilst being produced as a counter-discourse opposed to centuries-old scientific racism, bear similarities to the textual strategies of racialized scientific enquiry. That the two North American texts on which I focus have a largely undocumented but anecdotally significant following in the UK as well as in the USA suggests a disjuncture between those who promote what has come to be regarded as the dominant strand of contemporary black scholars' analyses of 'race' and those others who represent themselves as belonging to a definable, singular black, African-descended 'race'.[1]

The interaction between adherents of different black political formations is not, and never has been, simple or static, and the fault lines which have produced cleavages in the racial landscape during the last fifty or so years problematize any attempt at a unitary reading of black Britain. Important here is a shift in terms of defining what 'black' means. Up until the early to mid-1980s, in the British context 'black' had been used to indicate a certain inclusiveness, and the word carried a meaning that was concerned with the *politics* of solidarity across different racialized categories of people of colour, rather than being associated with the biological descriptors of racialized discourse. 'Black' was fluid enough to embrace various communities but predominantly referred to people of South Asian and African descent.

The current fragmentation of the sign 'black' is evidenced by the numbers of those claiming distinctive identities which are not felt to be best served by the former inclusiveness posited by 'black', and we now have the familiar but awkward juxtaposition of the disparate terms 'black' and 'Asian' to refer to communities of colour in Britain. Thus the struggle to continue using what many regarded as a broad, politically progressive term, whose function was to acknowledge a commonality of experience regarding racism, seems to have been lost. In some respects, however, the problematization of 'black' has been useful since it has allowed a space where suppressed differences and antagonisms within black communities may be discussed, in particular those relating to gender and sexuality and, increasingly, social and economic status.

In spite of claims to the contrary, the black/white dichotomy remains at the very centre of 'race' discourse, whether or not, and to whatever extent, 'race' is explicitly biologized or seen as an essential human property. The distinctive connotative properties of 'black' and 'white' maintain power and material reality, and it would be an act of disavowal to deny the significance of the visible markers of racial identity in contemporary Britain. Moreover, in spite of attempts to dislodge the legitimacy of the idea of 'race' in any context apart from reference to 'the human race', the force of the term is such that it constantly refuses to be bound by those boldly placed scare quotation marks.

A number of influential critics and academics working within an interdisciplinary cultural studies academic framework have sought to analyse developments within the sphere of black cultural production within what might be termed the postmodern and/or postcolonial theoretical sub-structure of cultural hybridity (see, for example, Mercer 1994; Hall 1987 and 1990; Bailey and Hall 1992; Bhabha 1990 and 1994; Gilroy (1993), though these accounts are differently inflected. Some of the most notable of these analytical accounts have focused on experimental, non-narrative, anti-realist film, photography and literature whose innovative qualities have gained some recognition in the form of public funding support. Identification of the hybrid text, moment or event – which occurs as diverse cultures are juxtaposed and interact, forming 'new', distinctive cultures – is a key component of such critiques, and the works analysed appear to be regarded as emblematic of the most exciting developments in the evolution of black British cultures. However, there is a danger of producing a very selective account of what constitutes contemporary black cultural production through constructing what amounts to a canon of texts which serve to confirm hypotheses regarding the hybridity of black cultural production. It is important to think through the implications of an intellectual strategy which does not give an account of that material which refuses to conform to a particular set of ideas about culturally plural, politically progressive work. Although some of the other kinds of material being produced and popularized outside of academic circles may not be so amenable to being discussed in the terminology and analytical framework of post-structuralism, such texts may be more widely known among the mass of black people and regarded by them as more relevant and useful than either the theory or key texts in much academic cultural criticism. This last point, together with the foregoing remarks about the tenacity of racism, underpins much of what follows in this chapter because it is central to the task of trying to understand the significance of the texts which I will be examining. Of course any critical history will be selective, but we have spent too much time in cultural studies questioning the absences, gaps and lacks that are evident in other disciplines, to ignore those which exist within our own field of study.

Telling hybrid stories

It might be useful at this point to think about whether it is worth trying to tease out some of the possible meanings attached to 'hybridity' Robert Young points to a definition of hybridity as ' "raceless chaos" which produces no stable new form but rather something closer to Bhabha's restless, uneasy, interstitial hybridity: a radical heterogeneity, discontinuity, the permanent revolution of forms' (Young 1995: 25). But nineteenth-century scientific racial discourse and early twentieth-century photographic images similar to that which adorns the cover of Young's book *Colonial Desire* speak of a differently inflected hybridity than the one with which cultural theorists have become so absorbed: one directly and explicitly linked to the sexual anxieties and desires which are an integral part of the term's historical provenance (Young 1995). Thus, for example, the expressions or manifestations of hybridity which both underpin and undermine the discourse of racial purity seem to haunt Nott – the prolific writer and editor of scientific texts – and his carefully constructed hierarchy of racial groups.

> What we term caucasian races are not of one origin: they are on the contrary; an amalgamation of an infinite number of primitive stocks, of different instincts, temperaments, and mental and physical characters. Egyptians, Jews, Arabs, Teutons, Celts, Sclavonians, Pelasgians, Romans, Iberians etc., etc., are all mingled in blood; and it is impossible now to go back and unravel this heterogeneous mixture, and say precisely what each type originally was.
>
> (Nott 1854: 67)

Interestingly, Nott's formulation of racial categories allows for some benefits: for whilst the polygenecist Agazzis claims that 'nobody can deny that the offspring of different races is always a half-breed, as between animals of a different species, and not a child like either its mother or its father' (Agazzis 1854: lxx), Nott declares,

'The infusion of even a minute proportion of the blood of one race into another, produces a decided modification of moral and physical character' (Nott 1854: 68).

During this period – the mid-nineteenth century – anxieties about racial purity, and thus interracial sexuality and the survival of the superior 'race' are embedded in the business of 'doing science'. As is demonstrated in the works of scientists such as Nott and Agazzis cited above, historically 'hybridity' was centrally concerned with the prospects for human fertility across or between 'races'. Young traces how this biological project was 'inextricably intertwined' with the cultural sphere, evidenced by the claims that the children of interracial sexual relations would bring about the degeneration of white societies and the debasement of their cultures.

Young's suggested definition cited above indicates how difficult it is to attempt to fix the particularities of the contemporary use of hybridity: how can we start analytical work on the basis of descriptors such as 'permanent revolution of forms', or 'radical heterogeneity'? Arguably, constructing definitions as an activity in its own right may prove in this instance to be something of a distraction. Ali Rattansi argues for critical and analytical work which does not seek to define complex terms like racism or identity, and, by extension, hybridity: since 'there are no unambiguous, water-tight definitions to be had of ethnicity, racism and the myriad terms in-between . . . There is a "family resemblance" between them, a merging and overlapping of one form of boundary formation with another, coupled with a strong contextual determination' (Rattansi 1994: 53).

The writings in Nott and Gliddon's extensive collections of essays, diagrams and drawings show that the hybrid figure emerged from observations of the practices of animal husbandry, and that the hybrid was most often sterile (Nott and Gliddon 1854). The slide of usage, then, from animal reproductive behaviour to interracial human sexual activity to human cultural and artistic endeavour is one fraught with difficulties. If hybridity is considered as a metaphor, then it is prone to some of the problems associated with the use of metaphor in science. Nancy Leys Stepan has argued that metaphor and analogy have played a significant role in producing inappropriate and destructive links between incommensurate subjects in scientific enquiry (Stepan 1993). Whilst the use of analogy – whether in the form of metaphor or symbol – may assist in a speedy appreciation of the broad principles at stake in a discussion or argument, the limitations need to be recognized and inform their use. The analogical term may become the 'reality' as we lose sight of the differences between the object under discussion and the object to which it is being compared. Thinking then of 'hybridity' as one of those 'myriad terms in-between' and firmly established as a key element in the discourse of 'race', it is necessary to recognize the extent to which it is a slippery concept which seeks to offer a description and an explanation of various disparate cultural phenomena, not all of which may be contained or clarified by the term.

Meanings, though, are important because people may act on the basis of what is implied by or inferred from a text or an utterance, and, by claiming that there are those who reject hybridity, I am suggesting that there is an identifiable cluster of ideas attached to the term. However, I do not want to get embroiled in a discussion of possible definitions, since the problems with hybridity go beyond matters of meaning, metaphor and semantic clarity. Its origins in a racialized scientific discourse which served as support for claims to white racial supremacy should encourage questions about the extent to which it is possible to disrupt or produce a radical discourse in spite of the history which is embedded within the word. There is a perception on the part of some community-based black activists that issues of racism as they affect black people's everyday lives have been marginalized and that critical discourses are far too obscure either to constitute or to contribute to meaningful political debate.

Hybridity and related concepts have not passed without critical, analytical comment. As well as critical assessments of the kind offered by those problematizing multiculturalism and hybridity from within the field (see, for example, Berlant and Warner 1994; Rattansi 1994; Coombes 1994), or scholars engaged in black nationalism, Marxist politics or working within other disciplinary contexts in both Britain and North America have accused the postmodernist, post-structuralist critics of being too dependent on western or eurocentric theoretical models, of evacuating all considerations of the material effects of racism from their intellectual work and of maintaining intellectual debate as the preserve of a middle-class, metropolitan elite (Asante 1996; Sivanandan 1989; Ahmad 1992; Friedman 1997). In addition the use of opaque critical theory is seen as being too distant from what is characterized as the realities of everyday black life in racist societies. Of course, there is nothing so simple as a 'western theory' or indeed a 'non-western' or 'Afro-centric' one, but the power of the apparently antithetical remains effective as a means of staking out intellectual territory. The tension between intellectual work which calls for the recognition of cultural polyvocality and heterogeneity, and that which invokes a set of 'authentic' black cultural practices and essential black subjects is indicative of some of the contesting strands of thought within black communities. The extent to which any of these formally opposed conceptual frameworks is able to engage adequately with the complex negotiations involved in being a modern black person living in 'the West' is open to question.

Melanin metanarratives

I now move to a consideration of the texts on melanin, but first I want to suggest that it is useful to bear in mind the features of racialized scientific discourse and to indicate possible readings of theories of 'race' constructed in opposition to such discourse but displaying similar discursive strategies. The two key attributes of racialized science may be identified as, first, a belief in a biologized definition of 'race' which posits common phenotypical characteristics, and crucially, second, the construction of a hierarchy which places the different 'races' in a relationship of inferiority or superiority (in terms of intellectual, moral and physical indicators of achievement). Traditionally, Euro-North-American systems of 'race' categorizations have positioned white people at the top and black people at the bottom of such hierarchies (Gould 1981; Gilman 1985; Goldberg 1993; Harding 1993; Rattansi 1994).

It seems that white scientific racism has gradually shifted its focus from visible physical characteristics to the powerful but invisible workings of genetic determinism. The racial theories generated by the black scientists and academics under consideration here discuss gene theory but the locus of their concerns is melanin, the substance which gives rise to skin colouring. This is a complex, interstitial chemical which is both invisible in terms of not being itself observable under ordinary circumstances and more or less visible in terms of its effects on skin coloration.

An important text for those black people seeking a counter to what are perceived as white racist eurocentric explanations of human evolution is Welsing's *The Isis Papers: The Keys to the Colors* (1991). The book proposes a version of the origins of humanity which claims that white people are the result of genetic albinism. Welsing's all-encompassing theory 'explains' the spectrum of white people's behaviour in terms of their alienation due to the lack of skin colour. Similarly, the central tenet of *Melanin: The Chemical Key to Black Greatness* (Barnes 1995) is that the concentration of melanin has properties which confer superior intellectual qualities on black people.[2] Barnes's tract on the abundant qualities of melanin provides the 'evidence' for its claims in a mixture of scientific and mystical terminology and in a manner which echoes the rhythms and exhortations of a religious sermon. Both *The Isis Papers* and *Melanin* deploy similar strategies to nineteenth-century racial ideologies as they draw on a number of scientific theories for the construction of their argument: the necessity for racial purity to maintain group integrity; the search for a biological justification for the racialization of difference; a typology based on the inferiority of the 'other' group in relation to the physical, moral and intellectual superiority of 'one's own'; an explanation for the deviant behaviour of those who have sexual relations beyond the assigned racial boundaries. Each of them also makes explicit the political imperatives underpinning the theories.

One intention of Barnes's report is to alert black people to the dangers of using drugs. These dangers are specific to black people, he argues, since the high levels of melanin present in our bodies bind with certain toxins, making us more prone to addiction than white people. Thus, although Barnes concedes that external economic and social factors exist, his view is that it is the very presence of melanin which engenders the problems, and he explicates the problem through a rather different, more directly sexual metaphorical use of 'hybridity' than the one which has become customary:

> If two chemicals have similar structures or functional groups, they will 'like' or fall in 'love' with one another. When they come into contact, physically and electromagnetically, they will 'marry', (dissolve into), or chemically react with each other . . .
>
> Once the marriage has taken place, the new mixture or chemical will show properties similar to both chemicals before the 'marriage', but properties

different from any one of the two original chemicals. A hybrid is produced! The sugar goes from being a solid to a liquid like water and the water goes from tasting neutral to tasting sweet like sugar. This is what happens in the case of harmful drugs [mixing with melanin] – a hybrid is produced!

(Barnes 1995: 74)

Having claimed that melanin holds the key to black people's superiority, Barnes proceeds to account for the lack of progress being made by black people, particularly in Europe and the Americas, and that is when social and environmental factors such as lack of economic power and poor education are cited. Black people, therefore have to be constantly vigilant lest their inherent, allegedly physiological propensity towards cocaine, heroin and so on overtake them.

Since there is so much invested in the idea of melanin, its properties are not denigrated: on the contrary, '*MELANIN* [*also*] *causes the expressive, flamboyant and cocky nature of the BLACK HUMAN (toughness)*' (Barnes 1995: 7). But melanin does not only cause certain character traits to be prevalent amongst black people, according to Barnes: it has its own unique 'character'. 'MELANIN has chemical and physical properties (personality traits) which distinguish it from other chemicals and is so fantastic it may be considered "DIVINE"' (Barnes 1995: 7). Amongst other signs of its divinity is the ability to 'keep you in constant contact with the chemistries of the universe!' (Barnes 1995: 8). Welsing invests melanin with similar exceptional communicative abilities. The success of George Washington Carver, distinguished nineteenth-century African-American scientist, is attributed not to his diligence and academic rigour but to the high concentrations of melanin in his body evidenced by the darkness of his skin colour which 'enabled him to communicate with the energy frequencies emanating from plants. Thus he was able to learn their secrets and purposes' (Welsing 1991: 233). For whites, the converse of this claim is that the 'absence of this black pigment in the skin and other aspects of the nervous system – critically impairs the depth of sensitivity of the nervous system and the ability to tune in to the total spectrum of energy frequencies in the universe' (Welsing 1991: 238). Not surprisingly, then, we are urged to ensure that our levels of melanin are continually 'topped up' – and Barnes does use the battery metaphor – through various means. This is how he sees melanin 'capturing energy':

Light energy from the sun or artificial sources like your indoor light bulb or vibrational sounds from your stereo, all cause MELANIN to be BLACK in color. For instance, a light wave leaves the sun or your stereo in the form of energy particles and/or vibrational sounds and travels in space until it contacts the MELANIN structure in your skin, and other areas of the body where it is absorbed by MELANIN.

(Barnes 1995: 15)

Once the attributes of melanin are established, the inadequacy of those who lack sufficient amounts of the substance may be assumed:

I reason then, that the quality of whiteness is indeed a genetic inadequacy or a relative genetic deficiency state, based upon the genetic inability to produce the skin pigments of melanin (which is responsible for all skin colour). The vast majority of the world's people are not so afflicted, which suggests that color is normal for human beings and color absence is abnormal.

(Welsing 1991: 5)

Barnes, too, claims black superiority in relation to what he claims to be white physiological inadequacy: 'The BLACK HUMAN'S body is the most refined, complex and sophisticated of any human species in existence today' (Barnes 1995: 4). According to Barnes, the properties of melanin manifest themselves in various ways:

This refinement shows itself in the high mental and physical capabilities as well as the tailored features and body structure of the BLACK HUMAN . . . Let me assure you that your MENTAL processes (BRAIN POWER) are controlled by the same chemical that gives BLACK HUMANS their superior physical (athletics, rhythmic dancing) abilities. This chemical, again my friends is MELANIN!

(Barnes 1995: 4)

Worth noting in these passages is the constitution of white as a 'lack'. Welsing invokes leprosy as another cause of the loss of skin colour, which inverts nine-teenth-century speculations about black skin colouring being the result of that disease and linked to syphilis (Gilman 1985). In contrast to nineteenth-century assumptions about the 'black' being equal to 'dark' and as such emblematic of the deprivation of light and colour, in Welsing's account, white is situated as the limited, inferior term. This stems from the central thesis of this and other melanin material 'that white-skinned peoples came into existence thousands of years ago as the albino mutant off-springs of black-skinned mothers and fathers in Africa' (Welsing 1991: 23). Both Welsing and Barnes pathologize 'white' skin by naming it as genetic deficiency and conflating it with albinism:

The albino (white man) has numerous body defects due to the lack of the genetic [*sic*] to produce EUMELANIN . . . their organs and systems which depend on melanin to work effectively do not operate well and may suffer numerous disorders such as rapid aging, cancer, poor physical and mental capabilities, low morals, racism etc.

(Barnes 1995: 21)[3]

At least one of the established scientific academic references cited in support of this statement is concerned with albinism, a genetic condition which occurs in all peoples rather than with white people.[4] Welsing claims that albinos are genetically inferior in terms of size and intellectual capacity, as well as – almost inevitably since this is a mirror-image of nineteenth-century racialized scientific racial discourse – being sexually deficient.

Implicitly or explicitly, sexuality is a key component of the discourse, especially in Welsing's account. The ambivalence and problems associated with white people's sexuality are, in Welsing's view, symptomatic of self-disgust at the inability to produce 'colour'. Welsing's 'explanation' of the desire for interracial sex on the part of whites is as follows: 'The [Cress] colour-confrontation theory postulates that whites desired and still do desire sexual alliances with non-whites, both male and female, because it is only through this route that whites can achieve the illusion of trying to produce colour' (Welsing 1991: 6). The potent mixture of desire, anxiety and repulsion historically attached to white people's engagement with interracial sex represents for Welsing 'the intense fear of the Black male's capacity to fulfil the greatest longing of the white female – that of conceiving and birthing a product of color' (Welsing 1991: 6). The *Cress Theory* (always italicized) accounts for lynching and the focus on the black male's genitalia thus:

> the testicles store powerful color-producing genetic material . . . the repeated and consistent focus on the size of black males' penises by both white males and females is viewed by this theory as a *displacement* of the fundamental concern with the genetic color-producing capacity residing in the testicles.
>
> (Welsing 1991: 7)

Thus, for Welsing, cross-racial castration anxiety and genitalia hysteria are not centrally concerned with the envy of an imagined hypersexuality or phallic power, indeed, the penis is – as it were – drained of its conventional symbolic power and reduced to the position of 'a less threatening object or symbol' since the real attention should be on black men's testicles as the storehouse of 'genetic color-producing capacity' (Welsing 1991: 7).

Homosexuality is 'explained' as an attempt by white men to ingest more maleness during anal intercourse, and to produce faecal matter in an attempt to replicate the originary black father: Welsing's theory is based on an assumption of 'maleness deficiency' which locates homosexuality as self-debasing behaviour. That homosexuality is an aberration is naturalized here, and white women are seen as being at fault in producing feminized men as a defence mechanism. It is explained thus:

> [in the white family] the white male's sense of genetic inadequacy causes him to project his sense of genetic inferiority onto the white female. She is forced to accept the concept of her own genetic inferiority compared to white males. In her angry reaction to the white male attack, she causes her white sons to negate their masculinity and to become more like herself as a female.
>
> (Welsing 1991: 47–8)

Welsing's conservative rhetoric assumes that homosexuals (males here) are essentially diminished females; that 'femininity' is a quality uniquely attached to the 'female'; that femininity negates masculinity and that they cannot coexist. For Welsing, 'white male and female homosexuality can be viewed as the final expression of their dislike of their genetic albinism in a world numerically dominated by colored people' and 'this dislike of their appearance, though deeply repressed, causes a negation of the act of self-reproduction (sex), in various forms' (Welsing 1991: 86). Black male homosexuality becomes a response to the powerlessness imposed under white patriarchal supremacy. Black women are advised to support black men and prioritize the needs of the black male ego to assert itself and resist its subordinate position. Black masculinity is best affirmed through the exercise of physical power, and the role of protector of 'their' women and children is often reiterated (Welsing 1991: 87)

Homosexuality and sexism, racism and genocide are analysed not as products of heterosexist conventions, patriarchal capitalism or institutionalised practices and policies with specific histories, but as 'necessary derivatives' of 'this finite unified behavior-energy-field' (Welsing 1991: 51), that is, white genetic deficiency-led behaviour. Whether discussing the ritualistic giving of boxes of chocolates, the significance of the different coloured balls in a range of sports, or the endemic racism in North American society, everything is analysed in relation to the *Cress Theory of Racial Confrontation.*

Welsing sees black women's function as being to serve black men's needs, whereas they are something of an underdetermined, vaguely troubling presence for Barnes, especially in their capacity as reproducers of the 'race'. He claims that, for black women, a lack or reduced level of melanin 'in the ectoderm causes the mother to lose the baby' whereas for white people the consequence of the lack of melanin, means that 'a defective species is produced because of low MELANIN in the "white" mother' (Barnes 1995: 38).[5] This 'defective species' is recognizable not only in physical terms but through the negative, aggressive personality traits displayed by whites which are directly attributed to the lack of melanin.

Just as in earlier scientific accounts of racial difference, the qualities of 'our' group are defined in opposition to those of the other, so it is with Welsing, 'I theorized that the presence of melanin in high concentrations in Blacks accounted for some of the observable differences in behaviour between Black and white (ie religious responsiveness, sensitivity levels)' (Welsing 1991: 232). The details of how 'religious responsiveness' or 'sensitivity' are measured are not clarified: Welsing's evidence consists of having apparently discovered that 'the most sensitive body areas are the areas most highly pigmented' (Welsing 1991: 232).

Barnes's racial typology is similarly vague about details of the rationale for his taxonomy. Ostensibly it is skin colour which determines the category into which people are placed, but there is little consistency. For example, type 4 in his numbered system of categorization consists of people who are 'whites who are lightly tan and include Japanese, Chinese, Italian, Greeks, Spanish, and Red Indians'. However, type 5 people are 'brown-skinned and include Mexicans, Indians, Malaysians, Puerto Ricans, and other Spanish speaking people' (Barnes 1995: 23). The position of peoples from the Indian subcontinent and from black Hispanic communities who display similar – though not identical – overlapping ranges of skin colouring is ambiguous. At the top of this melanin-based hierarchy are black people of implied 'pure' African descent; and the manner in which the 'facts' are laid out and the exhortative exclamation marks are typical of the way in which Barnes seeks to emphasise his point:

> Type 6 – These individuals are BLACK in color and include AFRICANS (EGYPTIANS, ETHIOPIANS, NIGERIANS, ETC.) AMERICAN BLACKS and AUSTRALIAN ABORIGINES!
>   Their eyes and hair are BLACK!
>   They virtually have no incidence of skin cancer!
>   They show skin aging after the age of 50–60 years.
>
> (Barnes 1995: 23)

It seems that there are no boundaries to the power and pervasiveness of melanin: it can 'cause altered states of consciousness such as those experienced in BLACK religious ceremonies . . . "improvisation", or creation of "jazz", "high five" and "telepathic communication"' (Barnes 1995: 39). Further, the principal characteristics of Barnes's black and white humans are attributable to their possession or lack of melanin: 'MELANIN is a civilizing chemical and acts as a sedative to help keep the BLACK HUMAN calm, relaxed caring and civilized!' and 'Individuals (whites) containing low levels of MELANIN will behave in a barbaric manner (or create a society not conducive to Blackness)' (Barnes, 1995: 40). Thanks to melanin, black people are

- EXPRESSIVE
- COLORFUL
- CREATIVE
- INDUSTRIOUS
- GENEROUS
- COCKY   (Barnes 1995: 40)

Much of Welsing's material about white envy of black people and how this is manifested in societies is based on an assumption that being a white person is the same as being 'white'. People in racially stratified societies learn how to live out a particular existence which calls upon them to behave in certain ways – we learn how to 'act' white and how to 'act' black. What it means to be 'white' – the assumption of privilege and superiority, white guilt and so on – are not inherent properties of whiteness or white people: the accumulation of these ideas has historical, social, political and cultural contexts which need close examination. If the forms of behaviour, activities, and modes of being outlined by Barnes and elaborated by Welsing are examined, exceptions to, and contradictions of, the rules as they state them are in evidence. For example, when Welsing writes of white people's desire for a tanned body as being solely about a desire to be black or to retrieve lost colour, she omits reference to class and social status, and the historical and social specificity of the continually shifting attitudes towards dark-skinned white people.

It is claimed that the benefit derived from these theories to black people is that, 'Armed with such insight, knowledge and understanding, non-whites will cease to be vulnerable to the behavioral maneuverings of individual or collective whites' (Welsing 1991: 13). And for white people? Welsing concedes that they could possibly benefit from such an analysis too, since they are frequently puzzled by their own actions: 'Perhaps some psychiatrist will develop a method of mass psychotherapy (ie therapeutic counter-racist theater) to help whites become comfortable with their colour and their numbers' (Welsing 1991: 13).

How this type of 'therapy' differs from white supremacist strategies for raising their feelings of low esteem through proto-fascist gatherings is not elaborated. Welsing does acknowledge, however, that not even mass psychotherapy will persuade white racists to give up the privileges they have gained over centuries. The realization that it is felt necessary to 'explain' whiteness will no doubt make some white people feel uncomfortable and re-evaluate their racial and ethnic identities: white is still taken for granted in its naturalness, even amongst some otherwise acute and scholarly observers of contemporary culture and society.

Neither Welsing nor Barnes has a problem with homogenizing 'BLACK HUMANS' since we are all seen as one people united by the presence of melanin. This allows a certain freedom to ignore the realities of difference within what they unproblematically constitute as a cohesive group. Diversity is either denied or attributed to deviance from Afro-centric norms because of the internalization of western or European influences: thus black people are capable of sorting out the problems which afflict us only 'provided the individual is "conscious" and has developed an Afrocentric mentality' (Barnes 1995: 5).

Typically, Welsing and Barnes support their claims with diagrams and formulae and, in the case of Welsing, with a form of psychological speculation derived from psychoanalysis. The use of rhetorical devices such as repetition, apparent transparent language, and emphatic delivery, the strategic deployment of scientific-sounding data, tables, and diagrams, and the strength of the internal logic of the analytical and explanatory methodology, can exert a strong emotional pull for those seeking some counter to white authoritative accounts of, and solutions for racial problems. Both Welsing and Barnes attempt to assimilate all social, political and sexual expression and activity into a grand theory based on the production of colour by melanin. There is an explicit belief in 'race' as an appropriate method of categorizing human beings and that different 'races' are separate species. The two texts present a refracted image of eighteenth- and nineteenth-century preoccupations with the identification of the body as racially marked. Welsing's and Barnes's epidermal aesthetic produces a shift by focusing on skin colour as an effect of melanin, rather than being a sign of 'race' in its own right. In one limited sense, this discourse is an example of hybridity, borrowing as it does from various cross-cultural sources. But this mode of hybridization is far removed from the intentionally ironic aesthetic syncretisms referred to by Hall and Bhabha. These ideas make sense to people who have little else by way of accessible critical narratives which they feel able to relate to their circumstances.

I would not want to suggest that these ideas should be endorsed simply because they are attractive to the disenfranchised: on the contrary, my view is that such 'explanations' of racialized behaviour and attitudes are not only inadequate as explanatory models, promoting ignorance rather than knowledge, but, like their white analogues, such theories serve to disempower black (and white) people from attempting to effect change. After all, if it is all down to the amount of melanin each of us has been allocated, how might we seek to transform racist societies? If George Washington Carver came to an understanding of botany because of high levels of melanin in his body, what is the point of a black person studying? If melanin and narcotics are a lethal combination, then it is not our fault if we are weakened by them, is it? If white people cannot get over being melanin-deficient, then how will they ever overcome their racism? The claims of this particular strand of Afro-centrist thought to be able to address the profound cultural and social disorientation which continues to be experienced by African-Americans and black Britons do not stand up to detailed examination. These continued investigations into biological explanations of what is constructed as racial difference is a product of a racist society, and participation in that most imprecise and pernicious discourse by black people does nothing to mitigate its worthlessness.

Conclusion

To return to the notion of 'black' as an organizing framework: the range of skin colouring and linguistic and cultural diversity in the Caribbean, North America, South America, Britain and Africa itself is broad and suggests that being black cannot ever be solely about the measurable amount of a particular chemical in the body. Black may be thought of as always already 'hybrid' and any attempt to use it as a homogeneous, self-contained category is contingent on a political interpretation not a biological one. Institutions – whether formal or informal – which lay down norms of behaviour, modes of dress and address, and regulations regarding the conduct of social and sexual relations will always fail in their attempt to normalize and discipline. That such attempts to establish such procedures and label them 'science' find acceptance within some communities is symptomatic of profound disappointment and despair over the perceived failure of 'integration', 'multiculturalism', anti-racist campaigns, class-based, economistic analyses of racial subordination, and postmodern theories of the subject. Current postmodern theoretical attempts to construct, or impact upon, effective programmes of political action seem to have accomplished little.

The expression of a need to make connections between African Diaspora communities still has currency, but for how much longer the extent to which it means something beyond a rhetoric of desire and fantasy is hard to assess. Increasingly in the context of the ascendancy of theoretical paradigms within which the notion of 'origins' or of 'authenticity' have been exposed as unsustainable positions, the insistence on a unitary point of origin becomes untenable and, indeed, politically undesirable. The desire to seek evidence of distinctive black identities on a global basis within a frame of reference constructed by black people for black people entails the notion of a shared *something*: that is crucial to making intraracial connections.

Analytical, evaluative accounts of the various modes of contemporary cultural encounters, the fluid circuits of identification, the instances of a double-consciousness which are concerned with the contradictions of being hybrid and essentialized simultaneously are required to help us understand our ever-shifting positions of identification. These critiques, whilst recognizing and clarifying links with and across moments, events and texts, would resist the lure of constructing under-interrogated universalizing narratives, instead seeking particularized examples for analysis.[6] It continues to be necessary to emphasize the asymmetries of political and economic power often involved in hybridized encounters, and these analyses should always identify the inequitable relations that underpin cultural transactions such as those enacted within the hierarchies of race, gender, class and sexual privilege.

The invocation of a discernible, essentialized blackness is often embedded in common-sense expressions of diaspora sensibilities. Such forms of black consciousness inform the anxieties which black people may have about what is perceived as a loss of cultural distinctiveness involved in recognizing the dynamic syncretism which characterizes so much of *everyone's* experiences. For many black people, the notion of a transnational black community is an empowering one because it provides a position of authority from which to speak. The hub of the problem for black academics, scholars and intellectuals seems to be that de-essentializing serves to undermine the authority of the black subject. And if black people cannot speak to, and from the (shifting) position of, the racialized subject, how can we speak at all?

Notes

1 Onyekachi Wambu has made a short film, *The Beginner's Guide to Melanin*, for *The A-Force* (1997), BBC2's black programming strand which included an interview with Dr Yorke, a British-based proponent of the powers of melanin. Other examples of this literature can be found in several black bookshops in London. Friends have spoken of finding *The Isis Papers* (Welsing 1991) on the bookshelves of relatives, and colleagues teaching in higher education have been taken to task by black students for not including Welsing's text on the list of recommended authoritative books. I've had a number of heated arguments with black colleagues who assert the intellectual and moral superiority of black people of African descent based on our allegedly inherent physical and mental supremacy. Frances Cress Welsing's melanin information service can be accessed through the Internet and there are any number of enthusiastic references to this material in publications as divergent as the diminutive, community-based booklet *Global Africa Pocket News* (London, Sukisa Publications Ltd); *Confronting the Color Crisis: Emphasis Jamaica* by Dr Louise Spencer-Strachan (1992), a populist, semi-academic account of what the writer locates as internalized self-hatred; and *The Color Complex: The Politics of Skin Color Among African Americans* by Kathy Russell *et al.* (1993), a mixture of empirical research, analysis and critical commentary on the conflicts produced by contesting notions of the importance of physical difference in black America.

2 Future references to Welsing's book are abbreviated to *The Isis Papers* and Barnes's to *Melanin*. All the emphases in quotations from *Melanin* are original unless stated otherwise: throughout the text key words are written in upper case and black people are referred to as 'BLACK HUMANS'.

3 It should be noted that melanin is present in all human beings and that the variation in the amount is actually quite small in spite of what are perceived as vast differences in the range of skin tones. Interestingly, a colour photograph of two 'black' men introduces the entry on albinism on the CD rom encyclopaedia *Encarta 1996*. Albinism, the more detailed text tells us, occurs 'in all races of humans, most frequently among certain Native American tribes of the southwestern US, but nowhere in large numbers'. Curious then that the encyclopaedist should choose this particular photograph as illustrative of albinism. 'Albino', contributed by Newton E. Morton. Microsoft ® Encarta ® 96 Encyclopaedia © 1993–5 Microsoft Corporation. All rights reserved © Funk and Wagnalls Corporation. All rights reserved.

4 Barnes lists several publications including 'Garber, SR, King, RA etc "Auditory Brainstem Anomalies in Human Albinos" Science, Vol. 209 (12) September 1980'. No page numbers are given in the original.

5 Barnes's endnote suggests that he has evidence to support his claims but when the reference is followed up, all that is cited is 'Stewart, M., San Francisco State University (Private communication)' (Barnes 1995: 99).

6 For an interesting article on the complex ways in which African-American students at very different universities settle upon what appears to be an eclectic, contradictory set of political principles, see Lemann 1993.

Bibliography

Agazzis, L. (1854) 'Sketch of the Natural Provinces of the Animal World and their Relation to the Different Types of Man' in Nott, J. C. and Gliddon, G. R. (eds), *Types of Mankind or Ethnological Researches, Based upon the Ancient Monuments, Paintings, Sculptures and Crania of Races and upon their Natural, Geographical, Philological and Biblical History*. Philadelphia, Lippincott, Grambo and Co., pp. lviii–lxxvii.

Ahmad, A. (1992) *In Theory: Classes, Nations, Literatures*. London, Verso.

Asante, M. K. (1996) *Afrocentricity*. Trenton, NJ, and Asmaria, Eritrea, Africa World Press Inc.

Bailey, D. and Hall, S. (1992) 'The Vertigo of Displacement: Shifts within Black Documentary Practice' in *Critical Decade: Black British Photography in the 80s*. Ten.8 Photo Paperback, 2, 3, Spring, pp. 14–23.

Barnes, C. (1995) *Melanin: The Chemical Key to Black Greatness – The Harmful Effects of Toxic Drugs on Melanin Centers Within the Black Human*. Houston, Texas, Melanin Technologies.

Berlant, L. and Warner, M. (1994) 'Introduction to "Critical Multiculturalism"' in Goldberg, D. T. (ed.), *Multiculturalism, A Critical Reader*. Cambridge, Blackwell, pp. 107–13.

Bhabha, H. (1987) 'Interrogating Identity' in Lisa Appignanesi (ed.), *Identity: The Real Me*. London, ICA Documents 6, pp. 5–11.

—— (ed.) (1990) *The Location of Culture*. London, Routledge.

—— (1994) *Nation and Narration*. London, Routledge.

Coombes, A. E. (1994) *Reinventing Africa: Museums, Material Culture and Popular Imagination*. New Haven and London, Yale University Press.

Frankenberg, R. (1993) *White Women, Race Matters: The Social Construction of Whiteness*. London and New York, Routledge.

Gilman, S. L. (1985) *Difference and Pathology: Stereotypes of Sexuality, Race and Madness*. Ithaca, Cornell University Press.

Gilroy, P. (1987) *There Ain't No Black in the Union Jack*. London, Hutchinson.

—— (1993a) *Small Acts: Thoughts on the Politics of Black Cultures*. London, Serpent's Tail.

—— (1993b) *The Black Atlantic: Modernity and Double Consciousness*. London, Verso.

Goldberg, D. T. (1993) *Racist Culture: Philosophy and the Politics of Meaning*. Oxford, Blackwell.

Gould, S. J. (1981) *The Mismeasure of Man*. New York, Norton.

Hall, S. (1987) 'Minimal Selves' in Appignanesi, L. (ed.), *Identity: The Real Me*. London, ICA Documents 6, pp. 44–8.

—— (1990) 'Cultural Identity and Diaspora' in Jonathan Rutherford (ed.) *Identity: Community, Culture, Difference*. London, Lawrence and Wishart, pp. 222–37.

Harding, S. (1986) *The Science Question in Feminism*, Milton Keynes, Open University Press.

—— (ed.) (1993) *The 'Racial' Economy of Science: Toward a Democratic Future*. Bloomington, Indiana University Press.

Kohn, M. (1995) *The Race Gallery: The Return of Racial Science*. London, Jonathan Cape.

Lemann, N. (1993) 'Philadelphia: Black Nationalism on Campus', *The Atlantic Monthly*, January, pp. 31–47.

Mercer, K. (1992) 'Back to My Routes' in *Critical Decade: Black British Photography in the 80s*. Birmingham, Ten.8.

—— (1994) *Welcome to the Jungle: New Positions in Black Cultural Studies*. New York and London, Routledge.

Nasmyth, G. (1971) 'A Critique of Social Darwinism' (1916) in Olson, R. (ed.), *Science as Metaphor: The Role of Scientific Theories in Forming Western Culture*. Belmont, California, Wadsworth Publishing Company Inc.

Nott, J. C. (1854) 'Geographical Distribution of Animals, and the Races of Men' in Nott, J. C. and Gliddon, G. R. (eds), *Types of Mankind or Ethnological Researches, Based upon the Ancient Monuments, Paintings, Sculptures and Crania of Races and upon their Natural, Geographical, Philological and Biblical History*. Philadelphia, Lippincott, Grambo and Co., pp. 62–80.

Nott, J. C. and Gliddon, G. R. (eds) (1854) *Types of Mankind or Ethnological Researches, Based upon the Ancient Monuments, Paintings, Sculptures and Crania of Races and upon their Natural, Geographical, Philological and Biblical History*. Philadelphia, Lippincott, Grambo and Co.

Nott, J. C. et al. (1857) *Indigenous Races of the Earth or New Chapters of Ethnological Enquiry Including Monographs on Special Departments of Philology, Iconography, Cranioscopy, Palaeontology, Pathology, Archaeology, Comparative Geography, and Natural History*. London, Trubner and Co.; Philadelphia, J. B. Lippincott and Co.

Rattansi, A. (1994) ' "Western" Racisms, Ethnicities and Identities in a "Postmodern" Frame' in Rattansi, A. and Westwood, S. (eds), *Racism, Modernity and Identity on the Western Front*. Cambridge, Polity, pp. 15–86.

Russell, K. et al. (1993) *The Color Complex: The Politics of Skin Color Among African Americans*. New York, Anchor Books.

Sivanandan, A. (1989) 'All that Melts into Air Is Solid: The Hokum of New Times', *Race and Class*, 31, 3, pp. 1–30.

Spencer-Strachan, L. (1992) *Confronting the Color Crisis: Emphasis*. Kingston, Jamaica, and New York, Afrikan World Infosystems.

Stepan, N. L. (1982) *The Idea of Race in Science: Great Britain (1800–1960)*. London, Macmillan.

—— (1993) 'Race and Gender: The Role of Analogy in Science' in Harding, S. (ed.), *The 'Racial' Economy of Science: Toward a Democratic Future*. Bloomington, Indiana University Press, pp. 359–76.

Tucker, W. H. (1994) *The Science and Politics of Racial Research*. Urbana and Chicago, University of Illinois Press.

Welsing, F. C. (1991) *The Isis Papers: The Keys to the Colors*. Chicago, Third World Press.

Young, R. (1994) 'Egypt in America: *Black Athena*, Racism and Colonial Discourse' in Rattansi, R. and Westwood, S. (eds), *Racism, Modernity and Identity on the Western Front*. Cambridge, Polity, pp. 150–69.

—— (1995) *Colonial Desire: Hybridity in Theory, Culture and Race*. London, Routledge.

Part III
Cultural translation

8 Translating the past: apartheid monuments in post-apartheid South Africa

Annie E. Coombes

In July 1992 the South African History Workshop in Johannesburg hosted a conference, 'Myths, Monuments, Museums', for which the logo was the representation of a crowd fighting over one of the national monuments most closely identified with the apartheid regime – the Voortrekker Monument (Figure 8.1). The effectiveness of the logo derived partly from its ambiguity. From one perspective the crowd is shoring up the monument but from another it is clearly intent on pulling it down. The thorny question of the fate of monuments erected to commemorate regimes which have since been discredited and disgraced is not solely a South African dilemma of course. In the recent past the future of most of the public statuary in Central and Eastern Europe as well as the infamous 'Wall' in Berlin has been the subject of intense debate. It is not surprising that similar scrutiny has been levelled at much of the monumental public sculpture set up over the long apartheid years to commemorate key moments and figures in the Afrikaner nationalist canon.

In the case of the Voortrekker Monument, arguments range from keeping the Monument as a reminder of the oppression of the apartheid era – to learn from the lessons of the past – to erecting an alternative monument (modelled on Mandela's hand) opposite the Voortrekker, as a kind of symbolic riposte,[1] to abandoning it altogether and demolishing the site. Unlike their Eastern European counterparts, however, those African National Congress (ANC) spokespeople involved in outlining cultural policy for the new government have been adamant that most of the Boer monuments should remain, including the Voortrekker Monument. Consequently, although in practice some have been destroyed (certainly the fate of most statues of Verwoerd – the man considered by many to be the major architect of apartheid), many of those most symbolically laden are still intact, including the Voortrekker and the Taal (Afrikaans Language) Monument outside Cape Town.

This chapter is an exploration of the possibilities and impossibilities for rehabilitating a monument with an explicit history as a foundational icon of the apartheid State. In particular, I am curious to know how far it is possible to disinvest such an icon of its Afrikaner nationalist associations and reinscribe it with new resonances which enable it to remain a highly public monument despite a new democratic government whose future is premised on the demise of everything it

Figure 8.1 Penny Siopis, Poster for the South African History Workshop
conference, 'Myths, Monuments, Museums', July 1992, Screenprint.
Courtesy of the artist.

has always stood for. How is it possible for different black constituencies simply to
accept the coexistence of such an oppressive reminder of apartheid? Conversely,
in the face of evident factionalism within the Afrikaner nationalist contingency,
since at least the early 1980s how do the Monument's fascist overtones square
with the requirements of what some have argued is an emerging Afrikaner middle
class with cosmopolitan and international pretensions (Hyslop 1998)?

I want to argue that the Voortrekker Monument of the 1990s has not simply
become a shadow of its former self as one might anticipate; that it is not lack of
interest alone (even were this figured as strategic disavowal) that makes it possible

for the ANC and others to enable this oppressive reminder of the recent past to remain in place. Rather I want to suggest that the Monument has in fact accrued significance, supplemental to and in some cases, of course, directly at odds with, its intended symbolic presence. I see this as not simply a symptom of the passing of time and the necessary sedimenting of meanings that accumulate as part of the process of historical change. My concern here is to reinstate the concept of agency as a way of understanding how this commemorative 'shrine' has been reinvented following the demise of apartheid. Sometimes serendipitous, sometimes strategic and sometimes opportunistic, it seems to me that the Monument has become a staging post for self-fashioning for both black and white constituencies across the political spectrum, from Afrikaner laager to Zulu kraal. These two images span the symbolic currency of the Monument today and help to resite the Monument. The semantic distance between them foregrounds the extent to which even an apparently stable signifier of monolithic nationalist associations can be undercut by the necessarily hybridizing effects of different acts of translation.

The concept of translation is helpful here, both in the Benjaminian sense of supplemental meanings which necessarily transform the 'original' through the act of translation but also in the sense that Gayatri Chakravorty Spivak suggests of an active 'reader as translator', capable of performing a reading against the grain and between the lines even in circumstances where the raw material reproduces a set of fairly standard colonial tropes (Benjamin 1969; Spivak 1993). While translation is something more usually associated with the word and text, on a simple level, it is perhaps appropriate in the case of a monument such as the Voortrekker where the iconographic register is particularly susceptible to this kind of linguistic model and the narrative of the interior frieze invites a performative reading. On a more complex level, translation offers a way of articulating the operations of agency in the construction of historical memory.

My argument turns on the fact that the Voortrekker Monument has a significance for all South Africans. Any acts of translation depend on a certain familiarity with the text, a getting inside the 'skin' of the writer. To the extent that the narrative of the Boer Trek was the imposed foundational narrative of the nation-state (the only legitimate history available at any level of education), and to the extent that Afrikaans was the imposed language at all levels of public intercourse (and often of private), the Voortrekker Monument attained a certain monstrous legibility – inescapable even to those who never visited the site. Most importantly the Monument had a historical status as the centrepiece of an orchestrated mass spectacle of Afrikaner unity and power – a legacy which has by no means receded and which provided a rallying point for various factions on the right up to and beyond the eve of the democratic elections in April 1994.

On 16 December 1938, the foundation stone of this central monument to apartheid was laid on a hill outside Pretoria (Figures 8.2, 8.3). It was also the occasion of an elaborate reconstruction of the foundational event of Afrikaner nationalism – the Great Trek of 1838 (Hofmeyr 1988; McClintock 1995). That year a party of Boer men, women and children, dissatisfied with British rule in the Cape and its inconvenient corollary of slave emancipation, set off in a convoy of

Figure 8.2 Laying the foundation stone of the Voortrekker Monument, December 1938. Board of Control of the Voortrekker Monument, *The Voortrekker Monument*, Pretoria, 1954.

ox wagons, on a gruelling journey from Cape Town in order to form their own independent republics in what were to become the Orange Free State and the Transvaal away from the interfering clutches of the British. One hundred years later in 1938, twelve replica ox wagons complete with costumed Voortrekker families set out from various parts of the country to restage that fateful journey and finally arrived (nearly four months later) at two of the most historically significant destinations – the city of Pretoria and the site of the battle of Blood River (Ncome River). The Voortrekker Youth Movement completed the staging of the event by forming a 'river of fire' with flaming torches lit in relay fashion by hundreds of young boy and girl Voortrekker scouts around the country starting in Cape Town and culminating in a torch-lit procession up the sides of Monument Hill – 'symbolic of the spread of civilization from the Cape to the far north' (Board of Control of the Voortrekker Monument 1954: 68). The mass spectacle which greeted the 1930s Trekkers, and which was orchestrated around the base of what would become the Voortrekker Monument, was a calculated attempt to invent a coherent Afrikaner identity where none actually existed, borrowing the language of theatre so successfully deployed by the National Socialists in Germany and epitomized by the Nazi rallies at the Nuremberg stadium (Hofmeyr 1987; O'Meara 1983; Vail 1989).

By the date of the actual inauguration of the Monument, ten years later, on 16 December 1949, it was clear that the theatrical orchestration of national unity was not the only thing which the South African leaders had borrowed from the Nazis

Figure 8.3 Celebrating the inauguration of the Voortrekker Monument, December 1949. Board of Control of the Voortrekker Monument, *The Voortrekker Monument*, Pretoria, 1954.

(Figure 8.4). Dr D. F. Malan, Prime Minister of the Union of South Africa, in his inaugural address, described the nineteenth-century Trekkers as

> Exclusively, and bound by their own blood ties, they had to be children of South Africa. Further, there was the realisation that as bearers and propagators of Christian civilisation, they had a national calling which had set them and their descendants the inexorable demand on the one hand to act as guardians over the non-European races, but on the other hand to see to the maintenance of their own white paramountcy and of their white race purity.
> (Historical Record 1949: 21)

Furthermore, this was not simply an historical condition relegated to the past but an ongoing ideal since Afrikaners were metaphorically still on the Trek road in 1949. Malan continued: 'On the Trek road! Whither? Look ahead and judge for yourselves . . . That which confronts you threateningly is nothing less than modern and outwardly civilised heathendom as well as absorption into semi-barbarism through miscegenation and the disintegration of the white race' (Historical

Figure 8.4 Crowd in Trekkers' costume on the occasion of the inauguration of the
     Voortrekker Monument, December 1949. Board of Control of the Voor-
     trekker Monument, *The Voortrekker Monument*, Pretoria, 1954.

Record 1949: 24). That same year the National Party passed the Prohibition of
Mixed Marriages Act.

   This huge monument still stands like some misplaced bakelite radio on one of
the hills outside the administrative centre of the South African Government in
Pretoria, ostentatiously positioned in the sight line of the Union Buildings which
were originally built as a symbol of South Africa's dominion status within the
British Empire (Delmont 1993: 80). Inside the Monument, in what is known as
the 'Hall of Heroes', is a carved marble frieze made up of twenty-seven panels,
302 foot in length and 7 foot 6 inches high (hailed at the time as the longest frieze
in existence) (Figure 8.5). Built to last, the frieze is painstakingly carved in Italian
Quercetta (rather than Cararra marble), known for its toughness under extreme
weather conditions. Together they narrate a version of the central incidents of the
1838 Boer Trek from the Cape to the Transvaal which became enshrined in
school history textbooks around the country – predominantly a tale of Boer
heroism and godfearing righteousness and of Zulu and Ndebele treachery and
savagery.

   Most significantly, as an early guide stipulates, the frieze is 'not only a represen-

Figure 8.5 Interior of the Voortrekker Monument showing sections of the marble frieze in the Great Hall. Board of Control of the Voortrekker Monument, *The Voortrekker Monument*, Pretoria, 1954.

tation of historical events. It also serves as a symbolic document showing the Afrikaner's proprietary right to South Africa . . . A people that have sacrificed so much blood and tears, have left their mark on such a country, and therefore spiritually and physically that country belongs to them and their descendants' (Board of Control of the Voortrekker Monument 1954: 34).

Historically then the Voortrekker monument is of critical significance for the foundational myths of Afrikaner nationalism. In particular the idea of the Trek as the moment of emergence of the Afrikaner as the founding ethnic group of a new nation, 'the white tribe', and also the 'divine right' of the Trekkers to the land (Delmont 1993: 77). These myths are embodied through the actual structure of the monument itself: first through the seductive resolution provided by the narrative of encounter and conquest represented by the interior frieze, and second through the fact that the edifice houses what amounts to a cenotaph on its lower level to the memory of those Trekkers killed en route, replete with 'eternal flame' (Figure 8.6). This was strategically positioned so that a shaft of sunlight would strike the tomb each year on 16 December (the 'day of the vow').[2] Third, of course, these foundational myths are reinforced through the prominent and confrontational positioning of the Monument itself on the hills outside Pretoria directly opposite the Union Buildings – the site of British legislative authority.

If the Monument had the power to muster symbolically a nascent Afrikaner

Figure 8.6 The cenotaph at the Monument showing the shaft of sunlight striking the tomb with two Voortrekker Scouts in attendance. Board of Control of the Voortrekker Monument, *The Voortrekker Monument*, Pretoria, 1954.

nationalism in 1938 and to consolidate this in 1949, by 1990 – just four years prior to the first democratic elections in South Africa – it still had the power to galvanize these forces. The changing fortunes of the Voortrekker Monument's appeal as a rallying ground for the forces of Afrikaner nationalism are a good barometer of the shifting allegiances within the white right in South Africa. In particular these mobilizations around the Monument in the run up to the elections, and the way they were dealt with by both the South African Defence Force (SADF) and the National Party (NP) who were in various stages of negotiation with the ANC by this time, serve to foreground the emergence of considerable fissures amongst the right in South African politics over this period.

It is clear that the constant regrouping of the far right into various alliances over the period 1990–3 was speeded by the cementing of the NP's defections under De Klerk from a truly segregationist apartheid and the consolidation of those liberal white supporters who were more concerned with the economic benefits of international acceptance than with maintaining Afrikaner ascendancy. As Jonathan Hyslop has observed, such splits had been underway for some time: 'The 1980's [then] saw a polarisation in Afrikanerdom between an elitist

National Party trying to restructure classical apartheid while retaining white control, and a Conservative Party [founded in 1982] committed to reimposing the fully segregated society envisaged by Verwoerd (Hyslop 1996: 148). One of the forms which this anxiety has taken is a contestation over representations of that founding moment of Afrikaner nationalism – the Great Trek – by the various factions on the right. Albert Grundlingh and Hilary Sapire trace the ways the Trek narrative has been variously recuperated by different governments (Grundlingh and Sapire 1989). Grundlingh and Sapire argue that by 1988 acute economic and political crises and challenges to the government both internationally and internally

> prompted Afrikaner businessmen and intellectuals to express their doubts about the feasibility of a system predicated upon racial division and state intervention in the economy and to pressurize the Government into making tentative moves of 'reform'. This programme required the support of English speakers and 'moderate' black groups, precisely those groups historically portrayed as 'enemies' in traditional Great Trek representations.
> (Grundlingh and Sapire 1989: 30–1)

However, rather than abandon the essentially traditionalist and archaic narrative of the Trek, this foundational story was 'translated' to suit the agenda of the newly reformist National Party.

By the 1988 150th anniversary celebrations of the Great Trek, the theme of 'Forward South Africa' was interpreted in a particular way. Instead of that aspect of the Trek narrative which foregrounded the early Trekkers' divine right to the land and the centrality of a divinely ordained racial segregation, the emphasis in the official literature and speeches for the 1988 celebrations was on the importance of learning the spirit of self-sacrifice and compromise from these heroic predecessors in order to promote the concept of 'power-sharing'. This concept extended, on that occasion, to acknowledging the role of various black constituencies in the historical Trek but also 'in contemporary South African political, economic and social life' (Grundlingh and Sapire 1989: 32). The contest over ownership of the Trek narrative and the legitimacy of other versions and interpretations of those historic events resulted in 1988 in an alternative celebration staged in opposition to the government festivities and orchestrated by the far-right Afrikaner-Volkswag (AV), who claimed that, 'like the Voortrekkers of 1838 who revolted against the "social revolution" at the Cape, the right wing of the 1980's is in revolt against the "social revolution" caused by liberalism and the 1983 constitutional arrangements' (Grundlingh and Sapire 1989: 36).

Despite the fact that lack of enthusiasm for the official celebrations suggests that a majority of prosperous middle-class urban Afrikaners were clearly far less identified with the values and lifestyle signalled by their Voortrekker ancestry – precisely those trumpeted by the far right – it is significant that the National Party evidently still felt it necessary to invoke the Voortrekkers to lend authority to their political agenda. In other words it is clear from Grundlingh and Sapire's research that both the reforming NP and other factions on the far right were considerably invested in the representation of the Great Trek and its associated Monument.

If by 1988 there were clear divisions between the prosperous sector of Afrikanerdom which had benefited from the embourgoisification of urban Afrikaner society and that sector which felt aggrieved at what were still perceived as the 'corrosive influences of liberalism, communism and materialism' manifest in the culture of the city, by 1990 these divisions had been exacerbated. One of the results of this is the stepping up of right-wing activism in relation to the contested terrain of the public representation of the Great Trek.

In May 1990 the Conservative Party chose the Monument as the meeting ground to stage a demonstration of right-wing Afrikaner solidarity against the prospect of political change presented by the forthcoming elections. About 65,000 people attended the rally – a smaller turnout than had been anticipated. Ferdie Hartzenberg, who was later to become the chair of the Afrikaner People's Front (AVF) executive committee, addressed the crowds on behalf of the Conservative Party, stirring his listeners with incendiary language which borrowed more than a little from earlier incarnations of gatherings at the Monument. He made it clear that 'the Conservative Party would resort to all possible democratic, constitutional ways to fight the political changes. "But if all those channels are closed for us," he continued, "we would regard ourselves as an oppressed volk. Then we would have no choice but to take the path of an oppressed nation to fight for our freedom"' (*Sunday Times* (Johannesburg), final edition, 27 May 1990). As Jonathan Hyslop has pointed out, this was no empty threat. The far right in South Africa, providing they cemented certain alliances, had a combined leadership comprising some of the top brass from the former South African Defence Forces and were fast amassing a considerable stock pile of military hardware (Hyslop 1996). Their success was partly due to the rise of the coalition Afrikaner People's Front (AVF) under the leadership of the influential Constand Viljoen (former Chief of the SADF and Angolan war veteran) whose message was neither the rabid racism of the AWB (under the extremist Eugene Terreblanche) nor the backtracking return to Verwoerdian apartheid measures of the CP but rather, as Hyslop points out, appealed on grounds of self-determination for the Afrikaner people. These were differences which would eventually split the right irrevocably and cement the ANC/NP option but which, at this time, presented the possibility of strengthening the right by drawing in other constituencies making similar claims, who were also antagonistic to the ANC/National Party negotiations, such as Buthelezi's Inkhata Freedom Party (Hyslop 1996: 154).

One year prior to the elections in December 1993, the area around the Monument was the focus of other acts of sabotage. Hartzenberg addressed another rally at the Monument, this time drawing a hundred thousand of the faithful. Another group of heavily armed right-wingers – the Pretoria East Boere Kommando – took over the Schanskop Fort situated directly opposite the Monument, in what was described by their leader, Commandant Willem Ratte (a former Angolan bush war veteran and intelligence agent), as ' "A symbolic gesture by the Boere Afrikaners to show their disgust with the implementation of the Transitional

Executive Council"' (the transitional government formed jointly by the ANC and the NP in December) (*The Citizen*, 8 December 1993). The main gate providing access to both the Fort and the Monument was besieged by a group of supporting right-wingers trying to get into the grounds but blocked by the police and a battalion of soldiers who had been mobilized after the siege. Considerable violence was narrowly averted but only through the deployment of significant numbers of government (National Party) military and police forces. One of the things this underlines is the need to see the military and the police force as bodies whose leadership at least, are no longer reducible to the lumpen racialist agenda of the far right but as bodies with vested (and opportunistic) interests in seeing the transition through to its conclusion.

The fact that panic over the impending elections manifested itself as restaking a claim to certain monuments associated with key moments in the Trek narrative – the Voortrekker Monument figuring particularly prominently – had a number of interesting repercussions. Specifically, concerns about the nature of historical writing and the stakes involved in the creation of compelling versions of a shared public memory became no longer the domain of the various factions on the left in South Africa – traditionally the stomping ground for such debates (Brown *et al.* 1991). Because of the very public nature of the struggle over monuments and 'heritage', aided by the new-found freedom of the press, a script which had been a naturalized version of historical events and the prerogative of a more solidly identifiable right-wing Afrikaner nationalist contingent is now a visibly contested domain where even the most rabid right-wingers are obliged to declare their investment in certain historical narratives *as opposed* to others which they are now forced to acknowledge (even while they may be misrepresented). As an example of this, in 1992 one of the organs of the far-right *Patriot* reproduced Penny Siopis's design for the History Workshop Conference with the caption:

> The destruction of a national cultural history is symptomatic of the current revolution. Revolutions force culture back to the year dot. The ANC wants history to be rewritten. They want Verwoerdburg to be Mandelaville and they want the Voortrekker Monument to become an ANC armed struggle museum in keeping with developments in the rest of Africa where the Communists took over. Already twenty years ago the National Party started to rewrite our history and to murder it, right in keeping with ANC ideas.
>
> (*Patriot*, 16 October 1992)

A further indication of this election panic and its resolution through action over a monument was when the main cultural organizations for the promotion and preservation of Afrikaner culture – the Federation for Afrikaans Culture (FAK) – formed a private company in 1993 and bought the right to control and manage the Voortrekker Monument, effectively taking it out of the control of the presiding National Party – but also, significantly, out of the control of any subsequent government. This prompted a flurry of responses from various factions of the national press. Journalists elaborated on what was fast emerging as a hot topic.

Even the Afrikaans national daily, *Die Beeld*, a fairly liberal paper with urbane pretentions, defended the Monument in grandiose terms: 'The VTM is one of the country's strongest reminders of a time when the Voortrekkers, through blood, sweat and determination, made South Africa their own.' Lorette Grobler went on to claim that 'In the eyes of the world the Monument is an important commemorator of SA history' (Beeld cuttings folder in the National Cultural Museum archive, pre-1993 but n.d.). She gives the final word however, to the head of history at the Afrikaans university of Potchefstroom, an institution with a solid reputation as one of the bastions of apartheid. The professor insisted that the VTM should be kept at all costs because it was 'indissolubly part of the total SA history. Maintenance of monuments is a cultural right and therefore the keeping of the VTM should not be a controversial matter.'

The confidence of this insistence on the maintenance of monuments as universally a 'cultural right' by someone whose primary concern is clearly the preservation of Afrikaans culture is telling. Because of the apartheid regime's denial or destruction of most historical cultural symbols belonging to the majority black communities in South Africa, this statement poses little risk to the speaker's cultural nationalist agenda. Such a legacy has implications for the level of engagement that some constituencies may feel is possible or impossible with debates around history, heritage and conservation. Indeed, as University of Cape Town historian Fereida Khan has pointed out, there are many reasons why black communities may be either apathetic or downright negative towards heritage or conservation issues and reluctant to engage in the debates around public culture (Khan 1992). Many of the buildings or other structures that had been proclaimed 'national monument' by 1992 by the National Monuments Council were sites which had more negative than positive connotations for the majority culture. What does it mean, for example, to preserve the Dutch Cape architecture and slave quarters of Groot Constantia, built on slave labour and thriving as a profitable vineyard to this day? Other commentators have pointed out that in some ways the general emphasis on conserving the built environment may also reinforce a divide between rural and urban communities (Frescura 1992). As Khan reminds us, the problem is exacerbated by the forced removals which were the direct result of the Group Areas Act in the 1950s and the subsequent demolition and destruction of areas which otherwise would have been ripe candidates for the conservation of a rich cultural heritage today. Two of the most controversial casualties are District Six in Cape Town and Johannesburg's famous suburb, Sophiatown (cynically renamed Triomf by the apartheid government).

Given this legacy, it is understandable that a certain degree of scepticism surrounds discussions about heritage. Nevertheless the media played a significant role in engaging a broader public in the monument debate in the lead up to the elections. First-hand accounts of visits to the Voortrekker Monument by individuals who would have previously felt excluded have been particularly effective here. Joe Louw, a well-known black photo-journalist famous for his photographs taken in the aftermath of Martin Luther King's assassination, writing in the *Saturday Star* pessimistically views the Monument as 'A concrete symbol of separate worlds'. Louw describes his feelings on encountering the Monument in 1992: 'Its immense box-like granite mass imparts the feeling of a fortress – defensive, mute and immovable. For a politically aware black person to even approach the thing requires some profound self-examination.' He attacks the guidebook's narrative, which constantly invokes the fiction of the interior as an uninhabited land – a point contradicted by the guide writer's own narrative since 'the rest of the trekker story is precisely about the bloody battles they had to fight in this supposedly "empty" country'. And finally, referring to the panel of the Zulu attack on the laager at Bloukrans as 'perhaps the most provocative and nauseating scene in which Zulus treacherously attack the trekkers – beating to death mostly women and children with sticks and assegais', Louw despairs of the kind of impression this must leave on the minds of both black and white children who visit the Monument. 'I left the monument in a profound state of sadness', he ends. 'Nowhere was there portrayed even a single gesture of kindness, mercy, magnanimity or heroism by any black. Instead they are shown either kneeling or killing. What a way to prepare the country, especially the country's youth, for the "new" era of mutual trust and tolerance' (*Saturday Star*, 7 November 1992).

In 1996 (two years after the election of Mandela's government), a visit to the Monument by another prominent black public figure made national headlines. Tokyo Sexwale, at that time the charismatic Premier of Gauteng Province, was photographed in a special spread in the *Sunday Times* (Figure 8.7). Gauteng, the recently renamed Transvaal, was, of course, the province historically most closely associated with Afrikaner nationalism. This is an interesting article for many reasons – and significantly different in tone from Joe Louw's earlier piece. Unlike

Figure 8.7 Tokyo Sexwale photographed in front of a panel from the marble frieze. *Sunday Times*, 15 December 1996.

Louw, who reports on the oppressive nature of the historical narratives represented in the Monument's frieze and the negative aspects of the representation of
black protagonists throughout – Sexwale, adopts a different strategy. While
Louw's consists of pointing out the absences and distortions in the Monument's
representation of the past, Sexwale reads this against the grain. He effectively
performs a 'translation' of inversion of the prime symbols of the Monument,
starting with the entrance. Noticing the granite laager of sixty-four covered
wagons surrounding the Monument, which symbolically was designed 'to protect
the tradition and sanctity of the [Afrikaner] nation against any attack' (Board of
Control of the Voortrekker Monument 1954), he is quoted as saying, 'Now I
understand the laager mentality. But I'm glad there is a gateway, or the whole
Afrikaner nation would have been trapped inside' (City Metro edition of the
Sunday Times, 15 December 1996). The gates themselves, which he insists on
being photographed opening, are in the form of assegais symbolic of Dingane's
power apparently blocking the path of civilisation (Figure 8.8). Sexwale's retort
to this is that 'It was precisely the assegais at its height that turned the tide.
Umkhonto we Sizwe, the spear of the nation, opened up the path of civilisation'
City Metro edition of the *Sunday Times*, 15 December 1996).

In a sense then, the Monument becomes the focus for an active process of
'translation' in terms of Gayatri Spivak's proposition of the 'reader as translator' – reading against the grain. Arguably, Sexwale's 'translation' of the symbolic
structure of the Monument is in some ways much more effective a strategy in the
case of the almost irredeemable Voortrekker Monument than it might be in
another example (say Robben Island) already associated with the heroic stoicism
of the liberation struggle.

More than this, however, Sexwale's inversion or 'Africanization' recalls a much
earlier moment in the Monument's history and reclaims for African consumption
what was identified at its founding as the hybrid nature of the iconographic
schema. By so doing, I want to argue, he attempts to render the structure 'safe'
and to disinvest the Monument of the power of its oppressive legacy as a hinge-
pin in the armoury of apartheid. In terms of the politics of national unity which
was so prevalent in 1996, his strategy may well have been motivated by the
diplomatic apeasement for which he became well known, but this does not dimin-
ish the broader effectivity of such a gesture.

As Elizabeth Delmont has pointed out, from its inception the Voortrekker
Monument was conceived as an architectural structure designed to cement the
historical legitimacy of an Afrikaner ascendancy (Delmont 1993). To this effect
the architect Gerard Moerdijk in his discussion in the guidebook on the design
and symbolism of the Monument places the Monument within a lineage of other
internationally significant locations, including the Mausoleum of Halicarnassus.
While acknowledging the disparity in scale, Moerdijk is not reticent about
marshalling the Hôtel des Invalides in Paris and India's Taj Mahal as points of
comparison. He points out that another detail such as the ornamental zig-zag
decoration above the large windows is borrowed from cuneiform writing to
indicate water and fertility with a reference to the importance of procreation for

Figure 8.8 Tokyo Sexwale opening the gates to the Monument. *Sunday Times*, 15 December 1996.

the Voortrekkers. Significantly, the two examples which he sees as most appropriate to the African context and which most effectively serve to bolster the ideology of the Afrikaners' right to the African soil are taken from Egypt and what was then Southern Rhodesia:

> Vastness is more than anything else a characteristic of Africa, a vastness that dwarfs the work of man. This is not so much a matter of actual size but rather one of appreciation and understanding. History teaches that one nation in particular could convey this characteristic of vastness in its works – the Egyptians. Even in their smaller edifices they succeeded in embodying a reflection of this greatness of Africa. Because of similar basic building principles it so happens that of all structures in Southern Africa this vastness of Africa is best reflected in the Zimbabwe Ruins in Southern Rhodesia.
>
> (Board of Control of the Voortrekker Monument 1954: 35)

The explicit reference to the Zimbabwe Ruins or 'Great Zimbabwe' (as it later came to be known) at the founding of the Monument is more interesting than at first it seems. Some scholars have dismissed this as simply another instance of invoking the degenerationist thesis which made it possible to praise certain apparently ancient civilizations in Africa without conceding to them a past which spoke of cultural and political greatness (Delmont 1993: 87).[3] This may well have been the intention. I think however, that this argument does not take into account that this was a highly contested topic at the time and its use may well forground the need to dispel any anxiety about the legitimacy of the Afrikaner's originary claims. Many South African intellectuals, amateur historians, archaeologists and certainly ideologues with an interest in constructing a historical and political lineage for Afrikaner nationalism were probably only too familiar with debates concerning the origin of the 'ruins'. As both Saul Dubow and Henrika Kuklick have pointed out, these debates have a long history which is intimately bound up with nationalist competition between South African, German and British archaeologists as part of the disciplinary history of anthropology and archaeology (Dubow 1996; Kuklick 1991). More to the point, however, in terms of how these debates might have impacted on the significance of the Voortrekker Monument, it is important to note that Gertrude Caton-Thompson's defence of Randall-MacIver's earlier claim for a 'Bantu' (that is African) origin for the 'ruins' comes to the fore in a series of highly public, volatile and entertaining debates in South Africa, widely reported in the national press at precisely the time when Afrikaner nationalism was beginning to be consolidated culturally (Hofmeyr 1987; Kuklick 1991: 152).[4] By the 1950s the controversy showed no signs of abating, and the literature on the mysteries of the origins of the 'ruins' was to continue growing exponentially well into independence (Kucklick 1991: 156). The fact that the official guidebook deliberately draws attention to an iconographic forerunner for one of the founding Monuments of Afrikaner nationalism – the 'Zimbabwe ruins' – whose public profile has been one of contestation around its African origins, speaks of the imperative for the Afrikaner nationalists to appropriate Africa to itself. But it was a risky gesture in the 1930s as it was still in the 1950s. The instability of the 'Zimbabwe ruins' as a sign ripe for recuperation during this earlier period has effectively and unambiguously been put to work for the 'opposition' in Sexwale's 'translation', while none the less offering conciliatory gestures to an anxious Afrikaner contingent very much in the way of another neat reversal of the 'concessions' made to the black majority in the opening speeches on the occasion of the consecrating of the Monument in 1949.[5] These are the complex underpinnings which I would argue make Sexwale's understated performance so compelling in the 1990s.

But potentially subversive readings of the Monument are not the monopoly of a single sector in the 'new' South Africa. Neither do they represent a simple choice between the revisionist critique offered by Louw or the 'reader as translator' offered by Sexwale. In June 1995 a new Afrikaans-language porn magazine, published by the owners of the South African edition of *Hustler*, hit the market. The title *Loslyf* roughly translates as 'Loose (body) living'. I want to argue here that the conjunction of image and text in the shoot featuring the Voortrekker Monument represents something more interesting than the usual disrespect for the boundaries between sacred and profane which is the staple of much pornographic literature and that it constitutes a more serious critique of the most oppressive version of Afrikaner ethnic absolutism. However, in order to make this claim one has to appreciate the context out of which the magazine is launched, the role of state censorship in South Africa and the emergence of an Afrikaner lower middle-class constituency which the editors of the magazine see as their readership along with a coterie of middle-class Afrikaner dissenters and intellectuals (which provide the bulk of the editorial staff) who are now even more intent on differentiating themselves from those ideally addressed by the symbolic litany of the Monument.

Flagged on the cover as 'Dina at the Monument', the feature is called 'Dina – *Loslyf*'s indigenous flower of the month' (Figure 8.9). This is no simple transgression being performed here but one which bears some analysis. That the photo-shoot is represented as taking place in the hallowed grounds of Monument Hill with the Voortrekker Monument looming large in the near background is one kind of slap in the face for the Calvinist puritanism of Afrikaner nationalists. But there are many other features which make this a more knowing trespass. I don't have the space to raise them all but two central conceits are crucial to its effectiveness in the South African context.

One of the primary conceits of this feature is that Dina is not just another porn star but is apparently related to one of the central figures in the Great Trek narrative commemorated by the Monument itself – General Andries Hendrik Potgieter, one of the Leaders of the Voortrekkers (Figures 8.10, 8.11). Mobilizing the very discourses through which Afrikaaner nationalism constituted itself as the guardian of the white race (civilization) – the indelible bonds of blood and family – Dina is quoted saying, 'My great great grandfather, Hendrik Potgieter, has been my hero since my childhood. He was the sort of man who inspired people to trek barefoot over the Drakensberg mountains so that us Boere could

Figure 8.9 'Dina – Loslyf's indigenous flower of the month'. *Loslyf*, June 1995.

be free and at peace living here in the Transvaal. If only we could have a leader of his calibre today' (*Loslyf* 1995: 125). To a South African reader schooled during apartheid this text is also clearly written as a pastiche of the standard children's history textbook version of the Trek.[6]

In addition, Dina, described as 'Loslyf's very first indigenous flower', devoid of the standard boudoir accoutrements of the other models in the magazine, is photographed *en plein air*, amidst the long grasses at the foot of the Monument. Traditionally the relationship of the Voortrekker to the concept of nature is a complex one. The idea of the Trekker as 'a child of the South African wilderness' was a myth obviously calculated to enhance the Trekker's claim to the land through demonstrating a special affinity with the rugged natural environment of the South African landscape. Dina's description and the 'natural' surroundings of the shoot clearly rely on this association while potentially exposing the contradictions of its sexual content.

Similarly, guides to the Monument refer to earlier Dutch or Portuguese settlers as finding 'the interior of Africa too vast, the forces of nature too strong . . . It was left to the Voortrekkers . . . to force, at a great price, an entry into the interior and establish a white civilisation . . . To achieve his ideal, he had to tame nature, conquer the savages and establish his state' (Board of Control of the Voortrekker Monument 1954: 31). In fact such copy could easily have found its way into the

Figure 8.10 The statue representing General Hendriek Potgieter at the corner of the Monument. Board of Control of the Voortrekker Monument, *The Voortrekker Monument*, Pretoria, 1954.

pages of a less knowing porn magazine verbatim, since it conforms creditably with most of the basic requirements of pornographic writing. The conceit of Dina as 'indigenous flower' plays with the implicitly sexual content of such an ideology and the violence which underscores it.

In the symbolic schema of the Voortrekker Monument, the Voortrekker ideal is achieved through the statue of the Voortrekker Mother and her two children representing 'white civilization', 'while the black wildebeest [in retreat] portray the ever threatening dangers of Africa' (Board of Control of the Voortrekker Monument 1954: 36) (Figure 8.12). Far from the Calvanist puritanism of the early Voortrekker dress and 'kappie', our 'indigenous flower' is confusingly kitted in an outfit more resonant of the threat of the African wild or of the male Voor-trekkers' attempts to tame it (especially in those shots of her posing in a man's bush jacket). Neither is motherhood the first thing on her mind. In fact she disrupts the versions of both femininity and masculinity (black and white) played out in the Monument frieze itself, providing a kind of composite figure where both gendered and ethnic identifications are deliberately confused. Dina's attire also makes reference to the pugilistic qualities of the Boer women, often indicated in histories of the Trek and immortalized in the Monument's own frieze. The

Figure 8.11 Dina photographed with the statue of Potgieter in the background. *Loslyf*, June 1995.

effect here is to display the contradictions of the image of the demure Calvinist home-maker and procreator of the Boer nation, by casting the Boer woman as Amazon: in other words, exposing the contradiction by explicitly sexualizing her warrior status.

In a timely finale, given the furore raging over heritage and monuments, the story line culminates with relentless punning: 'The 24-year-old nurse from Pretoria doesn't beat around the bush when she speaks of her love of Afrikaans language and culture. "All the people who are so eager to punish the Afrikaner volk by demolishing and desecrating our monuments are playing with fire. They should know: if you interfere with my symbols, you interfere with me"'. (*Loslyf* 1995: 125). There are many levels on which such appropriations might work as potentially transgressive strategies in relation to the primary myths of Afrikaner nationalism – not the least of which is that it breaks down the mythic conception of the Afrikaner as a homogenous mass completely in thrall to the doctrines of apartheid and their Calvinist origins – although the fact that such an image is still consumed within the context of pornography might clearly mediate any critical edge by turning back on itself, since the potential exposure of the sexualized violence of colonial and fascist discourse can become itself a source of titillation in its consumption as pornography.

Figure 8.12 Boer mother and child intended to represent 'white civilisation' with 'retreating' black wildebeest on either side intended to 'portray the ever threatening dangers of Africa'. Board of Control of the Voortrekker Monument, *The Voortrekker Monument*, Pretoria, 1954.

Other factors, however, support this reading of the feature as critique. The editor Ryk Hattingh has an interesting history in relationship to campaigns against state censorship (not just *vis-à-vis* porn) and has long been associated with an identifiable group of Afrikaans-speaking writers against apartheid who campaigned for freedom of speech. In 1988 he wrote and staged a play, *Sing Jy Van Bomme* (Singing about bombs), which created something of a stir because of its caustic critique of the South African military. He was also a journalist on the now defunct social-democrat independent Afrikaans weekly *Vrye Weekblad* and the monthly paper *Die Suid Afrikaan*, both (and especially *Vrye Weekblad*) known for their outspoken criticisms of the apartheid state. Journalists on both papers were frequently harassed and threatened, charged and faced suspension under the terms of the emergency media regulations imposed by the state during the period of draconian censorship in the 1980s (Tomaselli and Louw 1991: 90).

In addition, by the 1990s *Vrye Weekblad* had transformed itself into a bilingual magazine with a cultural and academic emphasis, with the editor Max du Preez arguing as justification in an interview on SABC English Service (*Weekly Mail and Guardian*, 12 March 1991) that an alternative newspaper was no longer an effective critical platform, 'It is yesterday's cause to be an alternative newspaper' (Tomaselli and Louw 1991: 226). Given this reasoning, one might ask (especially in a country where pornography of any kind was banned and where, after all, television was banned until 1975) whether a porn magazine might offer a more effective 'shock' vehicle and a space for critical intervention no longer available through the medium of the alternative press.

A further factor here is that in May 1995 Du Preez himself became directly involved in the monument and heritage debates. In this instance the monument concerned was that other canonical monument to Arikaner nationalism – the Taalmonument (Afrikaans Language Monument). Du Preez was responsible for an Agenda programme on the monument which resulted in a high-profile hearing by the Broadcasting Complaints Commission (BCCSA), with complaints being brought against the South African Broadcasting Corporation (SABC) by the Afrikaner Kultuurbond, D. J. Malan and others after the broadcast on 3 April, on the grounds that the language was objectionable and that descriptions of the monument as a penis were offensive (*Star*, 20 May 1995). Agenda won the case. Given this recent history, the repetition in *Loslyf* of a staged sacrilege featuring the Voortrekker Monument and deliberately signalling the wider monument debate gains a more critical dimension.

Finally, *Loslyf* appears at the same time that the Constitutional Court is decid-ing an important test case on the legality of banning pornography, with the Centre for Applied Legal Studies at the University of the Witwatersrand in Johannesburg arguing that it is not viable to contend that although 'free political discourse is an unassailable right, . . . expression on the level of pornography can justifiably be limited if this is in the common good'. Their opposition to such a judgement rested on the case that, 'with South Africa's history of censorship, all kinds of expression should be protected' and that, in answer to the Christian Lawyers' Association's position that pornography encouraged violence against women, there was little sociological evidence to support this (*Weekly Mail and Guardian*, 1 September 1995). That same year the new Film and Publications Bill, criticized in some quarters as 'the latest attempt to formalise censorship in [South Africa]' was also being debated.[7]

While censorship is always a hotly debated issue amongst defenders of civil liberties, the moral right and different factions of the women's movement (this latter particularly in relation to pornography), in the South African context its implementation has historically carried with it more serious penalties than in liberal democracies. Given the history of censorship in South Africa and its inextricable association with the apartheid state, it is understandable that those who have been most active in defending the rights of the individual against the limits set by the state are also those who are most anxious to ensure that such powers are never again available to the state even under the ANC.

It seems to me that the critical conjuncture of these factors occurring at the time of *Loslyf*'s launch combine to cement the view that it was certainly a strategic intervention by a knowing body of journalists (both men and women) associated very publicly with the censorship debate. Whether or not the magazine was widely circulated, it received enough attention to be reported in the progressive *Weekly Mail and Guardian*, where *Loslyf* editor Ryk Hattingh confirmed the view that the ideal readership was partly made up of the very Afrikaner constituency who were the lower-middle-class entrepreneurs whom we have seen growing steadily disaffected with the displays of 'traditional' volkishness of the far right and who wish (for whatever reasons, not all of which are in any way progressive) to differentiate themselves from this group (*Weekly Mail and Guardian*, 20 September 1996; Hyslop 1998).

It may not be insignificant, either, that *Loslyf* comes out of Larry Flynt's *Hustler* stable. According to Laura Kipnis, in an incisive analysis of *Hustler's* profile in terms of both gender and national politics *Hustler* is a clearly classed product intent on 'rampantly transgressing bourgeois norms and sullying bourgeois property and proprieties' (Kipnis 1992: 376). In this sense *Loslyf* shares something with its stablemate, particularly in its scatalogical humour and its refusal to buy into the tasteful rewriting of the Trek as a romantic narrative of ecological power-sharing between Boer, Ndebele and Zulu that has been a symptom of some aspects of the restaging of Afrikaner identity since 1994. As Hattingh says, 'Afrikaners have always been portrayed as khaki-clad repressed people and I wanted to show them as normal, sexual, fucking human beings' (*Weekly Mail and Guardian*, 20 September 1996). It also shares *Hustler's* outspoken and irreverent political satire, one difference being that the South African targets are, so far, more consistently levelled at the right than *Hustler's* idiosyncratic and highly problematic indiscriminate targeting.

Conclusion

Clearly the Voortrekker Monument of the 1990s is not quite the Monument it used to be. From a monolithic construction dedicated to a singular and for many years hegemonic version of the Afrikaner nationalist narrative it has effectively been transformed by various constituencies. Each of these constituencies has, for different and in some cases competing reasons, attempted to disrupt the hegemony of that version of Afrikanerdom symbolized by the Monument in the mind of so many South Africans. Because of these strategic and knowing interventions, the Monument has become a hybrid which, if not able to disinvest the monolith of its ignoble and oppressive past, does at least offer the possibility of indifference in its future.

Notes

This chapter is part of a larger book project on the role of cultural policy and visual culture in the construction of public memory in post-apartheid South Africa. I have been fortunate to benefit from the constant encouragement and critical insights of many colleagues whose own work on Southern African history has been indispensable to mine. Thanks to Shula Marks and Hilary Sapire for inviting me to speak in the Southern African Seminar at the Institute of Commonwealth Studies in London and for the constructive comments of many of the participants. Thanks in particular to Isabel Hofmeyr for frequent discussions and critical readings and for very generously translating large sections of Afrikaans. Thanks also to John Hyslop and Hilary Sapire for advice and information and to Jean Brundrit for sharing her copy of *Loslyf* and for translating much of the contents for me. Thanks also to Neil Lazarus for early discussions on the Voortrekker Monument and to Nico Coetzee for sharing with me his extraordinary wealth of knowledge on the history and iconography of the Voortrekker Monument and other Boer monuments.

1 The proposed monument of Mandela's fist was particularly controversial for two reasons. The suggested artist for the project was Danie de Jager, better known for his bust of Verwoerd and consequently not associated with a critique of the apartheid regime. Second, some sponsorship for the project was to come from Abe and Solly Krok, two businessmen better known for the fortune they made out of marketing a 'skin-lightening' cream.

2 The Day of the Vow fell on 16 December each year, and during apartheid was a public holiday which commemorated the moment when the Voortrekkers took a vow before God that they would hold this day forever sacred and commemorate it to his honour if he granted them victory over the Zulu. Following apartheid it is known as the day of reconciliation or goodwill. There is a nice irony here in that the shaft of light no longer hits its target owing to the idiosyncrasies of planetary activity.

3 For a further elaboration on the ways in which the concept of degeneration operated in terms of colonial evaluations of material culture from West Africa in the late nineteenth century, see my *Reinventing Africa: Museums, Material Culture and Popular Imagination in Late Victorian and Edwardian England*, New Haven and London, Yale University Press, 1994.

4 Kuklick argues, however, that certain aspects of Caton-Thompson's case for an African origin for Great Zimbabwe could also find favour with white settlers since she claimed to find traces of foreign influences in the buildings and they could latch on to such smaller qualifications in her argument.

5 See for example, the Historical Record commemorating the consecration of the Monument in 1949 where one of the opening speeches by General Smuts states, 'The Voortrekker struggle was not against the natives as such, but against barbarous chiefs who, with their Zulu doctrines, made the interior of Natal, the Transvaal and the Free State a wilderness and so unwittingly cleared the country for White settlement' (Smuts 1949: 32).

6 Thanks to Isabel Hofmeyr for pointing this out to me.

7 This Bill became law by October 1996 following much debate and also considerable antagonism from the ANC Women's League, who considered it to be too liberal.

Bibliography

Benjamin, W. (1969) *Illuminations*, New York: Schoken Books.

Board of Control of the Voortrekker Monument (1954) *The Voortrekker Monument Pretoria*, Pretoria: Board of Control of the Voortrekker Monument.

Brown, J., Manning, P., Shapiro, K., Weiner, J. (eds) (1991) *History From South Africa: Alternative Visions and Practices*, Philadelphia: Temple University Press.

Coombes, A. E. (1994) *Reinventing Africa: Museums, Material Culture and Popular Imagination in Late Victorian and Edwardian England*, New Haven and London: Yale University Press.

Delmont, E. (1993) 'The Voortrekker Monument: Monolith to Myth', *South African Historical Journal*, 29: 76–101.

Dubow, S. (1996) 'Human Origin, Race Typology and the Other Raymond Dart', in P. F. Alexander, R. Hutchison and D. Schreuder (eds), *Africa Today*, Canberra: Australian National University.

Frescura, F. (1992) 'Monuments and the Monumentalisation of Myths', unpublished paper, Johannesburg: University of the Witwatersrand.

Grundlingh, A. and Sapire, H. (1989) 'From Feverish Festival to Repetitive Ritual? The Changing Fortunes of Great Trek Mythology in an Industrializing South Africa, 1938–1988', *South African Historical Journal*, 21: 19–37.

Hofmeyr, I. (1987) 'Building a Nation from Words: Afrikaans Language, Literature and Ethnic Identity, 1902–1924', in S. Marks and S. Trapido (eds), *The Politics of Race, Class and Nationalism in Twentieth Century South Africa*, New York and London: Longman.

—— (1988) 'Popularizing History: The Case of Gustav Preller', *Journal of African History*, 29: 521–35.

Hyslop, J. (1996) 'Why was the White Right Unable to Stop South Africa's Democratic Transition?', in P. F. Alexander, R. Hutchison and D. Schreuder (eds), *Africa Today*, Canberra: Australian National University.

—— (1998) 'Why Did Apartheid's Supporters Capitulate: "Whiteness", Class and Consumption in Urban South Africa, 1985–1995', unpublished seminar paper.

Khan, F. (1992) 'Hidden Heritage: Our Past, Our Future', unpublished paper, Johannesburg: University of the Witwatersrand.

Kipnis, L. (1992) '(Male) Desire and (Female) Disgust: Reading Hustler', in L. Grossberg, C. Nelson, P. Treichler, *Cultural Studies*, New York, London: Routledge.

Kuklick, H. (1991) 'Contested Monuments: The Politics of Archaeology in Southern Africa', *History of Anthropology*, 7: 135–69.

Loslyf (1995) Johannesburg: J. T. Publishing.

McClintock, A. (1995) *Imperial Leather: Race, Gender and Sexuality in the Colonial Contest*, London and New York: Routledge.

O'Meara, D. (1983) *Volkskapitalisme: Class, Capital and Ideology in the Development of Afrikaner Nationalism 1934–1948*, Johannesburg: Raven Press and Cambridge: Cambridge University Press.

Spivak, G. C. (1993) *Outside in the Teaching Machine*, New York and London: Routledge.

Tomaselli, K. and Louw, P. E. (1991) *The Alternative Press in South Africa*, London: James Currey.

Vail, L. (ed.) (1989) *The Creation of Tribalism in Southern Africa*, Berkeley: University of California Press.

9 Technologies of conversion: cloth and Christianity in Polynesia

Nicholas Thomas

Like anthropological discourses, museum collections and exhibitions have long been sites for the invention and display of essentialized identities. Nineteenth-century ethnologists mapped out culture areas and painstakingly provenanced and described the repertories of ethnographic objects that belonged to particular peoples or tribes. This geographic and ethnic classification has remained the most widespread organizational principle in ethnographic museums: it is one that lends direct support to efforts of cultural typification, and marginalizes the historical formation of culture. Though many of these institutions' collections include remarkable objects attesting to cross-cultural influence and exchange, such as indigenous carvings representing colonial officials and missionaries, such pieces have generally been marginalized or wholly excluded from displays and published discussions, which instead use material culture to evoke cultures ahistorically.

The critique of anthropology's ahistorical biases has a long history. Though the argument for contextualization of the indigenous societies typically studied remained peripheral until the late 1960s, historical anthropology steadily emerged as a more rigorous and sophisticated approach through the 1970s and 1980s. Studies of indigenous art and material culture, however, lagged behind, and even when careful work was being done on 'cultural change', many museum ethnologists continued to work in an essentially descriptive manner, at considerable remove from debates concerning essentialism in cultural theory. It is not surprising, therefore, that around the time James Clifford's lucid account of the postmodern repudiation of cultural essentialism appeared, similar notions were being rapidly and sometimes uncritically embraced by curators, and others involved in the study and representation of indigenous material culture (Clifford 1991).

The 'new museology' has had many positive dimensions. In countries such as Australia, New Zealand, and the United States it has had profoundly important ramifications for the negotiation of indigenous and curatorial authority around acquisition, collection management, and curatorial questions. But the issue I want to address here has more to do with the framing of objects in ways that might refute essentialist ethnic and cultural typifications. Indigenous artefacts that incorporate western materials or that mimic colonial objects are immediately salient to this project. They attest to cultural traffic that belies the stability of cultural boundaries, while their vigour and apparent subversive mimicry also challenge those who expect cultural change to result in mere acculturation or westernization. The carving of the colonial officer, the mask that features a hurricane lamp (Figure 9.1), attests to a disorderly and fertile zone of hybrid, creolized cultural production. Objects and scenes of the type reproduced in Clifford's *Predicament of Culture*, and particularly in his set of 'affinity' images (which sketched out a critical alternative to the now-notorious MOMA exhibition on 'Primitivism in 20th Century Art')[1] exhibit the hybridizing tendencies that post-colonial curators and intellectuals have been anxious to identify, as the exemplifications of creative subversion in the global cultural order.

I suggest that it is necessary to work out a nuanced attitude toward this affirmation of transcultural artefacts. On the one hand, the older essentializing discourses and modes of exhibition were certainly highly problematic; they did and do represent factories for the materialization of colonial and neo-colonial typifications. (Though a great deal more might be said about the power and the workings of certain ways of showcasing indigenous pieces. Their essentialism may be notable, without it being their most compelling feature.) From this point of view, the exhibition of 'hybrid' artefacts that disrupt cultural boundaries remains highly attractive, and it is moreover the case that these 'hybrid' pieces reveal the extraordinary range of innovation in indigenous cultures of the colonial period, which has been rendered invisible by the stereotypes of traditional societies out of time. Hence exhibitions such as 'Paradise' at the Museum of Mankind in 1993, and the 1997 Osaka 'Images of Other Cultures' show, among many others, made important steps forward (O'Hanlon 1993; Clifford 1997; Yoshida and Mack 1997). However, it also needs to be acknowledged that the ground and the debate has shifted considerably. In markets around both African and Oceanic arts, neo-traditional colonial genres have received increasing attention. If some museums have remained deeply attached to ahistorical contextualization, collectors have not.

My main claim, however, is that the appeal of hybridity as a framing device must be seen primarily as a strategic one (Coombes 1994). That is, the presentation of objects as culturally mixed, as creolized or hybrid forms, is valuable for its contradiction of an essentializing order, and not because the 'hybrid' framing is necessarily at all apt to the historical context of the notionally hybrid objects. The substance of this chapter attempts to demonstrate that certain artefacts that are historically modern and innovative forms, that owe a good deal to colonial contact, are not productively seen as hybrid objects or as expressions of hybrid identity. It is arguable that they could best be seen not as objects at all but as techniques, as devices employed in projects of social transformation and self-transformation, which particular communities of Pacific Islanders were engaged in at particular times. The culturally 'mixed' nature of these objects does not somehow reflect or express a mixed 'identity' because it reflects no identity. If we describe the artefacts as bearers of a hybrid identity, we may be imprisoning them in a frame that is no less misleading and invidious than that of colonial ethnic typification. We do justice to their histories and stories only if we leave the

Figure 9.1 Eharo mask, Parimono village, Gulf Province, Papua New Guinea, before 1915, height 90 cm. Nature Focus/Australian Museum, Sydney, E23153.

globalized but originally western category of cultural identity out of the framing discourse altogether.

Polynesian barkcloth

Barkcloth, or *tapa*, is one of the material forms and – to adopt the term of an old-fashioned comparative ethnology – one of the cultural traits that manifests the affinities of peoples across Oceania.[2] It was produced all the way from insular Southeast Asia to Hawaii and Rapanui (or Easter Island). Though there were significant tapa traditions around coastal New Guinea, as well as in parts of the Solomon Islands, and in southern Vanuatu, Pacific barkcloth is associated above all with Polynesia, where its production and use were nearly pervasive.

The cloth, beaten from soaked strips of the bark of various ficus and paper mulberry trees, was nearly everywhere made by women, though it does not necessarily follow that it was defined as 'women's wealth'.[3] Much was undecorated, but much also was stained, rubbed, stencilled, stamped, or painted. Decoration often featured elaborate, optically dynamic non-figurative designs, some of which consisted of dense geometric motifs, and others of more open patterns and freehand elements (Figure 9.2). The material was used in garments, in various artefacts, and in rituals associated with hierarchy and reproductive exchange. There were generally various types and grades, ranging from heavy waterproofed clothes for common wear to very fine white tissue, often compared by early writers with muslin, which was monopolized by members of the elite. Though typically made and circulated simply in the form of sheets of cloth that were wrapped around the body, bundled, or extended in long strips, tapa was also sometimes used in figurative constructions, presumed to represent ancestral deities, notably in the Cook Islands, the Marquesas, and Rapanui.

The ritual significance of barkcloth related to identifications with the skin, which can be seen as 'natural' associations, in so far as the bark is the skin of the tree. What is more systematically fundamental, though, is the functional affinity between skin and cloth; both wrapped the body, containing contagious sacredness (*tapu*); additional wrappings were frequently required under conditions of peculiar ritual intensity or exposure, such as child birth, blood-letting rituals, and death.[4] Barkcloth certainly also marked the often-dangerous sacredness of a person or site. Mortuary places, the bodies of high-ranking people, and particular sacred artefacts, such as carvings of gods, were all consequently wrapped in tapa. Had an eighteenth-century Tahitian priest been transported through time and space to encounter one of the wrapped landscapes or buildings of the contemporary artist Christo, he would probably have had a much clearer idea of what the work meant than Christo ever arrived at himself.

In Fiji, Tonga, and Samoa, barkcloth making has never been abandoned. Tapa is still widely produced for huge presentations around events such as marriages, funerals, and high chiefly celebrations; it also features in contexts such as national and church diplomacy; through familial connections it is exported in considerable quantities for use among the Polynesia diasporas in New Zealand, the United

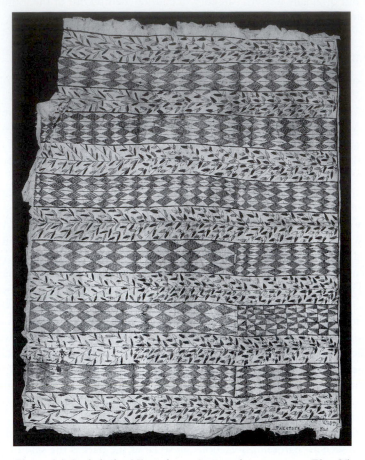

Figure 9.2 Barkcloth, Niue, late nineteenth century, *c.*72 × 95 cm. Nature Focus/Autralian Museum, Sydney, E2417.

States, and Australia; and it is also sold to tourists. In central and eastern Polynesia, that is in the Cook Islands, the Societies, the Marquesas, and Hawaii, tapa production on the other hand ceased at some point in the nineteenth century; perhaps as early as the 1820s or 1830s in Tahiti, and later in the nineteenth century in most island groups.

Even in those parts of western Polynesia where tapa is still extensively produced, its use as clothing has been long abandoned, except in exceptional ceremonial contexts and in cultural performances of various kinds. Hence it is partly misleading to speak of persistence in the west and abandonment in the east, since in both places shifts of a more diverse pattern have actually taken place, involving continuity in some domains, discontinuity in others, and new spheres of circulation, such as tourist markets.

Polynesian 'ponchos'

This history of the changing uses of indigenous and introduced textiles is intimately linked with the history of conversion to Christianity in the Pacific. As in
Africa, missionaries introduced manufactured cloth, and encouraged girls and
women to participate in sewing classes and to produce garments which missionaries' conformed to the standards of modesty, particularly for the purposes of
attending church. There is now an extensive literature on the ways evangelism was
not limited to changing religious beliefs, but entailed at the same time a far wider
conversion of 'social habits' of work, residence, conjugality, and gender roles
(Jolly and Macintyre 1989; Comaroff 1991; Thomas 1991; Eves 1996). Christianity brought not only new forms of worship and new beliefs; missionaries
attempted at least to impose new ideas of work, a new calendar, and a new sense of
the body. Sewing was important not only in itself but because its discipline
entailed the new way of being in the world that the missionaries sought to render
pervasive. Yet we cannot suppose that the Pacific Islander women who took up
sewing understood the practice in the same way that the missionaries did, nor that
they were necessarily transformed in the way that the missionaries desired. The
values of these new habits, modes of dress, and forms of worship for Samoans,
Tahitians, and other have to be investigated; we do not know what was received,
simply because we know what was being offered.

The most important Protestant mission in Oceania was the London Missionary
Society, which began work in Tahiti in 1797 and extended its efforts westward
from there to the Cook Islands, Samoa, Niue, and elsewhere in the first decades of
the nineteenth century.[5] In all these places progress was initially slow, but
indigenous elites as well as individual converts were gradually brought over to the
cause; the great majority of Tahitians were nominally Christian by the 1820s, and
by 1850 Christianity was well established also through most of western Polynesia.
The popular demonization of missionaries has obscured the point that evangeliza-
tion was effected, to a very substantial degree, not by white missionaries but by
Polynesian teachers and catechists. Though they were not, until much later, fully
ordained ministers, Tahitians, and later Cook Islanders and Samoans, were frequently landed by missionary ships and left to deal with hostile situations as best
they could, generally without the trade goods and other resources that gave the
white missionaries some nebulous measure of prestige. Even when a mission
was led by a white missionary and his wife, they were often accompanied by
several Polynesian families, upon whom much of the fraught business of cultural
negotiation and intervention presumably fell.

Not only was Tahiti the first base of LMS activity in the Pacific, it also happened
to be one of very few places in which there was any type of upper-body clothing.
Throughout Oceania, indigenous dress consisted in loincloths, waist-wraps, belts,
and skirts of various kinds; although flax and feather capes were made by Maori
and Hawaiians, the chest was generally routinely uncovered, except in Tahiti,
where early observers such as Cook and George Forster described garments like
ponchos, consisting simply of long rectangular pieces of cloth, bearing a slit or

hole through which the head was inserted. Although these were worn by both women and men, they were not so ubiquitous as to be remarked on by many observers, and the only early illustration of a *tiputa* being worn is of a chiefly man. There is no definite information suggesting that *tiputa* were worn only by persons of high status, but people of lower relative status were generally required to bare their chests in the presence of those more sacred, and it may accordingly be assumed that only those of high status routinely wore garments of this kind. A type of poncho was also worn in the pre-contact or at least the early-contact period in the Cook Islands; extant examples are often described as the dresses of high-born individuals, and are elaborately perforated with small diamond-shaped cuts, motifs associated in Cook Islands carving with sacred ceremonial adzes and the presences of deities.

At the time of the Cook voyages, Tahitian barkcloths in general were either undecorated, stained, or decorated in a minimal way, with circular motifs, stamped in red or black with the end of a cut bamboo. Even before 1798, however, a new style emerged, involving direct printing with leaves and ferns: 'they imprint sprigs and leaves on the cloth by wetting them with this juice, and impressing them on the cloth according to their fancy' (Wilson 1799: 371). Reasonably enough, Kooijman suggests that this was stimulated by printed trade cloth that was presumably introduced during the Cook voyages or subsequently. There is a good example of this type of *tiputa* in the collection of the Powerhouse Museum in Sydney, which was acquired by Lachlan Macquarie while he was governor of New South Wales, probably from a trader, between 1810 and 1822 (Figure 9.3),[6] and another in the British Museum, which combines similar stamped ferns with a denser body of botanical motifs within a clearly defined diamond-shaped area.

If Tahitian ponchos undergo local changes in the late eighteenth and early nineteenth centuries, the question of what *tiputa* are and where they are from becomes, soon afterwards, a great deal more complicated. There are many examples in museums that are decorated not with these stamped botanical motifs but with designs that are unmistakably western Polynesian; some of these are accordingly attributed to Samoa, Niue, or the Cook Islands, though others are said to be Tahitian, and even provenanced to collectors who visited Tahiti but not western Polynesia. If these pieces constitute a real anomaly, the wider phenomenon of the western Polynesian *tiputa* does not: it is clear that the Tahitian teachers who constituted the missionary vanguard in Samoa somehow managed to get the Samoans to adopt garments of this type, and that from the early 1830s to the 1860s, or perhaps later, they were made and worn by Christian Samoans, Niueans, and possibly Tongans. In the Cook Islands, older autochthonous poncho types were partially replaced by neo-traditional varieties associated with Tahitian missionary influence (Buck 1934). As imported cloth became more widely available, it came to be locally preferred, and, by the time islanders were being extensively photographed, nearly everybody was wearing European garments, except on occasions when 'traditional dress' was required. The journals of the enterprising John Williams (Figure 9.4), notable for their ethnographic acuity

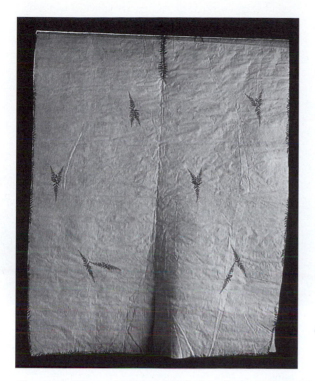

Figure 9.3 Tiputa, Tahiti, *c*.1815, length (unfolded) 234 cm, width 93 cm. Powerhouse Museum, Sydney, 86/395.

as well as their evangelical and imperialistic zeal, enable us to make some sense of the question of precisely why a change of dress might have constituted an issue, during the early phases of the conversion process in Samoa.

Thanks to Bougainville and many writers since, Tahiti has the reputation of being an 'island of love', while Samoa after Derek Freeman's supposed refutation of Margaret Mead is taken in contrast to have been a pretty repressed place. Going on the experiences of the Tahitian teachers deposited on Upolo by Williams in 1830, these images might be reversed: the Tahitians preached restraint while the Samoans paraded their sexual licence. The important point is not that the Tahitians were reputedly shocked by Samoan sexuality, nor that exhibitionism and orgiastic ceremonies loom large in Williams's account of heathen Samoan mores; it is rather that Tahitian teachers and Samoans alike evidently understood their differences in terms of the exposure and the display of the body.

When Williams returned to Samoa in 1832, he enquired of the Tahitian teachers whether 'they had not taught them [that is the Samoans] to make their nice white Tahitian cloth' (incidentally thereby indicating that the bark-cloth appealed to the missionaries because of its plain and chaste associations, associations that are hardly likely to have been present in Tahitians' minds).

Figure 9.4 George Baxter, *The Reception of the Reverend John Williams at Tanna in the South Seas*, 1843, oil print, 21 × 32 cm. Private collection, Canberra. This image of Williams's arrival in southern Vanuatu (formally New Hebrides) in 1839 draws attention to the fabrics and other objects that he brought as gifts.

They said they themselves had made a great deal for the Chiefs but they could not get the women to learn. They were so intolerably lazy. They liked the cloth very well to put round their middles but they could not induce them to cover their persons of which they are exceedingly proud especially their breasts which are generally very large. They are continually wishing the teachers wives to lay aside their garments & 'faasamoa' do as the Samoa ladies do, gird a shaggy mat round their loins as low down as they can tuck up the corner in order to expose the whole front & side of the left thigh anoint themselves beautifully with scented oil, tinge themselves with turmeric put a string of blue beads round their neck & then faariaria [make a display] walk about to show themselves. You will have, they say, all the *Manaia* the handsome young men of the town loving you then.

(Moyle 1984: 117)

Williams elsewhere reported that a young European whom he considered 'respectable' had initially been troubled by women removing their mats and exposing their genitals; his shy response prompted others to do the same and dance before him, 'desiring him not to be bashful or angry it was Faa Samoa or Samoa fashion' (Moyle 1984: 232). It appears, in other words, as though

Samoans, and Samoan women in particular, were responding assertively to Tahitian and European foreigners alike, insistently displaying their bodies, insisting on the pleasure of self-decoration, and on the value of these practices as Samoan practices.

Even in 1832, however, this was not a sustained or consistent line of resistance. Williams had learned even as he was approaching Upolo and Savai'i the second time that many of the people had turned to Christianity. This would seem an extraordinary development, if one understood Christianity as a European system that perforce had to be imposed by some powerful force of white missionaries; yet it is plain that Williams happened to bring the Tahitian teachers at a highly fortuitous moment, when a high chief and priest had recently been assassinated, when Malietoa, with whom Williams in effect formed an alliance, was in the ascendancy, (Moyle 1984: 10–11). The Samoan enthusiasm for Christianity at this moment thus seems to have had little to do with the concerns of the London Missionary Society, and Williams himself well understood that a plethora of motivations were at play, not least the fairly obvious interest in the acquisition of European wealth in various forms. Here again, though, we need to do more than merely note that islanders wanted guns or cloth, but ask what guns and cloth represented to them, and what guns and cloth enabled them to do.

It is notable that in Samoa, unlike neighbouring Tonga, and unlike Tahiti and the Cook Islands, barkcloth was not routinely used in ordinary garments. Dress consisted instead in several kinds of simple leaf skirts, and in a variety of grades of mats. The latter may have been held in place by barkcloth belts, but sheets of barkcloth themselves were not worn, except in exceptional ritual circumstances. The bride, for instance, wore a large piece of white *siapo* underneath her fine mats, and this piece was stained with blood when she was ritually defloured. The strong associations that barkcloth generally had with sanctity, and with ritually marked or dangerous states, elsewhere in Polynesia, can only have been intensified in Samoa, because it had fewer quotidian uses, though it's important to acknowledge that tapa was also used in household screens and in a few other situations, which were presumably not marked by peculiar sacredness.

It is striking that, if Williams's reports are to be credited, Samoan chiefs discoursing upon the merits of Christianity seem to have suggested that the religion was true because English people were visibly strong, and were visibly equipped with fine things, including especially clothes. He reported that one said 'Only look at the English people. They have noble ships while we have only canoes. They have strong beautiful clothes of various colours while we have only ti leaves. They have sharp knives while we have only a bamboo to cut with' (Moyle 1984: 237). Earlier, the chief Fauea, crucial as a go-between, had argued 'And you can see . . . that their God is superior to ours. They are clothed from the head down to the feet and we are naked' (1984: 68). I see no particular reason to suppose that Williams would have misrepresented these chiefs' statements, in the journal that he wrote up at the time; in any event, the suggestion that some spiritual condition is 'proved' by the efficacy and the well-being of the people concerned is very much in conformity with Polynesian rhetoric and ways of thinking. It is, however, interesting that well-being should be identified particularly with an abundance of clothing, and with the full covering of the body.

It would be hard to understand why a few fairly powerless Tahitians, or even one personally forceful Englishman, should have succeeded in imposing a Tahitian style of dress upon Samoans, whose political autonomy was in no sense compromised or threatened at this very early moment in contact history, and who clearly took pride in their own modes of comportment. But although Williams noted that some Samoan women sought to convert the Tahitian teachers' wives to the Samoan way rather than expressing any interest in changing themselves, some others however opted for cloth. Williams noted not only that 'Some few Samoans who have embraced Christianity have taken to wear cloth entirely' but also that 'On Sabbath days . . . the Teachers have succeeded in inducing the whole congregation men & women to attend properly clothed & decently covered' (Moyle 1984: 231). 'Cloth' means barkcloth and not mats, and 'decent covering' means that the women, or perhaps both men and women, were covering their breasts. Williams does not specifically mention *tiputa*, but these are presumably the upper body garments he has in mind, and there is one early Samoan poncho in the Australian Museum which is supposed to have been collected by him. Samoan *tiputa* were thus probably being made as early as 1832, or certainly by 1839, when the American explorer Wilkes noted that Samoans were wearing siapo 'wrappers' 'and the *tiputa*, a kind of poncho, of the same material, after the fashion of the Tahitians' (Wilkes, 1845, vol. 2: 141).

There are references in the missionary literature on Polynesia to converts wearing tapa ribbons to distinguish themselves from their pagan neighbours, but the point I want to make about these objects is that they were much more than mere markers of identities. To be sure, tapa clothes did indicate that a person was a Christian rather than a pagan Samoan, but I believe that the interpretative strategy of regarding things essentially as expressions of cultural, subcultural, religious, or political identities depends on too static and literal an approach to their meanings. We also need to go beyond another fairly obvious statement about these Samoan *tiputa*, which defines them as 'local appropriations' of a more pervasive form. Again, it is certainly true that these are Samoan variations upon a regional type, but it would be misleading if we suggested that 'localization' was a Samoan project, which motivated their production; it may rather be an aspect of their practice that has other motivations. Anthropological rhetoric at present tends to treat the global as something insidious, which locals have an interest in assimilating or incorporating, but the critical metanarrative of plural appropriations is ours rather than theirs; their investments may be in strategies that neither collude with nor resist global relations.

In this case, I suggest that the strategies used these material forms as a kind of technology, towards a new way of being in the world. Williams understood this; he was less interested in a badge or flag that declared a person's Christianity than in a technique of dress that altered the being of the convert, that manifested an inner redemption, or at least the scope for one. If it is unlikely that the Tahitian teachers shared this theology, they had in all likelihood adopted the notion of personal modesty, and saw the wearing of new garments as a means to that end. The Samoans too, would surely not have adopted these clothes had they not themselves regarded them as a technique of conversion; but what conversion meant to them, in 1832, is by no means easy to know. We can be sure that their ideas of self-transformation differed from those of Williams and the Tahitian Christians, and the most suggestive evidence lies perhaps in Fauea's observations on the strength and superiority of Christian people, with their ships and their full dress; this indicates broadly that the fully dressed body was an empowered body. We may infer, also, that the power of that body was conferred by tapa wrapping, by some kind of transmission of the sanctity that otherwise inhered in the use of tapa in more special ritual contexts. At any rate, if Samoans were transforming themselves, to some extent at the instigation of foreigners, they were also effect-ing a shift that was internal to Samoan culture and material culture. How far they were binding the values that cloth possessed in collective ritual uses in new forms that embraced the particular person is something that at this stage I can only guess about.

If *tiputa* started out, in Samoa, by bearing a Samoan strategy of empower-ment, these artefacts also entailed certain Christian values of individual self-presentation. The idea that a set of garments constituted one's 'Sunday best' implied both a new temporal order and a new spatial orientation, which made out of the church not only a space of worship but a theatre in which people might display their persons in a novel way.

Tivaevae

I want briefly to consider an entirely different type of material innovation. In the Cook Islands, the Society Islands, and Hawaii, barkcloth making declined and was abandoned over the course of the nineteenth century (earliest in Tahiti and towards the end of the nineteenth century in the Cook Islands). However women's efforts were transposed to the making of appliqué and patchwork quilts, known as *tivaevae* or *tifaifai* (in the Cook Islands and Society Islands respect-ively), which were never produced to a significant extent in places such as Samoa, Tonga, and Fiji, where barkcloth is still made in considerable quantities (Hammond 1986; Rongokea 1992; Thomas 1999). Hence it is broadly true that *tivaevae* are made where barkcloth is not, suggesting that quilts replaced cloth, and became valuable indigenous things because they took on the values that cloth once possessed. This would provide, then, a further instance of the argument of my book *Entangled Objects* that novel things may be assimilated to existing cat-egories (Thomas 1991). Although this argument attempted to demonstrate that indigenous peoples possessed the power to redefine introduced objects, it implied that their strategies were conservative, in the sense that they attempted to pre-serve a prior order rather than create a novel one. Here I seek to move beyond the constraints of an either/or approach. The value of *tivaevae*, I suggest, inhered in their doubleness; they were things that mobilized certain precedents, on the one hand, but possessed novelty and distinctiveness on the other.

The initial stimulus was provided by the New England missionary wives, who worked in Hawaii from the 1820s, and who immediately encouraged indigenous women to take up needlework. Quilts are referred to by travel writers from the 1850s onward, and are conspicuous in late nineteenth-century photographs. Though functionally identified as bedspreads, they seem frequently to be used as backdrops behind persons of high status, and are obviously items of display at ceremonies of various kinds. In the writing on the Society Islands and Cook Islands *tivaevae*, it tends to be assumed that these forms were similarly directly stimulated by missionary example, whereas it seems more probable that they were stimulated by contact with Hawaiians; while the English missionary wives certainly encouraged needlework to the same degree as the Americans, they did not bring nearly so developed a quilting tradition with them.

Appliqué quilts (Figure 9.5) are entirely different to traditional barkcloth, mats, and textiles in their methods of production and appearance, though there

Figure 9.5 A spectacular recent *tivaevae* by Maria Teokolai and others, *Ina and the Shark*, 1990, 257 × 247 cm. Collection of the Museum of New Zealand/Te Papa Tongarewa, Wellington, B24769.

are some continuities in the preponderance of botanical motifs, and in their uses. *Tivaevae* are hung up like curtains and adorn houses, churches, and spaces in which ceremonies are taking place. They are given to people to high status by being dropped before them or draped around them, in conformity with traditional presentations of tapa. In Niue and the Cook Islands, hair-cutting ceremonies mark a child's coming of age, and are occasions for major communal efforts, feasts, and gifts of cash. Quilts beneath and around the child recall the use of barkcloth in the traditional desanctifications of children and adolescents at successive points from the time of birth up to around puberty. It is unlikely, however, that many contemporary eastern Polynesians would acknowledge sustaining non-Christian notions of *tapu*, and an open question whether its operation in this kind of ritual would still be widely understood. The practice of hanging considerable numbers of quilts from church ceilings nevertheless suggests persisting associations with sanctity and rank, even if the old idea of contagious sacredness has been largely displaced by a generalized Christian notion of holiness.

Tivaevae are currently being embraced by art institutions and art dealers in Australia and New Zealand; they are being validated as cultural forms on the basis of their aesthetic qualities, and could be further affirmed, were it claimed that they have meanings that are derived from the meanings of barkcloth, and are therefore deeper than those of the antecedent white women's quilt forms. As I have already indicated, it is possible to make something of an argument along these lines. But the distinctiveness of this material form perhaps becomes more apparent if we consider its most obvious and quotidian function – as a bedspread – and its association with the household.

The evidence available to me concerning the early history of *tivaevae* and similar quilts is even more skeletal than the material I have already presented concerning *tiputa*. Hence it is appropriate that I offer no more than a sketchy reconstruction of their potential significance, in societies becoming Christian. As I noted earlier, conversion in the Pacific as elsewhere was much more than a matter of religious change. It also involved bringing the wider pattern of social life into some sort of conformity with English Christian ideas of marriage and familial life. This was arguably quite a task in eastern Polynesia, where residential and conjugal arrangements were highly various, and it could be argued that nothing approximating an English model domesticity really existed. Some food was gathered or produced by larger collectivities; some was obtained by individuals; men and women generally ate separately; men and women often slept separately; there was a good deal of recognized or *de facto* polygyny and polyandry; adoption was pervasive; and there were cult groups such as the Tahitian 'arioi that altogether removed youths from such domestic milieux as did exist. It is moreover notable that ordinary dwellings, and particularly their interiors, were not aesthetic foci in any sense. In fact, in general in eastern Polynesia, stone and wood carvings, and other architectural art forms, were situated around temple and mortuary precincts, rather than around chiefs' or men's houses, as was typically the case in western Oceania.

As objects, *tivaevae* could certainly be taken out of houses and used in various ritual contexts; but they were primarily associated with residential spaces and primarily displayed within them. In the Cook Islands, during the period of New Zealand administration, annual health inspections were conducted, involving visits to every house by government officials. These occasions were turned by Cook Islands women into a sort of competitive festival: the women would make their houses immaculate, and hang up as many *tivaevae* as they could bring together; houses were visited not only by the inspector, but by the entire community, who went on a sort of tour of everybody's residences. This custom was sustained after independence and remains a highlight of the calendar, I understand, in many parts of the Cooks today. I must admit that I do not know exactly when this started, or how *tivaevae* were initially used and displayed. My point is that their significance as artefacts lay partly in what they had in common with barkcloth, but that their special power lay in the ways they differed from it. Barkcloth was most typically produced in large sheets that were monopolized by chiefly people and transacted in the course of significant rituals. *Tivaevae* were and are often produced collectively by small groups of women (and by transsexuals), or by individuals, yet were located within particular households, and displayed, in order to display those households to advantage. They were, moreover, intimately connected with the bed, with the implication that particular people shared a domestic space.

In fact, the extent to which Polynesians such as Cook Islanders have really adopted the models of Christian domesticity and companionate marriage that the LMS advocated is arguably relatively limited; extended familial activities remain profoundly significant, as do sex-segregated ones, such as women's church activities and sports. What *tivaevae* have arguably done, though, is create an appearance and an aesthetic of domesticity, and it is in this sense that they can be seen as productive technologies that make social effects visible.

Conclusions

Tivaevae today are increasingly visible in Polynesian cultural festivals in New Zealand, which is becoming Aotearoa New Zealand – a Maori and Polynesian nation as much as a white settler one. They are, in other words, becoming expressions of a new Pacific identity (Figure 9.6). I do not deny that artefacts of all kinds can function in this way, as emblems of who people are or who they want to be. But my argument with respect to both *tiputa* and *tivaevae* is that this idea – that things may be simply markers of identities – impoverishes our sense of their workings. *Tiputa* were more than just Christian clothes; they were more than clothes that covered the body and effected a new modesty. They were also wrappings that were understood by Samoans, initially at least, to empower their bearers. And they were also Sunday best; they gave a new Christian calendar visibility and practical meaning; they were not part of a repressive missionary law as much as a productive effort, to teach people that their sense of self-worth and pride might be invested in their self-presentation on Sundays, on the path to the

Figure 9.6 Tivaevae (on bed and suspended from ceiling) incorporated into an instal-
lation presentation of a contemporary migrant Polynesian living room,
part of the exhibition, *Te Moemoea no Iotefa/The Dream of Joseph*, curated
by Rangihiroa Panoho, Sarjeant Gallery, Wanganui, New Zealand, 1989.
The fabric on the wall with grid patterning is a late nineteenth-century
piece of Samoan barkcloth.

church. What *tiputa* did for the body and the person, *tivaevae* did for domesticity
and the house. In both cases, these artefacts were not just expressions of a new
context but technologies that created that context anew.

This way of seeing things perhaps also helps us move beyond the categories
of identity that have shaped both colonial anthropology and that discipline's
post-colonial critique. People do not simply produce objects for the purposes of
social identification in traditional orders, or for the purposes of representing
and affirming identities in theatres of multicultural affirmation. Things do not
necessarily stand for cultures. People do not necessarily 'have' cultures that are
either integrated wholes or fused parts. They may have constructions of self,
history, and purpose that are indifferent to this language of cultural property,
that insists upon identity (whether stable or mixed) and upon identification via
artefacts.

Museum collections and exhibitions remain tremendously powerful and suggestive in many ways. If the historical dynamism of indigenous art traditions has

long been obscured, there are many reasons why the variety of innovation might be acknowledged now. It is important that the recognition of cross-cultural artefacts should not be limited to the celebration of their 'hybridity', their seeming exemplification of creolization. Artefacts such as *tiputa* and *tivaevae* can not only reveal the fissures and contradictions in the language of identity, they also suggest practices and histories that lie entirely beyond it.

Notes

1 See Clifford 1991: ch. 9.
2 See Kooijman 1972 for a good survey, albeit one that unavoidably leaves many questions unresolved.
3 As Annette Weiner generally argued in her important publications on gender and material culture in the Pacific (see, e.g., *Inalienable Possessions: The Paradox of Keeping-while-giving*, Berkeley, CA: University of California Press, 1992).
4 Gell 1993 *inter alia* provides useful discussion of rituals in which wrapping and tapa were crucial.
5 For the fullest review, see Gunson 1978.
6 On early post-contact changes in Tahitian barkcloth, see also Anne D'Alleva, *Shaping the Body Politic: Gender, Status and Power in the Art of Eighteenth-century Tahiti and the Society Islands*, Ph.D. dissertation, Columbia University, 1997.

Bibliography

Buck, P. H. (1934) *Arts and Crafts of the Cook Islands*, Honolulu, Bernice P. Bishop Museum.

Clifford, J. (1991) *The Predicament of Culture*, Cambridge, Mass., Harvard University Press.

Clifford, J. (1997) *Routes*, Cambridge, Mass., Harvard University Press.

Comaroff, J. and J. (1991) *Of Revelation and Revolution*, Chicago, Chicago University Press.

Coombes, A. E. (1994) 'The recalcitrant object: culture contact and the question of hybridity' in Barker, F., Hulme, P. and Iversen, M. (eds), *Colonial Discourse/Postcolonial Theory*, Manchester, Manchester University Press.

Eves, R. (1996) 'Colonialism, corporeality and character: Methodist missions and the refashioning of bodies in the Pacific', *History and Anthropology*, 10: 1, pp. 85–138.

Gell, A. (1993) *Wrapping in images: Tattooing in Polynesia*, Oxford, Oxford University Press.

Gunson, N. (1978) *Messengers of Grace: Evangelical Missionaries in the South Seas, 1797–1860*, Melbourne, Oxford University Press.

Hammond, J. D. (1986) *Tifaifai and Quilts of Polynesia*, Honolulu, University of Hawaii Press.

Jolly, M. and Macintyre, M. (eds) (1989) *Family and Gender in the Pacific*, Cambridge, Cambridge University Press.

Kooijman, S. (1972) *Tapa in Polynesia*, Honolulu, Bishop Museum.

Moyle, R. (ed.) (1984) *The Samoan Journals of John Williams, 1830 and 1832*, Canberra, Australian National University Press.

O'Hanlon, M. (1993) *Paradise: Portraying the New Guinea Highlands*, London, British Museum Press.

Rongokea, L. (1992) *Tivaevae: Portraits of Cook Island Quilting*, Wellington, Daphne Brassell.

Thomas, N. (1991) *Entangled Objects: Exchange, Material Culture and Colonialism in the Pacific*, Cambridge, Mass., Harvard University Press.

Thomas, N. (1992) 'Colonial conversions: history, hierarchy and difference in early twentieth century evangelical propaganda', *Comparative Studies in Society and History*.

Thomas, N. (1996) *Oceanic Art*, London, Thames and Hudson.

Thomas, N. (1999) 'The case of the misplaced ponchos', *Journal of Material Culture*, 2: 1, pp. 5–20.

Wilkes, C. (1845) *Narrative of the United States Exploring Expedition*, Philadelphia, Lea and Blanchard.

Wilson, W. (1799) *A Missionary Voyage to the Southern Pacific Ocean*, London, Chapman.

Yoshida, K. and Mack, J. (eds) (1997) *Images of Other Cultures*, Osaka, National Museum of Ethnology.

10 Re-dressing the past: the Africanisation of sartorial style in contemporary South Africa

Sandra Klopper

Following the unbanning of the African National Congress (ANC) and other political organisations in 1990, South Africa's formerly disenfranchised black majority began to reap the rewards of their painful but ultimately victorious struggle for freedom. Gradually attaining greater control over the country's economic and, more especially, its political future, those who led and supported this struggle against the Apartheid state's violent disregard for human life and dignity have either participated in or witnessed numerous events aimed at celebrating South Africa's transformation from minority to majority rule, especially after the country's first democratic election, held in May 1994. The role these public spectacles have played in reaffirming the eroded sense of ownership and belonging not only of former exiles but also of those who lived through the Apartheid era, is inestimable.

New and renewed visions of fashionableness have played a central role in these recent attempts to develop a post-Apartheid identity, in part because dress provides unlimited possibilities for the renegotiation and performance of notions of self. But, far from pointing to a clear and unproblematic development of new concepts of self, the clothing worn on official state occasions, and at other important public functions, ultimately serves to highlight not only the pride many people feel in being South African but, perhaps more especially, their increasingly complex understanding of themselves as Africans.

Since 1996, when the then Deputy President, Thabo Mbeki first unveiled his vision of an 'African Renaissance' – a rebirth of the continent predicated on the idea of cultural and especially economic partnerships between South Africa and the rest of the African continent[1] – this interest in South Africa's Africanness has given rise to a powerful and increasingly influential rhetoric. Mbeki himself has described his vision of this African Renaissance as a 'journey of self discovery and the restoration of our own self-esteem',[2] while Professor Musa Xulu claimed in a circular published by the Department of Arts, Culture, Science and Technology that the 'African Renaissance is becoming a factor in our lives. We need to work with each other as we define South Africa's Culture . . . The reality is that as we enter the world cultural arena, the world is increasingly expecting us to . . . be versed in our own South African and African culture first'.[3] In keeping with these sentiments, the pamphlet issued by the Design Institute of the South African

Bureau of Standards to advertise the 1998 Design Achievers Awards urged designers to head Africa's 'long and proud history of ingenious design' and argued that the continent is in the process of transforming itself 'from purely being a source of inspiration towards being a leading force in the design and production world'.[4]

In many respects, Mbeki's focus on South Africa's African roots, which alludes both to Fanon's interest in the retrieval of repressed indigenous traditions and Nkrumah's commitment to African unity and pan-Africanism, is predicated on the idea of celebrating diversity and multiplicity. His conception of the African Renaissance thus includes a concern not only to revalidate local ethnic signifiers but also to reframe and reinterpret these signifiers through the example of a broader African experience.

The lofty sentiments informing this vision of a post-colonial society notwithstanding, Mbeki's attempt at invoking a usable African past has proved to be quite problematic, mainly because it has spawned numerous commercial ventures aimed at marketing various products and tourist destinations (both to local and international customers) by appealing to the idea of Africa as a place of mythic primitivity. As I demonstrate throughout my discussion of these essentialist notions, however, they are constantly threatened and undermined by the messy contemporary reality of commerce in South Africa's informal sector, and in the clothing and beauty industries, all of which have witnessed the influx of economic refugees from West Africa. Working for or in competition with local entrepreneurs, these refugees include large numbers of highly skilled Ghanaian and Senegalese tailors and dressmakers, all of whom have benefited from the experience of training in and working for communities that have a long history of validating the role of dress in anti-colonial struggles.[5]

Whilst South Africa therefore has become a melting pot of cultures in recent years, it would falsify history if one were to suggest that ideas regarding the country's Africanness informed the thinking of the ANC's leadership when Mbeki and others first started returning from exile in early 1990. It was only after the country's first democratic election that this radical reappraisal of the country's economic relationship to the rest of Africa began to be formulated, and it was only in the immediate lead up to that election that South Africa's new black elite began to revise its attitude to African fashions.[6] Since the latter shift is reflected, most obviously, in the changing fortunes in South Africa of the Dutch textile company Vlisco, it is worth pausing to trace that company's attempt to enter the South African market after the unbanning of the ANC and other political organisations in February 1990.

In April 1992, Vlisco – which specialises in the production of cloth for West and Central African consumers – decided to rent a stall at Johannesburg's annual Rand Easter Show.[7] This was done against the advice of local chain stores, whose marketing managers claimed that South African tastes were too 'Western' for these textiles, and who argued that the company therefore would find it difficult to market their fabrics to South African buyers. At least initially, their advice proved to be correct: local consumers resisted buying the brightly coloured, richly patterned, and sometimes textured cotton fabrics first introduced into West and Central Africa by Vlisco's Dutch predecessor and various other European manu-facturers as early as the 1840s.[8] It has in fact been suggested that, if anything, it was a minority of anxious white South Africans seeking to demonstrate their acceptance of black majority rule who felt it necessary to wear African forms of dress in the early 1990s, ultimately embarrassing both themselves and their black hosts in the process (Lipkin 1996: 48).

As an anecdote recorded in the *New York Times* suggests, however, politically correct whites were certainly not alone in mistaking the sartorial preferences of South Africa's new leaders: 'The story is told of the 1991 gaffe when Mayor David N. Dinkins of New York and his entourage arrived for cocktails at Winnie Mandela's house in long, colourful caftans. The (African National Congress) elite met them in their uniform: dark business suits.' One of the South Africans is reported to have asked whether the New Yorkers were under the mistaken impression that they were on a visit to Cameroon.[9] This experience did not deter Mayor Dinkins from presenting South Africa's future president with an elaborately sewn *boubou*[10] that has since been placed on display in Mandela's former home, a museum that is now open to visitors.

Had Dinkins and his associates gone to South Africa three or four years later, they would certainly have spared themselves the embarrassment of their unfortunate visit to the Mandela residence in Soweto; for, following their 1991 visit, the sartorial style of South Africa's new leaders has undergone what can only be described as a radical transformation spearheaded by former exiles like Adelaide Tambo, wife of ANC leader Oliver Tambo, and President Mandela, who first started wearing brightly patterned silk shirts instead of business suits after a visit to Indonesia in 1993. Local couturier Chris Levin (who will probably be remembered mainly for his dubious decision to dress Marike De Klerk, the wife of former state president F. W. De Klerk, in a neo-colonial outfit complete with pith helmet, for President Mandela's Inauguration in May 1994) summed up this development as follows: 'There is a lot of what I call "political appeasement" dressing. With the swing to ethnicity, the code of formality has taken a back seat. South Africa is becoming an African country and Eurocentricity has found itself on the back burner' (*Style*, December/January 1996: 72).

The changing fortunes of Vlisco's South African operations provide a clear indication of the rapidity of this shift away from western codes and norms. In keeping with the tendency among consumers elsewhere in Africa, who often name the patterns found on African cloths of European. manufacture, local buyers have begun to refer to one of the Dutch company's designs as the ANC or Mandela print (predictably, this fabric is – like the organisation's flag – green, yellow and black in colour), while another, which has three gold leaves printed at intervals on a black, red, green or blue ground, is known as the 'three ministers' cloth. (It remains to be seen whether this reference to the principle of power-sharing under South Africa's short-lived government of national unity will survive.) Other fabric designs are named after famous individuals who have worn garments made for them. Among these are the singer Rebecca Malope, and

Figure 10.1 Dress using Vlisco fabric designed by Nandipa Madikiza, 1996. Courtesy Vlisco.

President Mandela's daughter, Zinzi, who appeared on the cover of *Time Magazine* (in the company of her father and American president Bill Clinton) wearing a Vlisco fabric.

A further measure of the unprecedented commercial success of imported 'African' cloth is provided by Vlisco's 1995 decision to introduce a new fabric inspired by the designs found, since the 1940s, on the house paintings of the Ndebele, some of whom still reside in a semi-rural section of South Africa's Mpumalanga province. This textile, which is now printed in fourteen colour ways, was the brainchild of veteran South African designer Peter Soldatos.[11] According to Soldatos, the idea of producing textiles based on local motifs first occurred to him when he attended President Mandela's Inauguration in May 1994. Convinced that there would be a renewed interest in what he called 'the ethnic look', Soldatos felt that Ndebele mural art offered an opportunity to create something distinctly South African – captured (according to him) in the stark, clean cut, geometric simplicity of this local art form. Soldatos's vision of a new, post-Apartheid South African style culminated in a visit to Prague, where several models were photographed wearing the new Ndebele pattern in garments conceived by the designer himself. Described by Soldatos as European in cut, but African in volume, some of these garments were inspired by the way cloth is draped to form a sari.[12]

Fuelled, no doubt, by a desire to exploit this growing interest in things African, South Africa's popular press has become remarkably bold in its attempts to promote values aimed at increasing the circulation among black readers of large glossies like *Cosmopolitan* and *Elle*. This is attested to not only by headlines like 'Back to black' (*Elle*, January 1998: 97) but also by the recently introduced annual competition, sponsored by a local television station, to find the 'sensuous and mysterious, demure yet regal . . . face of Africa.[13] Similar images of Africa are evoked in typical fashion features (disseminated through slogans like 'glamour tribe'), which invite consumers to 'mix home-grown couture with traditional jewellery . . . to tap into the soul of Africa' (*Elle*, April 1998: 94). In a bid to help its readers find their way 'through the African renaissance', *Elle* (South Africa) also included a feature article in which it suggested that 'South Africa is now seen as part of the chaotic, culturally rich, war-torn and vivid "dark continent" of European explorers' dreams' (*Elle*, April 1998: 64).

In recent years, many South African companies have also warmed to the fact that a mysterious, exotic conception of Africa is imminently marketable. Thus, for example, in a magazine and television advertising campaign featuring British supermodel Naomi Campbell, Africa is presented as a seductively inviting continent with a proud cultural heritage. Produced by Ogilvy and Mather for local chain store group Sales House – which also markets clothing based on indigenous forms by South African designers such as Nandipa Madikiza – this campaign relied on a series of evocative slogans rather than any particular sartorial style to communicate its message. In one advertisement, Naomi Campbell told her South African audience: 'My face is all over the world, but my soul will always be in Africa.' In another, she claimed that 'In Africa, I have to wear only one thing; my pride', while a third advertisement in this series showed her standing against a russet coloured backdrop partly covered in wild animal skins, with the slogan: 'My life has been a two million mile trip home' scrawled across the glossy surface of the magazine.

The essentialising clichés exploited in this advertising campaign were reinforced by the fact that Campbell was sometimes surrounded by artfully placed porcupine quills and cultural artefacts like a mask from central Africa and a sculpted bird from West Africa. Indeed, although the inclusion of these forms was probably intended to attest to the creative power of African artists, they ultimately served to reinforce the idea of Africa as a place of exotic, even 'primitive' beauty. As such, the Sales House campaign is obviously at odds with the self-consciously sophisticated notions of African empowerment invoked by politicians seeking to promote the concept of an 'African Renaissance'. In reality, though, these two notions go hand in hand, for they have contributed to an understanding among South Africans of Africa as a place of radical contrasts: a world in which it is possible to effect a fluid integration of past and present; where there is no necessary contradiction in juxtaposing notions of rural continuity with the idea of rapid urban transformation; a continent with a shared cultural heritage in which South Africans have a right to lay claim to newly discovered cultural forms from other African countries, while still paying homage to local forms and practices.

In some cases, the hybrid clothing styles that have emerged from this complex conception of what it means to be African are frankly excessive in their rich and layered allusion to various different traditions. By integrating ideas gleaned from local forms of dress with strips of kente cloth and beaded accessories that seem to allude to the bead art practised by a number of indigenous South African groups, these garments unashamedly celebrate the idea of African creativity and inventiveness. In other cases, designers and their clients seem concerned to overlay the style of ancient Egyptian headdresses with those worn by married women in rural KwaZulu-Natal, thereby evoking ideas both of African antiquity and local continuity. But there are also examples that eschew the past (both distant and recent) in favour of references to local forms of salvage sculpture and wire arts – the latter originally developed by children who had no access to commercially produced toys, using a technique that has since become increasingly popular in the production of anything from candle sticks to CD racks, for consumption by both local buyers and international tourists. These garments, produced for a clientele that is concerned to promote a self-consciously self-confident identity consistent with its new-found conviction that South Africa can no longer be regarded as a white colonial outpost, clearly are intended to evoke various and varied ideas concerning Africa, its history and its people.

In practice, however, a lot of the clothing that actually manages to assume a life beyond the hype of the catwalk and the showrooms of prominent designers is based on the Victorian-inspired garments and head wraps worn by Xhosa-speakers since they first came into contact with European settlers in the nineteenth century. The primary reason underlying the widespread preference for this Xhosa-style clothing – traditionally red/orange or white garments trimmed in black braid – is probably quite simple: unlike most other local clothing styles, these garments can be adapted to guard against potentially embarrassing displays of nudity. Equally importantly, they can be modified to provide adequate protection against the harsh climates of European countries. Often worn by South African diplomats and politicians in preference to similarly voluminous West African styles, these Xhosa-inspired designs are gradually assuming the status, albeit unofficially, of a national costume.

The interest less affluent consumers have expressed in Xhosa-style dress may also stem from the fact that the materials involved in the production of this clothing are relatively cheap. Thus although designers like Vuyokazi Bodlani (who produces garments for an elite market) have taken to using raw silk cloth in emulation of the loosely woven, textured cotton cloth adopted for the production of Xhosa clothing in the nineteenth century, many small businesses specialising in comparatively inexpensive cotton versions of this dress have sprung up around the

Figure 10.2 Euphenia Mayila wearing a contemporary Xhosa garment. Courtesy
Euphenia Mayila.

country in the course of the 1990s. Based in informal settlements as well as
established townships, designers of this kind are especially numerous in the
Eastern and Western Cape, where they service a mainly Xhosa-speaking market.
Unlike South African diplomats abroad, therefore, most of the consumers who
support small producers at the lower end of the market still view Xhosa-style dress
as a mark of ethnic pride and identity.

A status similar to that afforded Xhosa-style clothing by South Africa's new
leaders and diplomats has also been given to the patterns associated with the
mural art of the Ndebele. In keeping with this trend, Peter Soldatos, the designer
of the Vlisco Ndebele fabric, points out that, although it did not occur to him at
the time of President Mandela's Inauguration, he has since come to view the
kaleidoscope of colours found on Ndebele homes as symbolic of South Africa's
multicultural identity. Likewise, when Coca-Cola's southern African subsidiary

unveiled a larger than life 'Ndebele' beaded Coke bottle at the 1996 Atlanta Olympic games, it was described by the South African manager of the company as 'a symbol of our cultural heritage'.[14] This growing tendency to characterise Ndebele art as quintessentially South African has also led many people to suggest that South Africa's new flag may have been inspired by Ndebele mural designs, while local couturier Nandipa Madikiza uses a rural homestead covered in Ndebele-style paintings as the logo for her company.

This widespread local interest in Xhosa-inspired clothing and Ndebele-inspired fabric motifs notwithstanding, there are probably more differences than similarities between the work of prominent South African designers (among them, Vuyokazi Bodlani, Duval, Sandile Kula, Sister Bucks Mosimane, Sonwabile Ndamase, Nandipa Madikiza, and Nigerian-born Fred Eboka). While some of these designers are inspired, most obviously, by West African styles, others modify garments based on the work of Europe's major fashion houses. Almost all of them nevertheless are linked by their tendency to use large quantities of fabric in what amounts to an active rejection of the Western practice of highlighting the shape of the body. Nigerian-born Fred Eboka is especially eloquent in his articulation of this aesthetic. Arguing that beauty cannot be standardised, Eboka claims that African designers focus on ornamentation and colour rather than the production of tailored garments, because the latter tend to accentuate the contours of the body. According to him, the combination of bold colours and stark geometric patterns found on many of the fabrics conceived by African producers is so powerful that it alters one's perception of the person, always creating the impression that the wearer is large and, consequently, physically powerful.[15]

In the global fashion industry, where catwalk and photographic models continually reinforce images of anorexic womanhood, attempts to introduce large-bodied models like London-based Sophie Dahl have met with considerable scepticism, leading to assertions that the industry is desperate for novelty (*Cosmopolitan*, September 1997: 131). This helps to explain why local black consumers, many of whom clearly admire full-bodied men and women despite the insistent presence in South Africa's popular press of media icons like Naomi Campbell, often find it difficult to articulate their understanding of their own aesthetic preferences. Comments like those made by one black South African journalist, who attended the 'Versace for Africa' fashion show (held in Cape Town in February 1998), nevertheless provide clear evidence of this ongoing interest in full-bodied models: 'The highlight for me was Alek Wek, a very dark-skinned model from Sudan. People call her ugly but she is different – she has the body of an African woman, with hips and a healthy posterior' (*Sunday Independent*, 22 February 1998: 10).

Preferences of this kind help to explain why Sales House, the local chainstore group responsible for using super-slim Naomi Campbell in one of its advertising campaigns, now sells fashions 'for the fuller figure', described in one magazine spread as 'big, bold and beautiful'.[16] To promote this line of clothing, Sales House elicited the assistance of well-known South African singer Wendy Mseleku, thereby effectively reassuring their potential clients that big is really acceptable. To

Figure 10.3 Loose-fitting dress designed by Fred Eboka, 1996. Courtesy Fred
     Eboka.

reinforce this message, the company also pointed out that the full-bodied
Mseleku performed at President Mandela's Inauguration (as the country's first
black president) in May 1994.[17]

The fact that South Africa's fashion industry has taken to promoting bigness
suggests that it has finally come to the realisation that there is a widespread
acceptance among the country's comparatively new (but increasingly affluent)
black middle class that there is an intimate relationship between physical size and
social standing.[18] Thus, for example, when internationally renowned local actress
Busi Zokulfa[19] was asked whether her exceptionally ample figure posed a problem
to her career, she responded by saying:

> No. If an African woman is big, you're strong, bold and can tackle anything.
> If you don't put on weight, there is something wrong with you, you've got

Figure 10.4 Actress Busi Zokulfa as Ma Ubu in *Ubu and the Truth Commission*, 1998. Courtesy Ruphin Coudyzer.

TB. If a man has a skinny wife, he's maltreating her. I've never come across people who mock me. When I walk down the street people know this is a woman who doesn't take shit.[20]

Despite the obvious importance of physical stature in South African cultural perceptions of power and assertiveness, the desirability of bigness is certainly not restricted to the African continent: it is in fact only among economically privileged western communities that this complex concept, comprising, 'tallness, boniness, muscularity and fattiness' (Cassidy 1998: 181), lacks currency. Commenting on the tendency to celebrate bigness – throughout much of the world and even among the West's poorer neighbourhoods – Cassidy notes that 'Those who achieve this ideal are disproportionately among [a] society's most socially powerful' (Cassidy 1998: 181). As she also points out, however, 'In the secure West, fascination with power and the body has not waned, but has been redefined so that thinness is desirable. This apparent anomaly is resolved by realising that thinness in the midst of abundance . . . still projects the traditional message of power, and brings such social boons as upward mobility.' In a brutally blunt articulation of this western preoccupation with the embodiment of power on the catwalks of Europe, Suzy Brokensha noted in reference to well-endowed model Sophie Dahl that 'Most images of women in the media scream denial, or at the very least, restraint. Their subtext is all about disallowing certain things: the pleasure of eating, no not-exercising because you'd rather stay at home and watch TV . . . They're all about self-control . . . ' (Brokensha 1997: 131). In effect, therefore, many black South African designers and their clients are challenging western aesthetic norms not only by wearing African fabrics and favouring indigenous styles but also by rejecting the idea that there is a natural equation between thinness and physical beauty or desirability.

To suggest that these designers engage issues of power by challenging Western aesthetic norms is certainly not to imply that their language of form is crudely, or even necessarily oppositional. Far from it: comfort and convenience often are allowed to mediate between a vaguely articulated concern to give expression to a hybrid Africanicity and the realities dictated by a cosmopolitan fashion industry. The suits created by Fred Eboka for the leader of the Congress of Traditional Leaders of South Africa, Chief Phatekile Holomisa, are an interesting case in point. Although these suits are derived from European models, Eboka says that he actively deconstructs western fashions to create a more African look. This is achieved in part by fusing the idea of the jacket with that of the shirt, but also by adding beadwork embroidery to this hybrid under/over garment. Ultimately, and most importantly, Eboka's fusion of different garment types creates a greater sense of informality consistent with the growing trend among South Africans to challenge the principles of formality entrenched by the fashion houses of Europe in the early twentieth century.[21]

This important shift away from formality is probably best summed up by former President Mandela's recent dress code, described by some as accessible, by others (like former Nationalist Party politician Hernus Kriel) as an unacceptable break with the past. But while the debate fuelled by South Africa's presidential shirts in the mid-1990s undoubtedly was motivated by a deeply felt threat to the values celebrated by Mandela's former jailers and political opponents, it sometimes degenerated into pure farce: Hernus Kriel responded to this departure from wearing a suit and tie by trying to impose a more formal dress code in the legislative assembly of the Western Cape (in his capacity as leader of the still dominant Nationalist Party in the region). On the day following his decision to do so, leading ANC members deliberately turned up in richly patterned, loose-fitting embroidered shirts, thus challenging both Kriel's authority and the cultural norms he sought to impose. In the same vein, ANC cabinet minister Jay Naidoo challenged Archbishop Tutu's unexpected attack on the President's dress style –

Figure 10.5 Chief Phatekile Holomisa wearing a beaded suit designed by Fred
Eboka, 1997. Courtesy Anna Zieminski.

which blew up in the local press in 1995 after Tutu claimed that Mandela's
colourful silk shirts tainted the dignity of his office – by retorting: 'That's a little
rich coming from a man in a dress' (*New York Times Style*, 27 July 1997).

Although, unlike Hernus Kriel, Archbishop Tutu's outburst was obviously
motivated by a concern to protect South Africa's leader from his detractors,
President Mandela's tendency to wear loosely styled silk shirts – buttoned at the
top, but without either a tie or a jacket – has been taken as confirmation of the
widely held belief that he is a man of the people, uniquely able to bridge the gap
between the government and ordinary citizens. As such, Mandela's preference for
untucked, colourful silk shirts challenges what Fox-Genovese (1980: 30) has
rightly characterised as the only remaining fashion rule in contemporary society:
the adoption, virtually throughout the world, of the business suit as a kind of
corporate uniform that celebrates (male) economic and political power. This

Mandela's 'man-of-the-people' image is further reinforced by the fact that his Indonesian-inspired silk shirts are now widely believed to be African in inspiration. Mandela himself has never actually suggested that his dress code may be regarded as consciously African in style, but when he was asked by a ten-year-old Mozambican girl why he avoids wearing 'blazers and things', he told her that his informal clothing gave him a sense of freedom: 'you must remember [that] I was in jail for 27 years. Now that I am free, I want to feel freedom, and therefore I wear my shirts'.[22]

Significantly, this concern with freedom, as much from South Africa's past as from (western) convention, also underlies the history of the anti-Apartheid struggles of the 1970s. According to Sister Bucks Mosimane, who designs clothing for well-known South African musicians such as Miriam Makeba, there was a call to boycott 'white' clothes during the 1976 Soweto Student's Uprising.[23] The sentiments underlying this embryonic concern to reject South Africa's colonial heritage, which was actively promoted by the Black Consciousness Movement in the late 1970s and early 1980s, is summed up in her assertion that 'If you wear African clothes it is the start of going back to your culture'.[24] But, as she herself acknowledges, the principles underlying the work of many contemporary South African designers attests to a reliance on a rich and complex tapestry of forms and ideas, only some of which are recognisably African in origin. The producers involved in this fashion trend nevertheless insist that their hybrid solutions constitute an important expression of identity. As one designer claimed: 'It's a real identity, a new South African-ness that merges different cultures and helps us to become more tolerant of one another' (*The Argus*, 15 August 1996). Politically naïve though assertions like these might be, they fly in the face of the Apartheid state's characterisation of African traditions as backward (even barbarous), and they ultimately undermine its attempts to destroy the organic relationship both between different ethnic groups and between a proletarian urban population and its rural roots.

But while it is hardly surprising that the Africanisation of sartorial style in contemporary South Africa has been characterised by a complex re-evaluation not only of the past but also of the country's changing relationship to the rest of Africa, it is worth making the obvious point that attempts to understand the ways in which hybrid identities are negotiated tend to focus on the experience of socially and economically marginalised diasporic communities.[25] There can of course be little doubt that the reality of exile shaped the lives of many of South Africa's present leaders in ways that are undoubtedly analogous to that experienced by other diasporic communities. Indeed, as Nixon points out in his moving description of the life of exiled South African writer Bessie Head, the 'sheer force' of the dispossessions she suffered 'provoked her to pursue, with great vigour, alternative forms of belonging' (Nixon 1994: 102). As he also notes, the 'sprawling diaspora' of guerrillas, refugees and exiles who left South Africa throughout the 1960s, and in ever-larger numbers after the Soweto Student Uprising of 1976, 'had to piece together the most ironically hybrid identities on foreign shores' (Nixon 1994: 5).

For the most part, however, the painful reality of South Africa's diasporic experience – for some, in Europe and the USA, for others, elsewhere in Africa – ended quite suddenly following the unbanning of the African National Congress and other political organisations in February 1990. In the wake of that historic event, South Africans have sought, above all, to redefine their relationship to Africa and their own past rather than to the West. But while, in the process of doing so, they have developed hybrid forms and styles that repeatedly challenge western norms, the importance of this challenge lies above all in the development of a new sense of self; a sense of self achieved not through the painful experience of marginalisation but through the conviction that they are in control of their own destinies.

Notes

1 See, for example, the assessment of this idea by Thami Ntenteni, Director of Communication in the office of Deputy President Thabo Mbeki in *The Star*, 24 June 1997, entitled 'Mbeki's Africanism includes all'.

2 Speech by the then Deputy President, Thabo Mbeki entitled 'Africa's Renaissance Desperately Needs Your Help', *Cape Times*, 16 August 1998.

3 Circular from the Department of Arts, Culture, Science and Technology, 12 January 1998.

4 This information was taken from an entry form issued by the South African Bureau of Standards in early 1998.

5 On the subject of the West African clothing industry, the validation of tailors and dressmakers in Ghana, and the high percentage of economic refugees from the region see Manuh (1998).

6 This recent revision in attitudes to African fashion seems to be entirely unconcerned with earlier examples of the use of indigenous forms of dress in local anti-colonial struggles. For a consideration of the ANC's use of African dress as a symbol of resistance and validation in its confrontations with the Apartheid state in the early 1960s see S. Klopper and A. Proctor, 'Through the Barrel of a Bead: The Personal and the Political in Beadwork from the Eastern Cape', in Bedford 1993.

7 Unless otherwise indicated, the information provided here on Vlisco's activities in South Africa is taken from my interview on 24 June 1997 with Dean Trevis, Vlisco's Marketing Manager in South Africa.

8 For an account of the history of this and other European companies producing textiles for the African market, see R. Nielsen, 'The History and Development of Wax-printed Textiles Intended for West Africa and Zaire', in Cordwell 1979.

9 *New York Times Style*, Sunday 27 July 1997. I am immensely grateful to three very thoughtful friends, all of whom sent me copies of this article: Fran Buntman, Brenda Danilowitz and Gary van Wyk.

10 *Boubous*, which are long, loose garments, similar to kaftans, are worn in several West African countries.

11 Interview, Peter Soldatos, 24 June 1997. Soldatos himself developed only four of the fourteen colour ways. The others were developed by Vlisco's own designers in The Netherlands. Here, and elsewhere, I refer to Soldatos as a designer rather than a couturier in acknowledgement of his conviction that fashion is dead. According to him, it is no longer possible to dictate trends because the choices available to consumers have become so diverse as to be limitless.

12 See the article on the Prague trip in *rooi rose*, 5 March 1997. This local Afrikaans women's magazine described the style of Soldatos's clothing as Euro-ethnic.
13 See 'facevalues' *Elle* (South Africa), February 1998, pp. 100–3.
14 This information was gleaned from an Internet news listing. According to this listing, the bottle in question was created by six Ndebele women.
15 Interview, Fred Eboka, 12 June 1997.
16 *Pace*, November 1997, p. 40. *Pace* magazine aims to address the interests of a sophisticated urban black market.
17 *Ibid.*
18 It is nevertheless hardly surprising that younger black women are beginning to succumb to the global media pressure to equate beauty with thinness. *Femina*, a popular South African woman's magazine, recently included an article entitled 'Bulimia Strikes Our Black Women', in which the head of an eating disorder unit, Graham Alexander, emphasised 'the struggle young Africans face in their ambivalence between the pressures to conform to the Western cultural pursuit of thinness and the contrasting African traditional value attached to a fuller body shape' (*Femina*, May 1998, p. 64).
19 Since the early 1990s, Busi Zokulfa has been travelling the world with the Handspring Puppet Company and South African artist William Kentridge, acting in productions like *Woyzeck*, *Faustus*, and *Ubu and the Truth Commission*.
20 Quoted by Robertson 1998, pp. 34–5.
21 On the subject of Chief Holomisa's complex but sometimes quite ambiguous dress code see Klopper 1999.
22 From an Internet news listing.
23 This call was made by student leader Tsetse Mashing.
24 Interview, Sister Bucks Mosimane, 22 June 1997.
25 See Coombes 1994: 221. She points out that hybridity remains a term used to describe marginalised cultures.

Bibliography

Bedford, E. (ed.) (1993) *Ezakwantu: Beadwork from the Eastern Cape*, Cape Town, South African National Gallery.

Brokensha, S. (1997) 'The Next Big Thing', *Cosmopolitan* (South Africa), September, p. 131.

Cassidy, C. (1991) 'The Good Body: When Big is Beautiful', *Medical Anthropology*, 13, pp. 181–213.

Coombes, A. E. (1994) *Reinventing Africa: Museums, Material Culture and Popular Imagination in Late Victorian and Edwardian England*, New Haven and London, Yale University Press.

Cordwell, J. (1979) *The Fabric of Culture*, London, Mouton Publishers.

Fox-Genovese, E. (1980) 'The Empress's New Clothes: The Politics of Fashion', *Socialist Review*, 17 (1), pp. 7–39.

Klopper, S. (1999) ' "I respect custom but I am not a tribalist": The African National Congress, the Congress of Traditional Leaders of South Africa and Designer Tradition', *South African Journal of Historical Studies*, January, pp. 129–142.

Lipkin, M. (1996) 'How to Become Socially Desirable in the New South Africa', *Style*, June, p. 48.

Manuh, T. (1998) 'Diasporas, Unities and the Marketplace: Tracing Changes in Ghanaian Fashion', *Journal of African Studies*, 16 (1), Winter, pp. 13–19.

Mbeki, T. (1997) 'Mbeki's Africanism Includes All', *The Star*, 24 June.

Mbeki, T. (1998) 'Africa's Renaissance Desperately Needs Your Help', *Cape Times*, 16 August.
Nixon, R. (1994) *Homelands, Harlem and Hollywood: South African Culture and the World Beyond*, London and New York, Routledge.
Robertson, H. (1998) 'Size Counts', *Elle* (South Africa), January, pp. 34–5.

Part IV

Reconfiguring nation, community and belonging

11 Hybridity in a transnational frame: Latin-Americanist and post-colonial perspectives on cultural studies

John Kraniauskas

Other times

In 'Marxism after Marx: History, Subalternity, and Difference', the Indian historian Dipesh Chakrabarty provides a subalternist reading of the historicity of capital. Just as his *Subaltern Studies* colleague Ranajit Guha recovers the trace of subaltern agency in the historical narratives of the colonial and post colonial Indian states, Chakrabarty here reflects also on the coexistence of different temporalities within the time of capital: the temporality of commodified abstract labour that, in his view, underpins imperial history-writing, and the heterogeneous temporalities of subaltern 'real' labour that capital subsumes and over-codes, but which it cannot quite contain. 'If "real" labor . . . belongs to a world of heterogeneity whose various temporalities cannot be enclosed in the sign History', he suggests, ' . . . then it can find a place in a historical narrative of capitalist transition (or commodity production) only as a Derridean trace of something that cannot be enclosed, an element that constantly challenges from within capital's and commodity's – and by implication History's – claim to unity and universality' (Chakrabarty 1996: 60). Such heterogeneous social forms ('worlds') are thus only ever, for example, *pre*-capitalist from the point of view of capital's self-narration in a Euro-centred historicism – in Chakrabarty's words: 'secular History' – and its nation-based teleologies of progress (be they evolutionary or developmental) as they are imposed through colonialism. From a subalternist point of view, however, they mark the place of what Guha calls a 'semiotic break' (Guha 1983: 36) with such disciplinary history, and of alternative memories and non-secular temporalisations of experience, as well as alternative futures too:

> Subaltern histories are therefore [continues Chakrabarty] constructed within a particular kind of historicized memory, one that remembers History itself

First published, in *Nepantla: Views from the South*, 1:1, 2000, pp. 117–144 (Duke University Press).

as a violation, an imperious code that accompanied the civilizing process [here: the de-differentiation of labour[1]] that the European Enlightenment inaugurated in the eighteenth century as a world historical task. It is not enough, however, to historicize History, the discipline, for that only uncritically perpetuates the temporal code which enables us to historicize. The point is to ask how this imperious, seemingly all-embracing code might be deployed or thought so that we have at least a glimpse of its own finitude, a vision of which might constitute an 'outside' to it. To hold history, the discipline, and other forms of memory together so that they can help in the interrogation of each other.

(Chakrabarty 1996: 61)

But this 'outside' of the time of capital encoded as History, Chakrabarty insists in a Homi-Bhabhian rhetorical formulation, is grafted into the category 'capital', 'fractur[ing] from within the signs that tell of the insertion of the historian (as a speaking subject) into the global narratives of capital':

I think of it as . . . something that straddles a border-land of temporality, something that conforms to the temporal code within which 'capital' comes into being while violating it at the same time, something we are able to see only because we can think/theorize capital, but something that also reminds us that other temporalities, other forms of worlding, co-exist and are possible.

(Chakrabarty 1996: 62)

From the subalternist perspective of Guha and his colleagues, History as an institutionalized practice of writing emerged as a regulative apparatus of the colonial state in India. The presence of the subaltern within its historiography is thus defined by its negativity.[2] Here Chakrabarty gives this political story an economic twist, rereading commodification and value (abstract labour time) – the time of capital – as the site for possible re-memoration rather than reification (forgetting), and finding alternative histories in the heartland of ideology – in other words, cultural practices rather than mere false consciousnesses. Such, it seems to me, was the kind of critical space once opened up by the practices of history 'from below' and cultural studies in the UK, and now offered up anew by a post-Gramscian concept of 'the subaltern' as refashioned by Indian critical historians in their critique of the imperial political (state) economy (capital) of history.[3]

This is one reason why I have begun with Chakrabarty's reading of Marx against his evolutionary grain. Another is because it displays a set of ideas and images that underlies a tendential conceptual convergence in the increasingly institutionalised and interdisciplinary field of contemporary cultural studies in British and US universities (and beyond), particularly around the contributions of postcolonial criticism, on the one hand, and Latin-Americanist and Latino/a critical traditions, on the other. The work of Paul Gilroy and Angel Rama is an important case in point in such an intertext, for both, in their different ways, are concerned with reflecting on the processes by which historical memory is sedimented into contemporary cultural forms – novels and music – in ways that undermine 'civilizing' ideologemes of development: in Gilroy's work, the conventional sociological opposition between the temporalities of 'tradition' and 'modernity' and, in Rama's, the processes described in anthropology by 'acculturation'. Referring to black popular music and storytelling, Gilory observes that:

> narratives of loss, exile and journeying . . . like particular elements of musical performance, serve a mnemonic function: directing the group back to significant, nodal points in its common history and its social memory. The telling and retelling of these stories plays a special role, organising the consciousness of the 'racial' group socially and striking the important balance between inside and outside activity – the different practices, cognitive, habitual and performative, that are required to invent, maintain and renew identity. These have constituted the black Atlantic as a non-traditional tradition, an irreducibly modern, ex-centric, unstable, and asymmetrical cultural ensemble that cannot be apprehended through the manichean logic of binary coding.
>
> (Gilroy 1993: 198)

These 'tactics of sound', he goes on to say, become sedimented performatively in 'an alternative public sphere' that is also 'an integral component of insubordinate racial countercultures' (Gilroy 1993: 201, 200). What is alluded to in Chakrabarty as 'other temporalities, other forms of worlding' is thus concretely embodied and made present in dynamic cultural practices and alternative musical institutions in Gilroy.[4] Rama, meanwhile, writing in the early 1970s, finds the sounds of popular peasant and Indian cultures structuring the novels of writers like José María Arguedas, Juan Rulfo and Gabriel García Márquez – not now 'magical realists', but rather constitutive of what he calls a 'transcultural avant-garde' that rewrites the novel form with the resources of non-secular histories and alternative means of communication. From this point of view, Arguedas's novel *Deep Rivers* is not just a *bildungsroman* in(to) the European tradition but also an 'opera of the poor' founded on Andean song. The key concept enabling Rama's rereading of Latin American literary history is that of 'transculturation', coined originally by the Cuban anthropologist Fernando Ortiz to describe – in Gilroy's terms – the insertion of the black Atlantic into Cuba, the cultural counterpoint of the labour processes associated with the production of (American) tobacco and (imperial) sugar. For Rama the concept of 'transculturation' 'describes a Latin American perspective' on the experience conventionally referred to as 'acculturation', that is:

> resistance to being considered the passive or inferior element in the contact between cultures, the one destined to suffer most losses. The concept was born from a double recognition: on the one hand it confirmed the existence, in an already transculturated contemporary culture, of a set of idiosyncratic

values which could also be found in the remotest of its past history; and on the other, it simultaneously affirmed the existence of a creative energy acting, not only on its own inherited traditions, but on ones coming from outside too.

(Rama 1997: 158–9)[5]

Fundamental to Rama, therefore, was the critical registering in the concept of 'transculturation' of processes disavowed by the neo-colonialist concept of 'acculturation': of, in other words, the violent processes of *deculturation* associated with cultural colonialism and capitalist development in the countryside and, especially, the inventive ones of *neoculturation* associated with the transcultural renewal of cultural practices – and of which the novels of the 'transcultural avant-garde' are an example. In the interpretations of Rama and Gilroy, so-called 'tradition' produces the 'new' and thus confounds the narrative order and hierarchies of the ideologies of modernisation and modernism.

Different, although overlapping, historical forms of racism and subordination of 'heterogeneous worlds' to the time of capital are evoked in the work of these critics: slavery and debt-peonage in plantations, mines and haciendas at the colonial beginnings of modernity, as well as continuing processes of uprooting and dispossession, nation-building, proletarianisation and racist marginalisation. The memories of such processes, meanwhile, are recorded in and through cultural form. The difference, however, is that in the case of Rama, while the popular memories of and resistance to the 'civilising' processes of on-going primitive accumulation ('modernisation') – which, arguably, accompany capitalism rather than merely precede it – coexist with and interrupt the time of capital in a transculturated novel form, the latter does not return them to insubordinate alternative public spheres, as it does in the musical tradition described by Gilroy. Narrative transculturation thus possibly figures a process of contradictory cultural democratisation and integration, the widening of hegemony's cultural parameters under the impact of the expanded reproduction of capital and the ideology of development. This, of course, also says something about the particular socialities of the literature and music analysed by both critics – Rama is not analysing a process of transculturation 'from below'.[6]

The work of both Rama and Gilroy concretises Chakrabarty's deconstruction of History through reference to specific cultural practices, whilst Chakrabarty provides their work with a clear anti-capitalist and even utopian frame. All also partake, as I have suggested, of the kinds of interests, images and tropes marshalled in the critique of the rhetoric of 'progress' and 'development' that hold together important components of the field of contemporary cultural studies traversed by post-colonial and Latin-Americanist concerns and are centred on the idea of the production of a 'break' or 'disjuncture' in the dominant order, a 'trace of something that cannot be enclosed, an element that constantly challenges from within'. An 'outside' that is 'inside', and an 'inside' that is 'outside':[7] in Chakrabarty this oxymoronic outside–inside is real labour; in Gilroy and Rama it is the 'tactics of sound' carrying alternative memories. At another level, contemporary reflection on cultural forms and practices in an increasingly globalised world – the hybrid as specific global-local configurations – also stresses cultural mixture, and underlines the ways in which subjects are always already marked by 'others', identity by alterity. Indeed, this is a long tradition in Latin American critical thought. Similarly, while in her critique of sexual identity Judith Butler fore-grounds the ways in which the hegemonic imaginary is structured by what it excludes, Ernesto Laclau also theorises the mythic unification of the social around its 'constitutive outside'.[8] The keyword stitching together this field, however, is arguably the term 'hybridity', operating polysemantically at a number of levels, both inside and outside academic institutions. In this sense, as Alberto Moreiras has pointed out, one could say that it is a working, hegemonic idea (Moreiras 1998): becoming part of critical common sense, unifying and gathering together disparate themes – from the experiences of imperialism to subjectification – and different strands of thought – psychoanalytic and literary, sociological and histor-ical, passing through the philosophic – and fastening them into the interdisciplin-ary core of an increasingly internationalised and codified cultural studies. This means that the idea is also the site of a politics of theory in which alternative uses of the term – and alternatives to the term – fight it out, are articulated and unravelled.

Hybrid time

I would like to turn here to the work of a further two key writers in this field, Homi Bhabha and Néstor García Canclini, who, to simplify, we may take as representing the two halves of this – hybrid – interdisciplinary whole: the psycho-analytic and literary, on the one hand (Bhabha), and the anthropological and sociological, on the other (García Canclini). Their work also traverses the field of cultural studies from both post-colonial criticism (Bhabha) and Latin-Americanism (García Canclini) – which each has transformed considerably. The notion of 'hybridity' is central to both thinkers, and fundamental to their respective critical analyses of the cultural politics of the coexistence of different temporalities within modernity – that is, the kinds of issues and ideas set out by Chakrabarty on the disjunctive time of capital (although, as we shall see, neither Bhabha nor García Canclini *thinks* capital as such). Chakrabarty's image of a 'border-land of temporality' is especially apposite, for both García Canclini and Bhabha not only visit borders in their texts – indeed, their work meets and over-laps at one such border, the very particular border between the United States of America and Mexico – but also develop 'border epistemologies'.

'What is in modernity *more* than modernity is the disjunctive "postcolonial" time and space that makes its presence felt *at the level of enunciation*' (Bhabha 1994a: 251). Apart from its rhetorical and formal similarities to Chakrabarty and others' formulations of disjuncture, this brief quotation contains in condensed form some of the central ideas developed in the work of Homi Bhabha over the course of approximately fifteen years, and collected in his book *The Location of Culture*. I am thinking of the later, more recent essays in particular – including those that have been published since the book – in which the idea of 'hybridity' has become increasingly rethought from the point of view of time or, rather, 'the geopolitics of the historical present' (Bhabha 1994b: 210).[9] What emerges is an attempt to think an alternative temporality to established grand narratives, not from the point of view of their crisis as established by conventional postmodernist critique but their putting into question, their interruption from the point of view of a counter-modernity or, more specifically, a *post-colonial agency*. This agency is thought spatio-temporally in the concept of 'time-lag', and involves the hybridisation of time – which means, paraphrasing Chakrabarty, that it 'fractures the time of modernity' from within (Bhabha 1994a: 174, 252). In the paragraphs that follow I would like to trace a diagram of the mechanics of Bhabha's interpretative machine for reading/making this hybrid time.

Enunciation and disjuncture

As Benita Parry points out at the beginning of her recent critical review of *The Location of Culture*, the collection constitutes 'a strong articulation of the linguistic turn in cultural studies, distinguished by . . . [his] . . . recourse to Lacanian theories and hence foregrounding the instabilities of enunciation' (Parry 1994: 5). The specifically epistemological force of her subsequent critique then hinges on Bhabha's semiotic idealism, what she calls 'the autarchy of the signifier', whereby 'the generation of meaning [is] located in the enunciative act, and not in the substance of the narrated event' (Parry 1994: 9). Parry is right to foreground the act of enunciation. What is missing from her account of Bhabha's work, however, is precisely the intimate connection between it and a psychoanalytic account of the workings of the ego and unconscious – which she notes, but then immediately forgets. The point is that Bhabha's notion of post-coloniality actually *works* like the Freudian unconscious – its most basic dynamic being that of the return of the repressed in response to disavowal – and the site of this work is 'enunciation': enunciation without the unconscious is like post-colonialism without colonialism. Further: enunciation is to the unconscious as post-colonialism is to colonialism. Thus, what returns to modernity to make 'its presence felt' is precisely its colonial unconscious. Which means that post-coloniality is, in Bhabha's account, 'structured like a language' (Lacan), and the 'colonial', a mythical origin that is – like the unconscious – without history, but always already present, here and now. In this sense, Bhabha's interpretations approximate classic 'symptomatic readings', scanning the postcolonial present for the trace of its absent(ed) colonial cause (which it 'repeats').[10]

When Bhabha writes of enunciation he is articulating a specific conception of culture and thus intervening in the field of cultural studies itself. He is clearly uninterested in culture conceived as a given, pre-constituted 'epistemological object', that is, 'as an object of empirical knowledge' (Bhabha 1994a: 34). Taking the contemporary experience of racism and the historical experience of colonialism as his points of departure, culture becomes a specific kind of power-knowledge: 'Culture only emerges as a problem, or a problematic, at the point at which there is a loss of meaning in the contestation and articulation of everyday life, between classes, genders, races, nations' (Bhabha 1994a: 34). It is a practice; more specifically, an enunciative practice that emerges in a context marked by conflictual difference – which it attempts to negotiate and overcome (for example, in appeals to organic or homogenising notions of culture and community). The substance of the 'narrated event' referred to by Parry cannot, therefore, be unproblematically separated out from its performance or enunciation. 'The concept of cultural difference focuses', he goes on to say, 'on the problem of the ambivalence of cultural authority: the attempt to dominate in the *name* of a cultural supremacy which is itself produced only in the moment of differentiation. And it is this very authority of culture as knowledge of referential truth which is at issue in the concept and moment of *enunciation*' (Bhabha 1994a: 34–5). In uttering *that* culture, authority is *intimately* (and this is the force of Bhabha's use of enunciation to think the subject) implicated *in* and *by* it: outside–inside.

Why does Bhabha talk of the '*ambivalence* in colonial authority', of the '*attempt* to dominate'? It is almost as if in Bhabha's avening gesture colonial authority *qua* culture was defeated from its very inception. This is because the very practice of enunciation, the discourse of culture itself, undermines any attempt at narrative closure or cultural self-constitution on the part of the subject of power – here, the ideological constitution of colonial authority – even though this may have been what motivated its articulation in the first instance: 'The enunciative process', he says, 'introduces a split in the performative present of cultural identification' (Bhabha 1994a: 35).[11] Indeed, we are dealing here with something like transculturation in psychoanalytic mode. For example, the very articulation or performance of colonial stereotypification is marked by the cultural difference (the 'other') it negotiates. And it is this constitutive non-identity of the subject of/within enunciation – this splitting and this 'gap' – that provides Bhabha with his most important interpretative and critical resource: it makes the post-colonial perspective, its time and space, possible. In his essay 'The Commitment to Theory', from which I have quoted above, he calls this space 'third space'.[12]

Disjuncture and disavowal

We can now return to the relation Bhabha establishes between modernity and post-colonial time and space. He is concerned first, it has become clear, with modernity *as and when* it is enunciated, that is, with a particular narrative ordering of cultural difference (in the form, for example, of 'progress' or 'development'); and, second, with a supplementary force located within such discourse in the form of a disjuncture which splits the subject of enunciation (for example, in Chakrabarty's terms, the authority of Imperial history). Disjunctive enunciation, therefore, does have a contents – the differential object of narrative ordering and self-constitution – and it works as the discourse of culture's – in this case, modernity's – unconscious. In other words, the process of disavowal is welded into disjuncture.

The importance of the Freudian concept of 'disavowal' for Bhabha's work cannot be stressed enough. It provides a critic committed to a politics of cultural difference with an extremely simple but highly productive mechanism for generating critical interpretations from the 'postcolonial perspective'. Indeed, the idea surfaces in almost all of his essays, from 'The Other Question: Stereotype, Discrimination and the Discourse of Colonialism' – which I have referred to above – through ' "Race", Time and the Revision of Modernity' – from which I took the brief passage we are looking at – to 'In a Spirit of Calm Violence' where he 'discover[s] the postcolonial *symptom* of Foucault's discourse' – and in which his focus shifts from the ambivalence of colonial authority ('hybridity' and 'mimicry') as such to the question of post-coloniality ('time-lag'). Foucault, Bhabha insists, *disavows* ' "the colonial moment" as an *enunciative present* in the historical and epistemological condition of Western modernity' through a 'massive forgetting' (Bhabha 1995: 327–8) which, nevertheless, leaves its traces within his text. Freud's concept of disavowal emerges most clearly in his discussion of fetishism, and involves the simultaneous recognition and negation of difference in a displaced making of identity. In Freud's case, sexual identity. But in Bhabha's, racial and cultural identities: colonial stereotypification is the uneasy, anxious result of the recognition of difference, the generation of fear and attraction, and its negotiation through denial. But from the point of view of disavowal, and this is the crucial point, the recognition of difference does not disappear, it rather – as in Foucault's 'colonial moment' – haunts identity, making 'its presence felt', precisely, '*at the level of enunciation*'. Cultural difference thus accompanies the discourse of its negation and can be read symptomatically within the texts of both colonialism and modernity. This is a key idea, essential to Bhabhian critique.

The gap or disjunction within enunciation, the inter-subjective, now has a dynamic – of disavowal – that provides space – a 'third space' – for 'another place of enunciation': the 'other', so to speak, enunciates with(in) the 'self'. This is the effect of 'foregrounding the instabilities of enunciation' (Parry). Such a haunting, in Bhabha's view, opens up 'a narrative strategy for the emergence and negotiation of those agencies of the marginal, minority, subaltern, or diasporic that incite us to think through – and beyond – theory' (Bhabha 1994a: 181). Returning to our passage, then, it is possible to appreciate how colonialism and the cultures of 'resistance' and 'survival' accompany modernity in the form of a supplementary force (which will become 'agency') that has been disavowed, but which makes its presence felt – indeed, showing this, in a number of interesting and increasingly complex ways, is what Bhabha's critical practice is all about. But what is it that makes the colonial unconscious that interrupts narratives of modernity '*post*-colonial'? In other words, what is it that makes it a question of time? This question may be answered in two parts. The first refers to Bhabha's attempt to 'rename the postmodern from the position of the postcolonial' (Bhabha 1994a: 175). The second refers to a politics of time, that is, what Bhabha calls the 'time-lag'. Both are, of course, connected.

Time-lag

In his essay 'The Postcolonial and the Postmodern: The Question of Agency', Bhabha informs the reader that it is his 'growing conviction . . . that the encounters and negotiations of differential meanings and values within "colonial" textuality, its governmental discourses and cultural practices, have anticipated, *avant la lettre*, many of the problematics of signification and judgement that have become current in contemporary theory – aporia, ambivalence, indeterminacy . . .' (Bhabha 1994a: 173). The colonial past as interpreted by Bhabha thus illuminates the postmodern present, the crisis and critique of enlightenment paradigms and narratives – especially ideologies of progress – all of which were implicated in colonialism. But such a colonial 'unconscious' is not to be revealed in Bhabha's work through an inquiry into a set of historical determinations sedimented into the present as in the transcultural 'tactics of sound' that emerge in the criticism of Gilroy and Rama (although histories of the political economy of migration might provide such a possibility in his work).[13] Rather it comes through symptomatic and deconstructive readings that reveal the traces of disavowal in the discourses of culture articulated in the present, our present, marked by cultural difference. Contemporary neo-racism thus 'repeats' past colonialism, and it is the job of the post-colonial critic to articulate this 'unconscious' relation and to track the work of such repetition. The colonial past is thus *repeated, echoed,* though – more often than not – displaced into the metropoli.[14] This is the post-colonial time-space that interrupts the present: it is temporal in so far as it recombines the past and present as a deferred reinscription, and it is spatial in so far as post-colonial repetition travels – or migrates – and is experienced mainly in the metropoli. But how does this repetition work? Well, as expected, through the enunciative act, the rearticulating of discourses in the present such that it is interrupted, stalled or, as Bhabha says, 'lagged': 'disjunctive temporality is', he writes, 'of the utmost importance for the politics of difference. It creates a signifying time [via disjunctive enunciation (JK)] for the description of cultural incommensurability where differences cannot be sublated or totalized' (Bhabha 1994a: 177). This is why Bhabha underlines the fact that disjuncture – the return of the colonial repressed – happens in and through the *present* of enunciation. The time-lag is a 'temporal break in representation', the sign of temporal hybridity that, in Walter Benjamin's words, 'blast[s] open the continuum of history' (in the forms of historicism and progress) bringing it to a standstill (Benjamin 1979: 257). And this, of course, is where Bhabha also joins Chakrabarty in his critique of Euro-centred History. Postcoloniality is a form of counter-modernity, a disavowed colonialism made present, in the present, through the 'gap' (or 'fracture') in the enunciation of modern culture. Such also is Bhabha's heterogeneous temporality: it makes modernity *stutter*. In sum: 'the time-lag of postocolonial modernity moves *forward*, erasing that compliant past tethered to the myth of progress, ordered in the binarisms of its cultural logic: past/present, inside/outside' (Bhabha 1994a: 253).

What kind of agency is it that emerges from Bhabha's 'postcolonial archeology of modernity', his critical rereading of the conflictual present for the presence of the colonial? As his references to Walter Benjamin's 'Theses on the Philosophy of History' in his later essays on post-coloniality suggest, Bhabha is concerned with thinking about the materiality of the past in a non-positivist fashion. '*Time-lag keeps alive the meaning of the past*': it '*impels* the "'past", *projects* it' (Bhabha 1994a: 254) into the present that sparks it off. And in so far as it 'impels' and 'projects' the past through the speaking subject, the hybridising time of postocolonial agency would seem to take on the form of memory. It is not, however, a question of conscious memorisation, but rather – as we have seen – an unmediated force that brings the past to bear on the present *unconsciously*: the colonial past 'flashes up at a moment of [racist] danger' (Benjamin 1979: 257). In this respect, although responding to social conflict, it is an asocial agency. From Chakrabarty's point of view – which is influenced by Bhabha's – it is a temporality which may remind us of other 'forms of worlding', but which does not itself 'world'. There are, in other words, no equivalents to 'real' labour in Bhabha's symptomatic and revelatory readings, such as can be found in Gilroy and Rama's analyses of the historicity of cultural forms where heterogeneous histories flow into and nourish vibrant alternative and/or insubordinate worlds. On the contrary, in Bhabha's work the colonial – which, of course, has a variety of concrete instantiations – stands in *mythically* for such histories, as always already given and always already present, engulfing its future, our present, now. Whilst the only labour to be found is the critical labour of the analyst – which may explain the apparent voluntarism with which, despite the historical experiences of the colonised in the past, Bhabha refers to the 'ambivalence' of colonial domination (because, of course, on the one hand, a very anxious and ambivalent colonial discourse may play itself out in extremely unambiguous violence and, on the other, be experienced fairly unambivalently by the colonised themselves).[15] In his 'Theses on the Philosophy of History', however, Benjamin writes of the 'oppressed class itself' – which Chakrabarty might call 'the subaltern' – 'as the depository of historical knowledge'. Its task is social emancipation 'in the name of generations of the downtrodden' and for which, rather than images of redeemed 'future generations', the 'image[s] of enslaved ancestors' are crucial (Benjamin 1979: 262). Although Bhabha explicitly refuses alternative grand narratives to those of modernity, it is clear that Benjamin's allusions to historical forms of thinking *continuity* beyond 'now-time' – the idea of a class as a 'depository of historical knowledge' as well as the reference to 'generations' and 'ancestors'[16] – suggest that the 'flashes' of memory to be found in the reflections on history in both writers work best when fed into or read alongside (as mediating) alternative social forms of *conscious* memorisation. Forms which carry ongoing and renewed responses – narratives, images and histories – figuring (temporalising) experiences of subalternisation to the abstract 'time of capital'.

Differential historical time[17]

Psychoanalysis has – in a variety of guises – played a key role in metropolitan cultural studies, and coupled with semiotics has proven fundamental in reflections on questions of subjectivity, desire and identity. In Bhabha's work it provides the space opened up by *différence* with a very particular contents and time – the past – which haunts and hybridises the present and the subject of enunciation. Indeed, I have suggested that in fact the workings of the unconscious in his writings ontologise hauntology outside history – be it dominant or alternative – and does so through the mythification of the experience of the colonial. Within the context of Latin American cultural criticism, however, psychoanalysis is barely visible at all. This is so despite its very evident presence in a number of capital cities in the region as a clinical practice very much in demand amongst the middle classes, and notwithstanding the central importance of cultural identity to its traditions of thought and politics. Structuralist linguistics and semiotics have, on the contrary, been very important and, for example, transformed – dictatorships permitting – the disciplines of literary and media studies in institutions of higher education throughout the region between the mid-1960s and the early 1980s. The work of Néstor García Canclini comes out of this context – including the experiences of dictatorship in Argentina and exile in Mexico – and interconnects, moreover, with both sociology and anthropology, the other key disciplines associated with cultural studies. From the point of view of any discussion of 'hybridity' his recently translated work, *Culturas híbridas: estrategias para entrar y salir de la modernidad* (1990), is not only central but also helpful in so far as it uses the term at a number of levels, thus illustrating the conceptual field of its operation beyond psychoanalysis and deconstruction. The book presents itself as a socio-anthropological study of Latin American modernity, and in so far as it also attempts to provide for a historical account of cultural hybridisations, it may also be read as a critical counterpoint to Bhabha's psychoanalytic one.

Culturas híbridas is grounded in a set of hypotheses which attempt to formulate a theoretical approach to Latin American cultural history that is adequate to its object (that is, to a particular set of historical experiences). The object, as the title makes clear, is modernity; whilst García Canclini's proposal for theoretical adequation is suggested in another word included in the title: hybridity. The point is, of course, that not only is hybridity a feature of García Canclini's design for a 'trans-disciplinary gaze' (that is, interpretation), but of modernity in Latin America itself (the object of such interpretation): a transdisciplinary gaze for transculturated worlds. 'Nomadic' or 'hybridised' forms of critique would, he suggests in his first hypothesis, facilitate 'an alternative way of thinking about Latin American modernization: not as an alien and dominant force operating through the substitution of tradition and traditional identities ("lo propio"), but rather', and this is García Canclini's second – and, in my view, most important – hypothesis, 'as the projects of renovation with which diverse sectors take charge of the multi-temporal heterogeneity of each nation' – in other words, the specific character of Latin American modernity and its relation to tradition. Third, and finally, recognition of the cultural hybridity of modern Latin American nations illuminates 'the oblique powers that are involved in the mixing of liberal institutions and authoritarian habits, social democratic governments with paternalist regimes'. The political importance of the idea of hybridity as formulated in García Canclini's *Culturas híbridas* thus emerges as a response to the demands on the present made by 'this mixture of heterogeneous memory and truncated innovation' that is modernity in Latin America (García Canclini 1989: 14–15). The concept of 'hybridity' thus pertains to an epistemology of modernity, to its specific local characteristics and, finally, to its political significance.

It is clear that the demands made by García Canclini on the idea of 'hybridity' are substantial, for it is set to work at different levels. Hybridity as a form of transdisciplinarity, for example, does not simply mean the use of concepts derived from a variety of disciplines but, in some instances, their mutual transformation. For this reason, when investigating the 'theatricalisation of the popular' (García Canclini 1989: 191–235), he accompanies his deconstruction of the art-handicraft ('artesanía') opposition with a sociological critique of anthropological conceptions of the popular (associated with tribal and rural tradition) and an anthropological critique of sociological conceptions of the popular (associated with urban modernity). The effect of this conceptual confrontation and transformation is to illuminate what is conventionally thought to be a series of contradictions in terms: the aestheticising effects of commodification on a handicraft industry (now in the process of massification) usually thought of as traditional, folkloric and inimical to modernisation – in other words, cultural continuity and change through renewal, as in Gilory's analysis of black popular music (although, in this case, without insubordination). Elsewhere, he similarly confronts and transforms Gramsci's political concept of 'hegemony' with Bourdieu's sociological concept of 'reproduction'. At a more empirical level, the idea of 'hybridity' also has a more familiar function in García Canclini's descriptions of new urban landscapes, communities and identities – particularly at the US/Mexican border – that have been disconnected from specific locations and spatially reinvented through newly accesible communication technologies – processes associated, but at the level of practices and objects, with forms of cultural rearticulation he calls 're-conversion' and 'de-collection'. It is at these levels that the idea of hybridity as a critical strategy (interpretation and description) is, in my view, most productive.

More fundamental for his theory of Latin American modernity as such, however, and this is where García Canclini's reflections bring his work into the same conceptual space as Chakrabarty, Rama, Gilroy and Bhabha, are his references to 'intercultural hybridisation', 'hybrid sociability' and 'hybrid history' (García Canclini 1989: 264, 332, 69). Taken together, these references to culture, society and history testify to the apparent need to lift the idea of 'hybridity' from the realm of empirical description, via conceptual 'transdisciplinarity', into a totalising domain of theory that is adequate to the task of studying 'the hybrid cultures that constitute modernity and give it its specific Latin American profile' (García Canclini 1989: 15).[18] It is this theory of the particularity of Latin American modernity – its 'hybridity' – that is my principal concern in what follows.

Like the Brazilian critic Roberto Schwarz (1992), García Canclini correctly dismisses the idea held by many that modernism (and modernisation) is in some sense foreign to Latin America, or is a superficial transplant. He too points to the process through which 'misplaced ideas' (like, for Schwarz, liberalism's concept of 'citizenship' in a Brazil still dominated by slavery) become 'improperly' adopted but structuring components of national and regional cultural formations, and outlines '[h]ow to interpret a hybrid history'. It is here that the question of multi-temporal heterogeneity is discussed. Following in the footsteps of Perry Anderson's (1992) critique of Marshall Berman's homogeneous, unilinear and developmentalist theory of European modernism, García Canclini locates Latin American modernism at the intersection of 'different historical temporalities' so as to maintain, in an echo of his second hypothesis concerning Latin American modernity, that it 'is not the expression of socio-economic modernisation [as in Berman] but rather the way in which the elites take charge of the intersection of different historical temporalities and attempt to elaborate a global project with them' (García Canclini 1989: 71).

In his reading of *All That Is Solid Melts Into the Air*, Anderson suggests that an explanation of modernism can only be found in the *uneven* development of capitalism. Evoking Louis Althusser's conceptualisation of both conjunctural 'overdetermination' and the 'differential' historical time characteristic of all social structures, as well as Raymond Williams's temporalisation of cultural formations in terms of the 'residual', 'dominant' and 'emergent', he notes that '[s]uch an explanation would involve the intersection of different historical temporalities, to compose a typically overdetermined configuration' (Anderson 1992: 34): a still usable – aristocratic – *past* (in the form of artistic academicism), an unstable – bourgeois – *present* (characterised by technological revolution), and an uncertain – revolutionary? – *future* (revealed in the Russian Revolution).[19] What, then, constitutes the cultural content of such temporalities in Latin America? According to García Canclini, 'Latin American countries now are the product of the sedimentation, juxtaposition and intercrossing of Indian traditions (especially in the Mesoamerican and Andean areas), of colonial Catholic hispanism and of modern political, educational, and communicative practices' (García Canclini 1989: 71). This, it must be said, is quite a conventional picture of Latin American syncretism, separating out and identifying what is thought to be either 'traditional' or 'modern', so as to then – and only then – mix them. He goes on to maintain, however, that the dynamic of cultural hybridity results from the fact that the 'modern' has failed to 'substitute' the 'traditional'. Indeed, processes of modernisation have rather tended to reproduce and rearticulate 'tradition' – as in the case of the production of handicrafts – so that what has been usually defined socially, culturally or politically as 'traditional' and 'past' are still active in the present (such that they too are endowed with futuricity). Yet the key to Latin American modernity contained in García Canclini's outline of its modernisms is not to be found only in such transculturation, but rather in the ways it feeds into 'the way in which elites *take charge of* the intersection of different historical temporalities' (my emphasis) – the key hypothesis, as we have seen, concerning the particularity of Latin

American modernity that motivates the book as a whole. The main point here is that, given the historical absence of local centres of capital accumulation, strong civil societies and national markets – local manifestations of capitalism in a context of dependency – both modernism and modernisation have been thought of as *projects* whose concern is *to take charge* of temporal heterogeneity. In sum, what emerges without being explicitly addressed in *Culturas híbridas* – that is, despite García Canclini's culturalism – is the *political*, state-centred (rather than commodity-centred) dialectic of cultural modernity in Latin America. There are thus two interconnected levels of overdetermination at work here: first, the conjunctural intersection of different historical times (hybridity) which produces – and is at the same time reproduced by – a modernity in which, second, from the point of view of culture and the making or 'formation' of subjects, social relations with the nation-state (the political) predominate over social relations with the market (the economic).

This does not mean that a political history of modernity replaces García Canclini's hybrid history, but rather that each feeds on and informs the other. For as he points out, '[d]espite the attempts to give elite culture a modern profile, confining the Indian and the colonial to popular sectors, an interclass mestizaje has generated hybrid formations in all social strata' (García Canclini 1989: 71). It is this continual reproduction of cultural and social hybridity that provides the dynamic for the political character of Latin American modernity: 'truncated innovation' periodically demands processes of modernity that are conceived in political terms by Latin American elites, that is, as *projects* (modelled, in the main, on imperial conceptions of 'development' – the time of capital). And this is because each attempt at renovation fails to 'substitute tradition'. From this point of view, *Culturas híbridas* may be read as a response to Jürgen Habermas's question: 'modernity – an incomplete project?' In Latin America, however, modernity is not 'incomplete', it is 'truncated', and truncation – perceived as an effect of socio-cultural hybridity – constitutive of its political logic.

What is missing from García Canclini's account of hybrid history – although given the theoretical and empirical density of the text, it is perhaps asking too much – is some reflection on the history of the ways in which this truncated modernity has been thought, both culturally and politically, in post-colonial Latin America from, for example, D. F. Sarmiento in the 1840s to Angel Rama in the 1970s. For this may have critically illuminated the way in which the temporal and political logics of modernity as 'development' informed his own perspective on processes of hybridisation. Sarmiento is particularly relevant since he specifically addresses the question of the coexistence of at least two historical times in post-independence Argentina – he called them 'civilisation' and 'barbarism' – and set out 'to take charge' of them militarily and pedagogically: 'Both the nineteenth and twelfth century live alongside each other: one in the cities and the other in the countryside' (Sarmiento 1970: 63). Sarmiento's project was to reverse the situation in which, in his view, the Middle Ages had the upper hand and taken control of the state in the form of dictatorship. In other words, he proposes imposing the 'time of capital', the Europeanised city, onto the countryside, so as to bring the nation up to date by abolishing that 'other' heterogeneous time. The ideologeme under which such a project to 'take control of' heterogeneous time was thought was, of course, 'progress'. Rama, meanwhile – as we have seen – populistically inverts Sarmiento's problematic and attempts to read the dominant against the grain looking for the transformative effects of the heterogeneous.

From the point of view of this tradition of political and cultural interpretation in Latin America, it is thus not surprising that *Culturas híbridas* should suggest a modernising politics of its own that – with the help of recent postmodern critiques of modernist grand narratives of progress – attempts to overcome this opposition between modernisation and 'traditions that persist' (García Canclini 1989: 331). 'Perhaps the central theme of cultural politics today', says García Canclini, 'is how to build societies on the basis of democratic projects that are shared by all without equalising them, where disaggregation becomes diversity, and where inequalities (between classes, ethnic or social groups) are transformed into difference' (García Canclini 1989: 148). García Canclini recognises that one cannot just enter and leave modernity, that 'it is a condition that contains us, in cities and in the countryside, in the metropoli and the underdeveloped countries'. Here, however, he does not follow Anderson and advocate political rupture with modernity. He rather suggests that the only answer may be '[t]o radicalise the project of modernity . . . to renovate . . . to create new possibilities so that modernity can be something else and something more' (García Canclini 1989: 333). In García Canclini's view, such a politics would be new and arise from the contemporary 'cultural reorganisation of power . . . of the political consequences of passing from a vertical and bipolar conception of socio-political relations to a decentred, multidetermined one' (García Canclini 1989: 323) – in other words, I assume, the replacement of class politics by the disenchanted politics of social movements. What emerges, however, is a cultural politics in which a self-styled modernity identifies its own opposites, that is, those *traditions* it must overcome. *Culturas híbridas* may thus itself also be read politically – and 'obliquely' – as providing intellectual resources for such a democratic social and cultural project, for – in other words – 'taking charge of' the more recent configurations of modernity in Latin America.

Border times

In this context some of the transformations or hybridisations described by García Canclini in *Culturas híbridas* and elsewhere would seem to be over-optimistic and, curiously, subjectless, despite the importance of the concept of identity in his work (see García Canclini 1992 and 1995). This may be because of an over-emphasis on national and post-national identities at the expense of others, and the fact that the culture of the Mexican/US border – more specifically, the city of Tijuana – acts as a paradigm for his analysis of contemporary processes of hybridisation: '[t]he hybridisations described throughout this book lead us to conclude that today all cultures are frontier cultures', he says (García Canclini 1989: 325). This is a view shared by Bhabha. Indeed, he goes even further, inscribing his own thoughts on post-coloniality and counter-modernity in *The Location of Culture* into a politics of the 'borderline condition':

> [P]ostcolonial critique bears witness to those countries and communities – in the North and in the South, urban and rural – constituted, if I may coin a phrase, 'otherwise than modernity'. Such cultures of a postcolonial contra-modernity may be contingent to modernity, discontinuous or in contention with it, resistant to its oppressive, assimilationist technologies; but they also deploy the cultural hybridity of their borderline condition to 'translate', and therefore reinscribe, the social imaginary of both metropolis and modernity.
>
> (Bhabha 1994a: 6)

Thus, from the point of view of the working concept of 'hybridity' in the texts of both Bhabha and García Canclini, the border – especially the US/Mexican border where their texts meet – becomes both culturally exemplary, a 'third space', and an explicit epistemological position from which to read the texts and times of contemporary cultural formations.

Indeed, the realities of the US/Mexican border would seem to actualise in almost pradigmatic form what Chakrabarty calls a 'borderland of temporality' (see above) as well as the spatio-temporal tropes of 'transculturation', 'heterogeneity', 'inside-outsides' – that is, of 'hybridity' – that distinguish Latin-Americanist and post-colonial contributions to cultural studies in the form of critiques of the ideologies of progress and development, the 'time of capital'. The problem, however, and this is another characteristic the critical discourses of both Bhabha and García Canclini share, is that this 'time' is thought in such a way that cultural concerns – however dislocated and/or unconscious they may be – obliterate political economy, that is, capital as a determining – temporalising – instance (both of and by cultural form).[20] And this emerges particularly clearly in the way García Canclini's recourse to the idea of hybridity to analyse the temporal heterogeneity of Latin American modernity seems paradoxically to reconfigure and maintain, rather than subvert, the temporalisation of modernity and tradition as signs of the present and past it criticises. In his account of handicrafts, for example, a renovated traditional cultural form acquires the attributes of the modern and becomes new (via state subsidy and the comparative advantage of the marketplace). In such a context, what fails to renovate – including those branches of the handicraft industry that do not modernise – fails – and becomes 'past' – due to the truncating effects of a tradition 'that persists'. What this would seem to provide is not a critique of the logics of development but rather an example of *cultural* development in which, from the subalternist perspective of Charkrabarty, the chronological and abstract 'time of capital' not only remains intact but may even be strengthened.

The interrelated ideas of 'deterritorialisation' and 'reterritorialisation' used by García Canclini to describe the transformations of contemporary culture may provide a further illustration of the 'times' of García Canclini's critique, as well as a point of entry for critical reflection on both his and Bhabha's optimism with regard to the border chronotope – that is, a point at which, in García Canclini's own terms, socio-political bipolarity returns to organise multi-determination (García Canclini 1989: 288–305). According to Deleuze and Guattari '[t]he social axiomatic of modern societies is caught between two poles, and is constantly oscillating from one pole to another' (Deleuze and Guattari 1977: 260). Capitalism, in their view, 'is continually reterritorializing with one hand what it is deterritorializing with the other' producing 'neoterritorialities' (Deleuze and Guattari 1977: 259, 257). So enmeshed are these process that, they insist, 'it may be all but impossible to distinguish deterritorialization from reterritorialization . . . they are . . . like opposite faces of one and the same process': what Marx described as the tendency, and counter-tendencies, of the rate of profit to fall law immanent to the expanded reproduction of capital (Deleuze and Guattari 1977: 258, 259–60). The cultural content of Deleuze and Guattari's observations on processes of social abstraction – and what I have referred to above as 'ongoing primitive accumulation' – are glossed in the form of a culturalism by García Canclini as follows: 'I am referring to two processes: the loss of "natural" relations between culture and geographical and social territories, and, at the same time, certain relative and partial territorial relocalisations of old and new symbolic productions' (García Canclini 1989: 288). Migration is important to both Bhabha and García Canclini, in whose view the 'multi-directional migration' characteristic of contemporary transnational capitalism undermines bipolar – and 'relocalising' – conceptions of intercultural relations thought of in terms of dependency, centres and peripheries, and imperialism. It is in this context that the frontier, as a space of hybrid cultural intercrossings, a 'neo-territoriality', becomes paradigmatic.

But, as I have suggested, it is also the point at which the cultural contents of capitalist forms of social abstraction are lost. García Canclini does, momentarily, recognise that there may be suffering at the border: 'Intercultural movements show their faces of pain on both sides of the frontier: underemployment and the uprootedness of peasants and Indians who had to leave their lands so as to survive. But', he rapidly goes on to point out, 'a dynamic cultural production is emerging there too' (García Canclini 1989: 290–1). And he is right: hybridity, especially its border culture variant, is of increasing international exchange and exhibition value (see Coombes 1992). However, it seems to me that the suffering involved – what Benjamin may have called the 'barbarism', and by which I am referring to the violence contained in relations of exploitation and domination, the subordination to the 'time of capital' – is passed over too quickly and, curiously, this is because the processes of deterritorialisation and reterritorialisation described by García Canclini become binarised and, most importantly here, temporalised. He reports that in reactions to a series of photographs of Tijuana 'we saw a complex movement that we would call reterritorialisation. The same people that praise the city for its open and cosmopolitan character want to fix signs of identification, rituals that would differentiate them from those who are just passing through, be they tourists or . . . anthropologists interested in understanding intercultural mixing' (García Canclini 1989: 304). From the point of view of a contemporary modern (that is, what the author calls a 'decentred multidetermined') cultural politics, such fixing becomes a thing of the past – tradition, ritual – a politics signifying a time to be 'take[n] charge of, if it does not successfully 'develop' and become up to date.

The problem, however, may be that capitalist reterritorialisation does not present itself today only as *tradition*, or as what Deleuze and Guattari call 'neoarchaisms', but as the production of the new subjects of a socio-cultural order which is both specifically transnational (postnational) and one in which, from the point of view of time, the disavowal of coevalness that structures narratives of progress and development is being tendentially undermined by the new technologies allied to capital itself (see W. Mignolo 1998).[21] In other words, reterritorialisation may be located also – indeed, especially so – in a certain mobility – migration – and neocosmopolitanism: the ability, indeed the necessity at the Mexican/US border, to adopt a multiplicity of identities. That is, in Deleuze and Guattari's terms, reterritorialisation accompanies the ever-increasing need for social abstraction – what Chakrabarty refers to as 'abstract' rather than 'real' labour – of the capitalist machine (Deleuze and Guattari 1977: 258–9). As Stuart Hall has also reminded us, 'the so-called "logic of capital" has operated as much through difference – preserving and transforming difference . . . not by undermining it' (Hall 1994: 353) but by subordinating it to the logics of 'development', the time of capital that seeks to overcome traditions 'that persist'. If this were the case, the suffering García Canclini mentions so briefly may be more than just symptomatic of the 'loss' of traditional identities – that is, nostalgia. It may have critical content too, registering resistance and even possible alternatives to the new reterritorialised 'border' subjectivities being produced and replicated throughout the cities of the USA, and elsewhere, as 'disciplinary societies' are transformed into 'societies of control' (see Davis 1990 and Deleuze 1992).

Notes

I would like to thank Annie Coombes, Walter Mignolo, Mpalive Msiska, Alberto Moreiras, Peter Osborne and Carol Watts for their help (and patience) in writing this chapter.

1 '[T]his abstraction of labour as such is not merely the mental product of a concrete totality of labours. Indifference towards specific labours corresponds to a form of society in which individuals can with ease transfer from one labour to another, and where the specific kind is a matter of chance for them, hence of indifference. Not only the category, labour, but labour in reality has here become the means of creating wealth in general, and has ceased to be organically linked with particular individuals in any specific form. Such a state of affairs is at its most developed in the most modern form of existence of bourgeois society – in the United States' (Marx 1977: 104).

2 'The peasant obviously knew what he was doing when he rose in revolt. The fact that this was designed primarily to destroy the authority of the superordinate elite and carried no elaborate blueprint for its replacement, doesn't put it outside the realm of politics. On the contrary, insurgency affirmed its political character pre-

cisely by its negative and inversive procedure' (Guha 1983: 9). On the other hand, Guha underlines the fact that the colonial historiography documenting insurgency was a 'vital discourse for the state'. In it 'causality was harnessed to counter-insurgency and the sense of history converted into an element of administrative concern' (Guha 1983: 2, 3).

3 See my 'Globalisation is Ordinary: The Transnationalisation of Cultural Studies' (1998).

4 Other examples might, for example, include working-class institutions that keep the realities of 'real' labour alive. The question I am alluding to with this example is whether 'real' labour coexists with abstract labour for the working class in con-texts of real – or complete (if such a thing exists) – subsumption of labour to capital; that is, when labour is fully incorporated into the production process as variable capital.

5 These issues are developed in more detail in Rama (1982) – which also includes his reading of José María Arguedas's novel *Los ríos profundos* (*Deep Rivers*).

6 See Antonio Cornejo Polar (1998). In Cornejo Polar's work the difference of 'heterogeneity' – at the level of both culture and modes of production – constitutes the thorn in the side of transculturation itself.

7 See, for example, Jacques Derrida (whom Chakrabarty mentions): 'But this inside must also enclose the spectral duplicity, an immanent outside or an intestine exteriority, a sort of evil genius which slips into spirit's monologue to haunt it, ventriloquizing it and thus dooming it to a sort of self-persecuting disidentifica-tion' (Derrida 1989: 62). This philosophical formulation of 'hauntology' by Derrida – later developed in *Spectres of Marx* (1994) – is remarkably similar to Homi Bhabha's discussion of 'disjunctive enunciation' (see below).

8 In the words of Judith Butler: 'In this sense, then, the subject is constituted through the force of exclusion and abjection, one which produces a constitutive outside to the subject, an abjected outside, which is, after all, "inside" the subject as its own founding repudiation' (Butler 1993: 3); and Ernesto Laclau: 'we are faced with a "constitutive outside". It is an "outside" which blocks the identity of the "inside" (and is, nonetheless, the prerequisite for its constitution at the same time) . . . [T]he effectiveness of myth is essentially hegemonic: it involves forming a new objectivity by means of the rearticulation of the dislocated elements' (Laclau 1990: 17, 61).

9 In this sense, my account and critique of Bhabha's work is slightly different from Robert Young's (1990 and 1995) which are concerned with the ideas of hybridity in what we may call the 'early' Bhabha.

10 This is why, for example, one way of symptomatically describing the shift in the critical analysis of colonial discourse between Edward Said's *Orientalism* (1978) and Bhabha's own work is to note how Gramsci's notion of 'hegemony' – so important for Said's approach to colonialism – is dropped in favour of a psycho-analysis of politics.

11 Such an undermining of authority is central to Bhabha's concerns. As he puts it in another essay: 'I attempt to represent a certain defeat, or even impossibility, of the "West" in its authorization of the "idea" of colonization' (Bhabha 1994a: 175).

12 In this essay the full importance of Derrida's concept of *différence* for Bhabha's own analyses becomes very clear (see Bhabha 1994a: 19–39).

13 Many critics of post-colonial theory have related its emergence to migrant intellectuals who have risen in the academies of England and the USA. See, for example, A. Ahmad (1992).

14 See P. Osborne (1995: 199). This book has proved invaluable in helping me to think through some of the issues of this chapter.

15 See note 10 above and Bart Moore-Gilbert (1997).

16 The problem of thinking the continuity of subaltern cultural practices over time, and their significance, are tackled head on by Gilroy. For example: 'I believe it is possible to approach the music as a *changing* rather than an unchanging same. Today, this involves the difficult task of striving to comprehend the reproduction of cultural traditions not in the unproblematic transmission of a fixed essence through time but in the breaks and interruptions which suggest that the invocation of a tradition may itself be a distinct, though covert, response to the destabilising flux of the post-contemporary world' (Gilroy 1993: 101).

17 The section that follows is an amended version of Kraniauskas (1992). For a response, see García Canclini (1992a).

18 It is with the empirical and interdisciplinary meanings of 'hybridity' that US and UK cultural studies have been mainly concerned. As we have seen, its temporal meaning, on the other hand, has been the concern of critics of the practices and rhetorics of modernity, progress and development experienced as colonialism and imperialism.

19 See Louis Althusser (1966 and 1979: 91–118) and Raymond Williams (1977: 121–7). Post-colonial agency is, in Bhabha's account, a form of cultural 'emergent'.

20 On the ideology of cultural studies see Spivak (1996) and Kraniauskas (1998). For example, in their analysis of the Los Angeles uprising following the Rodney King verdict Melvin E. Oliver, James H. Johnson Jr and Walter C. Farrell Jr (1992: 122) refer to the contemporary political economy of the US/Mexican border: 'At the same time . . . well-paying and stable jobs were disappearing from South Central Los Angeles, local employers were seeking alternative sites for their manufacturing activities. As a consequence of these seemingly routine decisions, new employment growth nodes or "technopoles" emerged in the San Fernando Valley . . . In addition, a number of Los Angeles-based employers established production facilities in the Mexican border towns of Tijuana, Ensenada and Tecate. Between 1978 and 1982, over 200 Los Angeles-based firms . . . participated in this deconcentration process. Such capital flight, in conjunction with the plant closings, has essentially closed off to the residents of South Central Los Angeles access to what were formerly well-paying unionized jobs. It is important to note that, while new industrial spaces were being established elsewhere in Los Angeles County (. . . as well as along the US/Mexican border), new employment opportunities were emerging within or near the traditional industrial core in South Central Los Angeles. But, unlike the manufacturing jobs that disappeared from this area, the new jobs are in competitive sector industries, which rely primarily on undocumented labour and pay, at best, minimum wage.' Meanwhile, the territorial frontier provides very real opportunities for super-profits: on the Mexican side, in the maquilas (export-orientated assembly plants), forging, according to Leslie Sklar (1992), the formation of new transnational bourgeois strata mediating and linking national and international capital; and, on the US side, in the use of cheap – and illegal – immigrant labour power subject to increasingly racist legislation and discrimination. A slogan daubed on the border fence, 'Ni ilegales, ni criminales / Trabajadores internacionales', captures the contradiction produced there between a law that separates and an economic dynamic which joins, and that makes of the border zone it creates a place of extreme violence and exploitation.

21 I say 'disavowal' rather than the more usual 'denial' to underline the fact that coevalness is momentarily recognised before its denial (see J. Fabian 1983).

Bibliography

Ahmad, A. (1992) *In Theory: Classes, nations, Literatures*, London: Verso.

Althusser, L. (1969) 'Contradiction and Overdetermination', *For Marx* (1966), translated by B. Brewster, London: New Left Books.

—— (1979) *Reading Capital* (1968), translated by B. Brewster, London: Verso.

Anderson, P. (1992) 'Marshall Berman: Modernity and Revolution', in *A Zone of Engagement*, London: Verso.

Benjamin, W. (1979) 'Theses on the Philosophy of History' in *Illuminations*, translated by H. Zohn, London: Fontana/Collins.

Bhabha, H. (1994a) *The Location of Culture*, London: Routledge.

—— (1994b) 'Anxious Nations, Nervous States', in Joan Copjec (ed.), *Supposing the Subject*, London: Verso.

—— (1995) 'In a Spirit of Calm Violence', in G. Prakash (ed.), *After Colonialism: Imperial Histories and Postcolonial Displacements*, Princeton: Princeton University Press.

Butler, J. (1993) *Bodies that Matter*, London: Routledge.

Chakrabarty, D. (1996) 'Marxism after Marx: History, Subalternity and Difference', in S. Makdisi, C. Casarino and R. E. Karl (eds), *Marxism Beyond Marxism*, New York: Routledge.

Coombes, A. (1992) 'Inventing the "Post-Colonial": Hybridity and Constituency in Contemporary Curating', *New Formations*, 18, Winter.

Cornejo Polar, A. (1998) '*Indigenismo* and Heterogeneous Literatures: Their Dual Socio-Cultural Logic' (1976), translated by J. Kraniauskas, *Journal of Latin American Cultural Studies*, 7, 1.

Davis, M. (1990) *City of Quartz*, London: Verso.

Deleuze, G. (1992) 'Postscript on the Societies of Control', *October*, 59, Winter.

Deleuze, G. and Guattari, F. (1977) *Anti-Oedipus: Capitalism and Schizophrenia* (1972), translated by R. Hurley, M. Seem and H. R. Lane, New York: The Viking Press.

Derrida, J. (1989) *Of Spirit: Heidegger and the Question*, translated by Geoffrey Bennington and Rachel Bowlby, Chicago: The University of Chicago Press.

Fabian, J. (1983) *Time and the Other. How Anthropology Makes its Object*, New York: Columbia University Press.

García Canclini, N. (1989) *Culturas híbridas: estrategias para entrar y salir de la modernidad*, Mexico City: Grijalbo.

—— (1992a) 'Too Much Determinism or Too Much Hybridization?', translated by Margaret Smallman, *Travesía: Journal of Latin American Cultural Studies*, 1, 2.

—— (1992b) 'Museos, aeropuertos y ventas de garage: la cultura ante el Tratado de Libre Comercio', *La Jornada Semanal*, 14 June.

—— (1995) *Consumidores y cuidadanos: conflictos multiculturales de la globalización*, Mexico City: Grijalbo.

Gilroy, P. (1993) *The Black Atlantic: Modernity and Double Consciousness*, London: Verso.

Guha, R. (1983) *Elementary Aspects of Peasant Insurgency in Colonial India*, Delhi: Oxford University Press.

Hall, S. (1994) 'Culture, Community, Nation', *Cultural Studies*, 7, 3.

Kraniauskas, J. (1992) 'Hybridity and Reterritorialization', *Travesia: Journal of Latin American Cultural Studies*, 1, 2.

—— (1998) 'Globalisation is Ordinary: The Transnationalisation of Cultural Studies', *Radical Philosophy*, 90, July/August.

Laclau, E. (1990) *New Reflections on the Revolution of Our Time*, London: Verso.

Marx, K. (1977) 'Introduction', in *Grundrisse*, translated with a foreword by M. Nicolaus, Harmondsworth: Penguin.

Mignolo, W. D. (1998) 'Globalization, Civilization Processes, and the Relocation of Languages and Cultures', in F. Jameson and M. Miyoshi (eds), *The Cultures of Globalization*, Durham: Duke University Press.

Moore-Gilbert, B. (1997) *Postcolonial Theory: Contexts, Practices, Politics*, London: Verso.

Moreiras, A. (1998) 'Hegemonía y subalternidad', *Revista de crítica cultural*, 16.

Oliver, M. E., Johnston Jr, J. H. and Farrell Jr, W. C. (1992) 'Anatomy of a Rebellion: A Political-Economic Analysis', in R. Gooding-Williams (ed.), *Reading Rodney King/Reading Urban Uprising*, New York: Routledge.

Osborne, P. (1995) *The Politics of Time: Modernity and Avant-garde*, London: Verso.

Parry, B. (1994) 'Signs of Our Times', *Third Text*, 28/29, Autumn/Winter.

Rama, A. (1997) 'Processes of Transculturation in Latin American Narrative' (1974), translated by M. Moore, *Journal of Latin American Cultural Studies*, 6, 2.

—— (1982) *Transculturación narrativa en América Latina*, Mexico City: Siglo Veintiuno Editores.

Said, E. (1978) *Orientalism*, New York: Pantheon Books.

Sarmiento, D. F. (1970) *Facundo. Civilización y barbarie* (1845), Madrid: Alianza Editorial.

Schwarz, R. (1992) 'Misplaced Ideas: Literature and Society in Late-nineteenth-century Brazil' (1973), in *Misplaced Ideas: Essays on Brazilian Culture*, edited by J. Gledson, London: Verso.

Sklar, L. (1992) 'The Maquilas in Mexico: A Global Perspective', *Bulletin of Latin American Research*, 11, 1.

Spivak, G. C. (1996) 'Diasporas Old and New: Women in the Transnational World', *Textual Practice*, 10, 2.

Williams, R. (1977) *Marxism and Literature*, Oxford: Oxford University Press.

Young, R. (1990) *White Mythologies: Writing History and the West*, London: Routledge.

—— (1995) *Colonial Desire: Hybridity in Theory, Culture and Race*, London: Routledge.

12 Bad faith: anti-essentialism, universalism and Islamism

S. Sayyid

In recent years there has been a proliferation of political projects that claim to be manifestations of authentic cultural practices, untainted by western influences. These projects of cultural absolutism have an ambiguous relationship between what is problematically referred to as 'postmodernity'. Ziauddin Sardar argues that postmodernity is nothing more than the continuation of western cultural imperialism by other means (Sardar 1998: 8–9). I think he does this because he understands the postmodern condition to be associated with relativism and the valorisation of the hybrid (e.g. *ibid.*; Gellner 1992: 24). Postmodernists seem unambiguous in their rejection of cultural absolutism – that is, a set of arguments which see cultures as some invariant transhistorical set of specific practices and beliefs exclusive to a particular membership. Postmodernists would deny that cultures can be hermetically sealed units. They would favour arguments which advocate cultural hybridity. Advocates of cultural hybridity argue that cultures are not fixed or closed entities which enframe a particular membership; rather they argue that cultures are relatively open and intermeshed, thus it is difficult to decide upon the boundaries of any particular cultural formation, since cultural forms seep through attempts at (en)closure (Gilroy 1993: 7–8). Sardar thinks that the postmodernist rejection of cultural authenticity masks a promotion of western cultural values. I tend to agree with him, but I am not sure that the opposition between postmodernists and the rest is very helpful. I want to suggest that, under the slippery rubric of postmodernism, a critique of universalism and a rejection of essentialism, become conflated. The confusion arises when the critique of essentialism is given primacy over the critique of universalism. In other words, though postmodernism is blamed for being another attempt to reinforce the West's cultural hegemony, I think the project to inscribe western superiority goes beyond those who are by any stretch of the imagination postmodernists. The opposition, as I see it, is between those who represents western culture as universal and those who see these attempts as ways of trying to recover the authority of the West, in a context in which its cultural centrality is increasingly contested. In the rest of this chapter, I want to show how those who oppose the project of cultural authenticity rely on the rejection of essentialism. Anti-essentialism without a critique of universalism is simply another means of promoting and endorsing western hegemony.

Deconstructing Islam(ism)

Islamists (and even Muslims) are often accused of being terrorists, fanatics or fundamentalists. They are also charged with being intellectually duplicitous or incoherent. It is argued that, while they represent themselves as embodying auto-chthnous cultural practices, free from corrupting western cultural values, a closer inspection reveals, that despite their claims, they are riddled with western influences. The critics of Islamists often contend that despite their anti-western rhetoric they are, in fact, creations of the West. Variants of this argument are often deployed by opponents of Islamism both in the North Atlantic plutocracies and in the 'Kemalist' kleptocracies.[1] They claim to see western influences' behind their Islamist opponents (for example, the *mujahidin* who fought in Afghanistan), in the form of money, training, arms, and general support (Amin 1989: 133). The intellectual annexe to these narratives is provided by more imaginative writers who see western elements within Islamist discourse, not in terms of mere empirical referents but as an *aporia* – upon which it is possible to deconstruct the Islamist project. The work of Aziz Al-Azmeh provides a convenient entry point into this area as he is not only scornful of Islamist pretensions but also someone who is reluctant to accept that cultural differentia has any significance, apart from legitimising fascistic tendencies (see for example, Al-Azmeh 1993: 5–6, 21). Thus his critique of Islamism has an exemplary quality: it is illustrative of a genre of writing on Islamism which enjoys fairly wide acceptance (see for example Halliday 1996; Yuval-Davis and Sahgal, 1992).

According to Al-Azmeh, Islamism is invented by 'conjuration and proclamation' (1993: 7). It is a discourse 'conjured' around a fantasy of an essence of authenticity. That is, what the Islamists claim to be their discovery of 'real' Islam is nothing more than the fabrication of an Islamic tradition. He contends that cultural forms such as 'Islamic dress' or 'Islamic way of life' are recent inventions and not the recovery of sacral traditions (1993: 21). For Al-Azmeh, Islamism fabricates a 'true' Islam. It is a fabrication which is derivative and therefore inauthentic. He rejects the possibility of an Islamic essence, an invariant core which could generate the Islamist project as the internal working of its innate logic. In other words, when Islamists articulate their identities, they do so by using materials and resources which are not intrinsic to anything that could be remotely called Islamic culture. Despite the claims of the Islamists, Al-Azmeh seems to reject the idea that there is an authentic Islam.

While one could quibble about the details of Al-Azmeh's argument, from an anti-essentialist point of view he is surely correct: there is no essence to Islamism, despite what its adherents may or may not believe. Al-Azmeh's baroque prose, however, is replete with references to distortion and reality which can be sustained only in a theoretical scheme still dominated by essentialism. The idea of distortion implies an essential nature. It is only if something has an essence that it can be distorted or misrepresented. If there are no essences, then what we have are different constructions and not the distortion of a true nature. It seems that Al-Azmeh understands anti-essentialism as nothing more than a critique of the superstructural moment. He is happy to use the theoretical armoury of anti-essentialism to reveal the constructed nature of the 'phantasmagoric trend' of Islamism, but is unable or unwilling to accept that the logic of anti-essentialism entails the abandonment of foundationalism (1993: 8). This becomes increasingly clear as Al-Azmeh tries to demonstrate the inauthentic nature of Islamism.

He claims that the derivative nature of Islamist discourses arises from their dependency on western categories (1993: 10, 39, 41, 79). The reason the Islamists have to use the language of the West is that it is the only universal language. As Al-Azmeh states:

> I take it as an accomplished fact that modern history is characterized by the globalization of the Western order. Despite protests of a bewildering variety against this accomplished fact, it remains incontestable especially as, with a few exceptions of an isolated and purely local nature, these protests have taken place either in the name of ideologies of the Western province – such as national independence and popular sovereignty – or substantially in terms of these ideologies, albeit symbolically beholden to a different local or specific repertory such as the Iranian regime of the Ayatollahs
>
> (1993: 39)

The suggestion is that, when Islamists demand an 'Islamic state' or proclaim that 'Islam is the only solution', they are using the vocabulary of the West. Accordingly, then, the protests against the western order can be carried only out in the language inaugurated and enforced by that very same western order. Western discourse of self-determination, popular sovereignty, human rights, etc., which provide the means by which those who are subject to the West have been able to check or disrupt their subordinate status, are, in the final analysis, western. Even in circumstances in which resistance to the western order is couched in a language different from that sanctioned by the western order, the signifiers are different only tokenistically. This reduces the discourses of Islamism to being mere 'idioms', or dialects of a universal (i.e. western) language (Al-Azmeh 1993).

This insistence on the West as an embodiment of universal values is matched only by equally strident claims for the particularity of Islamism. For example, Al-Azmeh declares: 'The discourse of authenticity has rarely come into its own, outside Islamist circles, without being associated with some universalist discourse.' Such a statement suggests a rather limited awareness of the ambitions of Islamists. Islamist groups in general do not see their projects as being limited to any specific location, *ethnos*, or society. Islam is meant for all. Their projects are directed towards turning the world into the Muslim *Ummah*. There may be many pragmatic and contingent reasons why this global ambition may be restricted, but this does not mean that their ultimate aims are not universal. It is difficult to see how Islamists with their global ambitions can seriously be considered to be less universalist and more particular than even Serbian nationalists with their fantasies of an ethnically homogenised Greater Serbia.

This *fundamental* belief in the particularity of Islam(ism) makes it plain that the only region capable of generating the universal is the West. It is only by conflating the universal and the West that we can proceed with an analysis which recognises that the partaking of the universal also entails the internalisation of western categories (Al-Azmeh 1993: 34). By equating Islamism with particularity, Al-Azmeh is able to describe the Islamist project in terms of intellectual incoherence or charlatanism. This allows him to argue that, although Islamists reject the West, they have to partake of universalism – because they themselves, as manifestation of particularity, are external to any universalism. The universal categories, however, are at heart western, therefore the Islamists use western categories. This demonstrates the hollow nature of their claims to authenticity.

It is curious that, while Al-Azmeh identifies Islamism so closely with a particularity, he does not consider that the conflation of universalism and westernisation reduces the universal to the particular. But, if the 'universal' is based on the dissolution of all particularities, then how is it possible to identify western elements in the universal language used by Islamists? To get around this paradox, Al-Azmeh posits the idea of a multivocal totalising universal civilisation which contains historical formations such as 'the European, the Arab, the Indian' which themselves are internally heterogeneous (1993: 40). It is interesting to note that he uses broad geographical labels for European and Indian formations, but narrows his focus to one language group by writing about an Arab historical formation. Presumably, by an Arab formation he means Muslim – that is, a historical formation formed by the advent of Islam and including many constituent groups and languages. By recoding Muslim civilisation as Arab, Al-Azmeh silences its multivocal character and erases its non-Arab constituents (Iranian, Turkish, Malay, etc.). Such Arabo-centrism is a common trope in Arab nationalist circles, and it is strange that, while Al-Azmeh is keen to deny 'Arab exceptionality' *vis-à-vis* the West (1994: 115), he is apparently happy to collude with it in relation to Islam. The use of the signifier 'Arab' alongside signifiers such as 'European' and 'Indian' suggests a certain equivalence between them that is clearly unwarranted. The attempt to articulate such an equivalence suggests that Al-Azmeh's conception of a universal civilisation is rather inconsistent, if not a little confused. Of course, it is possible to defend Al-Azmeh's position by arguing that when he writes 'Arab' he means 'Arab' pure and simple – that is, an Arab formation of *jailiyha* and after. Such a position would be in keeping with his insistence that Islam is a religion and not a culture (Al-Azmeh 1993: 41). This line of reasoning is not a defence or resolution of the problem, however. By implying an equivalence between European, Indian and Arab, Al-Azmeh smuggles in a monolingual (univocal) subject as being comparable with multilingual subject positions, and thus undermines his own gesture towards multivocality and heterogeneity.

The undermining of the multivocal (universal) civilisation continues as Al-Azmeh goes on to inscribe universalism as primarily a form of westernisation. This multivocal 'universalism' is strangely monological: there are no references to the influence of Indian, Muslim or even Arab voices, and so, despite being multivocal, the universal civilisation seems to speak in one voice only. 'Multivocal', apparently, is only another name for the 'monolingual' white noise of the West. The universalism that Al-Azmeh puts forward proclaims universality while drawing on only one particularity. The linkage of the West with the universal in such a consistent manner establishes a privileged relationship between one particularity and what is counted as universal. This, of course, implies that the inclusion and dissolution of particularities within the universal is uneven: rather than universalism consuming particularities as Al-Azmeh thinks (1994: 34), universalism comes about by one particularity consuming all other particularities. This conspicuous consumption is possible only in a situation of power imbalance: what makes a particularity a 'universal' has less to do with its content and more to do with its power. In other words, universalism is the product of the exercise of *imperium*. This understanding of universalism means that it cannot be seen as merely the other of particularity: universalism is not external to the particular but, rather, it is the expansion of one particularity, so that it can consume other particularities. What distinguishes the universalised particularity from any other particularity is empire, in other words historical and contemporary forms of power relations.

Al-Azmeh's account of universalism is shot through with infelicities: if universalism is a pooling of various cultural formations, than it is difficult to describe Islam(ism) as a particularity, unless one excludes Islam from being one of the components of a universal culture. If one sees in the universal the dissolution of particularities, then there is the problem of identifying western tropes, without which the claim that Islamists are using western devices to further their anti-western ambitions becomes meaningless. If one claims that the universal and the western has become synonymous, this suggests an essentialising narrative of the West. These difficulties arise from trying to marry an anti-essentialist account with an affirmation of universalism of the western project. I shall describe the attempts to advocate equivalence between universalism and the West as forms of western supremacist discourse. Western supremacist discourses are an attempt to rearticulate the global hegemony of the West in the wake of decolonisation (however limited and unsatisfactory).

Falling down through the looking glass: Islamism and Euro-centrism

Western supremacists do not want the 'non-West' to be able to appeal to its traditions as a way of saying that it is incommensurable with western values; and in particular they do not want to concede to the claims of authenticity of Islamists. They do not want Islamists to be able to reject certain values by appealing to their Islamic heritage. Allowing Islamists to deny certain values on the grounds that these values are alien and artificial would, as Al-Azmeh argues, be an act akin to appeasement (1993: 20, 23, 34).

This charge of appeasement deploys notions which the white knights of the far right in the USA would instantly recognise and endorse (for example, their stories of how the defeat of American power is due to the 'liberal appeasement' of 'foreign i.e. Third World opponents'). Similarly, Al-Azmeh seems to see appeasement as being due to nefarious conspiracies (1993: 23, 32, 72), and, in his case these conspiracies have a 'petro-dollar' rather than a 'liberal' basis. This notion of conspiratorial appeasement seems odd for two reasons. First, he has chided the discourses of *asala* (cultural authencity) for trying to maintain the integrity of its subject, by postulating that change is due to sinister conspiracies such as imperial interference or internal subversion (1993: 42). Thus, it is strange that he resorts to similar strategies in his accounts of Islamism. Second, and more importantly, the exact nature of the empirical referents of Al-Azmeh's charges of appeasement are incomprehensible. The point is that the suggestion that Muslims (even in a sociological sense) are Islamists is most frequently used to legitimatise mass slaughter in which Muslims are often the main victims: Bosnia, Kashmir, Palestine, Tajikistan, Chechneya, South Lebanon, etc. Of course, it could be said that Al-Azmeh has in mind the appeasement of Islamists in the liberal West. Again it is difficult to see how one can sustain the idea of western attempts at appeasement of Islamicist given instances of restrictions on Muslim women wearing *hijab*, or the banning of various Muslim student organisations from campuses, or legislation threatening the funding of Muslim charities and welfare associations, or systematic vandalism of Muslim places of worship and residences. Or it could be that he is thinking of the 'appeasement' by Kemalist regimes in places like Algeria, Egypt or his native Syria, where in 1982 Assad, in a famous act of appeasement, wiped out the Muslim Brotherhood along with large sections of the city of Homs, including an estimated twenty to thirty thousand of its residents.

The idea of appeasement, however, is not a purely idiosyncratic gesture. Al-Azmeh also seems to consider the assertion of a Muslim subjectivity to be akin to 'apartheid' (1993: 40). This appears to be a rather parodic understanding of 'apartheid'. The suggestion seems to be that Muslim settlers in North Atlantic plutocracies are analogous to the Boer Trekkers, setting up their versions of Boerstats in Bradford, Marseilles, Berlin, Oklahoma City. This would seem to disregard the fact that one of the main causes of ghettos in the North Atlantic plutocracies has been 'white flight': ghettos are created when those with money and power do not wish to have black faces across their white picket fences. It is not 'Muslim settlers' who create ghettos, it is rather, that they are ghettoised. This generous reading of 'apartheid' as simply 'separate development' masks the play of racialised power which is as intrinsic to apartheid as any notion of closure or separatism. Al-Azmeh denies that racism has much of a part to play in the recent European representations of Muslim settlers (1993: 4), but it is surprising that he seems to be willing to ignore the racialised nature of apartheid.

Given Al-Azmeh's suspicion of Islamist claims, it seems curious that he appears to succumb to the ideologues of apartheid so swiftly, seemingly colaborating with the 'whitewashing' of racism out of apartheid. The extent of Al-Azmeh's misreading is made plain by the way his work often makes references to 'reverse-racism', 'counter-racism' 'reverse orientalism', 'racism-in-reverse' (1993: 9, 42). These notions of 'reverse-racism' and its cognates are currently in vogue among the advocates of the white backlash, being part of the Newspeak by which they advance their critique of multiculturalism (Bloom 1987; D'Souza 1991). But this rather quixotic critique of multiculturalism fails to acknowledge that the reverse of racism would be anti-racism, which is a rejection of the logic of racial hierarchisation. It is clear that what Al-Azmeh refers to as 'reverse-racism' is the refusal of South Asian settlers to accept metropolitan liberal discourse. Let us indulge Al-Azmeh and accept, for argument's sake, that one of the most pressing issues in contemporary Britain is that South Asian settlers are deploying a logic of 'racial' exclusion against white metropolitan liberals. Why is this reverse racism? As has been pointed out, racism is not something that can be reversed (Hesse 1996: 100, 103). To suggest otherwise means assuming that racism has a normative direction. Such a definition of racism suppresses its constitutive nature as an asymmetrical relationship of power (*ibid.*). Al-Azmeh's cavalier use of 'appeasement', 'apartheid', 'reverse-racism' firmly locates him within the logic of mirroring.

The logic of mirroring operates by transforming asymmetrical relationship into a relation of symmetry. This has a number of effects. First, it constructs the subordinate subject as an inversion of the dominant subject position. This obscures the possibility of any autonomy of the subordinate. The subaltern exists only as an effect of the hegemonic discourse. It is not that subalternity is merely the result of hegemony but, rather, that the status of subalternity exhausts the subjectivity of the subordinated subject. Second, it erases the dimension of power from any relationship. A relationship of power is a relationship of unevenness. Symmetry, obviously, denies hierarchy or oppression. The logic of mirroring is based on the assumption that the discourse of the dominant order produces its own resistance. That is, those who resist the hegemonic can do so only in the terms of that hegemony. It has the effect of transforming any struggle against a particular hegemony as another moment, in the expansion of that hegemony. Al-Azmeh is references to appeasement, apartheid and reverse-racism endorse the logic of mirroring. His entire argument takes its cue from a very popular idea (in the West), that resistance to the West is itself a gift of the West. If resistance to the West is another move in the inventory of the West, the West can have no limits. Projects such as Islamism, which ostensibly reject the West, could be seen as another moment in the drama of the West. This means that the rejection of the West becomes another form of its acceptance – the ability to reject is represented as a western capability (Sayyid 1997: 127–55).

How the West was won: the limits of universalism

A discourse becomes universal to the extent that it can erase the marks of its particularity. In semantics, marking within lexical structures is based around the differential distribution of morphologically or formally related lexemes within a language (Lyons 1966: 305–11). The lexemes that are marked tend to be more restricted in the range of contexts in which they can be used than unmarked lexemes. (For example, *lioness* refers to a female lion only, whereas *lion* refers not only to a male lion but also to the species as a whole.) An absolute universal discourse would be one that was totally constituted by unmarked elements. All projects, however, that are aiming for a universal status are confronted by a paradox that prevents their movement towards an absolute universalism; for marking works not only as a restriction on use but also as a form of identification. Absolute unmarking would remove the identity of the cultural formation, while absolute marking would remove its ability to transcend its cultural boundaries. For a discourse to erase all its marks would mean erasing its cohesion.

The paradoxical nature of universalism is clearly illustrated by the attempt to perpetuate the linkage between the western project and universalism. It requires using a notion of universalism that is able to fulfil two distinct tasks. First, universalism has to be conceptualised as a rejection of particularity. At the same time it has to be seen as the incarnation of one particularity, so that the western project can continue to be presented as universal. Both these plays on universalism can be illustrated by reference to Al-Azmeh. His efforts to project Islamism as an instance of particularity (that is, the incarnation of 'ontological irredentism') are based on the idea that universalism is a rejection of particularity (1993: 42). At the same time, to demonstrate the 'inauthentic' temper of Islamism, he is keen to locate traces of the West within Islamist discourses. To master this paradox writers such as Al-Azmeh rely on an essentialist reading of the western project.[2] This allows them to argue that Islamism is dependent on essentially western elements. The only way in which a critique of the essentialism of discourses of authenticity can be sustained is by evoking an essentialist notion of the West. That is, we can identify the western elements in Islamists' discourses only by claiming the persistence of western identity within the vocabulary of the Islamists. But this can be done only by invoking an essential West – a West that remains constant and invariant regardless of its articulations.

Thus, it would appear that an anti-essentialist critique of Islamism can easily operate by affirming an essentialist notion of the West: the affirmation of the particularity of Islamism is achieved by denying the particularity of the West. It would be naïve to assume that the problem with this approach is simply one of scholarly partisanship.[3] My point is not merely to highlight the inconsistencies and sleights of hand by which an apparent critique of cultural absolutism is itself based on affirmation of cultural exclusivity. Rather, it is to show that the problem faced by those who advocate western supremacist discourse is how to maintain the legislating performative of the name of the West, when the networks of power/knowledge that sustained that performance are no longer functioning as they once did. In the following section I want to demonstrate what the implications of anti-essentialism are for the possibility of a different construction of 'universalism'.

If we take a position consistent with anti-essentialism, then the West is nothing more than a construct produced by a variety of articulatory practices. The properties that have been historically sedimented as being associated with the West can remain so only in the context of the political project (empire) sustaining those articulations.

The identity of the West comes about, not as a working out of an intrinsically necessary essence but rather as an operation of articulation which tries to suggest that a contingent correlation of properties is, in fact, necessary. In other words, the West is a hegemonic project. What I would suggest is that it is more useful to understand the relationship between properties attributed to the West and the category 'West' itself in terms of articulation rather than in the working out of a destiny inscribed within the essence of the West. The 'West' is the name by which a number of discursive elements are structured, unified and given a destiny. In other words, the relationship between the signifier 'West' and the chain of signifi- cations articulated to it is a matter of historical contingency rather than teleology or necessity.

Drawing on the debate between the descriptivists and the anti-descriptivists, Slavoj Zizek concludes that the name *retroactively* constitutes the unity and iden- tity of the object (1989: chapter 2). The retroactive nature of naming also means that there is no primal baptism as a single foundational act. The relationship between signifier and signified is not fixed once and for all but rather the primal baptism is a horizon in which the moment of naming is constantly being re- iterated. It is not so much that some elements are western and others are not, but rather that some properties are claimed and attached to the 'West', while others are rejected and excluded. The constitution of the West requires the constant incantation of its name. For it is the name that acts as a mark of ownership and copyright and it is the name that makes possible the constitution of the unity of the object. Thus, the West acts as means of unifying a discourse.

As Said's inspirational work demonstrated, the ability of the Orientalist to dis- course about the Orient was founded on the dense network of political-cultural elements which supported the Orientalist. The Orientalist could speak for the Orient, because he could speak the language of science, rationality, progress. He could use a language by which other languages could be translated and tran- scribed. The Orientalist was part of a 'supercultural' formation reinforced by the facticity of European imperialism. With the breakdown of European imperial systems and the processes of decolonisation, the notion of a 'supercultural' forma- tion can no longer be taken for granted. Without the background which sustained the sovereignty of the West, the principle that the 'West knows best', which once used to inspire awe and agreement, is now more likely to provoke laughter and incredulity. If the name of the West can no longer perform legislatively (if it cannot sanction its visions), perhaps a new brand name might do the trick. Increasingly, the universal is used to smuggle in the western, while making half-hearted gestures to its 'multivocal' character.[4]

The supposedly Islamist rejection of the universal in terms of the rejection of the signifier western does not necessarily imply the rejection of what is being signified, but it is a rejection of that hegemonic operation, which claims what is being signified as a western patrimony. What this means is that the denunciation of Islamists for using western categories is, at the same time, the reconstruction and maintenance of particular genealogical traces. It is not that Islamists use ideas which are themselves 'western' in some essentialist sense, but the description of some values as 'western' retroactively constructs them as such. The contest between Islamists and their enemies is not a conflict between fundamentalists and liberals, as many maintain, but a contest between a discourses of western *asala* western supremacism) and a Muslim *asala* (Islamism). In this regard, Islamism or the western project are not so different. One may have one's own prejudices for preferring one to the other, but both are attempts to remake the world. Neither is sanctioned by any innate logic, both are themselves grand political projects: projects that aim to transform our cultures, histories and societies. Such projects are attempts to draw boundaries, they narrate themselves in terms of their destiny; projecting themselves into the future, but also projecting themselves into the past. The 'universal' is not a gift of history but the consequence of the failure or success of a political project: what is the universal at a given juncture is, to use the vocabulary of Husserl, the sedimentation of a particular political project – a sedimentation that is itself vulnerable to reactivation (Husserl 1970: 269–99).

It is not only Islamists who are engaged in an operation of fabrication (i.e. making up stories about their authentic selves). Those who reject Islamist narratives of authenticity also do so by fabricating stories about the West. The need to renew constantly the retroactive operation of constitution (naming) means that the 'universal' must be policed and constantly linked to the particularity of the West. This means that the link that is established between universal values and the traces of the West, in opposition to other particularities, is difficult to sustain within an anti-essentialist framework, since the identity of those values comes from their articulation, and not from their essences. The continued assumption of the universalism of the West is a consequence of historiography and not, as it is too often claimed (e.g. Halliday 1996), a matter of history.

Clearly, this conclusion might not find favour with those who, while opposing essentialism support the logic of euro-centrism. For example, Al-Azmeh's critique of Islamist essentialism is made within a context dominated by other kinds of essentialisms. His rendition of anti-essentialism illustrates very clearly the way in which anti-essentialism is increasingly used to inscribe 'universalism' and foreclose the possibility of any form of multiculturalism. The critique of universalism, within the emerging orthodoxy, assumes a secondary importance to the critique of essentialism. The postmodern critique of metanarratives raises questions about the essentialism of some of these narratives, but, at the same time, it reveals the limits of such critiques. Despite the current obsession with cultural hybridity and difference, it is clear that there is a reluctance to extend the logic of 'multicultural' beyond the superficial valorisation of ethnicity. Embracing the logic of the multicultural would mean abandoning the certitude and comfort of speaking from the centre. It would mean having to learn new language games. A 'violent hierarchy' (Derrida: 1973) between West and Rest continues to underwrite much of the current debate around themes of cultural difference and absolutism. As a result, anti-essentialism simply becomes another means of trying to defer considering the consequences of multiculturalism. Thus the critique of grand narratives is slowly brushed under the carpet by the attempts to articulate an implicit universalism from which anti-essentialism can be used to prevent the consolidation of the multicultural moment. Thus, it is not surprising that many advocates of postmodernity end up wistfully expressing a nostalgia for empire.[5]

The invocation of cultural hybridity as a solution to a globalising world presents a paradox. On the one hand, it seems to focus attention on the fragmentary nature of the hegemonic cultural formation, on the way their constituent parts were often marginalised and suppressed. At the same time as making possible the weakening of hegemonic cultural formation, cultural hybridity makes it impossible to displace the hegemonic formation, since the critique of cultural absolutism implied by cultural hybridity also makes it impossible to sustain any subaltern cultural formation. As long as the debate on universalism and particularism avoids taking into account the particularity of each and every claim to universalism, it cannot resolve this paradox.

The fear of relativism is the main argumentative plank for sustaining universalism. It is argued that, if we did not have the crutch of universalism, 'we' would not be able to defend ourselves from behaviour which 'we' find objectionable. Leaving aside the problem of identifying the 'we' (just as the common presentation of this type of argument does), such reasoning transforms political questions into a philosophical question. There is no philosophical way of getting around the problem that we all think and behave in the context of a particular cultural formation. Our desires, our values, our cognitive horizons are all conditioned by our insertion into a specific matrix of cultural practices. Cultures are not unitary, but at the same time they are not decentred. The quest for a decentred cultural formation inscribes the domination of one particular formation. A current example of this is provided by policies of the members of the European Union in regard to their Muslim minorities. Public policies of assimilation and integration are underwritten by attempts to decentre Muslim cultural practices. The critique of cultural absolutisim becomes the means of articulating *Festung Europa*.[6]

The postmodern-inspired critique of cultural essentialism too often refuses to distinguish between hegemonic and subaltern formations, and this has a number of important consequences, both at the level of policy-making and at the broader political cultural plane.[7] The ability to conclude multicultural alliances, or to renegotiate public spaces, depends on whether there is a dissolution of hegemony or its extension by other means. By attempting to 'deconstruct' every subaltern formation, anti-essentialism carries out a *de facto* endorsement of the hegemonic order. This is, why someone like Spivak suggests that we need a notion of 'strategic essentialism' as a means of allowing subaltern formations a fiction of essence around which political mobilisations and campaigns can be gathered (1987: 205–7 and Fuss 1990: 31–2). Fuss also acknowledges that essentialism has differential effects depending on whether essentialism is being used to entrench the domination of the hegemonic order or being deployed by subalterns to subvert a dominant order (1990: 32). The problem with this approach, as Fuss accepts, is that subalternity or hegemony does not tell us very much about the content of a political project, and that 'strategic essentialism' may be another way of reinscribing essentialism. Despite this, Fuss considers essentialism worth the risk (1990: 32). The difficulty with Fuss's approach is that it separates essentialism from universalism: this makes it possible to articulate an anti-essential universalism. What I want to suggest is that any critique of essentialism which is not also a critique of universalism is problematic, and should perhaps be understood as likely to serve as another strategic ploy within the armoury of western supremacist discourse. If a critique of essentialism is to be mounted, in good faith, it can be done only by extending the critique to universalism itself. No doubt Islamists make use of essentialism, but to point this out, without pointing out that the western project itself is also equally essentialist, seems to be at best eccentric and at worst mendacious. The conflict between Islamism and western supremacist discourses can be seen as a conflict between particularity and universalism only if one makes the particularity of the West unmarked and natural. The only way to avoid this reinscription of the West as the universal is to take seriously the logic of multiculturalism.

This logic should not be confused with recent debate regarding 'clash of civilizations' (Huntingdon 1993). Multicuturalism does not mean simply the recognition that there are many cultures, nor that cultures are inherently locked in mortal combat with each other. Nor should 'multicultural' be seen as a post-Holocaust euphemism for 'race' or 'nation'. The logic of multiculturalism is based on consequences arising out of the decentring of the West, in other words it is not an attempt to close the gap between the West and the centre; rather it is an attempt to explore the possibilities of widening the interval between the West and the idea of centre. This is terrain of the multicultural. The cost of making a multicultural move is the abandonment of any investment in the uncontested universality of the western project. This is a price that western supremcists are unwilling (or perhaps more charitably unable) to pay. Thus they deploy the logic of euro-centrism as a way of responding to the end of the European age. Euro-centrism then is an attempt to resuture the relationship between the West and the centre; one of the key strategies in this project is that of using critique of essentialism while avoiding a critique of universalism.

Conclusion

The problem of dealing with cultural formations that articulate themselves as being distinct from western formations become acute after the age of Europe. In this chapter I have argued that various attacks on the manifestations of Islamism, on grounds of its essentialism, are made possible only by articulating an essential-ist notion of the exceptionality of the West. The distinction between the universal and the particular is often no more than conceit of western supremacist dis-courses. The universal can no longer be a euphemism for the western project, nor can the particular be simply considered nothing more than the periphery of the West. The distinction between the universal and the particular, whereby the West is universal and the Rest is particular, ignores the particularity of the West itself. It is only by ignoring that particularity that one can claim that the West is universal. The continuing presence of various Islamist groups (and various other move-ments) indicates that the West can no longer be the uncontested template by which we give shape to the world. One of the reasons that Islamism is seen as a disruptive force is that it fails to accept this juridical role of the West. Many of the critics of Islamism are often merely content to try and reinscribe a *de facto* western hegemony in the guise of universalism, instead of recognising that there is a need to develop different language games which do not presuppose the juridical function of the West. There are many ways to forge a social order that one would be happy to live in. What Islamists challenge is the assumption that the only royal road to a better future is the one that has been pioneered by the West.

Notes

I would like to thank the following creatures of the night: Hatoon al-Fassi, Nasreen Ali, Avtar Brah, Pandeli Glavanis, Barnor Hesse, John Hutnyk, Ali Rattansi, Laura Turney, Katherine Tyler and Lililan Zac. In their individual ways they all make lovely music.

1 The discourse of Kemalism includes all political projects within Muslim communities (subsequent to the abolition of the Caliphate in 1924) which aimed at articulating a political community based around euro-centric notions of what was it to be modern. For more details see Sayyid 1997, pp. 52–83.
2 See for example Halliday (1996), Yuval-Davis and Sahgal (1992). One could cite many other examples.
3 One thing that Edward Said's work has made clear is that academic neutrality has been lacking in the study of the Orient. See for example, Brendan O'Leary's comments on the way Bernier's conceptualisation of oriental despotisim contradicted his own descriptions of Indian society (1989: 57), or Naqvi's commentary on Marx (1973: 66) or Springborg on Weber (1992).
4 The relationship between the universal and the West is central to maintaining the claim of one cultural formation to be the only legitimate form of power/ knowledge. One of the points that Said makes throughout his critique of Orientalism is the constant refrain in Orientalist discourse that the Orient cannot represent itself but needs the intervention of the (western) expert to be represented (Said 1985: 32–6). The questioning of this necessity of western intervention raises the doubts about the privileged position of the western canon. The conflict concerning the displacement of the western canon is a contestation about the possibility of getting along without Orientalism. To defend the centrality of the western canon and the impossibility of doing without Orientalism, it is necessary to extend and treat it as a universal canon containing all that is the best in human history. One strategy of doing this is to claim that when critics of the western canon voice their opposition they are actually still using the language of the West. Thus one way of perpetuating this universalist nature of the West is to relocate all attempts to resist it as mere illustrations of the universal nature of the West. This is done, for example, by making genealogical claims that elements of Islamist discourse are at heart western. The ability to recuperate discourses like Islamism rests on the ability to 'recover' the culturally copyrighted element in the discourse of Islamism. The battle between universalism and what are often described as particular claims of cultural authenticity can be seen as a conflict about genealogies: about how to narrate the future of the world. The western discourse is a product of several projects which narrate the world in terms of the continuity of the West. The limits of Europe emerge when groups of people begin to articulate their position by rejecting Europe's claims that the world is its patent.

5 See Slater's discussion of Baudrillard (1994: 94–6). Despite this complex relationship with postmodernity, Slater's critique of Islamism and valorisation of western exceptionality locates him with the problematic generated by attempts to sustain universalism within a terrain increasingly marked by the postmodern condition (Heller and Feher 1991: 12). Al-Azmeh's 'deconstruction' of Islam(ism) falls within the postmodern critique of essentialism. His use of anti-essentialism enables him to break with Orientalist accounts, which would see in the appearance of Islamism the culminating expression of a continuous Islamic essence.

6 See for example, the *Report on Muslim Voices in Europe*, University of Manchester, 1998.

7 While someone like Al-Azmeh rejects postmodernism, he is still willing to use many of the ideas associated with it.

Bibliography

Al-Azmeh, Aziz. (1993) *Islams and Modernities*. London: Verso.

Al-Azmeh, Aziz. (1994) 'Populism contra Democracy: recent democraticist discourse in the Arab world', in Salame, Ghassan (ed.), *Democracy without Democrats?* London: I. B. Tauris.

Amin, Samir. (1989) *Eurocentrism*. London: Zed.

Asad, Talal (1993) Genealogies of Religion. Baltimore: Johns Hopkins University Press.

Bloom, Allan. (1987) *The Closing of the American Mind*. New York: Simon and Shuster.

Connolly, Wiliam E. (1991) *Identity/Difference*. Ithaca: Cornell University Press.

Derrida, Jaques. (1973) *Positions*. London: Athlone Press.

D'Souza, Dinesh. (1991) *Illiberal Education: The Politics of Race and Sex on Campus*. New York: Free Press.

Fuss, Diana. (1990) *Essentially Speaking*. London: Routledge.

Gellner, Ernest. (1992) *Postmodernism, Reason and Religon*. London: Routledge.

Gilroy, Paul. (1993) *The Black Atlantic*. London: Verso.

Hall, Stuart. (1992) 'The West and the Rest: Discourse and Power' in Hall, Stuart and Bram Gieben (eds), *The Formation of Modernity*. Cambridge: Polity Press.

Halliday, Fred. (1996) *Islam and the Myth of Confrontation*. London: I. B. Tauris.

Heller, Agnes and Frenc Feher. (1991) *The Postmodern Political Condition*. Cambridge: Polity Press.

Hesse, Barnor. (1996) 'White Governmentality: Urbanism, Nationalism, Racism', in Westwood, S. and John Williams (eds), *Imagining Cities*. London: Routledge.

Huntingdon, Samuel P. (1993) 'The Clash of Civilizations', *Foreign Affairs*, Summer, pp. 22–49.

Husserl, E. (1970) *The Crisis of European Sciences and Transcendental Phenomenology: An Introduction to Phenomenological Philosophy*. Trans by D. Carr. Evanston: Northwestern University Press.

Kabbani, Rana. (1983) *Europe's Myths of the Orient: Devise and Rule*. London: Macmillan.

Kruger, Barbara and Phil Mariani (eds). (1989) *Remaking History*. Seattle: Bay Press.

Lyons, John. (1966) *Introduction to Theoretical Linguistics*. Cambridge: Cambridge University Press.

Lyotard, Jean-François. (1992) *The Post-modem Condition: A Report on Knowledge*. Trans. by Geoff Benninigton and Brain Massumi. Oxford: Polity Press.

Naqvi, S. (1973) 'Marx on Pre-British Indian Economy and Society,' *Socialist Digest*, 7, pp. 36–70.

O'Leary, Brendan. (1989) *The Asiatic Mode of Production*. Oxford: Basil Blackwell.

Rattansi, Ali and Sallie Westwood (eds). *Racism, Modernity and Identity: On the Western Front*, Cambridge: Polity Press.

Roy, Oliver. (1994) 'Patronage and Solidarity Groups: Survival or Reformation', in Salame, Ghassan (ed.), *Democracy without Democrats?* London: I. B. Tauris.

Said, Edward W. (1985) *Orientalism*. London: Routledge and Kegan Paul.

Sardar, Ziauddin. (1998) *Post-modernism and the Other*. London: Pluto Press.

Sayyid, S. (1997) *A Fundamental Fear: Eurocentrism and the Emergence of Islam*. London: Zed Press.

Slater, David. (1994) 'Exploring Other Zones of the Postmodern: Problems of Ethnocentrism and Difference across the North-South Divide', in Rattansi, Ali and Sallie Westwood (eds), *Racism, Modernity and Identity: On the Western Front*. Cambridge: Polity Press.

Spivak, Gayatri Chakravorty. (1987) *In Other Words*. London: Methuen.

Springborg, Patricia. (1992) *Western Republicanism and the Oriental Prince*. Cambridge: Polity Press.

Yuval-Davis, Nira and Gita Sahgal (eds). (1992) *Refusing Holy Orders: Women and Fundamentalism in Britain*. London: Virago Press.

Zizek, Slavoj. (1989) *The Sublime of Ideology*. London: Verso.

13 The scent of memory: strangers, our own and others

Avtar Brah

They all crossed into forbidden territory. They all tempered with the laws that lay down who should be loved, and how. And how much.

(Arundhati Roy, *The God of Small Things*)

This chapter is a meditation through a series of questions. A mediation, by definition, cannot presuppose answers or conclusions. I hope that this one develops into an open-ended conversation – a kind of graffito without finite beginnings and endings. My own meditation is in pursuit of what Donna Haraway so aptly designates as the need to consider how humanity might have a figure outside the narratives of humanism. What language, she asks, would such a 'posthumanist' figure speak?

I want to set aside the Enlightenment figures of coherent and masterful subjectivity, the bearers of rights, holders of property in the self, legitimate sons with access to language and the power to represent, subjects endowed with inner coherence and rational clarity, the masters of theory, founders of states, and fathers of families, bombs, and scientific theory . . . and end by asking how recent intercultural and multicultural feminist theory constructs possible postcolonial, nongeneric, and irredeemably specific figures of critical subjectivity, consciousness, and humanity – not in the sacred image of the same, but in the self-critical practice of 'difference', of the I and we that is/ are never identical to itself, and so has hope of connection to others.

(Haraway 1992: 87)

This would seem to be one of the most important tasks facing feminisms at this point.

Triggers

In late 1996, the British Sunday newspaper *The Observer* carried a review of a book titled *The Scent of Dried Roses*. The newspaper contained some excerpts from this autobiographical account by a son of his mother's suicide. What caught

---

First published in *Feminist Review*, No. 61, Spring 1999.

my eye were the contents of the mother's suicide note, especially the following line: 'This will be so bad for everybody but I hate Southall, I can see only decay. I feel alone.' This sentence reverberated in the quiet of the Sunday morning, compelling me to read the book. But why?

The word 'Southall' – ringing loud and clear in my ears – connected me across diverse, even disparate, life worlds to 'Jean' – this fifty-seven-year-old white woman who took her own life in March 1988. But what kind of a *connection* was it that beckoned me inexorably into her world? What clues did I expect to pick up about this woman by reading her son's account of her life? This was not really a question about the reliability of his account, not least because there is no guarantee that Jean's own account of her life would have rendered her any more transparently 'knowable' to me. The extent to which she becomes 'knowable' is not simply a matter of putting together fragments of information available about her according to some pre-given formula; nor can the task of making sense of Jean's universe only be an issue about the conceptual frameworks available to us for interpretation. Knowing is not so much about the assemblage of existing knowledge as it is about recognizing our constitution as 'ourselves' within the fragments that we process as knowledge; 'hailing' and being 'hailed' within the discourses that produce us and the narratives we spin; directing our socially, culturally, psychically, and spiritually marked focus of attention upon that which we appropriate as 'data' or 'evidence'. Hence, 'data' are neither more nor less reliable simply because of the nature of their source: whether the source in question is autobiography, biography, history, religion, or science. The boundaries between cosmology, history, religion, and science are far from clear cut as they are no more, and no less, than different ways of *trying* to know *that* which defies transparency. For example, what is 'history' if not an ongoing contestation of the very terms whereby the *term* itself emerged as a technology of eurocentric gaze. So that, a *specifically* embodied European subject such as Hegel could assert without an iota of self-doubt that Africa had no 'history'? What kind of a 'knowing' is this, where all human history is reduced to 'history'?

My point is: what is humanity if not an intricate mosaic of *non-identical* kinship?

Who was Jean? Is this a question about her alone? Why am *I* so exercised about this woman's fate? How am I implicated in *her world and she in mine*, by *my* asking of this question? Is my interest in her driven by a sense of affinity with her or by a sense of difference? Indeed, do these have to be bipolar alternatives? Clearly, these are not questions that can easily be accommodated within the frame of modernity's imperatives of rationality. As I tried to understand my agenda for reading the book, I gradually became aware that my reasons for wanting to 'read' Jean could in turn be 'read', at least in part, as an alibi for a certain desire: the desire of colonialism's Other to 'know' how differential forms of 'whiteness' are 'lived'? In a way, I was (am?) constructing her as my window on to 'working-class English whiteness'. But it was not just that. Which other, more intimate, chords had she touched in me?

What made Jean *hate* Southall?, I asked myself. Could one of the reasons be that it is one of those localities of London where the immigrants from Britain's former colonies – especially those from South Asia – came to settle in significant numbers? Was she amongst the white parents who in 1965 campaigned for bussing Asian children out of Southall schools if their numbers rose to one-third of the school population, because they were thought by these parents to 'hold back' white children? Was she at all like some of the white parents whom I interviewed as a research student in 1976? I had spent a considerable part of 1976 talking with fifteen-year-old students in three schools and their parents at home while trying to study the interplay – in the lives of 'whites' and 'Asians' – of the discourses of race, ethnicity, and class in *naming* identity. For several months I had sat in classrooms, observed what went on in school grounds, walked the streets, and visited homes in Southall, Ealing, and Greenford. All this had left indelible impressions of this heaving, bustling, culturally thriving locality of west London which was 'home' to a range of groups: Irish, Welsh, Polish, South Asian, and Caribbean descent groups alongside the 'English'. Jean was certainly within the same age-group as most of the white parents I had spoken to. Most of these parents had been incredibly outspoken and forthright in recounting what they thought about Asians in Southall. In some cases, my face-to-face presence during interview seemed to be completely obliterated, as if I did not exist, while they heaped a variety of derogatory stereotypes upon Asian populations. Did Jean experience them/us/me as a 'threat' in the same way as politicians such as Powell and Thatcher had been making out? Or could it be that her daily contact with Asian children through her job as a 'dinner lady' in a primary school with a predominantly Asian school population fostered bonds of connection and affection which served to refute the appeals of an essentialist Britishness of the Powellian–Thatcherite variety?

Origin stories

One 'white' mother whom I interviewed in 1976 had said to me: ' "Where did *they* come from?", my father used to say, "they were here, and then the shops opened up." ' The 'they' in this locution signified 'Asians'. 'She means people like me', I had thought to myself, feeling acutely 'othered', as my efforts at maintaining 'objectivity' (which my supervisor at university had insisted was critical for gaining academic credibility for my research) fast receded. I could not be a disinterested listener, although I listened attentively. My intellect, feelings, and emotions had all been galvanized by my respondent's discourse. I was framed within it, whether I liked it or not. What was it that made her referent 'they' instantly recognizable as 'Asians' to us both? I did not know her ethnicity. She could have been English, Irish, Welsh, Polish, or anything else in terms of her own 'background'. South Asians or 'people of colour' in general were not the only substantially large 'immigrant' group in Southall? Nor were they necessarily the most recent. The Southallian population at the time was continually renewed by, for instance, Irish immigrants. So, what was it that 'rang a bell' in the core of our sense of ourselves or 'interpellated' us relationally, simultaneously, with the result that we both understood who the 'they' in our conversation was? What non-logocentric discursive spatiality produces such electric moments of 'recognition'?

A digression through the idea of 'interpellation'

With regard to this question, I believe that there is much that is still of value in the Althusserian idea of 'interpellation', the concept that struggles with some of what I am trying to grapple with here, namely the making sense of being situated and 'hailed' socially, culturally, symbolically, and psychically, all at once. I am mindful of the critiques of Althusser's conceptual framework (see Hindess and Hirst 1975; Laclau and Mouffe 1985). Indeed, I too have some serious reservations about aspects of this discourse, including its economic determinism 'in the last instance', its class-centricity, and its structuralist formalism. Yet, to hold such reservations is not to deny the importance of economic and class relations.

A significant strength of the Althusserian discourse is that it takes seriously the relationship between the social and the psychic in the production of class subjects. It tries to stage, a critical and non-reductive dialogue between and across 'consciousness' (or 'conscious agency'), 'subjectivity', and 'identity'. The analytical reach of the *combined* Althusserian theoretical repertoire is profound, with its key concepts ranging from the notion of 'historical conjuncture', as the outcome of *articulation* of contradictions that defy simplistic reductionism; through the idea of overdetermination, as the *modes of articulation* incorporating a symbolic dimension and a plurality of meaning; to the concept of 'articulation' itself, as a metaphor used to indicate relations of linkages and their effects across different levels of socio-cultural formation such that, as Stuart Hall notes, 'things are related, as much through their differences as through their similarities' (Hall 1980: 320). The concept of articulation also embodies Saussure's insight that language is not a reflection of the world but produces meaning.

Hence, Althusser's claim that everything in the social is overdetermined highlights the processes whereby the social constitutes itself in and through the symbolic. And, therein lies the importance of the Althusserian reworking, following Gramsci, of the concept of ideology as not signifying false consciousness but referring, instead, to the complex matrices of meaning, concepts, categories, and representations in and through which individuals make sense of the world. That is to say that, individuals are 'hailed' or 'interpellated' within and across universes of representations and discourses of meaning in the process of our constitution into cultural or social subjects. The importance of the poststructuralist critique of the concept of ideology notwithstanding, I read interpellation as the process of signification whereby we come to 'live' (albeit largely unconsciously) our symbolic and psychic relationship to the social. I have sympathy with those critiques of the Althusserian paradigm which take issue with the functionalism embedded in his discussion of the relationship between 'interpellation' and the 'ideological State Apparatuses', but the concept of interpellation itself remains pertinent and useful. It places the question of the relationship between effects of capitalist social relations and subjectivity into the realm of productive interrogation.

A far more serious limitation of Althusserian structuralist Marxism, in my view, resides in its lack of attention to questions of women's gender (for the male gender is its norm), racism, ethnicity, and sexuality. My encounter with Jean within the pages of a Sunday newspaper and later in her son's autobiography, or with the white mother whom I had interviewed two decades earlier, cannot be understood outside of these 'other' contexts.

'"Where did they come from?", my father used to say . . .'

One straight answer would be that which was encapsulated in the contemporary political slogan: 'We are here because you were there!' This slogan referred to the history of British colonialism and imperialism, which resulted in Britain turning to its former colonies for the recruitment of workers to meet the post-Second-World-War labour shortages that befell capitalist economies of western Europe. Was my 'research respondent' familiar with this history? She easily might not have been, given, as I discovered during my research, a spectacular amnesia on this matter within the curriculum of Southall schools of the period, and presumably earlier. More worryingly, the school library in one of the three secondary schools still stocked reference books which discussed the anti-colonial Rebellion of 1857 in terms of the 'Indian Mutiny' and the 'Black Hole of Calcutta', without any evidence indicating that such texts were being subjected to critical scrutiny. But even if we assume, for the sake of argument, that my interviewee was singularly familiar with the history of British imperial adventures abroad, we cannot automatically deduce *how* such evidence would have been interpreted by her. Facts do not speak for themselves. How was she 'interpellated', as a working-class white woman with her *unique* autobiography, within the imperial discursive formations? Indeed, how did colonial discourses figure in the production of her subjectivity? How did they mark the minutiae of her everyday life? How and when did her father's rhetorical question, and the sense of threat and discomfort it conveys, become her own sense of her self?

We do not have the detail necessary to attempt any definitive answers (if, indeed, such a thing were ever possible). But some clues are available from the combined narratives of working-class white parents and school students I interviewed. A local (but not entirely localized) form of Gramscian 'common sense' – fragmentary, fragmented, and contradictory but one that could not be dismissed as irrational within the terms of its own internal logic – may be gleaned from their commentaries. The refrain of 'too many coloureds', 'within a month they were here like bees', and 'they have taken over, etc.' is a major theme within these representations. As one fifteen-year-old white boy said to me:

> Southall is too overpopulated with them. Such a lot of them. It is all right if they move up to Birmingham, somewhere different because they all like to come in one place . . . It makes some people not like them and they move out of the area. Some people can't afford to move and they are stuck by themselves.

What economists, sociologists, or geographers described as the 'white flight' from declining inner- or outer-city areas by upwardly mobile sections of the white working class in a period of economic boom is experienced by those who remain as a sense of having fallen behind those able to leave, 'stuck by themselves'. The resentment towards the upwardly mobile fellow whites is projected onto Asians and other 'people of colour' who are now blamed for the departure. The reams written about the role of global capitalism and unequal development in under-pinning contemporary labour migrations have little resonance in this explanation. They do not form part of the 'common sense' of this beleaguered identity.

A fifteen-year-old white girl confessed:

> I think they have taken over Southall. I suppose people just don't like the way they live, the smell of their food, it gets down your throat because you are not used to it. It is not so tidy as it used to be. I think they have mucked it up a bit really. A lot of old people, they complain, they say it used to be a nice country place and everything, and they have taken over all the shops, and it is horrible round here now.

Here we encounter feminized common sense with its fantasy of tranquil and tidy rural domesticity which is 'mucked up', disrupted by the 'intruders' with their alien foods and unfamiliar smells. There is an overwhelming feeling of being 'taken over', of being soiled and defiled, of things being 'horrible'. The 'intruder' is discursively embodied as a form of aggressive masculinity. This discourse con-structs Southall in terms of a vulnerable feminized space and displaces female anxiety about male aggression into a fear of the colonialism's 'Other'. This is partially achieved by transmuting colonial immigrant labour into the figure of 'colonizer': Asians come to be represented as having 'taken over', as the discourse converts the transgressed-against into the transgressors.

In contrast to the somewhat 'indirect workings' of racialized discourses in the girl's narrative, a father and son pair, conversing with me at their home, are positioned within an explicit and overt discourse of 'racial' superiority:

> Father: 'We have emigrated to other countries. Educated them, raised their standard of living, but they are allowing in too many. The black man is getting more educated and the white man doesn't like it. I was brought up to believe that the black man was a slave. Now they want the same standard as us! We don't like it.'
> Son: 'We resent them and we will influence our children. Even when I was five, you'd mix with them in school but never have them in your house. It is colour, not culture. You always feel you are white, you are brown, you are black.'

Far from being understood as a source of regret, the tales of colonial exploits and exploitation are refracted here through the ideology of 'civilizing mission' and absolutist racialized difference, and *experienced* as an intergenerational form of male bonding between father and son, whilst holding at bay the painful reality of the inferiorized position of working-class masculinity: 'the black man is getting more educated' (that is, getting ahead in class terms), 'and the white [working class] man doesn't like it.' The discourse of racial superiority may be understood here as *displacing* class antagonism while the father and son are transported into the realm of imagined and imaginary class-less and unified Englishness.

Similarly, a three-way discussion between myself and the parents of another student steers into focus the inconsistencies, dissonance, disavowal, and contradiction within the logic of narratives marked by racialized discourse:

> Mother: 'I am moving out because there is no future for my children in Southall. There are no shops or other facilities.'
> Father interjects: 'The facilities are there but proprietors have changed.'
> Mother: 'Indian shops are over-run by mice. We never used to get mice in our house until the Asians moved in next door. Look at their garden. It is filth.'
> Father protests: 'Our own garden too is over-run by weeds!'
> Mother: '*Ours is just overgrown. Theirs is filth and dirt*' (emphasis added)

The imagery of vermin, dirt, and filth is common enough in representations of all kinds of 'Others'. Here, it would seem to feature as a way of disavowing one's own sense of failure symbolized by the unkempt 'garden' while the neighbours' garden becomes the bearer of this self-disgust: 'Ours is just overgrown. Theirs is filth and dirt.' The very fact of having Asians as neighbours itself serves as a signifier of decline in this discourse. As regards future prospects for the children, it is arguable that the future of all children in this working-class London suburb in the throes of a recession at the time was far from sanguine. But the term 'future' may be understood as holding a double meaning here: referring to general prospects as well as to 'racial' destiny. A deeply felt concern that the more 'successful' white person was in a position to exercise the option of moving out is at the heart of this expression of acute anxiety. The father's interjection highlights inconsistencies within the discourse, but such contradictions are shored up by the mother's denial.

On the other hand, disavowal and denial are not the only vehicles for 'othering' processes. A subjective sense of resentment may persist even when the 'conditions underlying the recruitment of immigrant workers' and their 'contribution to the economy' is fairly explicitly invoked. Invocation, after all is not always the same as acknowledgement. Another mother, for example, observes:

> I was in Southall when the Indians came. They were brought in as cheap labour. They don't want to mix with us; don't try to learn the language. We try to get on. We feel resentful. My mother says that we were kicked out of India, now they are all here. People blame them for the economic crisis. But, our economy would fall down if they all went home. Who would run our buses, and our hospitals?

This discourse references the economic context within which workers from former colonies were recruited as replacement labour for jobs that white workers had abandoned in response to better opportunities provided to them by the postwar economic boom. It is couched within an acceptance, no matter how ambivalently articulated, of the proposition that the economic crisis of the late 1970s could not be blamed upon Asian or Caribbean descent people in Southall. None the less, these populations come to embody the site of difference and unfamiliarity where 'old ways of doing things' are in crisis. English ambivalence towards mixing with 'outsiders' and learning 'a new language' of communication is projected onto groups who, if the contemporary evidence of a thriving programme of classes in English as a Second Language is to be taken seriously, were exceedingly busy trying to learn English, as well as the wider cultural language of a rapidly changing late capitalist social formation. But everyday common sense of this discourse is not especially concerned about these seemingly 'distant' issues: 'we feel resentful', and a (mis)reading of the process of decolonization, 'we were kicked out of India, now they are all here', legitimates the logic of resentment.

How do we change this 'distanciation' of the 'macro issues' into more intimate conversations that foster connectedness and understanding?

This brief foray into excerpts from certain narratives – recorded in the 1970s Southall that Jean would have been familiar with as the mother of teenage sons – is not intended to suggest that there was a coherent, homogeneous, or uni-directional racialized discourse circulating in Southall; or to argue that the respondents involved were misinformed, irrational bigots. On the contrary, the point is precisely that the white young people and their parents were 'ordinary' (in Raymond Williams's sense of the term), everyday folk like you and me. Several admitted to having Asian and African-Caribbean descent friends, and a few counted individuals with these backgrounds as amongst their relatives. But none of this can be taken to work as a necessary inoculation against states of mind, emotions, values, and practices which may have ethnicist or racist effects. For example, a white mother with an Asian child is not, by definition, immune from positionality within racialized discourses and practices. Rather, the issue is much more about the position that we politically (in the widest sense) come to *practise*, and not merely *espouse*, as we 'live' (both consciously and unconsciously) the vicissitudes of our lives.

And, is this not one of the most difficult things to do, positioned, as each and everyone of us is, in some relationship of hierarchy, authority or dominance to another? How do we construct, both individually and collectively, non-logocentric political practices – theoretical paradigms, political activism, as well as modes of relating to another person – which galvanize identification, empathy and affinity, and not only 'solidarity'?

'"Where did they come from?"...'

Stories of origin abound in Southall as elsewhere. The local library stocks a pamphlet which holds that the 'Saxons' were one of the first to leave a permanent mark on this area (Kirwan 1965). The name 'Southall' is said to be of Saxon origin, meaning the south corner of a stretch of land. Were Saxons not a linguistic group then, instead of a separate 'race' as racial typologists claim? The Saxon invaders, according to this chronicle, were followed by the Danes, and later by the Normans. (And, 'Where did they come from?', I ask you). Until the nineteenth century, the majority of the inhabitants of Southall depended on agriculture for their livelihood. It is suggested that the farmers in the area were probably converted to Christianity by the missionaries of St Augustine in the eighth century. About this time, parishes were marked out and Southall became part of the 'Precinct' of Norwood. Southall began to lose its rural character at the end of the seventeenth century. The process would seem to have been initiated in 1698 when an influential local family succeeded in gaining a charter to hold a weekly market in the area; even today a market is still held on the same site. With the construction of a canal between Uxbridge and Brentford, and the building of the railway in 1838–9, Southall rapidly developed into an industrial town. The growth of industry and the availability of good transport facilities have played a critical role in attracting mobile labour to the area. Before the Second World War, the Irish and the unemployed from South Wales and the North of England constituted the major source of outside labour; immediately after the war, sizeable Polish enclaves also developed alongside South Asian and African-Caribbean groups. During the 1990s, the existing populations have been augmented by refugee groups, most notably from Somalia.

Who, in this fragment of global migrations, can claim to be 'native' of Southall?

The reason generally offered by academic discussions for the arrival of Asians in Southall during the 1950s was the availability of work at a rubber reconditioning plant, the Woolfs rubber factory, in Hayes, very close to the border of Southall. Owing to the unpleasant working conditions and the need for shift work, the company found it difficult to recruit white labour. During the Second World War, the personnel officer at Woolfs had apparently fought alongside Sikhs in the Middle East, and had been impressed by them. This ironical encounter between the colonizer and the colonized, away from 'home' on an imperial battlefield, was often cited to me by professionals working in the area as a watershed in the policy of hiring Asians. Soon, these workers were to combine into the Indian Workers Association and engage in a very British trade union activity of the period, mounting campaigns for unionization and improvement in working conditions (Harrison 1974). Yet, as we have seen above, class solidarity did not figure strongly in the white parents' accounts. A few of the white parents were born during the economic depression of the 1930s, and several recounted family and neighbourhood stories of hardship and scarcity. They spoke of the tradition of fierce pride with regard to skilled work which meant that a skilled worker would rather remain unemployed than engage in unskilled forms of work. In academic-speak the working class was internally fractured by the hierarchy marked by occupation skill and the ambition to succeed in life. It was also equally differentiated by gender and other modes of differentiation. But these internal fissions would be subsumed within the boundary of 'us' when facing comparison with the middle

classes. As a working-class locality, Southall was overshadowed by the more affluent, middle-class suburb of Ealing. As a community worker explained: 'Oh, yes
there has always been a feeling of "Us against Authority" – that the rules were
imposed from outside and pushed onto them. There was very much the element
that Southall was the back-end of Ealing. Southall residents would get angry,
would resent it. It was a dig and it made them even more united.' According to
the women, Southall was a close-knit community and social control was stringent.
'Most people lived and worked here. A lot of your relatives were in Southall. Most
people knew one another. You couldn't do anything without everyone knowing
about it', one woman told me. 'We wouldn't dream of going into Ealing when we
were youngsters – right up till I was twenty-one. Sunday night it used to be the
community centre . . . I don't have a clue what they do there now. Saturday we
used to be at the Dominion Cinema. That used to be a cinema for us, with a dance
hall at the top which my aunty used to be the manageress of.'

The point about not having a clue as to what 'they do there now' and, that the
Dominion 'used to be a cinema for us' is a reference to the fact that, when the
popularity of television during the 1960s resulted in a drop in the cinema-going
white audiences, the Dominion was bought by the Indian Workers Association to
hold Asian community events, including the showing of Indian films. Notwithstanding the fact that it was the play of economic markets which governed this
'take-over', what registers with segments of the white population is the fact that
the Dominion was now owned by an Asian organization. Asians are thus constructed as having usurped what is perceived by the white residents as *their* community resource. If, previously, intra-class boundaries were the primary signifier
of 'difference', it is a racialized form of ethnicity that now moves centre-stage as
the major axis of differentiation. The 'pub', a classic gendered signifier of
working-class sociality, becomes the point of condensation in naturalizing such
'difference':

> You don't find the white people going into the Victory. The Victory is for the
> Asians, the Black Dog is for the Jamaicans. We wouldn't dream of walking
> into the Victory or the Black Dog. That's just not on – we don't do that. We
> used to go to the White Swan – now it is mixed. We go to the White Hart
> over the bridge, which is ours, and the George is Irish. It's all segregated.

This multilayered discourse embodies the contradictory relationality of 'race',
gender, class, and differentialized ethnicity in the post-colonial spatiality of
Southall. The figure of the 'pub' articulates 'power-geometries of spatiality'
(Massey 1999) along these different signifiers of 'difference'. Its symbolism, partially communicated through the semiology of animal imagery, simultaneously
demarcates, transgresses, and erases a multiplicity of borders. The 'we' here is a
certain Englishness, differentiated from Irishness, with the 'difference' of the
latter signalled by 'The George'. The discourse marks the heterogeneity of 'whiteness', but it is a malleable boundary compared to that constructed against the
'Other' colour(s): 'we wouldn't dream of walking into the Victory or the Black

Dog'. But the 'Other' colour(s) is/are both similarized and differentiated: the Asian emerges as the victor, viewed as the 'colonizer' as we have already seen. The 'Jamaican' referring to African descent black people, on the other hand, is 'interpellated' across the long-established racist imagery of the African as closer to animals: the image of 'Black Dog', saturated with racialized meanings, conveys a sense of domesticated savagery. Whilst this common-sense discourse consciously invokes a situation where 'it's all segregated', it simultaneously undoes this claim by foregrounding subconscious anxieties about what might be going on at the 'White Swan', the feminine figure of racial and sexual purity, where the clientele is now 'mixed'. The White Swan was also the site of class ambivalence, for it attracted a higher class of 'racially' mixed clientele, 'not the general run', as one woman explained to me, to be found at the Victory, the Black Dog, the George, or, more significantly, at the White Hart – the very heart within this representation of this *particular* variety of working-class Englishness.

'"Where have they come from?"...'

The immediate context for the question was the summer of 1976. Which 'other' genealogies of Southallian Englishness, the ones in which my own Africanness, Asianness, Californianness, Englishness, Panjabiness – are allusions or illusions in this question? I can sketch only a few features here. As I retrace, certain contours begin to take shape: bodies, landscapes, sites, smells; sensations of fear and threat, of belonging, unbelonging, and sometimes alienation; of familiarity and estrangement, of love and hate; memories of blood on the streets, excitement of political mobilization, and optimism that comes in the wake of daring to imagine futures of hope when confronted with despair. Some memories, in particular, stand out. In Southall, Gurdip Singh Chaggar, a fifteen-year-old boy returning home from school is stabbed to death in front of the Dominion Cinema in April 1976. His death sends shock waves among Asian communities of Southall, and, it produces a resounding response as they (we) came out in force to demonstrate on the streets of Southall. At first, the media reports suggest that the attackers are three 'white' teenage boys. Some political activists discuss the incident as primarily a question of class – working-class communities torn apart by the dominance of the ruling classes. Then the media refer to one of the three as being 'mixed race' – in this case, meaning that he had one black and one white parent. His colour, light brown, becomes quite a significant political talking point. For some people this boy's involvement was a signal that this was not a racist murder, as if racism is coded in our genes. This position is not surprising, however, given that even in the late 1990s certain eminent socio-biologists continue to champion their troubling and troublesome thesis about 'selfish genes', 'homosexual genes', and so on (see Rose 1997 for a brilliant critique). For other commentators, this was a racist murder except that the brown boy had been deluded into thinking that he was white like his friends. But, whilst all positionality within discourse involves some disillusion on all our parts, racist or other *effects* of practices, whether they be scholarly treatise or actions such as stabbing, do not depend for their effectivity on the agent necessarily having to be white, gentile, male, or heterosexual (although of course these subject positions are implicated in the construction of racialized, gendered, or sexualized forms of power). If this were the case, we would not have any hope of, say, a white person ever being non-racist, or someone engaged in heterosexual practice ever being non-heterosexist.

While the political commentators, media pundits, and community activists debated the murder, the dead boy's mother wailed in agony the question: 'Why?' This is a question that no feminism worth its salt can refuse to address.

In East London, the proverbial 'gateway' into the 'heart' of London for a variety of immigrants over the centuries, incidents of racist attacks and violence continue to escalate throughout the 1970s, resulting in several cases of death. Two male students from Mile End are killed in 1976. During 1978, three men – Altab Ali in Whitechapel, Kennith Singh in Newham, and Ishaque Ali in Hackney – all die from wounds inflicted during street attacks. These deaths galvanize the East London Asians as well as some left organizations into public demonstrations (Bethnal Green and Stepney Trades Council 1978). In Notting Hill, there are massive confrontations in the summer of 1976 between the police and black young people as the latter try to stake their claim to this inner-city enclave of Central London where dire poverty jostles with fantastic wealth. The summer of 1976 was dubbed by the media as the 'long hot summer' as they relayed reports, television footage, and photographs of African and Asian descent protesters demonstrating publicly their anger and frustration at overt and covert forms of racism that were all but ignored by agencies of the state and rarely debated in public policy or other political forums, aside from certain research organizations. These public demonstrations were conspicuous, amongst other things, for the involvement of British-born young blacks and Asians who were asserting a new British political identity. Britain 'turned a different colour' in a million senses of this phrase, as Powellian constructions of 'whiteness' – British = White – were publicly interrogated, challenged, and decentred: a gesture that wordlessly, but not silently, declared, 'we are not just "in Britain" but rather are "of Britain", and we don't even care whether or not you agree'.

'"and then the shops opened up" . . .'

The high street of Southall in the late 1970s, as today, is indeed peppered with Asian-owned shops selling dazzling saris, beautiful *salwar-kameez*, exquisite gold jewellery, and restaurants offering all manner of delicious South Asian cuisine. To a casual visitor, of whom there are frequently many in Southall, the street exudes an atmosphere of wealth and prosperity. To the local white residents, the majority of whom are working-class, this apparent example of Asian entrepreneurship can easily seem, as we have already seen, like a 'take-over' because Britain in the 1970s is awash with constructions of 'the Asian' as an outsider *par excellence*. In the processes that mark the play of these signifying practices, local Asian shops become a sign of white working-class failure, a site of envy and desire. The 'Asian shop' assumes such a magnified visibility in the popular imagination that the presence on the high street of corporate businesses such as Marks & Spencer or Woolworths passes without comment. Even Woolworths, the chain-store owned by a USA-based firm, becomes 'our own' as against 'these Asian outsiders'. That is to say that, chromatism of the racialized imagination spotlights Asian-owned small business as a threat while rendering global operations of corporate business colourless and invisible. Yet, contrary to what this defensive 'Englishness' of a beleaguered subordinate class imagines, the grass is not greener on the other side. The shops are a façade. Behind the cheer and sparkle there is the grim 'Asian reality' of high levels of unemployment and rampant low pay, with many businesses – often set up under the noose of high debt in order to avoid unemployment – teetering on the verge of liquidation; overcrowding, a general lack of public amenities, and a growing presence of fascist organizations such as the National Front.

Which fragments of this reality did Jean connect with? With the glitter *as if it were a transparent sign of wealth* or with its opaqueness, signalling the much more complex and difficult terrain of hope, dreams, despair, and desire eked out on the margins of low income and poverty, where lack of money can easily come to stand for personal failure. What kind of 'puzzle' of loss and desire is figured in her suicide?

And the National Front comes marching in . . .

The year 1979 is the election year, and the National Front is fielding enough candidates nationally to win prime time on television for a political broadcast. Although the National Front had little support in Southall, they wished to hold an election rally in the local Town Hall. Despite petitions to the contrary made by local residents opposed to the fascists, the local authority grants them permission to hold their meeting. Escorted by the police, they begin their march shouting inflammatory slogans, calling for the repatriation of 'immigrants', a term that by now had become synonymous in popular consciousness with 'people of colour'. Their opponents have arranged a show of strength by planning a counter-march for the same day, and a route is agreed with the local police. In the event, the anti-fascist marchers are blocked from following the agreed route by the Special Patrol Group Units of the Metropolitan Police. During the confrontations that ensue, nearly seven hundred (predominantly Asian) men and women of all ages are arrested and bussed out to police stations all over London. Of these, 344 are charged and tried in courts. The building occupied by a black musicians' co-operative, including the band Misty in Roots, is raided by the police and the music equipment is all destroyed. The lawyers and the medical staff present are, according to their own accounts, forced out of the building amidst a barrage of racist and sexist abuse. Clarence Baker, the lead singer of Misty in Roots, is wounded and lies unconscious in hospital for some time. As a Report notes:

> 2,756 police, including Special Patrol Group units, with horses, dogs, vans, riot shields and a helicopter were sent in . . . the evidence of hundreds of

eyewitnesses shows that . . . police vans were driven straight at crowds of people, and when they scattered and ran, officers charged at them, hitting out at random . . . A Daily Telegraph reporter saw 'several dozen crying, screaming coloured [*sic*] demonstrators . . . dragged bodily along Park View Road to the police station . . . nearly every demonstrator we saw had blood flowing from some sort of injury; some were doubled up in pain. Women and men were crying.

(Campaign against Racism and Fascism & Southall Rights 1981: 2)

On that day, Blair Peach, a white teacher from East London, died from head injuries suffered, according to evidence presented to the courts, when he was hit by police officer(s) attached to the Special Patrol Group. I saw older Asian women file past his coffin, calling him '*put*' (my son) as tears streamed down their agonized faces. He was no 'outsider', as far as they were concerned, although they did not know him. He was very much 'our own', laying his life down for a future where racist and fascist activity would not stalk their neighbourhood. The women's lament was no superficial gesture of sentimentality, as some forms of 'hard politic' might maintain. It was a profound expression of love and inclusion. One of the many creoles spoken on the South Asian subcontinent is Urdu, which makes a distinction between 'ajnabi' and 'ghair'. An 'ajnabi' is a stranger; a newcomer whom one does not yet know but who holds the promise of friendship, love, intimacy. The 'ajnabi' may have different ways of doing things but is not alien. She could be(come) 'apna'; that is, 'one of our own'. The idea of 'ghair' is much more difficult to translate, for its point of departure is intimacy; it walks the tightrope between insider and outsider. The difference of the 'ghair' cannot be fully captured by the dichotomy of Self and Other; nor is it an essentialist category. Yet, it is a form of irreducible, opaque, difference. Although these three terms may often be used in contradistinction to each other, they do not represent opposites. To the women who mourned Blair Peach, he was an ajnabi but not a ghair. He was apna. The distinction is politically important. The world is full of ajnabis. There are feminists, for instance, whom I may never meet. They are 'ajnabi' but not 'ghair' because they are part of my imagined community. Unless, of course I meet one and she treats me as if I am 'ghair', because of, say, my colour. At that moment she steps out of my boundary of 'apne' (plural of 'apna': own kind) and begins to *feel* 'ghair'. We may continue to share political views, may even engage in common political projects. Yet, we will be divided by the boundary of 'ghairness' and our relationship will feel hollow. But, then again, her positionality could change – as has often happened through ani-racist projects – and the ghairness may be transformed.

In the aftermath of the events described above, Southall became the site of intense feminist, anti-racist, and other forms of political activity. Southall Black Sisters was formed. The Southall Youth Movement (a predominantly male organization) fought fascists but also came into conflict with feminist politics. Southall Rights and Southall Monitoring Group continue their advocacy work. A variety of Marxist groups, and various community organizations, still maintain their presence. But, political shifts marked by such terms as 'Thatcherism' (and now 'Blairism') have produced a significantly changed political terrain. This period, however, is not my focus of concern here, although I have discussed some features of this phase elsewhere (see Brah 1996; Southall Black Sisters 1989).

'Where did they (we) come from?': an origin story of the late 1990s

On 13 July 1997, *The Observer* carries the headline 'How I braved academic derision to prove we're really Africans'. The subject of this headline is Chris Stringer, a palaeontologist. Addressing the *Observer* readers, he writes how he was vilified when he first proposed the idea that 'they [the Neanderthals] are not our [read Europeans'] ancestors and humans are all Africans under the skin' (p. 12). So, are all *Observer* readers Europeans? That is an interesting presumption, or perhaps a subversive act begging the question about Europeanness. We are all, he says, Africans under the skin? The differences are only skin-deep? What does one do with the skin itself? What is the 'truth of the matter'? What is the matter of truth? The report outlines the controversy. Evidently it was generally accepted during the early 1980s that early humans known as *Homo erectus* had indeed emerged from Africa but nearly a million years ago. *Homo erectus*, the story goes, wandered the world, evolving into Neanderthals in Europe, Java Man in the Far East, and Peking Man in China (what a spectacle of male cloning, long before our very own dear 'Dolly', the sheep, came to fame in 1997). Chris Stringer accepted this hypothesis but only partially. Yes, *Homo erectus* had indeed evolved into the above eminent trio (where was women's lineage among all these men?), but they were not our immediate ancestors. Instead, Stringer contended that present-day humans are all descended from a second wave of humans who also emerged from Africa but approximately a hundred thousand years ago and replaced all the rest.

Stringer's thesis was based on the study of bones. The occasion for Stringer's *Observer* article is research published the previous week using DNA samples from bones. These studies by Alan Wilson's team at the University of California would seem to confirm Stringer's hypothesis that Europeans could not claim a separate line of descent from Neanderthals. This new evidence appears to establish that we must all have had a common ancestor: 'an African Eve, that had strolled *our* homeland a mere 200,000 years ago'. The image of a beautiful African woman walking tall and strong across thousands of miles we today call Europe is gloriously appealing. What was her name? Was she called Eve? Is it important what she was called? What would she feel if she returned today to find that some of her ancestors were enslaved, colonized, ethnically cleansed, subjected to rape, murder, and holocausts, and reduced to impoverished masses, largely because they were assumed to be 'different'. With which mother's tears would she cry? What collective achievements or acts of love, kindness, compassion, sensuality, beauty, or creativity could we name that would bring a smile to her face? 'Mother, are we all the same or different'? How would she/you reply?

The enigma of Jean

Jean unexpectedly entered my universe one Sunday morning in late 1996. Today we 'inhabit' Southall together as she 'lives' in the intimacy of my memory. I never met her. She was clearly an 'ajnabi'. But, somehow she had not felt like 'ghair'. I wanted to know what had made her hate Southall, a place which I had experienced so differently. I was also deeply touched by her words: 'I feel alone'. I had heard that note on the lips of several Asian mothers I had interviewed that summer so long ago as they traced memories of rural Punjab or East Africa, places where they grew up. They spoke of the pain of separation from family, friends, and the land they had known as 'home'; recounted the hardship of manual labour in London factories combined with the demands of 'woman's work' in the household; and, they described the pleasures as well as the trials and tribulations of having teenage children, just as Jean did. Their lives changed so radically when they boarded that plane to England. Stepping into Jean's neighbourhood was pretty traumatic for them. But, in time, Southall had become home and their locally born children were now approaching school-leaving age. There was so much that all women in Southall 'objectively' shared. But we do not 'live' lives objectively, nor is this a straightforward question of false consciousness, as we have seen.

Tim Lott's book, as one might expect, is not so much about his mother as it is about his own attempt to make sense of her suicide. Within its own terms, this is an honest, meticulous, deeply moving account of a son's inquest into his mother's death through a reconstruction of his family biography. It is a gripping narrative of the changing features of class during the twentieth century as 'lived' by an extended family. It is a chronicle of the upper or well-off sections of the working class who are listed as C2 on the Registrar General's classification of occupation, a group with more money than the Ds and Es, and a whole lot more ambition to succeed. Jean had been an attractive young woman with a beautiful cascade of chestnut-brown hair which she lost in the early years of her married life owing to alopecia. From then on, she wore a wig and never let anyone, including her husband and her children, see her without the wig. She even slept with a head scarf knotted tight in "gypsy style". What must it have felt like to live in fear of the 'wig' coming off? What constructions of female 'beauty' did Jean's mind occupy that she lived in terror of her 'camouflage' being discovered? It is only after her death that her son discovers how, as part of the treatment for alopecia, Jean had been prescribed a tranquilizer that was powerful enough to be used in serious cases of epilepsy. Later, for years she was put on drugs normally used in cases of schizophrenia. The doctor's note speaks of 'emotional factors playing a part' in the condition that resulted in her hair loss.

What *was* Jean's condition? The wider ramifications of the question is such that the question itself becomes virtually impossible to answer. Her suicide note points to a deep sense of alienation: 'I cannot keep up with this pretense. We have had so many happy year's [unhappy years?] and I can see the strain this is having on you [the husband], in the end you will grow to hate me. So it is time to get out of your life. You have so much to give such a bright mind and I am holding you back'. How far was the husband's 'lived' masculinity implicated in Jean's demise? This is not a question of apportioning blame, but rather a point about the psychological and emotional fallout of 'living' social relations of gender where the trope of 'good wife' works to make the woman feel so hopelessly inadequate that she must feel that she is 'in his way'.

In all this, Jean still remains an enigma, as she properly should. Who am I to 'analyse' Tim Lott's memory of a kindly and devoted mother? I still do not know how 'my kind' – the Asians – featured in her life world. *The Scent of Dried Roses* is largely silent about the questions that exercise me, which 'interpellate' me as a racialized gendered subject. Following Ruth Frankenberg, one could easily 'read' this book as a form of 'whiteness' that is blissfully oblivious of the 'social geographies of race' (Frankenberg 1993: 54) which constitute 'white' as a privileged signifier. What are the implications of this repression? I believe that the effects of both 'writing out' and 'being written out' are devastating for all concerned. The *repressed* eventually returns.

There is such a great deal of otherwise complex and sophisticated writing published today that still continues to 'forget' its own constitution in and through the discursive interstices of 'race'. Lott is very aware of the nuances of how class colours life but without acknowledging the 'colour' of his own class as compared to that of 'people of colour'. He knows that as, Annette Kuhn argues, class is not only about income, the nature of your job, your accent, how you dress, or how you furnish your home. It is more than that, for 'it is something under your skin, in your reflexes, in your psyche, at the very core of your being . . . ' (Kuhn 1995: 98). Precisely! But class does not operate independently of other axes of differentiation. It is gendered, raced, sexualized, etc. in precisely the same way. Accept that colour-based racialization is not merely *under the skin*. The colour of our skin is exactly what 'colours' us, our very being, across asymmetrical power relations. Lott speaks of how he and his two brothers loathed Southall, mentions the Asian presence in passing and declares that the whites and Asians were insular communities who were merely indifferent to one another. Is it mere indifference that leads to narratives such as those quoted and analysed above? Lott says that he and his brothers did not leave Southall 'because we disliked Asians':

> No, we bolted because Southall was a dump, because it was nowhere, like most of subtopian England. We hated it for the reasons we imagined our parents liked it – because it was predictable, safe, conservative and limited in scale and possibility. We hated because we could see that it didn't know what it was, or where it belonged, or what it was for.
>
> (Lott 1996: 29)

There is not the space here to fully address this perfectly plausible commentary on 'escapes', but can it really be understood independently of the resentful Englishness, discussed earlier, articulated by his peers and their parents who could not 'bolt'; or, indeed, outside the context of his mother's attempt at 'final escape'? In any case, with regard to Jean here, I am far more concerned about the genealogy of 'staying put' in the 'diaspora space' (Brah 1996) of Southall. Lott continues:

But Jean stayed, tending her isolated front garden, as the other gardens were paved over for car-parking space, as Sikh traditional styles – saris, turbans, salwar and kameez, dhupatas and guths – became more familiar sights than Arran sweaters or M&S belted raincoats. She would nod and say hello, always be polite and friendly, chat over the fence to Mr. and Mrs. Mukhrejee at No. 29. Perhaps, she was secretly prejudiced, although she never said anything.

(Lott 1996: 29)

Perhaps she was not 'prejudiced' at all, if she never expressed any such sentiment even to her loved ones. This is important to me. Like many of you, I have read scholarly treatises on prejudice and racism. I even confess to writing them! But, I have this fantasy that some disclosures – especially in relation to deep-seated feelings about issues of such unmentionables as racism or homophobia – are shared as secrets within the intimate space of friendship, family, and 'community'. My study in Southall had offered me some glimpses, but I did not have access to the 'intimate' history of such phenomena. I think I had hoped that Tim Lott's book would provide me that entrée. I am none the wiser about Jean, except for what is contained in the above quite telling observation by her son. Her map of suburban England had radically changed, for a million reasons: global and local economic restructuring; major political changes such as the impact of Thatcherism; the impact of new information technologies on daily life; and the broader social influence of late twentieth-century formations of globalization. There had been major cultural shifts rendering her kind of femininity in crisis (see Steedman 1986; Hall 1992; Skeggs 1997). All this clearly had a deep and profound effect on her. The growing presence of Asians might have been disconcerting to her; they (we) might have assumed iconic significance within her understanding of these topographies of change. But Jean did not demonize Asian presence. She did not blame 'us' for everything that had gone wrong in her life. OK, we did not become intimate. But nor did she treat me as a 'ghair'. In my story she becomes 'apni' (the feminine form of the term).

I began this meditation two years ago. It has taken me this long to reach this point in the narrative. I have managed to complete other projects since then but 'Jean' and her pain (my pain?) has been much more difficult to write about. Why? I keep thinking about how equally painful it had been to read Toni Morrison's *Beloved*. But, what a wonderful title – *Beloved*! Wonderful because it heals even as it opens all the intimate wounds. So, as Ann Michaels says:

Questions without answers must be asked very slowly . . . It's Hebrew tradition that forefathers [*sic*] are referred to as 'we', not 'they' . . . This encourages empathy and a responsibility to the past (all our pasts, I hope, for this is crucial if we are not to collapse into ethnic cleansings of all kinds) but, more important, it collapses time . . . If moral choices are eternal individual actions take on immense significance no matter how small: not for this life only.

(Michaels 1998 [1996]: 159)

Note

I wish to thank Ann Phoenix for her insightful comments about points raised here, and for her helpful comments on an earlier version of the chapter.

Bibliography

Althusser, L. (1965) *For Marx*, London: Allan Lane.

—— (1971) Lenin and Philosophy and Other Essays, London: New Left Books.

Bethnal Green and Stepney Trades Council (1978) *Blood on the Streets*.

Brah, A. (1979) *Inter-generational and Inter-ethnic Preceptions: A Comparative Study of English and Asian Adolescents and their Parents in Southall*. PhD thesis, University of Bristol.

—— (1987) 'Journey to Nairobi', in S. Grewal *et al.* (eds), *Charting the Journey: Writings by Black and Third World Women*, London: Sheba Press.

—— (1996) *Cartographies of Diaspora, Contesting Identities*, London and New York: Routledge.

Campaign Against Racism and Fascism & Southall Rights (1981) *Southall: Birth of a Black Community*, London: Institute of Race Relations and Southall Rights.

Frankenberg, R. (1993) 'Growing Up White: Feminism, Racism, and the Social Geography of Childhood', *Feminist Review*, 45.

Hall, C. (1992) *White, Male, and Middle Class: Explorations in Feminism and History*, London: Verso.

Hall, S. (1980) 'Race, Articulation and Societies Structured in Dominance', in *Sociological Theories: Race and Colonialism*, Paris: UNESCO.

Haraway, D. J. (1992) 'Ecce Homo, Ain't (Aren't) I a Woman, and Inappropriated Others: The Human in a Post-humanist Landscape', in J. Butler and J. W. Scott (eds), *Feminists Theorize the Political*, New York: Routledge.

Harrison, P. (1974) 'The Patience of Southall', *New Society*, 4, vol. 28, no. 600, April.

Hindess, B. and Hirst, P. (1975) *Pre-capitalist Modes of Production*, London: Routledge and Kegan Paul.

Kirwan, P. (1965) *Southall: A Brief History*, Middlesex: Southall Public Libraries.

Kuhn, A. (1995) *Family Secrets: Acts of Memory and Imagination*, London: Verso.

Laclau, E. and Mouffe, C. (1985) *Hegemony and Socialist Strategy: Towards a Radical Democratic Politics*, London: Verso.

Lott, T. L. (1996) *The Scent of Dried Roses*, London: Viking.

Massey, D. (1999) 'Imagining Globalization: Power-geometries of Time-Space', in A. Brah, M. J. Hickman and Máirtín Mac an Ghail (eds), *Global Futures: Migration, Environment and Globalization*, Basingstoke and London: Macmillan Press.

Michaels, A. (1998) [1996] *Fugitive Pieces*, London: Bloomsbury Paperbacks.

Morrison, T. (1987) *Beloved*, London: Chatto and Windus.

Rose, S. (1997) *Lifelines: Biology, Freedom, Determinism*, London: Allen Lane Penguin Press.

Roy, A. (1997) *The God of Small Things*, London: Flamingo.

Skeggs, B. (1997) *Formations of Class and Gender: Becoming Respectable*, London: Sage.

Southall Black Sisters (1989) *Against the Tide*, London: SBS.

Steedman, C. (1986) *Landscape for a Good Woman: A Story of Two Lives*, London: Virago.

Index

Added to page number, 'f' denotes illustration.